RECLAIMING A PLUNDERED PAST

RECLAIMING A PLUNDERED PAST
Archaeology and Nation Building in Modern Iraq

MAGNUS T. BERNHARDSSON

UNIVERSITY OF TEXAS PRESS   AUSTIN

Requests for permission to reproduce material from this work should be sent to:
Permissions
University of Texas Press
P.O. Box 7819
Austin, TX 78713-7819
www.utexas.edu/utpress/about/bpermission.html

⊗ The paper used in this book meets the minimum requirements
of ANSI/NISO Z39.48-1992 (R1997) (Permanence of Paper).

LIBRARY OF CONGRESS CATALOGING-IN-PUBLICATION DATA

Bernhardsson, Magnus Thorkell.
Reclaiming a plundered past : archaeology and nation building in modern
Iraq / Magnus T. Bernhardsson. — 1st ed.
    p.   cm.
  Includes bibliographical references and index.
  ISBN 978-0-292-72595-9
  1. Excavations (Archaeology)—Iraq—History—20th century. 2. Iraq—
Antiquities. I. Title.
DS70.B37 2005
935'.0072'0569—dc22

                                                    2005018747

TO MARGARET

CONTENTS

ACKNOWLEDGMENTS

One of the many joys of publishing a book is to publicly acknowledge the people and institutions who made this project possible. The book started at Yale University as a doctoral dissertation, which I completed in 1999. To my advisor and mentor, Professor Abbas Amanat, I owe the greatest debt of gratitude. His creative and insightful intellect, warm personality, generosity, and relentless enthusiasm were a constant inspiration that made this project worthwhile and enjoyable. He initially suggested this topic, and his sharp and artistic historical erudition greatly aided its development from a mere idea, into a dissertation, and finally into a book. I am truly fortunate to have him as my constant critic, role model, and friend.

In addition, I am grateful to the other members of my dissertation committee. Professor Benjamin R. Foster's vigorous, yet constructive, criticism and intellectual wisdom helped me formulate my own thinking about this project. I have also benefited from the reliable advice of Professor Frank M. Turner, who seems to have read everything by and about the Victorians.

I would also like to thank numerous other people in the Yale community: Ulla Kasten of the Yale Babylonian Collection; Simon Samoeil of Yale's Sterling Memorial Library; Lamin Sanneh at Yale Divinity School; Maryam Sanjabi; and those who were fellow graduate students at the time, such as Shahzad Bashir, Ahmed al-Rahim, Roger Kenna, Amir Arsalan Afkhami, Michael Rubin, Joshua Kronen, Heidi Walcher, and Arash Khazeni.

While I was conducting my doctoral research and while I was revising this book for publication, I was much enlightened by stimulating and informative conversations with Professor P. R. S. Moorey (Oxford

University), Professor Joan Oates (Cambridge University), F. N. H. al-Rawi (London), Abdul Amir al-Alawi (London), Lamia al-Gaylani Werr (London), Najdat Safwat (London), Venetia Porter (London), Professor Charles Tripp (London), Professor Eric Davis (Rutgers University), Professor Tom Patterson (Temple University), Professor Beth Kangas (Michigan State), Reeva Simon (Columbia University), Professor Jim Goode (Grand Valley State University), Mia Bloom (New York), and Joseph Greene (Harvard University). I am also thankful to Fadel Jabr for his insights. While at Hofstra University, where I started revising the dissertation, I benefited from conversations and support from Dean Bernard Firestone and my colleagues Sally Charnow, Dan Varisco, Simon Doubleday, Carolyn Eisenberg, Louis Kern, Stan Pugliese, and Susan Yohn. I would also like to thank my new colleagues in the History Department at Williams College for their interest and support. Finally, I have benefited greatly from the friendship of and endless conversations with Professor Michelle Hartman (McGill University). None of the people named above bears any responsibility for the opinions expressed in this book or for its shortcomings. For these, I am alone responsible.

I would also like to thank the archivists, librarians, and curators at the University of Newcastle, University of Hull, St. Anthony's College at Oxford, the British Museum Central Archives, the British Library, Harvard University, Rockefeller Center Archives, University Museum at the University of Pennsylvania, the Public Records Office in London, and Yale University for their assistance. Special thanks to Dominic Collon at the British Museum and also to Professor William Cleveland. Financial support came from Yale Graduate School, the Department of History at Yale, the Andrew Mellon Foundation, the Whiting Foundation, the Smith Richardson Fellowship at Yale's International Security Studies Program, the Yale Center for International and Area Studies, the Hofstra College of Liberal Arts and Sciences, and the Bernadotte E. Schmitt grant of the American Historical Association. I would also like to thank the committee at Yale that awarded the dissertation the prestigious Theron Rockwell Field prize at my commencement in 2000.

I am also grateful to the anonymous reviewers who read this manuscript for the University of Texas Press for their numerous suggestions. I am also very thankful to Jim Burr at Texas for his patience and support.

Finally, on a more personal note, I do not really know how to thank my parents, Bernhardur and Rannveig, who instilled an early love for books and ideas and have always been supportive of all my endeavors. My grandfather, Dr. Sigurbjörn Einarsson, has had a profound influence on my thinking. His exemplary lifestyle and profound knowledge of comparative religions are a source of inspiration. My grandmothers Magnea and the late Svava have likewise been admirable role models. My brother Sigurbjörn and my sister Svava were unwavering in their optimism and support. My in-laws, John and Karen McComish, have always been patient with their unconventional son-in-law.

My children, Bernhardur (aka Benni) and Karen Magnea, who have been both a delight and a welcome distraction, were born and learned how to kick a soccer ball while I have been working on this project.

Finally, my wife Margaret has tolerated with a calm sense of understanding the seemingly endless presence of this project. She edited the early version of the manuscript. I cannot possibly imagine finishing it without her. Certainly neither the book nor my life would have been the same. In appreciation of her patience, love, and tireless support, I dedicate this book to her.

RECLAIMING A PLUNDERED PAST

INTRODUCTION

May we throw a glance at our small museum and compare its contents with the objects unearthed in this country which have found their way into the museums which have been sending excavation missions into this country and find out whether our share has been a fair one or otherwise?

Sawt al-'iraq (Iraqi newspaper),
February 19, 1933

Why? How could they do this? Why, when the city was already burning, when anarchy had been let loose and less than three months after US archaeologists and Pentagon officials met to discuss the country's treasures and put the Baghdad Archaeological Museum on a military data-base did the Americans allow the mobs to destroy the priceless heritage of ancient Mesopotamia?

British journalist Robert Fisk,
The Independent Online Edition, April 13, 2003

During most of 2002 and 2003, Iraq was at the center of world attention and at the heart of an unprecedented international debate. Much of the discussion, prior to the invasion of Iraq in March of 2003, focused on whether or not military action against Iraq was justified. Once the war started the focus shifted toward the execution and strategy of the military campaign and the ensuing loss of human life. By mid-April, however, once it became clear that the government of Saddam Husayn was no longer in power, Iraq's antiquities and museums became part of the war's "collateral damage." For a few days in April, the questions and discussion of wartime strategy, links of Husayn's regime to al-Qaida, and the presence of weapons of mass

destruction were all temporarily swept aside and instead Iraqi antiquities took center stage. Eventually, archaeological artifacts became intrin-
sically linked to the execution of the war and perhaps symbolic of the
difficulties ahead in the reconstruction of Iraq.

This sudden interest in Iraqi archaeological artifacts was no mere
distraction, but the result of the catastrophic and unprecedented
destruction of Iraqi cultural heritage that took place in mid-April of
2003. In Baghdad were stored some of the greatest cultural achievements of human history, indicative of our shared history and accom-
plishments. But in a matter of a few hours, the Iraqi National Museum,
and numerous regional museums and libraries, were either destroyed
or looted for anything that seemed valuable. In the "cradle of civilization," which Iraq was often called in a tribute to its long and glorious
history, a particularly uncivil situation, caused by the power vacuum and
the destruction of local authority, shattered its many cultural remnants.

The National Museum, for example, housed important pieces from
such fabled historic cities as Nineveh, Khorsabad, Uruk, Hatra, Babylon,
Ashur, and Samarra. It thus contained some of the earliest pieces of
the human endeavor, whether of art, writing, or agricultural tools. The
actual scale of the destruction of the National Museum is still unclear,
though it obviously suffered considerable damage. According to preliminary estimates from the United Nations Educational, Scientific and
Cultural Organization (UNESCO) during the summer of 2003, around
three thousand objects were missing from the National Museum. In
November of 2003, Iraqi Culture Minister Mufid al-Jazaeri indicated at
a press conference that fourteen thousand objects had been looted and
that four thousand of those had since been recovered or reclaimed.
Among the missing pieces were unique artifacts such as the Warka vase,
an Assyrian ivory carving, a marble head of Poseidon, a relief-decorated
cult vase from Uruk, and painted ceramics from Arpachiyah from the
sixth millennium B.C.E. Some important items that have been returned
were the 330-pound copper statue from Bassetki, from around 2300
B.C.E., which bears the inscription in honor of Akkadian King Naram-Sin,
and the famed Warka mask.

It was not only the National Museum that was plundered. The Iraqi
National Library and Archives (Dar al-Katub wa al-Watha'iq) and the
Ministry of Holy Endowments and Religious Affairs (al-Awqaf) were set
on fire and/or looted during this same time period.[1] In addition to
these major cultural institutions, universities and other research and

cultural centers were also subject to considerable damage. The Iraqi National Library was subjected to at least two arson attacks. It is still not clear how much of its contents was actually destroyed by the fire and how much the Library staff was able to move to secure locations. The building itself is in disarray and deemed unusable by engineers. Furthermore, approximately fifteen hundred modern paintings and sculptures are missing from Baghdad's Museum of Fine Arts. Although the damage is not as devastating as initially feared, it is quite clear that Iraqi antiquities and archaeology suffered irreplaceable losses.[2]

This was not the first time that Iraqi antiquities had been plundered, stolen, or destroyed. But the conditions in which this destruction took place, and its magnitude and speed, were unprecedented. Furthermore, many observers maintained that this looting could have been prevented had the allied forces, particularly the American military, taken concrete measures to protect important cultural sites such as the National Museum.[3] What made this episode especially troubling was that the U.S. Department of Defense had met with a group of leading archaeologists and other experts prior to the war who had urged the military to protect Iraq's priceless antiquities, including those in its main museums, from potential looting.[4]

These disastrous episodes, however, underscored several themes in Iraq's often tragic history. As this book will demonstrate, archaeology and politics are often interconnected in Iraq, especially in relation to foreign intervention or interference. Ultimately, the demolition of much of Iraqi archaeological heritage was emblematic of the ruinous and violent politics of recent Iraqi history. In more peaceful times, antiquities were used by governmental officials for political purposes to foster national unity, and archaeological artifacts inspired Iraqi poets and artists.

But in April of 2003, during chaotic and violent days, when Iraq was united only in its anarchy, the symbols of the past were destroyed or stolen. Antiquities, after all, have more than political and cultural value: they are also valuable commodities tradable for currency on the international market. Thus, many Iraqis, whether working in conjunction with well-organized international art gangs or on their own, sought to remedy their desperate financial situation by stealing the priceless antiquities. Furthermore, the museums and other cultural institutions represented the central government and were in many cases closely identified with the government of Saddam Husayn. It is possible that many of those who looted or plundered were in effect extracting some form of vengeance against the recently fallen regime. Such behavior had been exhibited, for example, during the uprisings, or *intifada,* in 1991, or immediately after the first Persian Gulf War. At that time, museums in southern Iraq were attacked and looted by the demonstrators primarily because they were concrete vestiges of Husayn's government. These episodes confirmed the place of archaeology in the cultural and political discourse in Iraq. In the following pages, this book will explore the early history of archaeology in Iraq and analyze how archaeological artifacts would eventually become closely identified with the state and politics.

Situating archaeology in the nexus of imperialism and nationalism, this book explores the political struggle over Iraqi antiquities and demonstrates its intriguing implications for Iraqi national culture. Specifically, it highlights the transformation of an Iraqi interest in antiquities that manifested itself initially in a vibrant confrontation with Western powers and subsequently in a wide-ranging political negotiation regarding how to express a meaningful and effective national identity.[5]

The unifying thread in this battle over Iraqi archaeology is power—economic, cultural, and political power—and how people have used these powers to manipulate archaeology in order to preserve their authority and/or to maximize their access to archaeological finds.[6] This study, therefore, assesses how archaeology and the knowledge derived from it, contributed initially to European interest in the *land,* then eventually to the British delineation of the *country,* and finally to the affirmation of the Iraqi *nation's* sovereignty, independence, and identity. The Iraqi example, therefore, illustrates the processes through which archaeology and history can be used for the political purposes.

History is a critical ingredient in any nationalist discourse. In such narratives, the selective utilization of archaeology often serves important functions in articulating a conscious and deliberate national history. In twentieth-century Iraq, archaeology and ancient history has been intimately intertwined with the state-building process.

For most of the twentieth century, fashioning a distinct Iraqi national identity was a fundamental challenge in the political process.[7] Ever since the establishment of the Hashemite Kingdom of Iraq in August 1921,[8] the political leaders of the state have been faced with the formidable task of nation-building among peoples of diverse religious and ethnic backgrounds.[9] In the first few years of the nascent state, the Iraqi government and its British advisors had a difficult time convincing "Iraqis" of the legitimacy of the very idea of an "Iraq."

As political scientist Eric Davis suggests, two competing and seemingly diametrically opposed models of political community, one Iraqist and the other Pan-Arab, have clashed over which was to be the defining feature of Iraqi national identity. Davis argues that the Iraqi inability "to construct a viable model of political community explains to a large degree the country's political and social instability."[10] In other words, it has proven to be a particularly troubling and difficult enterprise for the nation-state to instill unity amongst people of diverse cultural traditions and multiple ethnicities.

Partly to overcome this complex political situation and the numerous competing claims for power, when the British were trying to organize the creation of the nascent Iraqi state in the early 1920s, they looked outside the country to find a suitable political leader. Iraq's first king, Faysal I, who hailed from the Hijaz, was foreign to Iraq. Yet his family subsequently played a central role in articulating and arguing for an Iraqiness under the rubric of the Hashemite monarchy that ruled Iraq between 1921 and 1958. Because of his impeccable religious credentials, as a direct descendant of the Prophet Muhammad and the son of Sharif Husayn, the custodian of the holy places in Mecca and Medina, and because of his family's integral role in the Allied war efforts during World War I, the British considered Faysal to be the ideal candidate to forge a unified nation out of Iraq's disparate elements. This process proved more problematic than anticipated. Eleven years into the state-building process, Faysal was speaking from frustration in 1933 when he exclaimed that in "Iraq there is still no Iraqi people . . . but unimaginable masses of human beings, devoid of any patriotic ideal, imbued with religious traditions and absurdities, connected by no common tie."[11] Thus, in the 1920s, the central political question the Iraqis asked was not "'Who should rule?' but 'Who are we?'."[12]

By the 1930s, however, the Iraqi political leaders turned to archaeology and ancient history to answer the latter question. Historical artifacts emerged as a useful and crucial foundation for the nation to build for itself a modern present based on a "modern" past. For example, in a series of speeches to Iraqi high school students in the mid-1930s, Dr. Sami Shawkat, the director of education of Iraq, observed that during the Baghdad-based Abbasid Caliphate in the eighth and ninth centuries the Caliphs al-Ma'mun and Haroun al-Rashid ruled over 200 million people all across the Middle East. For Shawkat, the lessons of the past were clear and had obvious contemporary implications regarding Iraq's role in the world. He stated that the spirit of al-Rashid and al-Ma'mun would lead Iraq to become a "formidable state, as it was under al-Rashid, to dictate its will to other nations of the Middle East . . . and not be a victim of exploitation and imperialism."[13]

Extolling the virtues of the modern Iraqi nation, Shawkat's didactic presentation of history was aimed at galvanizing patriotic sentiments among his young audience while validating Iraq's domestic and foreign policies. Furthermore, by drawing a connection between the contemporary state of Iraq and the glorious Abbasid Caliphate, Shawkat emphasized that Iraq's ancient history had important implications that were relevant and edifying for its present-day citizens. Like politicians all around the world, therefore, Shawkat took great liberties in his historical analysis, and his politically structured historical interpretation was useful for his government's political and nationalistic agenda.

In recent years, there has been a growing academic interest in the connection between nationalism and archaeology.[14] As several studies have demonstrated, nationalism influences the kinds of questions archaeologists have been willing to ask and determines what sort of historical sites to excavate and uncover. Nationalist ideologies can lead and have led archaeologists to present history as a nonproblematic, linear progression of a people often validating a specific nation-state's interpretation of its own history. Because of its potential to help define a people as distinct and unique, archaeology has proven to be a useful tool in the nation-building processes in many countries of the Middle East. There, as elsewhere, the borders of contemporary nation-states necessarily influence the tradition of archaeological research, and archaeology in turn can solidify the claims and legitimacy of the nation-state.

In the Middle East, this tendency was particularly visible in the foundational period between 1920 and 1950. After the downfall of the Ottoman Empire, when newly created nations in the Middle East were engaged in systematic state-building, ancient peoples and cultures were "rediscovered" and injected into nationalist discourse. Nations, just like their individual citizens, compete with one another to garner attention. In their quest to prove their worth to their own citizens and to the world at large, all nations seek to demonstrate their uniqueness and exceptionality. In these nationalist histories, whether that of Lebanon, with its interest in the ancient Phoenicians, or of Turkey, and its concerns with the Hittites, the activities and scope of ancient cultures and peoples, whose lives were not circumscribed by contemporary borders, were carefully articulated and manipulated so that they could be neatly fit into modern geopolitical spaces.[15]

The identification with ancient cultures, therefore, clearly served important utilitarian purposes for the nationalist enterprise. In a region where borders and frontiers were still fragile, fluid, and often contested, it allowed for the political expropriation of land. Furthermore, it served to convince the citizens of Transjordan, Egypt, or Syria, for example, that they were indeed—despite internal sectarian differences and some obvious religious and linguistic similarities with people outside their country—a community whose distinctiveness had historical roots. In the marketplace of identities, where the power to define is critical, selective interpretations of history helped legitimize certain governments and their views of what characterized a nation, at the expense of other groups or governments. The attempt to define and make distinct typically involves some form of exclusion, so prevalent in the nature of nationalism. Nationalism is thus often "negative" in the sense that it seeks to prove what the nation is not.

For example, historian Linda Colley has argued, in the case of Britain, "men and women decide who they are by reference to who and what they are not."[16] Another historian studying Western Europe, Peter Sahlins, has written that national identity is "contingent and relational: it is defined by the social and territorial boundaries drawn to distinguish the collective self and its implicit negation, the other."[17]

In defining its own nation, Iraqi nationalism has vacillated between a "positive" and "negative" identification. At times it has chosen to emphasize a negative stance ("us" [Iraqis] vs. "them" [everyone else]). However, because of the linguistic, religious, and ethnic cleavages in the country, even creating a plausible "other" from which to differentiate the nation has proven problematic. Iraq has thus, in contrast, primarily stressed a "positive" identity, whether it has been in the guise of pan-Arabism or a distinct Iraqi particularism.

This positive stance reaffirms or redefines the Iraqis against themselves. Instead of proposing that "we are who we are by what we are not," this position asserts that Iraqis are "who we are because of who we were." The nation has been presented as a commemorative group of past achievements of people living on Iraqi soil. Instead of identifying primarily with one ancient empire or people, primarily because it would be difficult to convince the Kurds, the Shi'is, the Sunnis, and the various Christian and Jewish communities of a common heritage based on one common ancestor, the contemporary spirit of the Iraqi nation has been identified, for example, in the law-abiding nature of Hammurabi's society, the fighting spirit of the Assyrians, or the scientific innovation of the Abbasids.

What makes the Iraqis interesting and distinct from some of their neighbors in the interwar years is that initially they did not identify themselves with a pre-Islamic empire. Unlike the celebrations of the Phoenicians in Lebanon, the Sassanian and Achaemenid Empires in Pahlavi Iran, and of the Hittites in Turkey, the Iraqi nationalist agenda did not "discover" an ancient people or empire with which to identify the nascent nation. In various stages, the government articulated a pan-Arab identity, whereas at other periods it sought inspiration in numerous ancient cultures both Islamic and pre-Islamic. Consequently, Iraqi nationalism has not always been constant, nor has it emphasized one epoch or period. Instead, it has sought paradigms from a variety of historical periods, depending on the political circumstances.

In Iraq, after World War I, forging a national identity has been a conscious, and not always a consistent, top-down process that was integrally tied to the government's foreign policy, so that the past was reconstructed and based on the reigning ideological stance. At certain times, Iraq's Arab/Islamic history has been emphasized if the government was interested in Pan-Arabism. At other times, ancient Mesopotamian history was given priority in order to underline Iraq's leadership role in the Arab world and hegemony in the Persian Gulf. For example, those governments in power between 1932 and 1941 and 1963 and 1968 emphasized archaeology and history connected to Iraq's pan-Arab and pan-Islamic ties, particularly its role as the seat of the Abbasid Caliphate. Others, in particular that between 1958 and 1963 and the government under the leadership of Saddam Husayn between 1979 and 2003, have stressed Iraq's particularism based on its unique pre-Islamic history, such as being the home of the Babylonian, Akkadian, and Sumerian civilizations.[18]

Overwhelmingly, the Iraqi national connection with the past has not been proposed as ethnic, but rather as cultural. Thus it was possible to make modern-day Iraqis the inheritors of ancient Mesopotamian culture. This cultural emphasis, what I refer to as *paradigmatic nationalism,* is predicated on sometimes vague and ever-shifting ideas of cultural paradigms. Because history offers so many possible and interchangeable motifs, it is a nationalism that is perhaps more fluid and adaptable than an identity built on race, language, or religion, as in other nations. Ultimately, though, like all nationalisms, it seeks national homogeneity and a common denominator.

Yet as the Iraqi experience suggests, the process in which nations attempt to create a "master narrative" that highlights their citizens' common past and legitimizes their aspiration for a shared destiny is, in actuality, dynamic and dialectical in character. In Iraq, as previously mentioned, the answers to the questions "Who are we?" and "What is the history of our nation?" have been subject to considerable debate. These debates were underscored in archaeology because the official emphasis in archaeology has deliberately been structured to fulfill ever-changing goals. These political goals were often antithetical to previous ones stressing radically different interpretations of what historically characterized Iraqis. "Iraq," in the rubric of paradigmatic nationalism, implies an "interpretive" or "recovered" community fueled, and perhaps restricted, by common historical experiences, though not necessarily common ideals and goals. Through archaeology, among other mechanisms, Iraqi politicians and scholars hoped to find, and use, historical artifacts and their corresponding legends to configure the Iraqi political and cultural community as one that had historical antecedents.

Thus, in a nationalism based on paradigms, complex historical events are also often reduced to basic plot structures that are easily packaged. For example, at a celebration to mark the first year of the Iran-Iraq War in 1981, the Iraqi vice president Taha al-Din Ma'ruf gave a fiery speech in which he led listeners back on a journey a few thousand years, stating that "when the mighty kingdom of Akkad and Sumer was founded, as an expression of the first Iraqi patriotic *[wataniyya]* unity in history, the unity of the homeland was exposed to a hateful attack by the Persian Elamites. . . . And when Iraq rose again and Sargon the Akkadian arose as the leader who united Iraq, the black Persian lust was reawakened. But the Iraqi leader Sargon repelled them forcefully. . . . Today your determined resolve was the mountain upon which dreams of the grandsons of Xerxes and Kisra were shattered."[19] For Ma'ruf, the contemporary war between Iraq and

Iran was merely the latest round of Persian-Iraqi enmity. Thus, according to this nationalist discourse, the Iraqi soldiers were historically destined to fight this battle.

This integration of ancient history and contemporary political concerns aims to convey that the spirits of the ancient civilizations are still alive and well in the modern nation. The modern citizens are thus direct descendants—culturally, politically, and even spiritually—of the great historic empires. Hence, contemporary cultural and political policies can be validated through historical precedent, and consequently political leaders imputed the trope of historical grandeur to archaeological artifacts.

In Iraq, the history and practice of archaeology have gone through three stages: The first phase, that of removal, was an "international" stage, and characterized by Western domination in which the Iraqis played a limited role—primarily supplying the manual labor at various excavation sites. Western archaeologists and institutions, not the inhabitants of Mesopotamia, sought to claim Mesopotamian antiquities as theirs. The second stage, during the interwar years, was a transitional period marked by intense negotiations and the beginning of the "national" phase of Iraqi archaeology. This epoch, or the period of negotiation, was dominated by the British but eventually became a struggle between Iraq and Britain over antiquities. In the third, from 1941 until today, Iraq has had full control of its archaeology, or at least until the decade of sanctions and the events of 2003. The focus in this book is only on the first two stages.[20]

The first period, the European, or Western, stage, should neither be isolated from the colonialist enterprise nor divorced from the general Western historical narrative of the "progress of civilization," which was necessary for the aims of a "civilizing" imperial mission. Mesopotamia was, after all, the cradle of civilization, the supposed site of the Garden of Eden and point of origin for everyone and everything. In this time period, from the 1830s to World War I, antiquities were "international." They were exportable and moved without many restrictions from the Middle East to European or North American destinations. In that part of the world, there was a growing market and demand for archaeological artifacts. Archaeologists from those areas were given considerable freedom and liberty to conduct extensive archaeological excavations in the Middle East and elsewhere.

Operating both within and outside of the 1874 Ottoman Law of Antiquities, they could roam the Mesopotamian countryside in an often frantic search for historical artifacts.

The scramble for colonies brought a parallel scramble for antiquities that was fueled by the frenzied competition of various national museums in Europe. The institutional desire to accumulate valuable antiquities was coupled with the private yearning of individuals to collect curios. In this time period, the selection of which sites and which ancient history would be interpreted reveals which history Westerners deemed important and relevant and also which history they felt was "theirs." The Westerners appropriated the history of Mesopotamia and brought back to Europe and North America nearly all of the excavated artifacts. In the hundred-year period between 1810 and 1910, nearly all major and minor excavations by Europeans and North Americans were conducted at pre-Islamic sites, such as Babylon, Khorsabad, and Nippur, which were considered exciting, interesting, and relevant because of their relation to the Bible. The histories of the ancient Sumerians, Assyrians, and Babylonians were studied, sometimes carefully, sometimes not. Islamic sites and history were overlooked and deemed neither valuable nor relevant, though there were exceptions to this rule such as the excavations at the Islamic site of Samarra led by the German archaeologist Ernst Herzfeld just prior to the outbreak of World War I.

In the second stage of Iraqi archaeology, starting in 1921 and ending roughly with the outbreak of World War II, historical artifacts became "national." Their export and movement were significantly curtailed, and they became tools in the agenda of the state, especially in writing and presenting a distinct national history. In this hybrid stage, archaeology was initially a British affair. The English politician and archaeologist Gertrude Bell was responsible for archaeology in the Mandate period. In the early 1920s, Bell became the first director of antiquities in Iraq and formulated the 1924 antiquities legislation that was beneficial to foreign archaeologists and validated the nineteenth-century Western claims to various sites. Though she experienced some resistance to her plans from influential Iraqis such as Yasin al-Hashimi, who was the prime minister in 1924–1925, and Sati' al-Husri, the minister of education during most of the 1920s, she was able to avert Iraqi pressure because of Britain's domination of Iraqi politics. Her encounters with the Iraqi politicians in this particular case are indicative of the general political atmosphere. The British politicians had to resort to some form of negotiation. The negotiations in the sphere of archaeology manifested themselves most visibly in discussions regarding antiquities law, especially how to divide archaeological finds between Iraq and the foreign excavator. During this time, however, nearly all decisions favored the British and the other foreigners—an indication of the power structure. For example, Bell was successful in asserting British domain through legislation and political power and devised an antiquities legislation that allowed for extensive exports of excavated antiquities. One major idea behind the legislation was that the archaeological artifacts were of universal relevance and belonged more in museums in Paris or New York than in Baghdad.

During the 1920s and early 1930s a number of large and ambitious excavations began in Iraq at pre-Islamic sites such as Ur, Kish, Warka, and Nuzi. As with the first stage in the nineteenth century, Arab/Islamic sites received scant attention despite the fact that Faysal's Hashemite monarchy derived its prestige and, to a certain extent, its legitimacy from its connection to early Islamic history.

The mood of this period began to shift in 1932, in the wake of Iraqi independence, when several Iraqi newspapers started an aggressive campaign concerning the state of archaeology in the country. The tone and direction of this discussion were unanimous and unequivocal: Iraq had been robbed and plundered by Western archaeologists, and the government should take concrete measures to immediately remedy the situation. The Iraqi newspapers complained about how modest Iraq's Mesopotamian archaeological collections were compared to those in foreign institutions and urged the government to train more Iraqis in archaeology in order to take precautions similar to those adopted by the governments of Iran, Turkey, and Egypt to protect their archaeological heritage. The Iraqi Parliament subsequently passed a new, more restrictive law that stressed the antiquities were the property of the Iraqi nation.

Furthermore, the Iraqi government took steps to reclaim its cultural property from the Western countries. This action was part of Iraq's overall struggle to recover more control of its resources, both natural and cultural, from the Western powers. Thus, attempts at reclaiming its plundered past had begun. During these efforts, I argue, archaeology entered Iraqi politics in a profound manner, thereby laying the foundation for archaeology and nationalism to intersect and thus become inseparable in Iraqi politics in succeeding decades. This junction is the theme of my book and suggests, as previously mentioned, how inter-twined archaeology, imperialism, and nationalism have been in the modern history of Iraq.

The time period under consideration in this book, especially between 1921 and 1941, is also interesting from a number of other angles. Like many other features of Middle Eastern political and cultural life, the politics of archaeology went through a "hybrid" transitional stage in which the state-building processes of the newly established nations left their mark on the practice of archaeology. Thus in an attempt to be more fully in control of their destiny, the new governments in the Middle East fought with the old imperial powers and structures in order to exercise full authority over cultural resources and assume the power to articulate a relevant and feasible history, based on their archaeological heritage.

The book starts in the "international" stage. The first chapter exam-ines the early excavations that took place in Iraq in the nineteenth cen-tury. In particular, it analyzes the philosophical assumptions behind the archaeological enterprise in order to understand the Western impulse to appropriate Middle Eastern antiquities. The second chapter focuses on the first two decades of the twentieth century, especially the British occupation during World War I. The politics of the Mandate period (1921–1932) is the theme of the third chapter. During the Mandate, the British made critical decisions regarding the basic political institu-tions of the nascent state, including those related to archaeology. Chapter 3 describes the beginning of the hybrid stage of archaeological excavations, when foreign archaeologists were operating under prime conditions in Iraq and the Iraqi political establishment had only a passing interest in this archaeology.

The final two chapters focus on the development of the "national" period in Iraqi archaeology. In Chapters 4 and 5, I examine the increas-ing Iraqi involvement in the archaeological enterprise and the ensuing negotiations to gain full control of the nation's antiquities. The trans-formation of archaeology from being primarily a Western affair to one that Iraqis felt that they should dominate was drastic. Furthermore, the accompanying nationalism and the critical reassessment of the history of Iraq's relationship with Western powers generated a certain propri-etary stance concerning Iraq's archaeological heritage. This develop-ment was coupled with the attempts of Western archaeologists and politicians to prevent any significant changes in archaeological policy in Iraq. It was essentially a battle of power—the battle over Iraq's historical artifacts was ultimately a struggle over Western involvement in the Middle East.

Two events, 130 years apart, reported in newspaper articles, one in London and one in Baghdad, best illustrate the level and nature of this transformation. On July 27, 1850, the *Illustrated London News* published a series of articles on recent archaeological excavations in the Middle East. It stated: "It is gratifying that England has not only rendered herself the first of the nations by those sterling qualities which so strongly characterize her natives—that she uses these means to extend and disseminate the wealth, and comfort, and advantages produced by the arts of civilization, at the same time that she administers happiness and contentment by inculcating the tenets of pure religion."[21] This text was accompanied by an illustration that depicts the process of removing a one-hundred-ton sculpture, the Great Bull of Nimrud, from its site in Iraq to a transport ship bound for London, where it was installed and, to this day, remains in the British Museum. As C. M. Hinsley points out, the central contrast in this illustration lies between the passive, onlooking native population and the impressiveness of the British technological feat they were witnessing. Although the "local flagpole stands flagless, the Union Jack frames the right side of the picture."[22]

One hundred thirty years later, in August 1980, a leading Iraqi governmental newspaper, *al-Thawra (The Revolution),* announced that

Removing the Great Bull of Nimrud as depicted in the *London Illustrated News* in 1850.

Iraq had solicited a United Nations resolution calling for the restoration of antiquities to the country of their origin. The article explained the rationale behind the UN resolution: "The stele of Hammurabi awaits impatiently in the Louvre, and the library of Ashurbanipal is in the British Museum . . . [both] are languishing sadly . . . in the museums of the world and their inability to return to the homeland from which they emerged is a cultural calamity and a major crime."[23] Several months later, when the French Prime Minister Raymond Barré visited Iraq to discuss an oil deal, he was stunned when the Iraqi president, Saddam Husayn, changed the topic of conversation and demanded that the Louvre return the stele of Hammurabi.[24] Husayn believed that the stele was Iraqi property and that it would be most appropriate that France return the stele to Iraq.

In the Iraqi-scripted scenario, in contrast to the depiction in the *Illustrated London News,* the Iraqis were no longer passive onlookers but rather proactive initiators. They were not admiring the technology of foreigners but rather using their leverage as suppliers of oil to discuss

The 1970s and early 1980s witnessed close relations between the Iraqi and French governments. The two governments signed several commercial treaties. In this illustration, President Saddam Husayn celebrates an agreement with French Prime Minister Jacques Chirac in 1974. It was at a similar meeting in 1980 with French Prime Minister Raymond Barré that Husayn brought up the return of the stele of Hammurabi. © Henri Bureau, Sygma/Corbis.

the fate of antiquities. Furthermore, the Iraqis were taking an ethical and nationalist stance by accusing the French, and by extension the West more generally, of past cultural wrongdoing that should be remedied immediately. Husayn was interrupting sensitive, and potentially lucrative, negotiations in order to reclaim this cultural treasure from France. Yet in the end, the Iraqi government did not make the return of cultural property a condition for its economic relationship with France. To this day, the stele of Hammurabi still sits on display in the Louvre, leaving the question of its return unresolved. However, this symbolic moment suggests the degree to which Iraq's views of its antiquities had changed.

The twin themes of removal and return are indeed central elements in the historiography of archaeology. The discussion and illustration of the removal of antiquities in the *Illustrated London News* characterize how the history of archaeology in the Middle East has generally been written and interpreted. As Hinsley suggests, the entire process of archaeological retrieval was divisible into three stages that form a mental geography of the archaeological enterprise in the nineteenth century: the site of discovery and excavation, the means of transport, and the final resting place in a European urban center.[25] The excavation site is typically presented as a barren landscape of the lost grandeur and the fate of ancient empires populated by a passive, unenlightened population. (The "empty space" motif is characteristic of nineteenth-century European and American travel literature describing the Middle East.) The means of transport (the ship) indicates the technological ingenuity and military prowess of Western civilization. Finally, the objects' resting place is represented by the sophisticated display in a museum or university where the object could be observed and appreciated by enlightened Europeans.[26] Therefore, the final result of this discourse is to underscore the valuable contributions of the Western world in "discovering" and "preserving" these historical treasures for the benefit of humanity as a whole.

In contrast, the latter theme, return, traditionally has not been discussed in the literature on archaeology. In recent years, however, this theme has increasingly emerged as an important topic and will probably become the primary focus in the politics of archaeology in coming years. Especially in light of the looting of 2003, this issue will demand wide-ranging cooperation among relevant authorities. Because of the complex and controversial nature of this topic, in addition to its novelty, this theme has yet to be shaped.

In addition to analyzing the archaeological enterprise in Iraq and its connection to nation-building, this book also combines the removal and return themes by discussing the early, and largely unsuccessful, attempts by the Iraqis to reclaim cultural property from the Western world. The topic of removal, however, was the prominent subject in the time period under consideration, and, consequently, the bulk of my analysis examines the means through which Western institutions sought to maximize their access to Iraqi antiquities. Their attitudes, methods, and ultimate success may help explain why many Iraqis viewed these activities with suspicion; archaeology was not perceived to be a neutral science, but an integral part of the imperialist enterprise. Many Iraqis, often with good reason, came to view most of the earlier archaeological missions as aggressive campaigns to plunder Iraqi antiquities. Archaeology was a treasure hunt, and the prizes were on display in the West.

With the development of an Iraqi national consciousness, these antiquities, even though many had been exported under lawful conditions, became philosophically, politically, and emotionally part of the Iraqi heritage. Just as Westerners felt the urge to bring the antiquities "back home," Iraqis believed that these artifacts were Iraqi property destined to be restored to Iraqi soil. Mirroring so many aspects of the Western-Iraqi power struggle during the interwar years, archaeology was a contested terrain. Yet in contrast to their failure in other matters, such as controlling oil resources, the Iraqis were able to successfully challenge the stronghold in archaeology. As archaeological relics became the heritage of Iraqi culture, representing the sovereignty of Iraq over its land, treasures, and history, this heritage provided the Iraqi politicians with the pretext and the context to negotiate other features of their general political and economic relationship with Britain and other Western powers. In the decades after World War II, archaeology no longer served as a vehicle of anti-imperialism and the Iraqi state's assertion of its authority vis-à-vis Britain. Rather, the archaeological heritage became associated with the Husayn government. At sensitive and volatile political junctures, such as during the uprisings of 1991 and in 2003, archaeological sites were targeted by the general populace for not only their monetary value but also because of their links to governmental policy. Archaeology, therefore, played a significant role in helping promote nationalism in the age of decolonization of Iraq and provided tangible objects for defining the nation in the era of a strong, centralized nation-state.

The political and cultural history of archaeology in Iraq has thus witnessed numerous impressive cultural victories and at the same time depressing cultural calamities. What started out as the endeavor of a few committed individuals eventually became a massive state-sponsored and -sanctioned enterprise. Ultimately, the fate of Iraqi antiquities has been interlinked with the general political history of the area and the world at large.

Gertrude Bell, director of antiquities in Iraq
between 1921 and 1926. By permission of
the University of Newcastle-upon-Tyne.

Excavation at Babylon, ca. 1914. Photograph by Gertrude Bell.
By permission of the University of Newcastle-upon-Tyne.

Ashur in 1911. General view of excavation site and workers. Photograph by Gertrude Bell. By permission of the University of Newcastle-upon-Tyne.

Samarra, Iraq, in 1909. The Great Mosque of al-Mutawakkil. Photograph by Gertrude Bell. By permission of the University of Newcastle-upon-Tyne.

Gertrude Bell in Iraq, probably near Babylon, in 1909. By permission of the University of Newcastle-upon-Tyne.

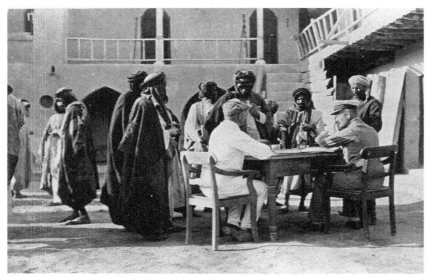

The German archaeologist Julius Jordan paying local excavation workers. Taken in Ashur, Iraq, in 1911. By permission of the University of Newcastle-upon-Tyne.

The Shah of Iran visits the Iraq National Museum accompanied by Seton Lloyd. Date unknown. By permission of Dominique Collon.

The weekly tour of the Iraq National Museum in the 1940s headed
by Seton Lloyd. By permission of Dominique Collon.

Naji al-Asli, Seton Lloyd, and Sir Archibald Creswell at the ruins
of Mustansirriya College. By permission of Dominique Collon.

Removing the sculptures at Khorsabad and re-erecting them at the entrance of the new National Museum in Baghdad. By permission of Dominique Collon.

Sati' al-Husri, director of
antiquities in Iraq between
1934 and 1941. With permission
from William Cleveland.

U.S. military tank in front of
damaged National Museum in
2003. The lions from Khorsabad
are still standing. Photograph
by Ramzi Haidar/AFP/Getty
Images. © Getty Images.

Iraq's National Museum Deputy Director Mushin Hasan holds his head after the
National Museum was ransacked in 2003. Photograph by Mario Tama. © Getty Images.

1

EARLY EXCAVATIONS IN MESOPOTAMIA

With its ties to biblical history and the absence of an authority protecting its archaeological sites, the area we now know as Iraq was an attractive destination for European and American archaeologists. The region then called Mesopotamia, a Greek word meaning the land between the two rivers, offered boundless opportunities for the burgeoning new science of archaeology. Up until the twentieth century, archaeology was primarily a Western enterprise, and the pioneering archaeological efforts in Mesopotamia, both in terms of method and in their relation to local peoples and cultures, were characteristic of the Western cultural and political involvement in Asia and Africa. Middle Eastern antiquities became the latest trophy; another valuable resource to exploit and conquer. Archaeology was one mean toward the end of acquiring the latest imperial prize.

The story of the early archaeological endeavor in Mesopotamia, so often funded and validated by the new fledgling (and competitive) national museums, is a particularly interesting and significant one. The characters who entered this volatile stage were certainly dramatic and colorful, and their scientific achievements were no less than remarkable despite their rudimentary, and often destructive, methods. In a few decades these explorers recovered the magnificent artifacts of earlier history and deciphered the long-lost dead languages of ancient civilizations. They introduced nontextual forms of evidence, thus supplanting that role of the Bible. The testimony of artifacts allowed scholars to reach beyond romantic-nationalist histories toward the identification of cultural areas. The practice of archaeology resulted in an explosion of interest in epistemological methods, which emphasized studying cultures based on firsthand knowledge through primary sources. Archaeology revealed that the hitherto authoritative corpus of historical knowledge (i.e., the Classical authors and the Bible), which had been recycled and synthesized by numerous authors through the centuries, was in itself inadequate for an accurate understanding of the past. The archaeological artifacts therefore contributed to a sentiment that regarded human history as something more objective, tangible, and real, and ultimately relevant and accessible to the population as a whole.

Archaeology, as a science and philosophy, was one outcome of the ideas of the Enlightenment, the economic prosperity brought by colonialism, and the inventions of the Industrial and Scientific Revolutions.[1] At these junctures, European intellectuals came to foster a culture consisting of simultaneous adulation of and optimism about the idea of progress, coupled with a reverent fascination for their past.[2] Progress, as historian Herbert Butterfield suggests, was an act of faith, a secularization of Messianism, which entailed a verdict on the tendencies of the past coupled with a hope reaching out into the future.[3]

The unprecedented acceleration of the development of material civilization created intense and serious tensions in European and American society. This era of massive industrialization technologized the landscape, both physical and psychological, with fascinating and frightening results. The transition required developing new values for the complex industrialized society.

During this transformative stage, the lessons of history offered both comfort and directives to those intellectuals committed to the idea of progress. The legacy of the past, they believed, could be used to ascertain a general trend in social and economic development as well as offering verification and justification of their own values and aesthetics. In Britain, for example, this tendency resulted in a blossoming of interest in ancient Greek culture. Greek culture and art were deemed to contain a certain purity that provided a model of Western moral values.[4] The ancient Athenians, as historian Frank M. Turner points out, provided the British with a "reflection of their own best selves."[5]

Thus the study of history, with its material and scientific proofs of the progress of human culture, replaced philosophy as the fundamental cultural symbol of the age. With it came an efflorescence of the historical sciences, which inaugurated the avid study of everything that could be understood as "history" in diverse disciplines. This historical emphasis inaugurated an age of classification, in which the British, for example, sought to divide humans, and the natural world, into genera and species revealing distinct differences in civilizations and historical cultures.[6]

Yet these reflections did not necessarily reveal that human progress and development were definitely linear. Those who had received a classical education and were well versed in various Classical Greek writings, such as Herodotus, were familiar with the notion of the ancient Greeks that civilizations are organisms and go through cycles of birth, growth, and death.[7] Europeans were therefore acquainted with the cyclical notion of history, which they adapted into their own linear, progressive view of history.[8]

Instead of just thinking about history, the scholar's duty at hand was to find the physical remains of history—unearth history, to retain and then make history. The events of the past were therefore studied because they were useful and relevant. Material things, such as buildings and statues, vestiges of the past, were now clues that would provide for the re-creation of the past. Consequently, scholars demystified history, as its sources were no longer limited to the Bible or Classical works, and were made more tangible. In this process, history became property, in a sense, since it was no longer solely a text but a physical entity that could be owned as well. A person did not only belong to history; history belonged to him or her.

The appearance of objects and things as viable sources for historical interpretation epitomizes this development. This sense of belonging was evident in the rise of antiquarian research and in the appearance of persons known as antiquarians, who accumulated and collected historical things. As Arnaldo Momigliano observes, this rise of antiquarian research was a revolution in the historical method.[9] The search for evidence outside the literary sources made the need for new histories apparent. These objects were believed to extend knowledge of how people lived and felt in earlier centuries. History, historical objects and historical peoples, therefore, became elements directly related to one's contemporary situation.

Antiquities and archaeological remains emerged as viable sources for the study of the origins and development of culture. Given that humanity has left material traces of its history in and on the earth, such artifacts became obvious tools in the historian's armory. What initially was an unsystematic hobby of collecting antiquities soon became a discrete scientific, academic discipline. In the search for physical verification of the material progress made by modern societies, archaeology provided the tools and basis for much such speculation. In a textual world, dominated by the Book, where only a few could write, archaeology would soon contribute to an expanding epistemological universe. The text was supplemented, or in some cases undercut, with other physical truths that archaeology would help supply.

Most historians of archaeology trace its origins as an academic discipline to Jacob Spon, a French physician and antiquary who traveled to Greece and Asia Minor in 1675–1676 to make firsthand observations and studies of antiquities.[10] Presumably, it was Spon who first coined the word *archaeologia* from the Greek words *archaious* and *logos*, meaning discourse about the past, or about origins. Spon used the word *archaeologia* to describe what antiquarians did when they studied objects and monuments from the past.[11]

By the late seventeenth century, Classical antiquity had aroused the intense curiosity of scholars and collectors all over Europe. French and British architects and antiquarians produced massive tomes on the subject of Greek art; many of these men had even traveled to Greece to see these artworks themselves.

The steady acquisition of antiquities, whether by chance discovery or excavation, soon posed the problem of classification, in this age of categorization, as the artifacts were clearly not all of the same age. The classification problem was addressed in 1806, by the Danish government, for instance when it set up a commission to research Denmark's geology and natural history. Christian Jorgensen Thomsen was secretary to the commission. When a national museum was created in 1816, he became its first curator. While organizing the collection, Thomsen arranged objects according to the material of which they were made; stone, bronze, and iron. It was a simple, yet effective, step to recognize the three groups of artifacts as representative of three chronological periods. This "three-age system" became widely used. For example, it appeared in the writings of Sven Nilsson (1787–1883) and J. J. A. Worsaae (1821–1885). In 1865 John Lubbock published a history based on archaeological syntheses called *Prehistoric Times*. In this work he divided the Stone Age into an earlier phase of flaked stone tools (the Palaeolithic) and a later period of polished stone axes (the Neolithic). The "three-age system" attracted a wider interest among both the educated public and scholars working in the field of ethnography. Sven

Nilsson applied the system to argue for a sequence of four socioeconomic stages: savagery, nomadic pastoralism, settled agriculture, and civilization. Nilsson's comparative method was adopted by the Oxford anthropologist Sir Edward Tylor (1832–1917), who suggested a threefold division: savagery, barbarism, and civilization.[12]

It was during this period of systematic collections that national museums began to be established.[13] The age of the "cabinet of curiosities" was coming to an end, and the great private collections of the aristocracy and royalty became public institutions.[14] With the formation of grand national museums in Britain, Denmark, France, Germany, and Italy, museums became manifestations and sources of national pride, rather than the personal prestige associated with private collections, and were expected to play socially useful moral and educational roles.[15] The very structure and philosophy of a museum presupposes the ability to organize and display human history—elements so critical to the archaeological enterprise. Museums present history and art in a systematic, classified manner offering their viewers a distinct outlook on the progress and development of history. In the halls and display cases of museums, history was no longer a mythical, superstitious entity. Rather, it was something more tangible, more physical, less text-based—appropriate for the rational scientific society.

These new national museums in Europe also exhibited the diversity and immensity of the respective empires. A central component in the British Museum and Louvre, and to a lesser extent in Berlin, was to display the fruits of the imperial labor. As their sponsoring nations scrambled for colonies and their commodities, these museums were useful barometers of the pressures, successes, and achievements of that endeavor. And just as they reflected the competition in the imperial field, the museums themselves soon became the locus of the rivalry, which was intensified by new discoveries in the rich archaeological fields of Egypt, Palestine, and Mesopotamia.

The activities and writings of the early anthropologists and archaeologists and the establishment of national museums instituted solid foundations for the general acceptance of the idea of progress. According to this view, the highest stage of social development resembled the societies that were emerging in the rapidly industrializing regions of Europe, whereas the earlier stages conveniently evoked images of various native peoples in the Americas, Africa, and Asia. By incorporating ancient history into a universal framework that traced the technological and scientific progress of humanity through distinct stages, ancient history, in effect, became vital material evidence of the economic success story of the Western world. Although this idea of progress tended to stress the superiority of Western civilization, it also suggested, within its universal scope, that the origins of Western civilization were not limited to the Western world. Scholars analyzed the physical remnants of ancient civilizations in Africa and Asia in order to trace ultimate sources of Western progress. Indeed, in order to gain a more complete picture of the development and nature of the mature societies of the Western world, archaeologists and other scholars felt it was imperative to go back to their origins, to search for their own roots beyond Greece, by seeking civilization in its infant, pristine form. This endeavor necessitated finding and analyzing the "cradle" of civilization.

The innocuous term "cradle of civilization" referred to the pristine beginnings of human development. For example, when the archaeologist Austen Henry Layard visited Mesopotamia in the middle of the nineteenth century, he described its landscape as "the plain to which the Jew and Gentile alike look as the cradle of their race."[16] The archaeological enterprise, or the unearthing of the lost fragments of ancient history in the Middle East, and in particular in Mesopotamia, can thus be viewed as an attempt to reconstruct this cradle in order to relive and understand that youth. And since the biblical accounts of creation and early human history were accompanied by seemingly specific geographical descriptions, Europeans focused on Mesopotamia—the area also known as the "cradle of civilization."

For centuries, Europeans did not doubt the historical accuracy of the biblical story in Genesis about the beginnings of humanity in the Garden of Eden. According to Genesis, Eden is said to be set among four rivers, including the "Tigris which flows east of Assyria and . . . the Euphrates." This account gave rise to a vast literature, especially in the sixteenth and seventeenth centuries, on the geographical details of this earthly paradise and its possible location.[17] The early and medieval Christian cartographers' pictures of the world incorporated depictions of paradise that reflected the belief that earthly paradise still existed somewhere on earth.[18] On the maps, and in particular ones that accompanied commentaries on the Apocalypse, Eden was most often situated among the names of the Caucasus, Assyria, Persia, Chaldea, and India. By the eighteenth century, however, paradise practically disappeared from any major maps. Significant progress in cartography, due to advances in the marine and navigational sciences, resulted in more realistic and accurate maps.

In tune with the idea of progress and the forward-looking orientation of the day, the early archaeologists who traveled in Mesopotamia gave no indications that they were looking for the remnants of the Garden of Eden or somehow hoping to regain the paradise that was lost. Rather, they were products of a culture whose historical imagination leaped forward to the eventual eschatological City of God, not backward to the original Garden of Eden.[19] The role of Mesopotamia in the archaeologists' imaginative constructs, and its apocalyptic connotations, were suggestive of the historical developments taking place in their own society and were pointed reminders of the vulnerability of human society and progress.

MESOPOTAMIA AND THE APOCALYPSE

Even before systematic diplomatic and commercial excursions into Mesopotamia, its history, fables, and geography were vividly present in Western religious and cultural attention. The histories of Herodotus and Josephus, as well as biblical accounts, had already ensured that Mesopotamian civilizations, such as the cities of Babylon and Nineveh, took on mythical, and therefore exaggerated, proportions in Western imagination. These ancient civilizations figured largely in the literature and the arts, as they were integral to Christian religious thought and were especially critical components in any apocalyptic configuration.[20] In the twenty-first century, particularly in evangelical Christian literature in the United States, the apocalyptic associations are still vivid and potent and continue to play important cultural and political roles.[21]

The lands of Mesopotamia had the potential for evoking awe-inspiring reactions touching on central themes of Western civilization. The biblical tales from Babylon and Nineveh represented the integral elements and motifs of Christian faith and action—sin, punishment, reward, providence, freedom, certitude, resurrection, and everlasting life.

For many Christians, the biblical tales from Mesopotamia served as a historical example of the weighing of souls and the fate of the damned in the Last Judgment. For example, when the German traveler Leonhard Rauwolf traveled to Mesopotamia in the sixteenth century and stood on top of what he believed were the ruins of ancient Babylon itself, he would gaze with astonishment as he remembered this great city, which was now "reduced to such a desolation and wilderness that the very shepherds cannot stand to place their tents there to inhabit it." For Rauwolf, this was a "most terrible example to all impious and haughty tyrants . . . [to] leave their tyranny and cease to persecute the innocent," since God would certainly punish them, like he had those of Babylon.[22]

In a world where history was interpreted as a moral text, the allegorical and apocalyptic significance of the stories from Mesopotamia was often considered suggestive of the cosmic meaning of current events. During the intense religious debates preceding and following the English Civil War of the seventeenth century, the identification of Britain with the Whore of Babylon was a staple of religious invective.[23] In later years, the revilement of England was specifically focused on London. For example, in Byron's play *Sarandapalus,* set in ancient Nineveh, Byron depicts that city, as Marilyn Butler has maintained, "as a richly imagined Otherworld, which is the familiar world—London— at once turned upside down, and satirically reproduced."[24]

The Mesopotamian apocalyptic images found their way into a variety of writings. In a 1806 British book discussing current municipal problems of London, particularly the status of the Thames, the author states: "If this river were rendered unnavigable, London would soon become a heap of ruins, like Nineveh or Babylon."[25] In Eugene Roche's poem *London in a Thousand Years* (1830), Revelation's destroying angel brings the end upon London. Somehow the narrator survives, to awaken a thousand years later to find "Babylon" covered in a green mantle, and starts recollecting about the sinful place that was once London.

Mesopotamia therefore played a complex and multifaceted role that often seemed paradoxical. It was an area whose history was clearly associated with the beginnings of human history, and yet its relationship with the End was also becoming increasingly acute in the late eighteenth century. In popular and religious imagination, Mesopotamian themes were critical ingredients in the recipes of eschatological doom, which despite the seeming decline in authority of the biblical record were particularly potent in the nineteenth century. These complex dualistic, antithetical, yet ultimately interconnected, roles endowed Mesopotamian ancient history with special urgency. This feature was particularly evident in the visual arts.

MESOPOTAMIA IN THE ARTS

I n the late eighteenth and early nineteenth centuries, religious elements, albeit in different, new forms, became increasingly visible in the literature and arts of Western Europe and North America.[26] The new Christian images typically stressed earthly tragedy or heavenly grandeur in immense depictions of landscape. Edmund Burke's *Philosophical Enquiry into the Origins of our Ideas of the Sublime and the Beautiful* (1756) became a major aesthetic source, with its evocations of terror, vastness, obscurity, and horror, for the first generation of Romantic artists in search of overwhelming and fear-inspiring experiences.[27] This exploration and its "divinity of landscape"[28] led inevitably to depictions of the "landscape of belief,"[29] which often had apocalyptic undertones.

This biblical sublime movement was particularly prominent in England, where artists such as J. M. W. Turner, William Blake, John Martin, and Benjamin West sought inspiration from biblical tales. This fascination with the apocalypse was not limited to the visual arts. In one guise or another the apocalyptic theme of world destruction appears in Byron's *Sarandapalus* (1821) and *Heaven and Earth* (1823), William Wordsworth's *Ode* (1815), Edward Bulwer-Lytton's *The Last Days of Pompeii* (1834), Mary Shelley's *The Last Man* (1826), and Edwin Athersone's *The Fall of Nineveh* (1828).

In 1819 John Martin displayed his critically acclaimed panoramic *The Fall of Babylon*. The reaction to the painting was immediate and unanimous. Its exhibition was well attended, and a contemporary critique stated that it united "all the great essentials of an epic poem; and is one of the most astonishing productions of modern art."[30] Martin's portrayal of Babylon was based on images, such as docks and warehouses, of his own day, yet also contrived to cater to the increasing taste for distant eras. This imagery may also have suggested, as art historian William Feaver has argued, that London was the "New Babylon," yet also stressed the reflection of present times in the past.[31] In his painting, Martin emphasized the architectural grandeur of Babylon, with its colossal promenades, canals, and viaducts. These images inspired awe for such an achievement, while also, through historical knowledge, giving the benefit of insight into the vulnerability of the ancient kingdoms—which had clear implications for the present age.

Martin's painting was inspired by the publication of the book *Memoir on the Ruins of Babylon*, written by Claudius James Rich, British Resident in Baghdad. This book, published in 1815, described prominent aspects of the site, such as Babil and the Ishtar Gate. Rich also published a plan of the city by an earlier traveler, James Rennell, which shows the Tower of Belus across the Euphrates and opposite the imperial palace. This plan was adopted by Martin in his painting of Babylon. Martin also adopted the eight-storied form for the temple that Rennell outlined in an insert to his map of Babylon.

Despite the seeming prosperity of the British Empire, there was nevertheless prevalent among artists what one critic has called "the sense of an ending."[32] Such a sense is manifested in the increasingly popular depiction of the catastrophic history of the Deluge. As Lynn Matteson observes, from 1780 to 1840 the Deluge was to become the subject of no less than twelve ambitious dramatic poems and nineteen paintings in Britain alone.[33]

In 1828 Martin exhibited *The Fall of Nineveh*,[34] the last painting in Martin's Mesopotamian trilogy, indicating that Martin, like Turner and West before him, was especially concerned with the tottering empires and epic catastrophes that the Bible detailed. This fascination with the cataclysmic end of ancient cities supports the theory that the theme conveyed a far more profound meaning than the mere re-creation of a historical event. To the Romantics the destinies of Babylon and Nineveh stood as a testimony to the tragic destiny of all things human, namely their eventual extinction. The destruction of a city was employed as a microcosm of world destruction and understood as a gloomy metaphor of the fate of civilization.[35]

The fable of Babylon's fall, seen as the just result of internal vice and corruption, seemed an obvious lesson for the British Empire, which, in its eighteenth-century global expansion, seemed to be suffering the ill effects of excessive luxury and pride.

This apocalyptic feature became clearly evident in early 1821 or at the same time, when the first British archaeologists were making their first surveys in Mesopotamia. The London art scene became aghast at the display of a new, titanic painting by John Martin called *Belshazzar's Feast*. As Feaver asserts, Martin's special contribution was to popularize and make immediate long-vanished civilizations: "While offering little or nothing in terms of original research, he turned literary references into *visual* reality."[36] (Several years later, as a result of Austen Henry Layard's excavations in Mesopotamia, which will be discussed below, ancient history became a *physical* reality.) Martin's *Belshazzar's Feast* places the story amidst a staggering and exotic architectural setting. In trying to make his setting imaginatively true, Martin incorporated much of what was then known about Middle Eastern architecture.[37] There is an enormous central atrium bordered by two rows of columns supporting the hanging gardens above them. The sense of exoticism is heightened by details like the signs of the zodiac that decorate the lower colonnades, an Oriental-type ziggurat, and the Tower of Babel hovering in the background.[38] With his powerful contrasts of light and shadow displaying God's authoritative power and frightened human gestures, Martin contributes to the sublime of terror so common in contemporaneous Romantic paintings. According to Morton Paley, the painting was enormously popular. However, there was a division between the painting's popular appeal and the artistic establishment's response. The most important artists of the Royal Academy, such as the critic Charles Lamb, who found *Belshazzar's Feast* vulgar and bombastic, remained indifferent or even hostile to Martin. This reaction would foreshadow the reaction to the Assyrian art that Layard uncovered and was later displayed in the British Museum.[39]

Therefore, at the time when apocalyptic landscape became a central element in the artistic sentiment, archaeologists—themselves the products of the new scientific empiricism and the age of classification and progress—traveled to the land associated with apocalypticism to literally unearth its history in a relatively systematic scientific manner. Relishing the experience that aroused the instinct for self-preservation in the face of the excitements of the unknown and unfamiliar, the archaeologists eagerly sought out lessons about the remote past among remote people in remote places. The historic treasures, with their indisputable links to biblical history, challenged, however, the reigning Classical aesthetic norms and values. Archaeologists found strange objects and unreadable scripts. Yet, somehow these scholars and later the public sensed some affinity because they believed these artifacts were integral elements of their own heritage. This sense of belonging is evident in the fact that it was popularly considered necessary to bring the objects "back home."

The first British archaeologists who ventured to Mesopotamia in the first half of the nineteenth century were very much products of a society still firmly entrenched in religious beliefs and influence. When the earliest archaeologists were making their initial forays into Mesopotamia, they felt they were proceeding onto what they considered to be known grounds. The biblical landscape they were entering had been prominently and dramatically imagined in their own cultural milieu. Their extensive knowledge of both biblical history and the accounts of Herodotus and Diodorous had already given them a familiarity with the history and legacy of the area before they ever set their eyes upon it.

The early Western archaeologists encountered locals who, rather than sharing the intense Western interest in Mesopotamian antiquities and their Christian religious connotations, were largely uninterested in any archaeological endeavors. Most commentators have suggested that their apathy was born out of a sense of discontinuity with the ancient civilizations that once flourished in their countries, due to the linguistic and religious gulf between the modern Middle East and its pre-Islamic past.[40] This chasm was supposedly manifested by Islam's own unconcern, even condemnation, of the ancient past, its "*jahilliya,*" as an age of ignorance.[41]

In this land of magnificent ancient history, the local inhabitants seem to have been apathetic to that history and its artifacts. Since Western archaeologists were able to start their excavations on virgin soil, it suggests that the locals had not made serious attempts at uncovering antiquities. The absence of such activities does not reveal a sense of proprietorship over or assigning value to these historic artifacts. Many of the Western archaeologists complained of this attitude, the ignorance of locals and their failure to appreciate the value of the antiquities. Although this lack of interest was one primary justification of the Westerners' removal of the artifacts from Mesopotamia, it also contributed to the acquisition of great Mesopotamian antiquities by various museums and private collections in Europe and North America. Yet what role did the ancient history actually play among the inhabitants of Mesopotamia of the nineteenth and early twentieth centuries? Why didn't they regard the artifacts as having any particular value and worthy of excavation and public display? One reason that these artifacts did not attract the attention of the inhabitants was that they did not represent epochs or events that were extensively discussed in their literature, both secular and religious.

In contrast to its treatment in the Bible, the city of Babylon does not figure prominently in the Qur'an and is referred to in only one passage (2:95) as the location where the two angels, Harut and Marut, descended onto earth.[42] According to various legends attached to this passage, the angels in heaven had spoken contemptuously about the sinful practices of humans. When God said that they would not have done any better in the same position, the angels did not agree and received permission to send two of their kind to earth as an experiment. Harut and Marut were the ones chosen and were ordered to abstain from the various worldly sins such as idolatry, whoredom, and murder. Once on earth, however, the angels became fascinated by a beautiful woman and were led astray, and when they were discovered they killed the man who had found them. They were given the choice between punishment in this world or the next. They chose the former and were incarcerated in Babylon, where they have since suffered atrocious torments.[43]

Despite numerous apocalyptic passages in the Qur'an that refer to the coming of the Hour,[44] a prelude to the *eschaton*, which will be characterized by the darkening of the stars and the movement of the mountains (81:2–4), a mighty earthquake (99:1–3), and the appearance of a Beast (27:82), neither Babylon nor any other Mesopotamian city is mentioned in the apocalyptic scenario. These cities did not intrigue the Islamic apocalyptic imagination, their dramatic associations not being the same as those in Christianity. Rather, in the Islamic context, it is the city of Jerusalem that plays a key role in the eschatological drama as the site of the second coming of Jesus Christ, which inaugurates a new age and a new earth. The cities of Nineveh and Babylon, therefore, did not evoke complex allegories that might have made their histories and ruins more relevant and intriguing for the local populations.

Yet despite the lack of apocalyptic connotations in the Qur'an and its scant discussion of the ancient civilizations of Mesopotamia, those civilizations would figure more prominently in succeeding Islamic writings. Beginning in the eighth century C.E., Islamic historiography had, as one of its main concerns, the problem of the ancient nations and their relationship to the Islamic era. As historian Tarif Khalidi suggests, "The Muslim historian was faced with the spectacle of many great nations, ancient as well as contemporaneous, which rose to heights of glory without their having an Islamic heritage."[45]

The historians Dinawari, al-Tabari, Mas'udi, and Ya'qubi all strove to incorporate pre-Islamic history into their overall history. For the influential historian al-Tabari (839–923), the primary value of studying ancient history was didactic. That history would reveal more insights into the workings of God while also highlighting the "moral," i.e., the struggle between the righteous and unrighteous, of pre-Islamic history in general.[46] Since al-Tabari was greatly interested in Persian history,[47] which he intertwined with biblical and, later, pre-Islamic Arab history, Babylonia figures prominently as a Persian regional seat of government.[48] Further, al-Tabari devotes considerable attention to the famous accounts of Sennacherib and Nebuchadnezzar.[49] For these historians, Babylon did not necessarily signify a place of lust, corruption, and evil as it did later in European art and literature. Rather, it is portrayed as a seat of government of colorful monarchs who initiated many critical developments such as the mining of iron and copper, the digging of canals, and the investigation of the properties of light and color. It therefore played a critical role in the development of Middle Eastern societies that would reach its zenith with Muhammad and the emergence of the Islamic faith.

Later Muslim writers and geographers would incorporate these histories in their discussion of the ancient civilizations. Although they were both vague and sometimes imprecise about its history and its exact locations, they generally agreed that, for example, the ancient city of Babylon had been at the location of a current small village called Babil (or Babel). For example, the tenth-century Arab geographer Ibn Haykal notes that Babel was a small village, whose buildings were the most ancient in Iraq, with many ruins of great edifices. Ibn Haykal states that in Babel Abraham was thrown into the great fire and there are two heaps in which the ashes still remain.[50] The European travelers who first visited these sites starting in the twelfth century would relay similar information concerning the condition of the antiquities.

In his influential *Muqaddimah,* the historian Ibn Khaldun (1332–1406) only presents a brief summary of the history of pre-Islamic peoples. He was aware that powerful, ancient civilizations once flourished in the area: "The old Persian nations, the Syrians, the Nabataeans, the Tubba's, the Israelites and the Copts, all once existed. They had their own particular institutions . . . their own politics, crafts, languages, technical terminologies, as well as their own ways of dealing with their fellow men and handling their cultural institutions. Their relics testify to that."[51] Ibn Khaldun stated that Iraq, specifically, was "ruled continuously by the Nabataeans and the Persians, that is the Chaldeans, the Kayyanids, the Sassanians, and after them, the Arabs."[52]

Generally speaking, therefore, the medieval Islamic travel books and geography did mention certain wonders *(aja'ib)* such as the arch of Ctesiphon *(Iwan Kisra)* and the ruins of Babylon. Yet of more interest were the various Islamic shrines and sanctuaries of Mesopotamia, such as the burial places of Ali and Husayn and the numerous tombs in Kufa, Basra, and Baghdad. These works, though, are typically more concerned with commerce and agricultural production. Therefore, the date palms of Basra, for example, and the city's extensive textile industry receive extensive discussion and analysis. When history or culture is mentioned it usually involves a discussion on local manners and customs. Therefore there is more emphasis in classical Islamic literature on the cultural and economic conditions of Mesopotamia than on the ancient historic artifacts.

In stark contrast to the Islamic writings, the main preoccupation of Western writings on Mesopotamia of the same period was the exact opposite: much on the antiquities and less on the contemporary human element. The antiquities were one of the primary reasons Westerners were interested in the region. The local peoples were perceived as unfortunate and irritating occupiers of sacred space who could only hinder or obstruct any major activity.

WESTERN ARCHAEOLOGISTS IN MESOPOTAMIA, 1808–1899

The early travelers and archaeologists who in the eighteenth and nineteenth centuries ventured into Mesopotamia to explore the land and culture were not necessarily investigating or opening up a new frontier. Mesopotamia was not a total terra incognita. Although they did not feel kinship with the local populations, they conversely sensed an affinity with the land and its history. In a sense they were returning to their infancy—to their "cradle"—and as they started to dig into the earth to find traces of those roots, they somehow naturally felt the need to relocate those artifacts to their current home. This sense of owner-ship was evident in that up until World War I most sites that were exca-vated were ones somehow directly related to biblical history—a history perceived by the Europeans as their own, along with its artifacts, and a history of which they were the representatives.[53]

The exotic lands and cultures of the Middle East also lured adven-turers seeking encounters with both the known and unknown. Their interest was further piqued because these treasures could easily be unearthed, bought, or removed due to local apathy toward these ruins. These explorers could transport them back home because of European imperial political and naval strength. With a sense of great urgency, ambitious and talented scholars and archaeologists traveled to Persia, Egypt, Palestine, and Mesopotamia hoping to unearth great historical treasures while tracing the roots of their own civilization.

The beginnings of archaeological work in Iraq date back to rough-ly the same time as the beginning of Egyptology, or the early years of the nineteenth century.[54] Unlike Egypt, Iraq had few surviving spectacular buildings or monuments to remind people of the splendors of ancient civilizations.[55] Therefore, as art historian Frederick N. Bohrer demon-strates, ancient Mesopotamian antiquities never had a hold on popular imagination in Western countries similar to those of ancient Egypt.[56]

Given the relative inaccessibility of Mesopotamia, until the late nineteenth century it was only the odd traveler or diplomat who encountered any remnants, or what were believed to be the ruins, of the ancient Mesopotamian civilizations. The only evidence these Western travelers of the seventeenth and eighteenth centuries saw were great mounds of earth covering sites identified by native traditions, both Jewish and Arab, as the ancient cities such as Babylon or Nineveh. The barren state of these remains was compelling for Westerners, since their condition seemed to fulfill biblical prophecies proclaiming the utter desolation of these great capitals.[57] For example, the Book of Jeremiah (51:43) stated, "Her cities are a desolation, a dry land and a wilderness, a land wherein no man dwelleth." Even though the early explorers did not encounter distinct monuments, these travelers came across bricks, potsherds, and fragments of tablets covered with a curious writing similar to inscriptions on certain old Persian monuments.[58] The void of Mesopotamian antiquities stood in stark contrast to the magnificent Egyptian ruins, as well as those of Persepolis, Palmyra, and Petra. As the English clergyman Thomas Maurice stated, "From the perishable nature of materials of which Babylon was constructed, no remains of the magnificence prodigious as those of Egypt are there to be found."[59] Similarly, the Dane Carsten Niebuhr, who visited both Egypt and Mesopotamia in the eighteenth century, wrote, "When one reflects on Babylonian antiquities, one must not expect to find magnificent monuments such as one encounters in Persia and Egypt."[60] The barren and covert nature of Mesopotamian antiquities stood in stark contrast to the fluid, fertile, and distinct character of Mesopotamia in the Europeans' religious and historical imagination. The archaeologist Austen Henry Layard later would convey such sentiments when he wrote in 1849: "A deep mystery hangs over Assyria, Babylonia and Chaldea. With these names are linked great nations and great cities; mighty ruins in the midst of deserts, defying, by their very desolation and lack of definite form . . . the fulfillment of prophecies."[61]

The desolate nature of Mesopotamian antiquities is evident in the fact that nearly all the early travelers speculated on the exact locations of noted biblical sites such as Babylon and Nineveh and came to different conclusions. Even though the Islamic geographers and historians such as Ibn Haykal and Ya'qubi gave fairly accurate indications of the position of ancient Mesopotamian cities, which were further supported by vague local traditions, the Western explorers ignored those authorities in their own speculations.[62]

The initial European explorations in Mesopotamia were neither systematic nor a concerted effort of any particular nation. Rather, given the difficulties, dangers, and unpredictability of international travel, the pioneering explorers were an impressive collage of personalities who represented myriad nations. These extraordinary men included the Spanish Jew Benjamin of Tudela in the twelfth century, the Germans Johann Schiltberger in the fourteenth century and Leonhard Rauwolf in 1574, the Italian Pietro Della Valle in 1616, the Dane Carsten Niebuhr in the 1770s, and the Frenchman Abbe de Beauchamp in the 1790s.

The earliest recorded Western explorer, Benjamin of Tudela, who traveled from his native Spain all the way to China between 1162 and

1173 to evaluate the living conditions of Jews in the diaspora, visited Babylon and commented on the antiquities. He stated that the ruins of the palace of Nebuchadnezzar were still to be seen and that the local synagogue had been built by the prophet Daniel himself.[63] Benjamin misidentified the ruins of Birs Nimrud (ancient Borsippa), which lie south of Babylon with the Tower of Babel. The German Schiltberger, who visited the ruins three centuries later and wrote one of the first German travel books, made a similar incorrect assumption, which, as the historian John M. Lundquist points out, is probably because they relied on the inaccurate testimony in the Talmud for information about the layout of Babylon.[64] When Rauwolf of Germany surveyed the area in the sixteenth century, he imagined that he had found the site of Babylon at Fallujah, a town on the Euphrates.[65] Although Rauwolf noted that the region surrounding Fallujah was so dry, barren, and incapable of cultivation as to make it an improbable location for a great and powerful capital such as Babylon, Rauwolf was nevertheless convinced that Fallujah was the site of ancient Babylon due to its "situation, and several ancient and delicate antiquities that still are standing hereabout in great desolation."[66] Rauwolf also thought he saw the Tower of Babel in the ruins near Fallujah, although contemporary travelers such as Cesare Federici, who visited Baghdad in 1563, Ralph Fitch (1583), and John Eldred (1583) identified that biblical site with the ruins lying near and to the west of Baghdad.[67]

The learned Italian traveler Della Valle examined the area more thoroughly in 1616. Della Valle states in his travel account that Babylon "appears [like] a heap of ruined buildings, like a huge mountain, the materials of which are so confounded together that one knows not what to make of it." He maintained, furthermore, that apart from the mass of ruins, there was no sign of anything to show that there had been in that place the great city that Herodotus described. Della Valle contended that the location of Babylon was at the site of the modern town of Hillah, yet he was the first to report a relatively accurate description of the area and to bring back inscribed cylinder seals.[68]

In Niebuhr's *Description of Travels in Arabia*, based on his travels in Persia, India, and Mesopotamia in the 1760s, he describes and illustrates several Mesopotamian ruins, including Babylon and Nineveh. He firmly asserts that the mounds he visited opposite Mosul were the ruins of Nineveh.[69] Niebuhr also speculated about the location of Babylon, which he claimed was near the town of Hillah. Niebuhr was also erroneous in his assumption that Birs Nimrud was the Tower of Babel.[70] His book, however, is most noteworthy for his accurate copying of the inscriptions of Persepolis. By identifying the existence of three distinct scripts, one of the alphabets with forty-two signs, Niebuhr laid important foundations for deciphering these lost languages.

Shortly after the travels of Niebuhr, the Frenchman de Beauchamp explored the sites of Mesopotamia. In an article in *European Magazine* in 1792 de Beauchamp refuted the assertion of Della Valle that the city of Hillah was the site of Babylon. According to de Beauchamp, the hills that contained the ruins of Babylon were visible only to the attentive traveler. Yet, it was not as obvious that these mounds were the seats of physical remnants of that kingdom. Beauchamp noted that only by digging in the mounds could the human structures be made visible. As de Beauchamp wrote, "The mound is so little elevated that the least ruin we pass in the road to it conceals it from the view. To come at the bricks, it is necessary to dig into the earth."[71]

These travelers conveyed extensive new information about the cultures, landscapes, and people of the Middle East. It is particularly striking how capriciously the biblical framework determined their description and analysis.[72] In their accounts, the travelers quite naturally wrote with an eye to their particular audience back home. Such an awareness undoubtedly affected the travelers' perceptions and influenced them to select specific examples of the geography and culture, ultimately stressing aspects that would most easily find popular resonance, as well as examples of how the people and the landscape resemble biblical descriptions. Rauwolf, in his narrative, frequently alludes to biblical imagery, as when, tasting honey in travels between Raqqa and Baghdad, he commented that it reminded him of the food of St. John the Baptist as described in Matthew 3:4.[73] These associations lingered for later travelers. For example, the artist David Roberts, on his travels in the Middle East in the 1840s, observed the departure of a caravan from Cairo to Mecca and wrote in his journal that it recalled "vividly the children of Israel bearing the ark through the wilderness."[74]

While the landscape and history of the area had strong biblical reverberation that clearly appealed to the writers, the role of the Middle Eastern peoples themselves was more ambiguous. Therefore, as has been aptly documented, the travelers went to the Middle East with

specific stereotypes in mind, and their writings would typically perpetu-
ate the stereotype asserted in earlier accounts.[75] Rather than being the
reflection of themselves, as were the classical Greeks, the inhabitants
and cultures of ancient Mesopotamia were most often
portrayed—invoking the phrase of Frank Turner—as the opposites of
their own best selves. The Orient aroused the image of the "Other,"
allowing poets, painters, and authors to produce realizations of what
England and Western civilization were not.[76] In the case of the Middle
East, the travel literature is overflowing with references to the seemingly exotic and even erotic aspects of Middle Eastern cultures, which were
eagerly read by the audience back home.

FROM LITERARY REFERENCES
TO HISTORICAL PRESENCE

While the references to and images of the ancient Near Eastern
civilizations were primarily based on allusions in literature, in
the early years of the nineteenth century this situation began to change.
The Western nations started to increase their missionary, commercial,
and diplomatic activities in the Middle East, forcing Westerners to be
more knowledgeable about Middle Eastern countries and cultures.[77]
These diplomatic and commercial contacts opened new opportunities
for more systematic and thorough research on the antiquities of the
Middle East.

In the eighteenth and nineteenth centuries, the Ottoman Empire
was in a state of transition. It was uneasily and cautiously adapting to the
new and modern geopolitical realities. This vast empire, with its diverse
populations and difficult natural terrain, struggled to maintain some
level of credible control and coherent integrity. Due to the arduous task
of governing this complex and delicate empire, the Ottomans decided
to rule distant provinces such as Mesopotamia indirectly. Although the
Ottomans had conquered the Mesopotamian region in the sixteenth
century, its incorporation into their empire was sporadic. In return for
taxes and some level of formal submission, the local inhabitants were
basically left to administer themselves. The region, therefore, was controlled through local tribal chieftains, provincial notables, religious
leaders, and Ottoman administrators.[78]

Because of the decentralized political structure of Mesopotamia, a
permit was required from local authorities to pursue archaeological

excavations in an area. The writings of the archaeologists themselves are full of vivid descriptions of these procedures, which necessarily accentuate the exotic features of Middle Eastern governments such as the practice of giving *bakhsish* (bribes) to facilitate transactions. Although the impatient archaeologists vehemently complained about the apathy of the local authorities in archaeological matters (an attitude that actually was ultimately beneficial to the archaeologists, since it allowed for the massive export of antiquities), one should not rush to judge the authorities in question. It is quite natural that the chieftains were suspicious of this newfound interest of Westerners in their countryside. Most commentators have claimed, relying on the writings of the archaeologists themselves, that the local authorities' suspicion stemmed from the belief that the Europeans were looking for some sort of treasure, such as gold (which in a sense they were), or that the Europeans were gathering evidence through the ancient inscriptions to support a demand for repossession of the land.[79] Heinrich Schliemann's removal from the Ottoman Empire in 1872 of the gold artifacts from Troy known as "Priam's Gold" and the removal of the Great Altar of Zeus from ancient Pergamon (modern Bergama in western Turkey) to Berlin in 1879, only confirmed the Ottoman suspicion that these collectors acting as archaeologists were primarily interested in treasures.

The first piece of Ottoman legislation to deal specifically with antiquities was enacted in 1874.[80] It placed all archaeological excavations in the empire under the supervision of the Ministry of Education. It also included provisions dividing finds among the excavation team, the landowner, and the state.[81] This division is reflected in the *firman* awarded to Hormuzd Rassam, which allotted one third of the finds to the British Museum, one third to the Imperial Museum in Istanbul, and the last third to the landowner. Under the auspices of the state museum, a school to train Ottoman archaeologists and museum curators was opened in 1875. In 1884 a new antiquities legislation was enacted that involved a significant change. In this new act, the state itself became the sole owner of all antiquities, and in the 1906 law of antiquities the export or removal of antiquities was prohibited unless a special license was provided.

Concurrent with the increasing Western commercial and political involvement in the area, field archaeology began in Mesopotamia with the appointment of Claudius James Rich (1787–1821) as British Resident in Baghdad in 1808—a position that primarily entailed watching over the interests of the British East India Company. Rich, who had managed to learn Turkish, Persian, Arabic, and Hebrew, visited, in his leisure time, the sites of ancient Mesopotamian cities. During his first visit to the ruins of Babylon in 1811 he made a thorough survey and examination of the site. Later in 1815, when he published the results of his investigations, his book aroused considerable attention and became a best-seller in both Britain and France.[82] Although Rich did not base his discussion on scientific excavations or on deciphered cuneiform scripts, he was able to make pointed observations about the layout and architecture of the area and the position of the inscriptions, which laid foundations for much later work.

When Rich died of cholera at Shiraz in 1821, the British Museum bought his archaeological collection and subsequently displayed it to the public. Posthumously another memoir was published in 1836, edited by his wife.[83] This publication included his detailed measurements and maps of Nineveh. He also identified the major mounds called Kuyunjik and Nebbi Yenus (named after the prophet Jonah). His rather modest collection had a profound impact on people's views of ancient civilizations in the Middle East. For example, in a pamphlet distributed during the exhibition of *The Fall of Nineveh* in 1828, John Martin, who previously had been very concerned with the ancient civilizations in his paintings, wrote that the "mighty cities of Nineveh and Babylon have long since passed away. The accounts of their greatness and splendour may have been exaggerated. Into the solemn visions of antiquity we look without demanding the clear daylight of truth."[84] In light of Rich's recent writings and discoveries, Martin was obviously very concerned to depict as accurate a reconstruction of Nineveh as modern research could permit. The modest archaeological findings of Rich were clearly already starting to have a profound impact on the reconstruction of ancient biblical civilizations.

The French government, impressed with the findings of Rich and concerned to not be outdone by England in this field, realized the possibilities of active archaeological work in Mesopotamia. France, having already considered appointing a consul in Mesopotamia so that Britain would not have the area entirely to itself, now saw new impetus for such an appointment.[85] Julius Mohl, a member of the French Asiatic Society who had seen Rich's collection at the British Museum, insisted that the French agent have some experience in archaeology and that he be instructed to collect antiquities for France.[86] Finally, in 1840, the French appointed Paul Emile Botta as French consul in Mesopotamia and stationed him in the city of Mosul.[87] He began excavating at the colossal mounds at Nineveh in 1842 and Khorsabad in 1843—tasks for which the existing methods of archaeology were hardly sufficient. During this first systematic excavation in Mesopotamia, Botta found at Khorsabad the first major Assyrian discovery. Botta's excavations unveiled an enormous and complex series of sculpture-lined limestone slabs picturing wild beasts, winged animals, and bearded men in long gowns. These slabs were rooms later recognized to belong to a palace of Sargon II. Although it was not clear at the time what exactly Botta had uncovered, his findings were nevertheless published in the *Journal Asiatique,* primarily in the form of his letters to Mohl.[88] The French government arranged for the sculptures to be transported to France in 1846.[89] Botta's expedition, which at a later stage included an illustrator, Eugéne Flandin, was well financed by the French government. Botta was able to publish his findings along with Flandin's drawings in the impressive and elaborate *Monument de Ninive.*[90]

The public exhibition of the Mesopotamian artifacts was held the following year at the Louvre in Paris.[91] The objects on display often generated curious reactions. In his 1877 novel *L'Assommoir,* Emile Zola describes a working-class group visiting the Louvre in the late 1850s. "[They] wandered into the Assyrian gallery where they were somewhat taken aback. . . . They thought the sculptures very ugly. One knew a jolly lot better than that nowadays how to carve stone. An inscription in Phoenician characters stupefied them. It was not possible, no one could ever have read that scrawl."[92]

Paralleling these French efforts, the Englishman Henry Austen Layard (1817–1894), an unpaid attaché to the British Embassy in Istanbul, began his excavations at Nimrud in 1845.[93] In his prior travels to Mesopotamia, he visited some of the mounds of the alleged biblical sites and met with Botta. Just like other Western travelers before him, he was, as he recalls in his autobiography, "deeply moved by their desolate and solitary grandeur . . . and I felt an intense longing to dig into them."[94] The British Museum was more parsimonious than the Louvre in its support of archaeological activities in Mesopotamia.[95] In contrast to the generous official backing of Botta, Layard first arrived into Mesopotamia with no official financial support. Instead he was armed with £100—a private grant from Stratford Canning, the British ambassador to the Ottoman Empire. In addition to the desire to compete with the French in order to acquire antiquities, it is also likely that Canning's support and Layard's mission had intelligence-gathering motives.

Because Layard considered the local governor at Mosul obtrusive and he did not have any of the requisite official excavation permits, Layard decided to start his excavation covertly 25 kilometers from Mosul at Nimrud.[96] At Nimrud, which Layard had visited several years earlier, there was a large mound with a pyramid-type structure on its northwest corner of the mound.

In one of the most unbelievable episodes in the history of archaeology and one unlikely to occur ever again, Layard quite literally stumbled over a rock on his first day. After Layard and his workers had removed the earth around it he found rooms of palaces subsequently identified with the Assyrian kings Ashur-nasir-pal (883–859 B.C.E.) and Shalmaneser III (858–824 B.C.E.). During the succeeding weeks, Layard found a large number of sculptures, often of huge animals, and bas-reliefs that were, as he was surprised to note in his account, elegant and aesthetically pleasing, and quite suitable for display in England.[97] Unlike many of his countrymen, Layard was adamant in his appreciation of Assyrian art. Even before his first excavation he described the sculptures found by Botta at Khorsabad in an article in the *Athenæum* in 1845 as "immeasurably superior to the stiff and ill-proportioned figures of the monuments of the Pharaohs."[98]

Layard's most significant find was a black obelisk. Although he did not realize it at the time, the text and pictures give an account of Shalmaneser III's campaigns, including the submission of the Jewish king Jehu. These findings were encouraging for Layard, who was excited about the prospects of transporting them back to England for public display. Through Canning he applied for extra funds for the complicated and rigorous task of removing the delicate, voluminous objects in the middle of the Mesopotamian desert all the way to the halls of the British Museum.

As he was waiting for further funds, Layard sent some specimens to Henry Creswicke Rawlinson (1810–1895), British consul in Baghdad, who was also a leading authority on cuneiform.[99] Rawlinson, whose impressive linguistic abilities were useful in his official duties as an officer cadet in the East India Company and later in various posts in Iran,

India, and Mesopotamia, became instrumental in deciphering the Old Persian, Babylonian, and Elamite texts. Rawlinson's work established that Babylonian was a Semitic writing, eventually paving the way for both the Babylonian and Assyrian inscriptions to be translated.[100] This accomplishment was primarily because Rawlinson was able to copy (with the help of an anonymous Kurdish boy) and translate from the famous, and inaccessible, trilingual inscription engraved in 516 B.C.E. on the great rock of Behsitun, thirty kilometers east of Kermanshah, which tells the story of the Persian King Darius's fight for the throne.

In a letter written to Layard, Rawlinson was tepid in his enthusiasm for the artifacts that Layard had just discovered: "The battle pieces . . . are curious, but I do not think they rank very highly as art. . . . I must confess I think the general style crude and cramped but still the curiosity of the thing is very great, if not a full compensation."[101] In a similar letter written later that month, Rawlinson reiterated his position and stated that the Assyrian sculptures have "nothing whatever to do with value. You ask by what standard I compare them. Why of course, in any abstract matter we adopt the highest standard available—and I say therefore the Elgin Marbles. . . . And I still think the Nineveh marbles are not valuable as works of art."[102] Rawlinson only saw a scientific utilitarian purpose for the Assyrian sculptures to fill in the blanks in the knowledge of ancient history.

Rawlinson's reaction was a disappointment to Layard, who was naturally excited about his recent finds, which he considered superior to those of Botta. Rawlinson's response reflects the prevailing artistic and aesthetic appreciation at the time in England, in which everything was compared to the ideal fundamentals of Greek art. Such a reaction may have convinced Layard that in order to attract attention to his discoveries, and thereby increase his reputation, he should not rely on the authorities at the British Museum or in the government, but instead appeal to the public by popularizing the subject. And in that endeavor, Layard later proved to be particularly successful. His discoveries were already becoming public knowledge in England. During his first expedition various English papers and magazines reported on Layard's findings. One leading magazine, the *Athenæum*, even criticized the government for its stinginess toward Layard.[103]

Eventually, the British Museum secured funds for the transportation of the objects back to England.[104] When the Mesopotamian artifacts arrived in England, their aesthetic value was hotly debated among the trustees of the Museum and even became the subject of an inquiry by a British parliamentary committee.[105] As historian Ian Jenkins observes, the British Museum officials considered the primary value of these artifacts pedagogical because they were examples of the most primitive attempts in the evolution of the arts.[106] Compared to the penultimate Greek sculptures from the Parthenon recently brought to the Museum, the artifacts from Mesopotamia were considered second-rate. Even someone as involved in Mesopotamia as Rawlinson, as previously mentioned, distinctly disavowed any interest in the pieces as art. He did not hesitate to state plainly that "I regard inscriptions as of infinitely greater value than sculptures." Insofar as he considered the artifacts as sculpture, he found them "valueless, for they can neither instruct nor enrapture us."[107] William Hamilton, a senior trustee of the British Museum, went even further in his criticism of the relics. He considered Layard's artifacts as a "parcel of rubbish," which he wished to see displayed only "at the bottom of the sea."[108] Richard Westmacott, the sculpture advisor to the Museum, stated that the value of the "Nineveh Marbles" will be in the history that the inscriptions relate, "for it is very bad art. . . . The less people, as artists, look at it, the better."[109]

Amidst this internal controversy, in 1853, the British Museum opened its "Nineveh Gallery," thus enshrining Layard's findings. This decision may have been influenced by the immense success, in 1848–1849, of Layard's book, called *Nineveh and Its Remains.* In contrast to Botta's grand, opulent publication, Layard wrote an accessible account that aimed to cater to the public interest in biblical history written in the style of popular travel accounts of the time. Layard had corresponded with his American friend, the painter Miner Kellogg, about his plans to publish this account, which he expected would garner much attention among Bible-reading Americans. A letter from Kellogg to Layard confirmed Layard's assumption when Kellogg wrote back eagerly: "You can scarcely dream of the importance of which your solitary labors may have upon the right understanding of the Historical and Prophetical parts of the Holy Word. Every image that you uncover, may add a link in that chain of interpretation."[110] It seems that Layard had come upon a formula that guaranteed success and popularity. As a commerce-minded friend of his suggested prior to the publication: "Write a whopper with lots of plates . . . fish up old legends and anecdotes, and if you can by any means humbug people into the belief that you have established any points in the Bible, you are a made man."[111] His mentor Stratford Canning suggested an addition to the biblical angle, advising Layard to write about the Mesopotamian relics to "make the public understand that they have got a prize."[112]

It is hardly surprising, given Layard's seemingly well-planned marketing strategy, that the book attracted immense attention. This popular account—one of the earliest and most successful of archaeological best-sellers, and certainly not the last work of archaeology to enjoy popularity—aroused great interest in the Nimrud sculptures at the British Museum. The fact that these inscriptions and artifacts were filled with biblical characters such as Sennacherib, and kings of Israel such as Jehu and Hezekiah, greatly excited the general public, and in particular the lower to middle classes, whose purchase of the book accounted for more than two-thirds of its total sales.[113] The *London Times* was lavish in its praise for Layard's work, reporting that "this is, we think, the most extraordinary work of the present age, whether with reference to the wonderful discoveries it describes, its remarkable verification of our early Biblical history, or of the talent, courage, and perseverance of its author."[114] Layard became the talk of the town and was subsequently awarded numerous prestigious honors, such as an honorary doctorate from Oxford University and a gold medal of the Royal Geographic Society.

Furthermore, Layard's work and the display of the Assyrian antiquities also added to the debate over the historicity of the Bible. By associating his sculptures with distinct biblical events, Layard, perhaps unwittingly, contributed to the prevailing belief in the historical chronology set forth in Scripture. Despite numerous challenges from many scientific disciplines, English society in the 1850s and '60s generally still clung to a biblical interpretation of history.[115]

In his second expedition to Mesopotamia in 1847, Layard turned his attention to Kuyunjik, where he discovered the remains of the palace of Sennacherib (704–681 B.C.E.), the largest known Assyrian palace. He was able to prove that Nineveh existed at this large site opposite Mosul, not at Khorsabad or Nimrud as previously thought.[116] He also greatly increased the number of inscribed cuneiform documents with his discovery of the library of King Assurbanipal. These documents were shipped back to the British Museum.

Concurrent with Layard's expeditions, critical developments were being made in deciphering the languages of the ancient civilizations.[117] The decipherment of the ancient cuneiform script, which was a gradual and long-term collaborative effort by numerous gifted linguists, is one of the more impressive scientific and cultural achievements of the eighteenth and nineteenth centuries.

In the geographic area that symbolized and inaugurated the confusion of tongues through the Tower of Babel, archaeologists now sought to understand the long-lost languages of that era and perhaps find remnants of a original universal language from before the curse of Babel.[118] Such an accomplishment would reveal new information about the history and culture of those civilizations. The successful advancement in decipherment enabled scholars to focus on the primary sources themselves, making the Classical and biblical sources somewhat marginal in the quest for accurate information about the past. Even a staunch traditionalist such as Rawlinson declared: "I throw all Greek traditions regarding Assyria to the winds."[119] Therefore, the decipherment of the extinct languages of the cylinder seals opened up a new world, independent of the recycled accounts of earlier travelers and historians, resulting in a new history—making the history and civilizations more tangible, manageable, and scientific.

The decipherment of cuneiform writing was first successfully and systematically attempted following the travels of Niebuhr, the great Danish scholar, to the Middle East. In his travels to Persepolis, Niebuhr observed that the Persepolitan inscriptions contained three kinds of script, which probably represented three different languages.[120] Later in 1798 Frederick Münter hypothesized that the contents of the texts were the same in the three different languages, representing different developmental stages of Persian.

It was up to a relatively unknown and unassuming German schoolteacher, Georg Friederich Grotefend (1775–1853), to provide an essential key to decipherment. Supposedly, he made a bet with his friends at his local pub that he could read the ancient inscriptions of Persepolis. This innocuous wager subsequently resulted in Grotefend presenting a learned paper to the Academy of Sciences in Göttingen in 1802 about his findings. Grotefend substantiated that the cuneiform characters were a form of writing and not decorative inscriptions. He also correctly assumed, which in hindsight seems so obvious and simple, yet at the time was perplexing, that the script included certain introductory or salutatory phrases. Grotefend then extrapolated that the most frequently repeated group of wedges stood for the word "king" and, after consulting his Greek histories for the names of Persian dynasties, concluded that the names Darius and Xerxes fitted most easily into the inscription pattern.[121]

In 1835 Rawlinson began his work of copying the inscriptions at Behistun. Not far from the site of Babel, Rawlinson was constantly reminded of the practical implications of the mythical story of the confusion of tongues. As he was laboring intensely in an effort to understand the strange writings and inscriptions that Layard had uncovered or the ones he himself had copied, an elderly pastor in faraway rural Ireland, Edward Hincks, was making great strides in decipherment. In 1837 Rawlinson had previously published the results of his decipherment of the Old Persian cuneiform in the *Journal of the Royal Asiatic Society*. Roughly ten years later, Hincks published a letter in the London magazine *The Literary Gazette* that offered a solution to reading the Old Persian alphabet. However impressive these discoveries may seem today, they were at the time greeted with a degree of skepticism. Segments of the academic community and the general public were not convinced that these translations were verifiable or sound.

In 1857, the Royal Asiatic Society, in response to the concern with the validity of the cuneiform decipherment and in an unusual move in the academic world, decided to put the accuracy of the translation to a test. Unbeknownst to the people involved, it sent the same copy of a newly discovered Assyrian inscription independently to four leading cuneiform experts, Rawlinson, Hincks, Jules Oppert, and William Talbot, and asked them for a translation of this text. When the four translations were returned they were in agreement on the most important points. The Society then published the results, which were convincing proof of the scientific accuracy of cuneiform decipherment. As William Stiebing points out, the Mesopotamian remains "could once again speak for themselves after two thousand years of silence."[122]

"THE UNEDIFYING SCRAMBLE"

In 1852 Victor Place, the second French consul in Mosul, reopened the excavations at Khorsabad. Place had met Rawlinson in Turkey on his way to Mesopotamia, and they discussed the renewed official interest in excavations. Just as the British and the French reconfigured the borders in the Middle East after World War I, Place and Rawlinson agreed that Khorsabad should be French territory and Kuyunjik should be divided between the British and the French.[123] In 1851 and 1852 Place systematically explored the areas that Botta had left untouched. This resumption of French archaeological activity inaugurated a frantic race for antiquities between British and French representatives which archaeologist Seton Lloyd has characterized as a time of "unedifying scramble."[124] As Mogens Larsen points out, Place had received instructions from the French Academy to "procure the largest possible number of sculptures, vases, jewelry, cylinder seals and objects of all kinds."[125] Despite the prior gentlemen's agreement, both Place and Hormuzd Rassam, a former assistant to Layard, tried to claim as many mounds as possible.[126] The increasing public interest in the development of Mesopotamian archaeology after the publication of Layard's books intensified the race to uncover the buried treasures scattered throughout the Middle East.

Rassam is essentially the first "Iraqi" (although that denotation would have been foreign to him) to have conducted a scientific archaeological excavation. This interesting character was born in Mosul in 1826 and belonged to the Chaldean Christian community, which accepted papal authority. Due to the influence of English Protestant missionaries, Rassam converted to Protestantism as a teenager and remained faithful, with strong convictions, for the remainder of his life. He later became a British citizen and was intensely loyal to his adopted country. A biographer of Layard, Gordon Waterfield, quotes Rassam as saying, "I will sacrifice myself for England and worship forever the pure religion of Great Britain. I would rather be a chimney-sweeper in England than a Pasha in Turkey."[127] His determination to further British interests in his archaeological work resulted in his almost bitter rivalry with French archaeologists.

Because the archaeological regulations of the Ottoman Empire were only haphazardly enforced in the remote Mesopotamian provinces, it had become standard practice among the British and French that rights to a site belonged to the nation whose representative first excavated it. Thus, Place and Rassam each sent groups of workmen scurrying around the countryside digging in every mound in sight that seemed promising.[128] The attempts to achieve political gains and brag-ging rights sacrificed scientific and academic results. The frenzy of this scramble resulted in the destruction of many ruins and artifacts and caused irreparable harm not only to the antiquities themselves, but to historical scholarship as well. Archaeologists, diplomats, and politicians all took part in this race. For example, in the early 1850s, Canning wrote to the British Prime Minister Robert Peel, "M. Botta's success at Nineveh has induced me to venture in the same lottery, and my ticket has turned up a prize . . . there is much reason to believe that Montague House [the British Museum] will beat the Louvre hollow."[129] This senti-ment also prevailed among the archaeologists themselves. As Rawlinson wrote to Layard in 1840, prior to Layard's first excavations, "It pains me grievously to see the French monopolize the field, for the fruits of Botta's labors . . . are not things to pass away in a day but will constitute a national glory in future ages."[130]

The outbreak of the Crimean War in 1855 brought a temporary halt to British and French archaeological excavations in Mesopotamia. Scholarly emphasis, therefore, shifted to the thousands of tablets and inscriptions uncovered during the previous decade and a half. The French scholar Jules Oppert demonstrated that the strange non-Semitic text on cuneiform tablets from the libraries of Sennacherib and Assurbanipal was not Akkadian, but Sumerian. In 1872 George Smith, an assistant in the Assyrian section of the British Museum found a tablet that seemed to be part of a legend or myth of a flood. Although the tablet was not whole, Smith announced his discovery in a paper read before the Society of Biblical Literature. Public interest in this find was so great that the *London Daily Telegraph* paid Smith a thousand pounds to equip an expedition to Nineveh to search for the missing section of the narrative.[131] In an incredible episode, once in Mesopotamia, Smith actually found the missing part of the tablet con-taining a "Chaldean account of the Deluge" that seemed similar to the Hebrew story in Genesis. In an era when the historical veracity of the Bible was increasingly being questioned within the scholarly commu-nity through the publication of such studies as Julius Wellhausen's *Prolegomena to the History of Israel*[132] and from the new ideas from the natural sciences, especially those deriving from Darwin, Smith's dis-covery was therefore a double-edged sword. Believers in biblical inerrancy argued that the Mesopotamian story proved that the flood had really occurred; others maintained that it revealed how the Israelites had borrowed this story from Mesopotamia, thus demonstrating that there was nothing particularly unique about the Bible.

By this time, the French and the British were no longer acting alone in Mesopotamia.[133] In the late nineteenth century, German-[134] and American-sponsored archaeological expeditions began to make their presence felt.[135]

AMERICAN EXPEDITIONS

Americans entered the field of Mesopotamian archaeology in the late nineteenth century. Their expeditions, supported by generous private contributions from wealthy individuals such as J. P. Morgan and John D. Rockefeller Jr., often had ties to religious institutions or causes. In fact, American archaeological missions into the Middle East are distinct from those of the British, French, and Germans in that they were generally financed by private individuals and received little official backing or diplomatic support.

For Bible-reading Americans, the geography and history of the Middle East were familiar, and irresistible for evangelical work and subsequently for academic research. American missionaries stationed in the Middle East undertook numerous field trips surveying potential populations for evangelical work and wrote many reports and letters about Middle Eastern cultures, geography, and religions.[136] They published their findings in journals such as *The Missionary Herald,* which were eagerly read in the United States. Following in the footsteps of the missionaries, American academics soon followed suit in the Middle East. For example, Edward Robinson, who later became professor at Union Theological Seminary in New York, published a topographical and geographical study of Palestine.[137] Incorporating historical research into his firsthand ethnogeographic survey of the area, Robinson was able to identify more precisely the actual location of biblical sites.[138] By making biblical history correspond with contemporary reality, Robinson not only challenged numerous older travel accounts with his empiric scientific research, but also brought that history alive.[139] He was instrumental in founding the American Oriental Society (AOS) in 1842–1843, which encouraged research in any culture known as "Oriental," yet was initially primarily involved in the investigation of the Bible lands. Shortly after the American Civil War, the

Palestine Exploration Fund—an organization inspired by Robinson's research—was established to seek the "systematic investigation of the archaeology, topography, geology . . . manners and customs of the Holy Land, for Biblical illustration."[140] In 1879 Charles Eliot Norton of Harvard established the Archaeological Institute of America (AIA), whose original function was primarily to recover Greco-Roman art and which also supported Mesopotamian archaeology. In 1880, a group of scholars started the Society of Biblical Literature (SBL).[141] As historian Bruce Kuklick has argued, Mesopotamia became the core of the American conception of the ancient Near East particularly since the pivots of inquiry were derived from scriptural study.[142]

American scholars were determined to join in on the archaeological enterprises in the Middle East. An 1884 meeting of the AOS in New Haven, Connecticut, encouraged its members to join England and France in their fledgling archaeological activities.[143] The first American expedition into Mesopotamia, the Wolfe Expedition, was named after its chief financial backer, Catharine Lorillad Wolfe, a New York tobacco heiress. Under the direction of William H. Ward, a New York City newspaper editor who had taken an interest in Mesopotamian archaeology, this exploratory mission conducted brief preliminary surveys in Mesopotamia in 1884–1885. Ward, upon his return to the United States, recommended that Nippur, an ancient Sumerian city, should be chosen as the first site of serious American archaeological activities.[144]

Two years later an Episcopal clergyman, John Punnett Peters, who had been present at the 1884 AOS meeting in New Haven, was instrumental in the creation of the Babylonian Exploration Fund (BEF) after diligently soliciting funds among wealthy philanthropists with evangelical leanings. This group subsequently formed a close relationship with the University of Pennsylvania.[145]

In 1888, Peters led to Nippur a group of scholars who encountered tremendous difficulties in its first seasons, such as strenuous weather, tribal strife, and disagreements between Peters and Hermann Hilprecht, the expedition's leading Assyriologist. Although Peters had shown impressive administrative abilities in his quest to raise funds for the expedition, his management in the field was suspect. According to Hilprecht, he became preoccupied with recovering impressive artifacts that would satisfy his financial backers and was less concerned with maintaining scientific standards. His conduct led to tense relationships with other scholars on the expedition, such as Hilprecht and Robert

Harper, which in later years led to an intense controversy between Peters and Hilprecht over the ownership of the tablets found at Nippur.[146] Although Peters resigned after two expeditions, excavations in Nippur sponsored by the University of Pennsylvania and the BEF continued on and off for twelve years under different directors.[147] The expeditions employed around 350 workmen and uncovered a multitude of tablets, which were, after considerable delay and lengthy negotiations with the authorities, sent back to the United States. The tablets preserved numerous works on Sumerian literature, and so were one of the great literary finds of archaeological history and were instrumental in deciphering the ancient Sumerian script.[148] As Kuklick demonstrates, the Christian commitment of most American archaeologists in Mesopotamia was absolute in their wish to secure the truth of the Old Testament. However, this endeavor often had different outcomes than they envisioned since it often resulted in the weakening of their faith. As Kuklick says, "The paradox in the evolution in Near Eastern Studies was the manner in which the pursuit of the Bible might undermine the truth of the Bible."[149]

John D. Rockefeller Jr.'s financial contributions were instrumental in the establishment in 1892 of the University of Chicago, which installed the archaeologist William Rainey Harper as its first president. In the course of the next decades, Rockefeller would contribute significant sums toward Mesopotamian archaeology. In 1903, he gave a large amount to the university, which Harper used himself to establish the Oriental Exploration Fund and to support excavations by his brother Robert at Adab in Mesopotamia. The Oriental Institute, liberally supplied with Rockefeller money, undertook ambitious projects in various Middle Eastern countries including Khorsabad and the Diyala basin in Iraq.

GERMAN "KULTURPOLITIK" AND ARCHAEOLOGY

Germany was a relative latecomer to the Middle Eastern scene. Its imperial and commercial ambitions in the area were not evident until the last decades of the nineteenth century. Germany's cooperation with the Ottoman Empire, in particular in military affairs, increased dramatically during the reign of Sultan Abdul Hamid II (1876–1909), when the Ottomans sought German help in their continued efforts to modernize their army and reform the government of their vast and delicate empire.

Since the 1870s, a small group of German officers had been serving in the sultan's army. From 1882 onward, Germany's military presence was substantial, with German officers advising the Ottomans on military organization and training procedures. In return, the sultan offered the Germans various concessions, culminating in the Berlin-Baghdad Railway concession.[150] Started in 1899, the railway was seen by the sultan as a vital strategic link across the mountainous backbone of his territories that would link Berlin to Istanbul and ultimately with Baghdad and the Persian Gulf.[151] For Germany, the railway would be instrumental in its quest to exploit raw materials in the Ottoman Empire, as well as develop markets for German goods inside the Ottoman state. This project, the greatest scheme of German imperial economic endeavor in the Ottoman Empire, also symbolized the aggressive emergence of German interests into areas that traditionally had been the domain of other European powers.[152]

At the same time, Germany was not satisfied to compete with the other European nations only in political, military, or commercial spheres. At the turn of the century, when the British-German naval arms race was breaking out,[153] Germany's rise to world-power status created a desire to bring the Berlin Museum collections up to the level of those of the Louvre and the British Museum. The German archaeologists, as Johannes Renger notes, were closely following developments in London and Paris and were determined not to allow the two traditional powers to monopolize archaeological activities in the Middle East.[154] When the German consul in Baghdad suggested that Germany start excavating at the site of Uruk, the German Academy of Sciences reacted enthusiastically, stating that such an expedition would be of great profit "to science in general and to German science in particular, as well as to our public collections."[155]

Concurrent with the economic and political concessions from the Ottomans, German archaeologists were also able gain access to some of the Ottoman Empire's archaeological treasures. In 1898, a year before the beginning of the construction of the Berlin-Baghdad Railway, the Deutsche Orient-Gesellschaft (DOG), a leading institution for German archaeological activities, started expeditions in Mesopotamia.

DOG relied extensively on private financial support, while enjoying official diplomatic backing. A prominent and visible spokesman for the society was Friedrich Delitzsch, a professor of philology in Berlin and the first director of the Ancient Near Eastern divisions of the State Museums. In 1902 and 1903 Delitzsch delivered several lectures on ancient Near Eastern religions that aroused considerable interest and controversy. In these lectures in the Royal Palace, which were attended by Kaiser Wilhelm II, Delitzsch argued that Babylon was the ultimate source of various religious practices of the ancient Hebrews, including monotheism, the keeping of a holy seventh day, and the tradition of a deluge, or flood.[156] Delitzsch's position caused considerable uneasiness among theologians and other leaders of the church, since his emphasis seemed to discard any notion of the ancient Hebrews as God's chosen people—a cardinal tenet in the Old Testament.[157] The kaiser himself took a great interest in these debates, as he was intrigued by biblical history. He avidly sponsored archaeological missions both in Greece and Asia Minor and went on an official visit in 1898 to Palestine, where he personally dedicated a new Protestant church in Jerusalem.

One of the most often-voiced motives underpinning German intervention in the Ottoman Empire, as Suzanne Marchand demonstrates, was the notion that Germany had been entrusted with a special mission to bring *Kultur* to the unenlightened Turks, which "aimed at the creation of a spiritual bond between the two nations."[158] The Germans took great pains to promote this *Kulturpolitik,* which complemented the German diplomatic efforts, and stressed that its cultivation was by disinterested, apolitical scholars who were solely seeking new and pure knowledge.[159]

This dual political and cultural effort generated an immense expansion of German archaeological expeditions in the Ottoman Empire between the years 1899 and 1913. State-affiliated agencies, private associations, and the kaiser himself funded these expeditions. During these years German expeditions were sent, for example, to Baalbek, Pergamum, Hattusa, Borsippa, Axum, Jericho, Tel El Amarna, and Milteus. In the years prior to World War I, therefore, the Germans made heavy investments—scholarly, political, and psychological—in archaeology in the Ottoman Empire.[160]

The first of the German endeavors in Mesopotamia was led by Robert Koldewey to Babylon in 1899 and sponsored by DOG.[161] A subcommittee within the DOG lobbied the German government to put diplomatic pressure on the Turkish authorities so that this expedition would be able to circumvent the antiquities law and get exclusive long-term rights on the site. This ambitious project ultimately became one of the most successful and long-lasting undertakings in Mesopotamian archaeology.

When Western archaeological endeavors in Mesopotamia in the nineteenth century are examined, several distinct national trends are discernible. The Americans arrived late in the Middle East under an evangelical call, privately financed, eagerly seeking plausible scientific evidence for their beloved Bible.

Conversely, the Germans entered Middle Eastern archaeology at about the same time as the Americans, yet were fueled by a competitive imperial stimulus under the rubric of *Kulturpolitik,* which they practiced enthusiastically in order to acquire artifacts in numbers similar to Britain's or France's. The German archaeological expeditions received a mixture of private and governmental funds, and the archaeologists used the close diplomatic ties between the Ottoman Empire and Germany to receive favorable concessions. Although Edward Said claims that German Orientalists stand apart from their American, French, and English colleagues because of their peculiarly nonpolitical, almost exclusively "classical," interest in the Middle East,[162] a closer examination into German archaeological activities in Mesopotamia prior to World War I in fact demonstrates that the German scholars had more in common with their European counterparts than Said recognizes.

The French used Mesopotamian archaeology as a trophy to glorify their own culture. They displayed the antiquities in their magnificent and impressive national museums and published the results of their research in elegant and expensive publications that were an indication of the exquisite level of French culture. Ever since Napoleon's foray into Egypt, French archaeologists were closely aligned with the state, and they primarily received official financial support.

The British, whose archaeological expeditions in the nineteenth century were not as extensive as the other nations, combined all three approaches. Like the Americans, they were influenced by certain religious trends; they sought ancient artifacts to bolster their national collections, although they did not necessarily appreciate their aesthetic value; and just like the German archaeologists, they benefited from British political clout, since their politicians also practiced a version of *Kulturpolitik* in the Middle East.

As in nearly all other aspects of life there, the Great War drastically altered the archaeological landscape in Mesopotamia. As a result of the war, the British gained preeminence in Mesopotamia and occupied it militarily. That military and political situation made the British instrumental in archaeological matters for the next twenty years.

2

WORLD WAR I AND THE BRITISH OCCUPATION (1900-1921)

At the beginning of the twentieth century, German excavations dominated the archaeological scene in Mesopotamia. The Germans had several extensive archaeological missions at work in Babylon, Assur, and Samarra. In contrast, the Americans had by this time discontinued their excavations at Nippur, and the British and the French were conducting only minor, fragmentary soundings. By the end of World War I, however, the German presence had disappeared. And just as Britain had conquered the area militarily, so, too, it dominated the archaeological landscape of Iraq.

The new century signaled few changes of horizon for the peoples of Iraq. The Ottoman Empire still maintained nominal, indirect control in the area. The *vilayets,* or provinces, of Mosul, Baghdad, and Basra, which later comprised the Iraqi state, were geographic frontiers of the Empire. They were also political and cultural frontiers, isolated and distant from the Empire's epicenters. Most histories of Iraq, particularly those by mid-twentieth-century British historians, have painted a picture of a dormant, backward, and anarchic nineteenth-century Iraqi society. This portrayal is presented as a stark contrast to the modernizing and state-building efforts of the British in the 1920s.[1] Although this depiction may have some truth to it, it exaggerates the direct positive impact of Western influence. For example, Western ideas and technology were only available to certain segments of the population, particularly those in the major cities. In addition, these studies fail to recognize the fluidity of the culture, particularly by overlooking the effects of critical political developments taking place in neighboring Iran and in the structure of the Ottoman government that influenced the political culture of Iraq.

When compared to either its neighbors or to Western countries, Iraqi society had not experienced similar economic, cultural, and political developments, in particular attempts at constructive state-building and centralization. In the words of the historian Hanna Batatu, the "Iraqis were not one people or one political community," but rather a "congeries of distinct, discordant, self-involved societies."[2] Such conditions made large-scale centralized economic, political, or cultural reforms, such as were attempted in Egypt or Iran, difficult in the regions of Iraq. Communications among towns such as Baghdad, Basra, and Mosul were tenuous; in turn, each town differed in its economic orientation. Mosul had close ties with Syria, Baghdad with Iran, and Basra with India. Different schemes of weights and measures, variations in commodity prices, and even different currencies all fostered a strong spirit of localism.[3] Furthermore, Iraq did not experience the same nationalistic ferment or dramatic discussions of modernity that were taking place in Istanbul and Tehran, for example, and that resulted, respectively, in the Young Turk movement and the Iranian Constitutional Revolution. Although Iraq lacked such dramatic episodes, several subtle, yet drastic, developments were taking place.

Since 1858, the Ottoman Empire had actively pursued a centralization policy in Iraq that aimed at governing the region more efficiently.[4] Particularly by introducing the Land Code of 1858, it sought to centralize the collection of taxes. This code was part of the Ottoman Empire's Tanzimat, which aimed at reasserting the powers of the central government and restructuring and modernizing key societal institutions such as the army and the bureaucracy.[5] In the context of Iraq, this policy seems to have had the effect of strengthening the position of powerful landlords.[6]

These reforms also went along with systematic efforts of recruitment by the Ottoman army. By the end of the nineteenth century and in the first years of the twentieth century, more and more Arabs from central Iraq, especially from the middle classes, went to Istanbul for military training. These young soldiers would eventually form the influential society Al-Ahd, a secret society with a pan-Arab nationalist political platform. Many of its founding Iraqi members, such as Yasin al-Hashimi, Nuri Fattah, and Nuri al-Said, would in subsequent years play integral roles in Iraqi political history. More and more Iraqis were thus gaining political and military experience and being exposed to the integral issues of the day such as nationalism.

These economic and political transformations went hand in hand with a stimulated literary life, particularly following the restoration of the Turkish Constitution in 1908, which brought an end to the reign of Abd al-Hamid II and the beginning of the Young Turks' rule and their Committee of Union and Progress.[7] Even though it was on a relatively modest scale, new journals and newspapers began to be published, and influential Arabic magazines such as *al-Manar* and *al-Muqtataf,* which were printed in Beirut and Cairo, were allowed to circulate freely.[8] New ideas and new forces infiltrated the society. Therefore, trade and migrations among the different provinces, coupled with increasing communications, made the ground in Iraq ripe to bear new fruit. The British archaeologist and traveler Gertrude Bell commented on feeling a sense of change in 1909 among the inhabitants of Mesopotamia, who were asking themselves, "Liberty—what is liberty?"[9] Bell suggests that people articulated these questions in an unsystematic manner not directed toward specific ends, such as political independence from the Ottoman Empire or demands for a new constitution for Iraq. There was, Bell pointed out, "little to encourage an unqualified confidence in the immediate future,"[10] since no cohesive political unit within Iraq seemed able to challenge Ottoman control and influence.

Little did Bell realize, however, that in less than a decade she herself would have tremendous impact on the political future and configuration of Mesopotamia and the formation of modern Iraq. World War I brought drastic changes for the Middle East as a whole, and to Iraq in particular. Bell served in the political unit of the British military and played an influential role in the postwar settlements that produced a new map of the Middle East, with new nation-states and new geopolitical realities. Moreover, she was particularly critical in archaeological matters in Iraq, since she would go on to draft the first antiquities law, serve as the first director of antiquities, and establish the Iraq Museum. In order to understand the development of archaeology in Iraq in the twentieth century, an examination of Bell's career is necessary.

GERTRUDE BELL AND MESOPOTAMIAN ANTIQUITIES

At the dawn of the new century, Gertrude Bell stood between two centuries and between two cultures.[11] An enigmatic, energetic, and erudite figure, Bell was an example of the few somewhat atypical, yet significant, British Victorian women who felt oppressed in their home country but were able to find liberation in their extensive travels abroad.[12]

Born in 1868 to a wealthy family of industrialists in northeastern England, Bell graduated from Oxford University in 1888 with a First in History, the first woman ever to do so. After having spent some time traveling and climbing mountains in Europe,[13] she first traveled to the Middle East four years later on a trip to Tehran.[14] In her *Desert and the Sown,* an account of her travels, she conveys the sense of excitement, emancipation, and adventure that the travels in the Middle East brought her:

To those bred under an elaborate social order few such moments of exhilaration can come as that which stands at the threshold of wild travel. The gates of the enclosed garden are thrown open, the chain of the entrance of the sanctuary is lowered, with a wary glance to right and left you step forth, and behold!—the immeasureable world. The world of adventure and of enterprise, dark with hurrying storms, glittering in raw sunlight.[15]

Bell represents a new and different traveler to Mesopotamia—one who had been exposed to its ancient history and archaeology. She reaped the fruits of Layard's and Rawlinson's archaeological and linguistic labors by visiting the Assyrian collection in the British Museum on a number of occasions. She had, therefore, been introduced to a history of the area that was not confined to the Bible or Classical texts like Herodotus. In contrast to earlier travelers, therefore, she did not resort solely to biblical metaphors in describing the area and peoples. Instead, she appreciated and used the archaeological artifacts, conveying a clear sense of fascination with the living, historic continuity of the present with earlier civilizations. In a 1909 letter to her mother, she stated that "yesterday I saw the Arabs swimming across the Euphrates on inflated skins just exactly like the Assyrian soldiers on the bas reliefs in the British Museum."[16] Her descriptions depicted a yearning for the romanticized quaintness of a past era. She wrote to her father during a visit to Babylon, "I heard the Mesopotamian nightingale and remembered that these were the same sights and sounds that Nebuchadnezzar had known and even Hammurabi. Were they, I wonder, comforted and sustained by the eternal beauty of the earth and the simple country life of field and river, that springs and dies and leaves no marks and never alters?"[17]

In contrast to the tranquil, seemingly unchanged setting she was describing, Bell would leave her mark and significantly alter the political and cultural landscape of the region. After some time in Iran, where she mastered the Persian language and translated the poems of Hafiz into English, she traveled to Jerusalem to study Arabic in 1899. From there she made numerous trips to the desert, where she became intimately familiar with the peoples, politics, and cultures of the region.

In 1905, she started to work on her *Desert and the Sown,* a title taken from Omar Khayyam's "The strip of herbage strown that just divides the desert from the sown," which she hoped would inform the English in all aspects of the East—its ancient history and archaeology, its current literature and poetry, and its future prospects. She traveled extensively through the eastern Mediterranean and described local cultures and landmarks. At the same time, Bell's travels were also important intelligence-gathering missions. She was constantly checking the accuracy of British maps of the area and conducted extensive interviews with prominent local politicians. When the book was published in 1907 both the British and American press gave it rave reviews. Both the book itself and its reception established Bell as an authority on the ancient history, as well as the contemporary politics, of the Middle East.[18] Bell's erudite literary output made her, according to historian David Fromkin, the "best-known British writer about Arab countries."[19]

In 1909, the same year that T. E. Lawrence made his first trip to the Middle East, Bell went to Mesopotamia and traveled extensively throughout the country. She planned to write an account that would follow in the wake of her previous literary success. The result, her *Amurath to Amurath,* published in 1911, reveals her fascination and sense of proximity to ancient Mesopotamian history. In her preface, which is dedicated to Lord Cromer of Egypt, she stated that those with

experience of the East, have learnt to reckon with the unbroken continuity of its history. Conqueror follows upon the heels of conqueror, nations are overthrown and cities topple down into the dust, but the conditions of existence are unaltered and irresistibly they fashion the new age in the likeness of the old . . . past and present are woven so closely together, the habitual appreciation of the divisions of time slips insensibly away. Yesterday's raid and an expedition of Shalmaneser

fall into the same plane; and indeed what essential difference lies between them?[20]

Bell's account is full of observations and views on the contemporaneous political conditions of the area. In fact, one primary reason for the journey in 1909 was to "discover the Asiatic value of the great catchwords of revolution,"[21] and she concluded that "fraternity and equality" were dangerous concepts in a region where different ethnic and religious communities coexisted uneasily.[22] A complete absence of what Bell called the "Anglo-Saxon acceptance of common responsibility in the problems which bested the state" among the peoples of the Middle East ruled out their future participation in any form of democracy.[23] Her opinions there foreshadow her own important and decisive political decisions a decade later, when she was pivotal in the creation of the modern nation-state of Iraq.

Her accounts contain thorough and astute descriptions of Middle Eastern ancient architectural structures and antiquities at sites such as Ukheidir, Samarra, and Babylon. Even though she had previously published articles in archaeological journals and made extensive surveys of archaeological remnants, Bell had never actually conducted an excavation. At this point in her life, Bell was probably not sure what she was or what sort of career lay ahead of her. She did not seem to envision a career in politics (which was not easily open to women at the time anyway); in fact, she had been active in the antisuffrage movement in England. She did not view herself as an archaeologist or an antiquarian. Rather, she looked upon herself as an educated traveler and writer who could bring out the intricacies of Middle Eastern cultures and history to the British reader. In a letter to her mother she stated, "Sometimes . . . I think I'm something of an archaeologist myself—but of course that's going too far."[24]

That caveat notwithstanding, Bell described the antiquities and excavations she encountered with an expert eye and presented her views to the general public in England. In 1909–1910 she wrote a series of articles for the English newspaper *The Times* that detailed the ancient history of the area and assessed the excavations then taking place.[25] At each excavation site, she had lengthy conversations with the archaeologists, and she did not spare her criticism of their method and interpretations if she felt that was necessary.[26] For example, T. E. Lawrence, who at the time was conducting archaeological excavations at Carchemish, wrote nervously to his mother that he and his colleagues were expecting Bell and that she would probably be critical of their work. When she eventually arrived, she told them their ideas of digging were "prehistoric."[27]

When she visited the sites in Mesopotamia where the British had excavated in the nineteenth century, she was shocked to see the remnants of their work. Their unscientific methods were evident, and the mounds bore witness to their unsystematic scramble to uncover precious relics. In a letter to her mother describing a visit to Nimrud, where Layard had excavated, she wrote, "The state of the mound is a disgrace to us. The British Museum has the right to carry on excavations; it does nothing and allows no one else to do anything."[28] In her book, she was not as explicit in her criticism (probably so as not to offend the archaeological establishment, which she felt, or was aspiring to become, a part of), stating that Nimrud is "a pitiful sight for English eyes."[29] But in her newspaper articles for *The Times,* she declared that the British had neglected the mounds of Nimrud, suggesting that "for the sake of our honour it would be well that we should take steps to preserve the works of art that remain in it. If no arrangement can be made to transport them to the museum of Constantinople, we might at least employ a few men to rebury them."[30]

In contrast to the British mounds, however, she was much impressed by the German excavation missions she visited at Samarra, Assur, and Babylon. She maintains that the neglect evidenced by British mounds stood in sharp contrast with the "pious care" that the German excavators were expending on their ruins.[31] She was highly impressed, for example, by the methodical excavations at Babylon directed by Robert Koldewey. She reminded her readers that "if [Layard's] distinguished labours, together with those of Botta and of Place rescued the most remarkable monuments which have yet been found in Assyria, the work which is now being done under the auspices of German excavators, is of no less importance to Mesopotamian archaeology."[32] She had extensive and interesting conversations with the German excavators about ancient history. In her diary she recounted the substance of these discussions, stating that Koldewey maintained that the ancient East had nothing to do with Parthian, Sassanian, or Islamic civilizations, but rather Roman. Koldewey supported this theory-in-progress by stating that when they found Roman terra-cottas there, it suggested Roman civilization had been there whether Romans were there or not. He maintained, furthermore, that "art was divided by time, not by geographical conditions, and at a given moment all over it was more or less the same."[33]

And once again at Babylon, ancient history became alive for her. She wrote, "I have seldom felt the ancient world come so close . . . the great hall where Belshazzar must have held his feast . . . the remains of the platform in which Nebuchadnezzar used to sit when it was hot."[34] She imagined Alexander the Great sleeping in Babylon the night before he died, stating that "the memory of the Conqueror of the World was very vivid to us among the solid ruminating figures. 'He was mad in Babylon,' said Dr. Koldewey, 'his perpetual drunkenness, the blood he spilt, he was mad with wine, love and power.' And must he not be mad who conquers the world?"[35] For Bell, the ancient history was evident in the present. Even "as you climb the stairs of the German house you will become aware of the characters that spell the king's name upon the steps beneath your feet."[36] She also recounted how for centuries the remains at Babylon had been used for building material by the neighboring populations, "No man building in its neighbourhood was at the pains to construct brickkilns, but when he needed material he sought it in Nebuchadnezzar's city. Greek, Persian and Arab used it as a quarry."[37] As someone who remained unmarried her whole life, Bell devoted her attention to the region. Her obsession, enthusiasm, and love for the country and its history are most visible in an unpublished, undated essay she wrote. She stated, "I have written of politics, of commerce, of steamships, of locomotive engines, but I have not pronounced the word which is the keynote of Iraq. It is romance. The great twin rivers, gloriously named, the huge Babylonian plains, now desert, which held once the garden of the world, the story stretching back into the dark recesses of times—they shout romance!"[38]

Bell's travel accounts, letters, and diaries reveal her tremendous respect for and knowledge of the antiquities in Mesopotamia. She was struck by the magnitude of history and its role in forging current situations. Antiquities were not just curiosities or trophies—rather, they represented a living history, remnants of civilizations—something that was to be respected, studied, and preserved.[39] In her writings, Bell acknowledged that ancient history is paradigmatic, and for her the antiquities offered the best possible sources for the study of history. She wrote,

> **History in retrospect suffers an atmospheric distortion. We look upon a past civilization and see it, not as it was, but charged with the signifi- cance of that through which we gaze, as down the centuries shadow overlies shadow, some dim, some luminous, and some so strongly coloured that all the age behind is tinged with a borrowed hue. . . . I had determined to journey back behind this great dividing line, to search through regions now desolate for evidences of a past that has left little historic record, calling upon the shades to take form again upon the very ground whereon, substantial, they had played their part.**[40]

Bell's keen sense of historical curiosity and her respect for the ancient civilizations and their remnants guided her views when in 1922 she was responsible for formulating a new archaeological policy for Iraq. Her views on the method of archaeological excavations and on the intellectual and scientific approaches to the interpretation of artifacts and their relation to the overall site were also influenced by the German excavations in Mesopotamia that she visited in 1905 and 1909. She had the opportunity to follow the excavations closely, discuss the archaeolo- gists' findings with them, and collaborate in postulating new theories of the ancient civilization in ways that she had never done before and would not, to the same extent, be able to do later. These German exca- vations were model excavations in Bell's view, in particular when com- pared to earlier British excavations in Mesopotamia and the current project at Carchemish in Syria. They, therefore, formed the basis for Bell's thinking about the practice of archaeology when she devised the antiquities act for Iraq between 1922 and 1926.

GERMAN EXCAVATIONS IN MESOPOTAMIA

The increasing political and economic cooperation between Germany and the Ottoman Empire in the last years of the nine- teenth century created numerous and lucrative opportunities for German archaeologists in Ottoman domains. As discussed in Chapter 1, the first German excavation mission sent to Mesopotamia had been to Babylonia in 1899 under the direction of Robert Koldewey. The German excavations differed from other excavations in several signi- ficant ways. First, they were funded and performed by archaeological societies, not museums, in order to "insure preservation of the artifacts for future generations and to avoid reputation-damaging charges of 'interested' acquisitiveness."[41] Second, the Germans were not concerned only with biblical sites, but were also attracted to early Christian and even Islamic ruins. Conrad Preusser explored ancient Christian churches and Muslim shrines,[42] and Franz Sarre and Ernst Herzfeld excavated among the ruins of the Islamic city of Samarra.[43] Third, the Germans had a different academic background than their predecessors. Instead of being diplomat-archaeologists, in the mold of Layard or Rawlinson, or trained in biblical studies or Assyriology, typical of the American excavators, many of the German archaeologists were trained as architects, including Koldewey, Walter Andrae, Ernst Herzfeld, and Julius Jordan and were therefore more concerned to investigate the architectural and social context of the artifacts. Fourth, the Germans carried out the most deliberate scientific excavations of the era. And finally, German archaeologists worked under a unique secret 1899 agreement between Germany and the Sublime Porte. This agreement ensured that the results of the excavations would be divided evenly between the Ottoman state and the excavator.

Since 1897, when the Kommission für die archäologische Erforschung der Euphrat- und Tigrisländer (Commission for the Archaeological Study of the Lands of the Euphrates and Tigris) was established, the Germans sought an exclusive arrangement in Mesopotamia similar to what the French had obtained in Iran.[44] Although the Germans did not receive exclusive rights, they started excavating at Babylon in 1899 and by 1903 had succeeded in excavating large portions of the famed city walls and had filled hundreds of crates of the monumental Ishtar Gate façade.[45] Their excavations at Babylon were primarily concerned with the Neo-Babylonian period and remains of the seventh century B.C.E. This was, furthermore, the first complete and scientifically conducted excavation of a large site in Mesopotamia. This was a giant undertaking, with around 250 Arab workmen laboring both winters and summers to uncover remains that were often over 20 meters beneath the surface.[46] Until then, most ancient remains discovered in Mesopotamia had not been more than 6 meters beneath the ground.

Under the direction of Walter Andrae, excavations began at Ash Shargat (ancient Assur) in 1902 and, under Herzfeld, at Samarra. At

Assur, the first capital of the Assyrian nation, the Germans tried an experimental application of stratigraphical analysis, enabling them to gather detailed evidence of Assyrian religious ceremonies.

Probably owing to their architectural background, the Germans were less concerned with the individual object than the structure and the site as a whole. Koldewey had little interest in inscriptions and refused to disfigure architectural structures to seek them.[47] Bell noticed this on her visits. She stated that unlike previous excavators, these Germans were not governed by the purpose of acquiring as many valuable objects as possible. For them, archaeology was not trophy-gathering; rather, "the task he [Andrae] is engaged in now is one from which he can't get any popular fame. They find no splendid museum objects. . . . There is no guess work here and no scamping—but observation so minute . . . and true respect for ancient monument and ancient art."[48]

These German expeditions continued sporadically until 1914. Their extensive excavations, conducted under the often brutal conditions of Mesopotamian weather, were labor-intensive and required significant physical and intellectual commitments. As Bell commented, "until you have seen them at it you can scarcely guess what labour and self-denial that means."[49] Koldewey and his crew uncovered and recorded in commendable detail a remarkable series of palaces, temples, and other houses from the time of Nebuchadnezzar such as the Ishtar Gate and the Processional Way. At Babylon and at Ashur the Germans set standards in stratigraphic investigation and observation that would form the basis for later Mesopotamian archaeology.

Although the German excavators benefited from the close political ties between Germany and the Sublime Porte, those arrangements did not always materialize as the German archaeologists had hoped. As Marchand demonstrates, the German-Ottoman relationship was delicate, unpredictable, and unreliable, and the source of anxiety and misunderstanding between the Turks and the Germans.[50] Although the German politicians aggressively pursued their archaeological diplomacy, with full support from the kaiser himself, they did not feel that they reaped the full fruits of their labor and money invested. In addition, Turkish politics underwent profound transformations with the rise and fall of the Young Turk movement, which introduced additional complexities to the relationship. And the outbreak of World War I terminated, temporarily at least, all hopes that Mesopotamian treasures would soon fill German museums.

WORLD WAR I AND ARCHAEOLOGY

Although Mesopotamia had long remained detached from major events in Europe, after the war broke out in Europe in 1914, it soon became an arena in which European rivalry was fought out. The Ottoman Empire initially declared armed neutrality, but soon thereafter signed a secret treaty with Germany and thus in effect joined the Central Powers. In August of 1914, the pro-German position of the Empire was officially expressed when it granted asylum to two German battleships. That October, Britain, France, and Russia declared war on the Ottoman Empire and thus were finally confronted with some of the practical aspects of the "Eastern Question."

The "Eastern Question," a term referring to the European diplomatic, strategic, and economic problems created by the perceived decline and gradual dissolution of the Ottoman Empire, had been a focal point of European diplomacy since the eighteenth century.[51] When the Sublime Porte entered the war in 1914 on the side of the Central Powers, it meant a triumph for German statecraft and the expansion of a theretofore European battle into a world war. The entry of the Ottoman Empire also posed very difficult questions for the Entente Powers, in particular for Britain, regarding the ultimate war aims since it would possibly entail the reallocation of the Asian territories of the Ottoman Empire.

In order to formulate war aims in Asia, the British Prime Minister H. H. Asquith established an interdepartmental committee under Sir Maurice de Bunsen. The committee's June 1915 report provides a useful summary of Britain's prewar interests.[52] The de Bunsen report, whose views were dominated by Mark Sykes,[53] pointed out that Mesopotamia could become an outlet for Indian colonialists and, with irrigation, a valuable producer of grain. Given the committee's emphasis on British access to and control of the Persian Gulf, it deemed it important to secure control of Basra. The committee believed, furthermore, that if Basra was acquired, the two more northerly provinces of Baghdad and Mosul should also be secured, since the security of Basra against encroachments by powers such as Russia was contingent upon the control of the other two provinces. Even before World War I, Lord

Hardinge, the viceroy of India, favored its annexation into India and believed that with irrigation it would become "one of the granaries of Europe."[54] He also envisaged lower Mesopotamia as a fruitful area of Indian colonization and trade, and hoped that with development it would become a "second Egypt."[55] However, Sykes was against extending India into Mesopotamia, which he believed would be a "profound . . . mistake." Rather, Sykes suggested starting a provisional government "with a well-paid native administration with British advisors."[56]

Before the war, British influence in the area was confined to commercial activities and political representation. However, with increasing tension, Britain realized that "to safeguard the routes to India" it must assume "political control direct or indirect . . . over territories through which lay actual and potential highways to her indispensible Eastern possession."[57] Furthermore, the recent discovery of massive oil resources in Iran ensured that Britain would "secure, once and for all, by the establishment of political control, the Mesopotamia portion of the land route to India."[58]

Inevitably, the archaeologists were drawn into the war effort, many of them playing critical roles. They became useful assets in the war-making effort because of their familiarity with the region's geography, peoples, and languages. The British war operations were even steered by a former archaeologist, Horatio H. Kitchener, who as a young man in 1878 conducted extensive surveys of Palestine for the British Palestine Exploration Fund. These surveys produced a very detailed map, including all recognized ruins, at a scale of one inch to a mile.[59]

Others, such as T. E. Lawrence, Leonard Woolley, and David Hogarth, who worked in archaeology prior to the war, became important British intelligence officers based in Egypt.[60] Although Lawrence's wartime activities in Arabia, made legendary in the Academy Award–winning film by David Lean, captured the popular imagination, his work at other Middle Eastern sites—as an archaeologist-in-training—remain much less familiar.[61] His archaeological activities and interest in ancient history influenced the military and political role he would later play in the Middle East.

Lawrence received his training at Oxford, where under the auspices of David Hogarth, keeper of the Ashmolean Museum at Oxford, he developed an interest in crusader castles in the Levant.[62] In order to do research for his B.A. thesis, Lawrence went on his first trip to the Middle East in 1909. Upon his graduation in 1910, Hogarth secured a scholarship for Lawrence to go to Syria to assist him on an archaeological excavation he was conducting at Carchemish, the eastern capital of the ancient Hittite Empire.[63] At Carchemish, Lawrence worked both with Leonard Woolley and Reginald Campbell Thompson, who both, either during or after the war, worked extensively on archaeological excavations in Iraq. From an archaeological point of view, the findings and the excavations themselves were initially far from satisfactory and somewhat disappointing to Lawrence and his colleagues.[64] Consequently, there has been some debate whether the excavations at Carchemish were also used as a cover for intelligence missions, particularly to observe the progress of the Berlin-Baghdad Railway, which was being built by the Germans near the Carchemish excavation site.[65] Woolley describes their intelligence work quite openly in his memoir, stating that they not only observed the construction of the railway itself, but also secured all of the blueprints for it from a disgruntled Italian engineer.[66] Furthermore, in 1913 they were directed by the British Museum, which had now taken over the excavations, to go on a six-week survey of the Sinai and southern Negev Deserts for the Palestine Exploration Fund. Although officially the purpose of this mission was archaeological exploration of biblical and Byzantine sites, the real object of the survey, as Lawrence would write to his mother, was to observe the Turkish defenses near the Suez Canal.[67] This experience enabled Lawrence to better understand the strategic landscape of the Middle East as well, which became critical when the war broke out in 1914. At that point, Woolley and Lawrence suspended their excavations at Carchemish, and they joined the war effort by joining the British Intelligence Unit in the Middle East and eventually were assigned to the Arab Bureau.

The Arab Bureau was an assortment of British intelligence officers who congregated in Cairo in 1916 for the purpose of centralizing the collection and dissemination of intelligence about the Arab world.[68] The Arab Bureau's policy was based on its vision of a postwar Middle East composed of various Arab states loosely bound together under Sharif Husayn's family, through which the British could have indirect and direct control. As previously stated, the Arab Bureau included the archaeologists Bell, Lawrence, Woolley, and Hogarth. The Arab Bureau came to follow a controversial policy that sought to unify the Arab world under the leadership of Sharif Husayn of Mecca and his family. This group had identified Husayn as a suitable successor to the Ottoman sultans as the primary religious, and thus by implication political, leader in the Islamic world.

One of the Arab Bureau's first projects as war broke out was to liquidate a British military disaster by the shores of the Tigris River in Mesopotamia. In November of 1914 the British had invaded southern Iraq, conquered Basra, and started to march toward Baghdad. The initial military objective was to protect Britain's oil supplies from Iran, particularly to protect the oil refinery at Abadan at the head of the Persian Gulf. However, after meeting with feeble Turkish resistance at Basra, the British became more ambitious and sought to gain control of both the Baghdad and Basra provinces. As the British troops advanced north toward Baghdad, their progress was impeded at Kut al-Amara, where they were surrounded by Ottoman forces and forced to surrender.[69] In early 1917 the British launched a new offensive, reaching and conquering Baghdad in March. At the end of the war, therefore, the British exercised political and military control over Mesopotamia. And as they held the keys to the political future of the area, they were also in the position to unlock and tap into some of the Mesopotamian resources, now at their disposal. These included natural resources, such as minerals and oil, and cultural ones such as antiquities.

ARCHAEOLOGY DURING THE BRITISH OCCUPATION OF IRAQ (1917–1921)

Despite being in the midst of a prolonged war effort, the British military leaders in Mesopotamia started paying increasing attention to the state of antiquities in the region. In the last years of the war, when it was becoming somewhat clear that Britain would win the war in Mesopotamia, issues such as the preservation of the ruins and excavations, and export of antiquities became increasingly acute. The British military and political leader started to debate how to approach archaeological matters in the region. This tedious, somewhat avaricious debate had the unforeseen consequence of actually forcing the issue of antiquities onto the table. Eventually the discussions influenced how archaeological policy was subsequently formulated when the modern state of Iraq was established in 1921.

When this debate is examined in greater detail, it displays not only the politics and rivalry of the administrative offices involved (such as the India Office [IO], Colonial Office [CO], and Foreign Office [FO]), but also, more interestingly, accentuates the critical debate over what level of political and administrative control should be maintained in the area. What may seem to be a petty intergovernmental rivalry actually had critical repercussions for the status of antiquities and archaeology in Middle Eastern nations under British influence. This discussion occupied the attention of several influential British politicians and academics such as Winston Churchill, then at the Colonial Office, Lord Curzon at the Foreign Office, Edwin Montagu at the India Office, and Frederick Kenyon, president of the British Academy, who was also the director of the British Museum. Such high-level attention suggests how important this matter was considered.

The primary reason that this debate reached the most powerful British politicians was the question of what to do with certain valuable Mesopotamian antiquities that had been left behind by German excavators. Since the British army was occupying the region, many felt that these artifacts could be taken as war trophy. However, because of Allied criticism of German looting during the war, the British officials were sensitive to outside criticism that they were acting like Germans. The controversies also centered around the question of how large a share the home country should receive in exchange for allowing foreign archaeologists to excavate. Another question was how, as a memorandum from the India Office put it, "to reconcile the rights of national ownership with the supra-national rights of science and scholarship."[70] Further, the wartime debates highlight the role of cultural institutions such as the British Museum and the Victoria and Albert Museum, which urged the government to use its power and status as the occupation force in Mesopotamia to bolster British national collections. The discussion also reveals to what lengths these museums were willing to go to acquire more Mesopotamian antiquities and how they used their neutral, scientific façades for that very purpose.

One theme that is also present in the discussion, although it is never systematically explicated or defined, is the question of value. It is taken for granted that antiquities are valuable, both as possible commodities on the open market and in the cultural, political, and scientific, and, ultimately, in the sentimental sense.

This debate and discussion therefore conveys the confusion, disagreements, and opinions of the time, primarily surrounding three collections of Mesopotamian antiquities. The sagas pertaining to the Samarra, Lisbon, and Hall/Campbell Thompson collections raised intriguing questions about the value and ownership of Mesopotamian antiquities and their role as war trophy.

ANTIQUITIES AS WAR TROPHY

A s the events in Iraq in 2003 demonstrated, antiquities are often vulnerable during times of warfare. Typically, however, throughout history, it was the invading army that was primarily engaged in the plundering. Indeed, for centuries war has been the means by which states have secured both territory and property, including cultural artifacts. For example, the celebrated stele of the laws of Hammurabi was found by the French excavators at the Elamite capital of Susa in Iran. The stele had been brought home as a trophy when the Elamites briefly conquered Babylon in 1160 B.C.E.[71] Another famous example is how the Babylonians under King Nebuchadnezzar sacked Solomon's Temple in Jerusalem in 586 B.C.E. The Hebrew Bible records that "what was gold the captain of the guard took away as gold, and what was of silver, as silver."[72] On the eve of the retreat from Moscow, Napoleon wasted time deciding what trophy to drag home. In more recent years, London's Victoria and Albert Museum formerly contained the entire regalia of the Burmese kingdom, taken in the conquest of Mandalay in 1885, but the ornate ruby-encrusted objects forming the regalia were returned to newly independent Burma after World War II.[73]

Condemnation of the looting of cultural property during war and the corresponding principle that plundered property should be returned to its country of origin were first addressed on an international scale by the 1815 Convention of Paris. At that convention, various nations rallied against Napoleon's acts of plunder. The Duke of Wellington, who observed that the systematic looting by Napoleon of cultural property was "contrary to the principles of justice and the rules of modern war," stated the allies' position.[74] Even though Napoleon's actions were condemned and despite several attempts to codify the principles of the protection of cultural property, such as the Lieber Code of 1863, the Declaration of Brussels in 1874, and the Oxford Manual of 1880, it was not until the early years of the twentieth century that an international agreement was completed.[75]

In 1907 many nations, including the Ottoman Empire, Germany, France, and Britain, ratified the Convention Respecting the Laws and Customs of War on Land (also known as the Hague Convention), the first international treaty to codify the protection of cultural property during war.[76] Its Article 56 stated that "all seizure of . . . historic monuments, works of art and science, is forbidden, and should be made the subject of legal proceedings." The Hague Convention is significant since it, for the first time, represents the international community's codification in writing of the notion that the cultural property of each nation is so important that it must be afforded special protection—especially in time of war.[77]

Yet even after an international agreement such as the Hague Convention is signed, its success ultimately depends on the voluntary compliance of the signatory states. This feature is one predicament of international law, because the world has no universal system of enforcement of international laws similar to the police and courts of individual states. Indeed, the Hague Convention failed to prevent the wanton destruction and plunder of cultural property during World War I, a foreshadowing of the failure of international laws to prevent such acts during World War II. During the First World War, the Central Powers systematically violated the Convention by following the example of Napoleon and carrying off all forms of plunder, whether or not of military value. These acts were vehemently criticized in the Allied press, in particular the burning of the great library of Louvain in Belgium, where ancient manuscripts and books were stored, and the destruction and bombardments of various European cathedrals such as in Rheims. The German military even went so far as to systematize the plundering of cultural objects by attaching to their military units art experts who could decide which objects were valuable, and also to protect and preserve the cultural property under their control.[78]

When the British occupied Mesopotamia militarily during the First World War, they initially considered the antiquities of the region as essentially spoils of war. The military authorities received an encouraging letter from the keepers of the British Museum that evinced this belief in archaeology as trophy-gathering, declaring that the "British Museum is the central archaeological museum of the capital of the empire and that science, fully as much as political considerations, demands that its contents should represent the archaeology of the British possessions."[79] In this view of archaeology, antiquities collection was an end in itself. Archaeological artifacts were to adorn the museums and thus decorate the British nation with historical treasures. The collecting of archaeological artifacts was but one of the many forms of collecting in which the British and other Western Europeans indulged. And, therefore, during World War I, when military and political conditions provided the British with the opportunity to collect antiquities in Mesopotamia, this became a somewhat systematic activity under the auspices of the military authorities. There were several significant cases when the military officials encountered large collections of antiquities, their actions largely demonstrated their view that, given their military victory and occupation, these antiquities were the rightful property of the British government.

Yet the question of Mesopotamian antiquities was not a simple one. The British anticipated that they would eventually have to administer this region. They had portrayed their occupation of Mesopotamia as a liberation of its peoples from foreign Turkish despots. Consequently, Britain's future considerations in this area dictated its military occupation. As opposed to the American occupiers of Iraq of 2003, who initially did little to prevent the systematic looting and destruction of cultural property, the British military authorities did pay attention to the cultural artifacts. Although much of this attention was self-serving, there was at least some level of realization that archaeological artifacts needed protection and preservation. Initially, though, the British sought to extract as many antiquities as they could, especially the large collections of antiquities that they found at German excavation sites in Mesopotamia.

In June 1917 Cecil Harcourt Smith of London's Victoria and Albert Museum (VAM) wrote to Sir Reginald Brade at the War Office (WO), stating that he heard privately that the Mesopotamian Expeditionary Force (MEF) had discovered numerous cases left by the German expedition at Samarra which had been packed and intended for dispatch to Berlin. As previously mentioned, German expeditions conducted excavations at Samarra. The city of Samarra, which is located around 125 kilometers north of Baghdad, was established in 836 C.E. by the Abbasid Caliph al-Mutasim as the new administrative capital of the Caliphate. Samarra was largely abandoned in medieval times, only to be rediscovered by the German archaeologists at the beginning of the twentieth century.

In his letter to the WO, Smith was inquiring as to the fate of those cases, as well as the fate of other antiquities found in Mesopotamia. He politely, yet assertively, suggested to Sir Brade that "in such cases I hope very much that the claim of this Institute may be recognized."[80] Smith pushed the nationalistic sentiment and current competitive animosity toward Germany further, declaring, "I believe it is the case that the Germans usually arrange that the interest of their National Museum shall be properly represented in any military expedition they send out, where artistic treasures are likely to be forthcoming." Smith continued, adding pressure on the government official, by arguing that it had often proved to be a misfortune in the past that the English government had not followed this example, and that he hoped that something would be done to "remedy this defect, and that if artistic treasures of any kind are discovered . . . they may be sent to this country . . . for the national benefit."[81]

The India Office (IO), which deemed Mesopotamia as its responsibility, heard of this matter and contacted Percy Cox, then chief political officer of the MEF.[82] He told the IO that "93 cases from Samarra are stored in my office. Miss Bell examined one of the Samarra cases and found it to contain valuable fragments of early Moslem pottery and glass."[83] Cox went on to state that he had arranged for a representative selection to be sent to the Victoria and Albert Museum and had "always had in mind claims of museum on this important material."[84]

Then for almost a year this case lay dormant until the WO suddenly got involved once again. The British War Trophies Committee of the WO independently considered this issue, stating that these German cases "are of great value," and allotted them to the British Museum.[85] The committee suggested, furthermore, that preparation for transport be initiated. Arnold T. Wilson, then civil commissioner in Baghdad, received a cable with instructions he found confusing, so he sought the IO's advice. Wilson mentioned in his cable to the IO that the cases had been packed and were in storage in Basra.[86]

Wilson's cable caught the IO by surprise. In interoffice notes accompanying this cable, John Evelyn Shuckburgh, an IO official, raised some points which clearly show that the IO was initially reluctant to allow the export of antiquities from Mesopotamia in general.[87] He noted, "It seems undesirable that any objects of archaeological interest should be sent out of the country . . . to remove these antiquities from their natural home raises a large question of policy."[88] An office memo that circulated throughout the IO office and allowed various members of the department to state their views strongly criticized the Trophies Committee's decision, and two officials, Arthur Hirtzel and Edwin Montagu, the secretary of state for India, stated in it that this matter was "most discreditable."[89] Further, this matter was embarrassing in view of a recent American journalist's interview. In it, the British secretary of state made special mention of Mesopotamian art treasures and contrasted the English policy of leaving such objects in their own country with the methods of "wholesale pillage pursued by the Germans in Territories under their military occupation."[90] It was in this context that Montagu stated to his colleagues that the WO decision should have been in consultation with the IO, since this was an issue in which "political, as well as military, considerations come into play."[91] Montagu's remarks reveal that for the politicians involved, antiquities were not merely artifacts that were interesting from a historical or archaeological point of view, they had a distinct political dimension as well.

Somewhat harsh exchanges between the WO and IO followed this first memo. The two offices disputed who had the authority to decide the fate of the antiquities. Next the Foreign Office (FO) got involved. The FO sided with the IO, stating that it strongly deplored the projected removal of antiquities, "in view of the fact that it is of a nature to expose the British administration of occupied territory to criticisms of enemy propaganda."[92] This concern was further voiced in a memorandum by Montagu: in it he stated that the issue "raised a large question of policy directly affecting the good name of the British Government in the eyes of the world."[93] In view of Britain's charges against Germany of war pillaging, Montagu urged that the British should "avoid any action that could give a pretext for similar charges against ourselves."[94]

Another memo, by Arthur Hirtzel, argued that the Samarra objects were not spoils of war in any real sense, since although their immediate possessors had been Germans, they had appropriated them from the Turks. Consequently, Hirtzel recommended that this issue be governed by an international statute, which stated that any seizure of historic monuments be made the subject of legal proceedings.[95]

Next, the Eastern Committee of the Cabinet discussed the issue in a meeting on August 20, 1918. It overruled the WO decision and declared that it was "desirable that the treasures should remain in Mesopotamia."[96] Interestingly, the Committee temporized, since it went on to state that if the antiquities in question consisted of Assyrian antiquities they should "appropriately find a place in the British Museum"; otherwise, if they were from a "mid-Arabian period . . . they should properly be reserved for a museum at Baghdad, if such were ever created."[97] This was the first time that the idea of establishing a museum in

Baghdad ever appeared in any official documents. It reveals that these influential British politicians, who were so instrumental in the initial state-building process in Iraq, envisaged a state that had a museum, a museum that should appropriately contain Islamic monuments rather than pre-Islamic ones. It is also noteworthy that the British officials considered the Assyrian antiquities as more appropriately theirs rather than the Islamic antiquities.

Although she seems not to have been aware of the Eastern Committee meeting, Gertrude Bell, then in Baghdad, added to the confusion by issuing a memorandum called "The Safeguarding of Antiquities in the 'Iraq."[98] In this report, Bell documents the state of archaeological matters in the region and tries to set the record straight. She states that during the occupation of Samarra, ninety-six cases were found in the town, containing plasterwork and fragments of pottery collected by Professors Sarre and Herzfeld. This collection had been transferred to Basra. As mentioned above, Cox stated that ninety-three cases were in his office.[99] Bell states, "Their proper destination, if they are sent to England, is the Victoria and Albert, not the British Museum, and Sir Cecil Smith [VAM] has been informed that they will be delivered to him as soon as there is reasonable prospect of safe transport by sea."[100] The British political officers at Basra worked closely with the WO in this matter and considered themselves as having the authority to unilaterally decide the fate of the antiquities. In this memo, Bell, foreshadowing her own important role in this respect, pointed out that the British would be in the future called upon to provide for archaeological regulations on as large a scale as in Egypt. Bell writes, "We may take for granted that this will imply the foundation of an adequate museum in this country, probably in Baghdad, with arrangements as in Egypt for sharing with excavators, of whatever nationality, their possible finds." Bell went on to reassure that neither the objects at Babylon nor Samarra need fall retrospectively under arrangements of this nature. However, as she pointed out, at Babylon were many duplicates that the British Museum would not need, and these might form the nucleus of the Baghdad Museum.[101]

Bell's report surprised the IO, which responded with a cable reiterating once again that the British government was unwilling on broad grounds of principle to sanction the removal of the cases from Mesopotamia unless their contents were such that the custody in a European museum would be clearly more appropriate than their retention in their country of origin.[102] An IO departmental minute in December 21, 1918, summarized the issue, stating that its intervention had been on grounds of high principle. However, this minute also reveals that the IO had slightly modified its position. Now the IO was suggesting that the antiquities be lent to a London museum pending the establishment of a museum at Baghdad. The basis for this arrangement was that they needed to be in London "if they are to be of any use to scholars, until Baghdad is easily accessible by air. . . . They [the Samarra relics] are of no use to anybody at Baghdad now, and provided that they may some day be recalled, they may quite well be exhibited here in the meantime."[103] Hence, the historical artifacts should be on loan until the circumstances were ripe to return them to Baghdad.

The officials at the BM and VAM, however, were determined not to allow this golden opportunity to be decided by governmental bureaucrats. In an effort to pursue the Samarran and Babylonian artifacts, Frederick Kenyon, director of the BM and president of the British Academy, initiated the establishment of the Joint Archaeological Committee. The officials at the IO were quite skeptical, almost cynical, about this new entity, which was supposed to promote the wishes of the respective museums under the façade of a neutral scientific organ. One official described it as a "rather elaborate scheme . . . [that] cannot be regarded as a practical proposition."[104] The Foreign Office subsequently reminded Kenyon of its view that in principle it was averse to exporting antiquities from the country of origin unless they were duplicates or had little or no connection to the area. Interestingly, the British foreign secretary, Lord Curzon, stated that he anticipated that the Middle Eastern countries would soon take a great interest in their own archaeological remains, which made him disinclined to allow their removal from the area.[105] This matter even reached the corridors of the British House of Commons, in April 1919, when Sir Martin Conway inquired about the German antiquities, wondering if they had arrived in England.

The antiquities in question were then examined by H. R. Hall, a senior assistant in the Department of Egyptian and Assyrian Antiquities at the BM who had been stationed in Mesopotamia during the war. According to his examination, the collection at Basra contained 126 boxes in all: 86 from Samarra (down from 93, which Bell had reported), 17 from Babylon, and 23 from other unknown sites. The boxes from Samarra contained primarily plaster relief work, frescoes, and carved wood work from the Islamic Abbasid Caliphate around 850 C.E. The other boxes contained Assyrian and Babylonian stone sculptures, cuneiform tablets, and pottery. Not surprisingly, Hall recommended that, although the contents were not of first-class importance, "their custody in a European Museum would be more appropriate than the retention in the country of origin."[106] Hall then suggested that the whole collection be sent to the BM, which would then distribute a significant portion to the VAM. Not unless it was definitely intended to found a national museum in Baghdad, Hall contended, should duplicates be made available for that museum, and then only when it was actually in working order. Hall argued, "There is such a thing as 'cruelty to antiquities' . . . which consists in keeping the product of excavations shut up in boxes, where nobody can see or study them."[107]

Upon receiving Hall's report, the IO officials still felt there were not adequate grounds for removal of the antiquities and strongly urged the British authorities in Baghdad to start collecting a nucleus for a museum in Baghdad.[108] Wilson responded in a letter to the IO that such a possibility had been considered, but he claimed that the antiquities did not appeal to the public in the region. Moreover, he also argued that if they were stored in Baghdad they would not be sufficiently accessible for European scholars. Therefore, Wilson suggested, like the earlier IO position on the matter, that they all be sent to the BM and at some subsequent date a representative collection could be sent to Baghdad. Wilson, however, also pointed out that both the French and the Americans had expressed interest in resuming archaeological excavations and would expect to be allowed to remove their finds, a request that would be difficult to refuse. Wilson then formulated an idea that would later guide antiquities legislation in Iraq. The concept was based on the idea that foreign missions would be allowed to export their finds. It also required the excavations to "make an adequate return to the Central Museum [of Baghdad] when established[.] I believe this administration would assist the cause of science, and at the same time obtain the willing co-operation of the various institutions in the formation of a local museum."[109]

Upon reviewing this matter, Curzon of the FO suggested that the safest policy was one of absolute prohibition on the export of antiquities from Mesopotamia.[110] Kenyon at the BM, however, reiterated his view that keeping the antiquities there could cause permanent damage to them and, therefore, once again, suggested that they be sent to England.[111]

Despite the BM's valiant attempts, Curzon's view and policy were upheld, and for the next fourteen months the antiquities stayed at Basra. In February of 1921 Percy Cox cabled the IO, reminding the authorities that a national Iraqi government was about to be formed, so "we might lose sight of the antiquities in question." He once again suggested that arrangements be made for sending them to England.[112] At this point the Colonial Office (CO) became involved. Winston Churchill, colonial secretary, wrote to the FO stating that a certain risk would attend its detention of these "valuable antiquities . . . and that it would be unwise to delay a decision as to their disposal any longer."[113] Ostensibly, the rationale for removing the antiquities from Iraq was that if they remained there much longer without skilled attention they would "deteriorate greatly in value."[114] Although Churchill was officially seeking the FO's approval, a letter written the same day by T. E. Lawrence to Frederick Kenyon of the BM stated that Churchill had already given Cox the authority, without the FO's approval, to send the antiquities to England. Lawrence stressed, however, that no decision had yet been taken as to their final destination.[115]

When the FO heard about the correspondence between Cox and Churchill, its officials reminded Churchill that the "policy of despatching such antiquities to this country is in entire contradiction with that which has been pursued by HMG since 1914." Consequently, the FO urged that the order to Cox be suspended while the matter was discussed further.[116]

A later letter from Cox in Baghdad to the CO, however, demonstrates Cox's true rationale for sending the antiquities to England: "My hope in sending home the Samarra antiquities before the Iraq Government succeeded the British administration was that they could be regarded as spoils of war taken by our troops . . . and to discuss them with the Iraq government would be unnecessary."[117] Despite lofty ideals such as the question of accessibility to Western scholars and the wide-ranging debates within the British government involving some of its most influential foreign policy figures calling for the antiquities to stay in Iraq, the British political leaders at Basra ultimately unilaterally made this decision.[118] Perhaps Cox was sensing that the end of an era was approaching in the Middle East. Previously, European travelers and

archaeologists brought back antiquities and works of art without hin-
drance. Now, with new modern governmental structures on the horizon
for Iraq, Cox seized the last opportunity he had to bolster British
national collections.

Once the antiquities reached England, the British authorities invited one of the original excavators from Samarra, Ernst Herzfeld of
Germany. Churchill also appointed T. E. Lawrence to represent the CO
in examining the collection. Herzfeld and Lawrence issued a report
stating that of the 105 cases packed by Herzfeld at Samarra, 79 had
arrived in England. Since Hall had counted 86 cases in Basra, 7 boxes
were lost since their arrival there. They stated that the "condition of the
antiquities leaves a good deal to be desired and it is evident that they
have suffered much through their long detention in Mesopotamia."[119]
A majority of this collection, or 79 cases, were from Herzfeld excavations at Samarra. The collection also contained approximately 40 boxes
with artifacts from the German expeditions in Assur and some
Babylonian relics, presumably a detached group from the so-called
Lisbon Collection.[120]

According to a report by Herzfeld, the finds at Samarra were miscellaneous, ranging from stucco wall reliefs, marble decorations, and
frescoes to smaller finds such as fragments of pottery and glass, copper
implements, and marble vases.[121] Herzfeld also addressed the value of
the collection and how it should be divided. He maintained that for
science and museum purposes by far the most important finds were the
stucco wall decorations that were still in the government's buildings in
Samarra, which were about 1 square meter in size. He suggested that
these stucco decorations would be given to the Imperial Museum in
Istanbul, the future museum in Baghdad, and to the original expedition. Of the collection that was now housed at the British Museum,
Herzfeld stated that there were several objects of special importance,
including big, rude jars showing portraits of male and female figures.
These portraits were unexpected finds, as they were hardly characteristic of Islamic art. In his report, he begged that he be given these jars,
some of which were only in fragments.[122]

In general, Herzfeld and Lawrence suggested that the artifacts be
divided among museums in Europe, North America, and the Middle
East. They recommended that Iraq primarily receive various marble
fragments, since "a European museum would but little care to possess

these objects."[123] Herzfeld also pointed out that the objects most desirable for a European museum, "and at the same time least connected with the place of their provenance,"[124] were the ceramics—pre-Islamic, Islamic, and imports from China from 838–883 C.E.

In the end, the collection was split amongst seventeen institutions.[125] In most of these cases, the British Museum suggested an exchange, with corresponding museums receiving, for example, Danish porcelain for Abbasid glazed tiles.[126] Many of the museums only received pieces of minimal value. For example, in a letter to the shipping company Messrs. E. W. Morgan regarding the shipment to the Royal Ontario Museum, the British Museum stated that there was no need to insure the shipment, because it "contains fragments of pottery of glass of nominal value only—say £5."[127] The British Museum and the Berlin Museum received the largest and most impressive pieces of the collection. The Louvre and the Victoria and Albert Museum also received sizable portions.

Upon receiving the report from Lawrence and Herzfeld, Churchill and his staff at the CO wrote a letter to the FO that recounted the whole story of the antiquities. They stated that it was inadmissible to treat the antiquities as war trophy. They pointed out, however, that Churchill's concern that the antiquities would deteriorate greatly if they remained in Iraq induced him to permit their export. Since there was no museum in Iraq and funds for establishing an Iraqi museum were presently unavailable, they recommended that the collection be divided among ten or twelve museums, primarily in Western Europe, "where [its] value would be appreciated."[128] However, because the collection contains dozens of duplicates of all kinds, they suggested that the interests of the future Iraqi government be safeguarded by keeping in England a representative set that would be handed over to the Iraqi government, free of charge, "as soon as they are prepared to receive it."[129] In a letter to the BM, Churchill stressed that a delegate of his office (Lawrence) would assist in choosing a representative, duplicate set for Iraq. Further, Churchill ruled that the question of the antiquities of the Babylonian, Assyrian, and Parthian periods, which also came along with the Samarra collection, would be dealt with separately.[130]

This intergovernmental discussion about antiquities reached the British delegation at the Paris Peace Conference. It cabled the IO asking for a list—to be inserted eventually in an appendix of the Treaty of

Peace with Turkey—of objects of archaeological interest removed from the Ottoman Empire.[131] Subsequently, Article 421 of the peace treaty with Turkey stated that the Turkish government would abrogate the existing law of antiquities and that it would enact a new law of antiquities ensuring the perfect equality among all nations. Article 422 stated that all objects removed since August 1, 1914, from any of the territories detached from Turkey would, within twelve months from the coming into force of the present treaty, be restored by the Turkish government to the government of the territory from which such objects were removed. Despite these articles of the peace treaty, portions of the Samarra antiquities were not handed over to Iraq until 1936. As will be discussed below, that share had deteriorated and was hardly representative of the overall collection.

THE LISBON COLLECTION

At the same time as the question of the Samarra antiquities went back and forth between different governmental entities, the British officials were also squabbling over another Mesopotamian collection. The strange saga of the Lisbon Collection reveals further insights into the role of antiquities as war trophy and the question of ownership during a transitory time.

Just prior to the outbreak of the war, the vessel *Cheruskia* left Basra with instructions to convey its cargo, which consisted of 448 cases of antiquities from the German excavations at Assur, to Hamburg for dispatch to the Deutsche Orient-Gesellschaft in Berlin. While the ship was at sea, the war broke out. Consequently, the vessel sought refuge in Lisbon.[132] Since the antiquities left Mesopotamia prior to the outbreak of the war, they were not subject to Article 422 of the peace treaty with Turkey and could therefore be considered a prize of war.[133]

The German government tried to pressure the Portuguese government to transfer the antiquities to Germany.[134] Despite German efforts to resolve this matter covertly, diplomatically, and even militarily, the presence of these Mesopotamian antiquities in Lisbon was brought to the attention of the archaeological community. The archaeologists in turn alerted the relevant political officials.[135] In the British press, there was some discussion on how these antiquities should be disposed, particularly given Britain's current role as occupation force in Mesopotamia.[136] Mesopotamian antiquities were once again discussed in the British House of Commons on August 18, 1919, when it was declared that all possible steps should be taken to retain the Lisbon Collection for England.

From the British point of view, the question of the antiquities was more a question of justice. The British maintained that the antiquities had been removed by the Germans illegally. Major Young of the FO, who had visited the German excavators in 1913, recalled that they admitted they were not entitled by law to export the antiquities, but "rejoiced in the fact that they freely did so."[137] The British seemed unaware of the secret 1899 agreement between the Ottomans and the Germans. They were therefore guided by the still current Ottoman antiquities law, which during the period of the war remained in force, which stated that all objects excavated in the Ottoman dominions should either remain on the spot as the property of the country or be transported to the museum in Istanbul as the property of the state.[138]

In this case, when they were not on the receiving end, the British appealed to a principle which hitherto had not been much of a concern for them. Although this principle had not been discussed in the Samarra antiquities affair, the British representative in Lisbon emphasized to the Portuguese authorities that restoring the antiquities to Germany would denote "the greatest mockery of the most elementary principles of justice."[139] Concurrently, one of the original German excavators, Walter Andrae, wrote to Gertrude Bell in Baghdad, appealing to their friendship before the war and her "fair international reasoning in regards to scientific things." Asking for the return of the objects to Berlin, he stated that they were being used as a "political object instead of being treated as things of international value."[140] Bell cast aside any personal ties she may have had to the German archaeologists. She had in fact visited Andrae in 1911 and wrote to her mother on that occasion, "I found great profit from endless talks with Dr. Andrae. His knowledge of Mesopotamian problems is so great and his views so brilliant and comprehensive. . . . He put everything at my disposal, photographs and his own unpublished ideas. I don't think that many people are so generous."[141] Bell had also written to the German archaeologist Herzfeld during the war and stated, "Let us remember that for us at least friendship is stronger than war."[142] Yet in contrast to Andrae's passionate plea, Bell's cool reply maintained that whether the antiquities belong to the German or to the Turkish government, the Portuguese government had every right to consider them as war prize. She added that on behalf of the "future Mesopotamian State for which we regard ourselves as trustees we should like to acquire them if after examination this seems to be desirable for the Museum which will ultimately be established in Baghdad."[143] Bell continued acrimoniously, reminding Andrae that "fair international reasoning" could cut both ways. "For example, I have reason to believe that you have in the Kaiser Friedrich Museum certain moulded bricks of the fourteenth-century inscription from the liwan in the courtyard of the Marjan Mosque in Baghdad. I know that these were removed by the Germans here during the war and I hold that on fair international reasoning they should be returned."[144] In this matter, Bell took a pragmatic view of the situation. Instead of being sympathetic to the personal ties she had fostered with the German archaeologists or keeping the scientific wholeness of the collection at heart, Bell responded as a British politician rather than an archaeologist.

A miniconference was held at the India Office in May 1920 to consider what further action should be taken regarding the Lisbon Collection.[145] E. Budge, from the BM, (incorrectly) stressed that under the terms of their concession, the Germans could not export their antiquities. In this case, Budge referred to the 1874 Ottoman Law of Antiquities, which stipulated that all excavated antiquities were the property of the Ottoman state. A. S. Yahuda, of the University of Madrid and special British envoy in this matter, pointed out that the Portuguese recognized that these were stolen property, but would not surrender them without some sort of compensation. Despite Yahuda's reservations, the officials from the IO and FO suggested that diplomatic, as well as scientific (i.e., appeal to considerations about what contributions these artifacts could make to science in preserving the collection as a whole unit), pressure be put on Portugal. They suggested that the government of Portugal be asked to surrender the antiquities "as an act of grace, on a guarantee that the British Museum would examine the antiquities on behalf of Mesopotamia" and then either give Portugal a portion of the collection or sell the other with Portugal receiving the proceeds.[146] The British would stress that the collection would initially go to the British Museum for examination and classification, then ultimately return to Baghdad. It is not clear from the documents whether that was indeed the plan or whether they hoped that the collection would stay in the British Museum.

Although the British officials were clearly going to use scientific and political arguments to pressure the Portuguese, they were also very concerned with the value of the collection. As a report from a British Treasury official attending the conference reveals, the collection was believed to be worth around 100,000 pounds sterling.

The British ambassador in Portugal was instructed to approach the Portuguese government and point out that Iraq had recently become a British Mandate.[147] He should initially attempt to persuade the Portuguese that these antiquities were stolen property and should, therefore, be returned to the Mesopotamian administration. If necessary, he could offer the Portuguese between fifteen and twenty thousand pounds, "an amount which could probably be realized by the sale of these articles in the collection which could be dispensed with."[148] The amount which the otherwise frugal British Treasury was willing to pay, even at this time when England was rebuilding after the war, reveals how valuable British officials considered these antiquities.

The Portuguese authorities shunned British diplomatic pressure, deciding to keep the antiquities in Portugal, where they claimed they could be readily available for anyone interested in studying them.[149] This decision may have been because the Portuguese press devoted considerable space discussing the fate of the collection. Newspapers urged the authorities, because of the lack of such objects in Portuguese museums, to keep the artifacts in return for Portuguese sacrifices in the war.[150] Thereafter, the British decided not to revive this question until a "new 'indigenous' administration of Mesopotamia has been placed on a permanent footing."[151]

Eventually, in 1926, the Portuguese returned some of the antiquities to the Germans in exchange for various valuable Portuguese paintings then housed in Germany, plus scientific instruments.[152]

THE HALL/CAMPBELL THOMPSON COLLECTION

When the British occupied Mesopotamia during the war, they were in a position to exploit some of its resources, both natural and cultural. Since they were the occupation force, the British became the proprietors of the antiquities. And because there was not a local scientific establishment in place to deal with these antiquities, the

British forces in Mesopotamia had no local interests to monitor their activities, nor did they feel restricted by the current Ottoman antiquities law. As they gained control of the land, the state of the antiquities was brought to their attention.

The British Museum authorities were not satisfied with receiving antiquities solely as war trophy. At the same time in which they were active in the war trophy discussion, they felt that British control of the area could obviously facilitate the Museum's archaeological expeditions in the area. In a letter to Mark Sykes, Kenyon, of the British Museum, urged that the British authorities take advantage of research "as may be compatible with the exigencies of war and generally show interest in the history and ancient civilization of the countries in our occupation."[153] Kenyon suggested that such a mission would be best placed in the hands of the British Academy, since it was "disinterested" and had no ends to serve "except the interest of civilized studies."[154] Kenyon also alluded to the close ties between the archaeological and intelligence community in stating that "presumably they would be attached, as the archaeological representative of the British Museum has hitherto been, to the Intelligence Branch."[155] And Kenyon did not sit idle as he saw an opportunity arise in Mesopotamia.

Upon occupying Mesopotamia, the British war authorities had issued a proclamation that "throughout the Occupied Territories all antiquities . . . which formerly were the property of the Ottoman Government or shall hereafter be discovered are the property of the Administration of the Occupied Territories acting on behalf of the said Territories."[156] The BM subsequently applied to the WO for the attachment of archaeologists to the British forces in Mesopotamia "with a view to the preservation of the ancient sites . . . and the conduct of such research as might be practicable under existing condition."[157] Reginald Campbell Thompson, until then a sedentary scholar of linguistics whose specialty was the deciphering of Hittite seals and who had excavated with Lawrence and Woolley at Carchemish prior to the war, joined British Military Intelligence in Mesopotamia to decrypt Turkish-German wireless messages. In 1917 he was discharged from his duties and conducted brief excavations at Abu Shahrein and Tell Muqayyir. When Campbell Thompson had to return to England in 1918, the BM made a request to the WO that H. R. Hall, who was senior assistant in the Department of Egyptian and Assyrian Antiquities at the BM, also be relieved from military service so that he could undertake archaeological soundings in Mesopotamia.[158]

Hall reported to the BM that he had completed excavations at "Southern Babylonia" at Tell Muqayyir. Hall was happy to relate that he had been assigned seventy Turkish prisoners of war, "which simplified the labour problem" as well as saving money.[159] In cooperation with Wilson and particularly the military authorities in Baghdad, Hall arranged for the export of the antiquities from his and Campbell Thompson's excavations. Hall wrote to Kenyon stating that not all authorities were enthusiastic about permitting their export, particularly those politicians whose allegiance was to the IO.[160] This export arrangement, about which some of the local British authorities were fully knowledgeable, was against official governmental policy. These objects were subsequently exported to England and arrived there, without customs inspection, by action of the military authorities.[161]

The IO officials were furious when they heard that this shipment had arrived at the BM, since they had sent a telegram to Wilson, the civil commissioner in Baghdad, specifically forbidding the shipment. Shuckburgh noted that "these people are always trying to 'suck' us," while Hirtzel stated that it was altogether "improper for the British Museum to send out people to pillage Mesopotamia under cover of the military occupation."[162] The IO officials sought full explanations from the BM authorities. Curzon, at the FO, also heard of the matter and stated that "it looks as though the order of the Secretary of State had been deliberately disregarded. . . . We must have a clean sheet in these matters and if the articles ought not to have been brought here at all, they should be sent back."[163] After an IO official inquiry into whether the antiquities had actually reached England, Kenyon confirmed that they had indeed reached the BM, stating, "If any official of the India Office cares to come and see them, I think he will be satisfied that whatever may be the ultimate destination of the objects, it was essential that they should first be brought to England and receive skilled treatment."[164] The IO subsequently once again commissioned T. E. Lawrence to inspect Campbell Thompson's collection. Lawrence stated in his report that the antiquities were from three sites, Abu Shahrein, Ur, and El Obeid. The collection from Abu Shahrein was fairly large yet "nothing of any outstanding value and as a whole the objects are not of great importance." And once again, Lawrence recommended against sending any of it back to Mesopotamia, since "for less than the cost of carriage from London an equally good selection could be made from Abu Sharein . . . and sent to Baghdad."[165] The Ur collection did not, according to Lawrence, contain "a single valuable piece," although it was of "particular interest" to the authorities of the British Museum, since it was a representative set of pottery complementing the museum's Assyrian sculpture collection.

Lawrence concluded his report by stating that some pieces in the collection had some importance for the study of early Mesopotamian art. Therefore, it was desirable that they be represented in the local museum, when one existed. However, it would not have been possible to leave them there when they were found because of their poor condition and the lack of expertise in Mesopotamia in treating them. Lawrence apologetically argued that to have delayed the export of these delicate objects from Mesopotamia would have been improper and to send them back was impossible. He therefore recommended that the whole collection should be ceded permanently to the BM, while stipulating that the Mesopotamian government should be supplied with reproductions of these objects, "since they are of greatest rarity and interest and should certainly be represented at Baghdad."[166]

The IO and FO were generally impressed by Lawrence's report. However, they drew the conclusion that objects so valuable and delicate may suffer irreparable damage from the lack of immediate preservative treatment on the spot. For those very reasons, as well as to "prevent the wholesale pillage for the benefit of foreign museums," they recommended that further excavations should be prohibited in Mesopotamia until an adequately staffed department of archaeology had been created there.[167] They informed the BM that the Hall/Campbell Thompson Collection could be permanently retained in England under the following conditions: (1) that it was recognized that the objects are the property of the Mesopotamian government and that they are described as being lent by that government; (2) that a formal receipt for them be furnished together with an inventory of the major objects; and (3) that the Mesopotamian government be supplied with reproductions (casts or copies) as may hereafter be required by local museums.[168] The BM responded that it had acted throughout with the full authorization of the relevant authorities, first through the WO and later through the civil administration in Baghdad. It had even informed the IO that Hall was leaving for Mesopotamia to excavate. Therefore, if it was now desired to claim all the objects discovered belonged to the Mesopotamian government, the BM felt that the government should reimburse it for all the expenses incurred in the expedition. Moreover, if the objects were to be regarded as a temporary loan, it would be impossible to spend money from the BM budget for their restoration, "a restoration which is so necessary that without it the most valuable objects will perish, and even after which it would be highly dangerous to send them out again to Mesopotamia."[169] Kenyon suggested that the collection in the Museum be formally presented to the BM by the Mesopotamian government, on the understanding that when a museum was established in Mesopotamia, the BM would "assist the Mesopotamian Government to secure a representative collection of the antiquities."[170] The IO suggested, however, that any monies spent on the restoration of the antiquities should be refunded to the Museum trustees by the Mesopotamian government if the objects themselves were eventually returned to Mesopotamia. Although IO officials could not definitely pledge the future Mesopotamian government's acceptance of this view, they suggested that the BM administrators "consider themselves sufficiently protected by the assurance that HMG will, if the occasion arises, take such steps as may be within their power to secure its acceptance."[171]

Although the politicians had surrendered to make this decision, they were not oblivious to how paradoxically they were behaving toward Mesopotamian antiquities. In fact, one official asked during the course of the Lisbon affair, "If we question the propriety of the Portuguese attitude, what are we to say if they question the Thompson-Hall Collection? It is true that we have stipulated that these objects must be regarded as the property of the Mesopotamian Government; but the Portuguese might question in their own minds the *bona fides* of this arrangement."[172]

Comparing the cases of the Samarra, Lisbon, and Hall/Campbell Thompson collections reveals intriguing questions about the ownership and propriety of the antiquities. In each of these cases, it was ambiguous who exactly owned the antiquities. It was not clear if they should belong (1) to the country in which they were found, (2) to the excavator's nation, (3) to the nation that funded the mission, (4) to the presiding political power, or (5) to the nation that could most easily appreciate their value. Although the question of value presumably meant its historic and scientific value, the monetary value of the antiquities was also a significant factor.

Despite their seemingly self-serving acts in archaeological matters, the British took their role as occupying force in Mesopotamia seriously. To their credit, they took several measures to preserve and repair some Mesopotamian monuments. In a memorandum from September 1917, the general commanding officer of the MEF brought the fragile state of the ruins at Ctesiphon to the attention of the chief of the general staff in India.[173] The officer suggested that an archaeologist should visit the ruins and make the necessary repairs. Subsequently, the Foreign and Political Department in India wrote to Edwin Montagu, the secretary of state for India, on the subject of preservation of the ancient ruins of Mesopotamia.[174] The department requested that the director general of archaeology of India visit the sites in Mesopotamia in order to make the necessary repairs, because "the preservation of these and other interesting ruins we consider to be the business of the Government in occupation."[175] In an IO office note accompanying this letter, Shuckburgh affirmed the belief that Britain should be responsible for the antiquities of the area, pointing out that "the matter is one that is likely to arouse widespread interest and HMG will be held closely responsible by the world at large for the proper preservation of these famous monuments of the past."[176]

When this matter finally reached the political officer in Baghdad, who obviously felt other matters needed more immediate attention in Mesopotamia, he recommended to the IO that all research and excavation be postponed, yet that preservation of specific sites (such as Ctesiphon, Ukhaidar, and Samarra) be undertaken immediately.[177] Some minor repair work was performed at Ctesiphon, and the sites at Samarra and Babylon were put under guard to prevent further damage and theft. Furthermore, the British issued a proclamation that made any removal of antiquities without official permission unlawful and subject to significant fines.[178]

When it became clearer that Iraq would become a British Mandate, the British sought to organize a modern state there with all the relevant institutions. Given the confusion surrounding the status and ownership of the Mesopotamian antiquities during the war, and in recognition of "the morals of antiquity-hunting being what they are,"[179] as one British politician lamented, antiquities legislation and the establishment of a local museum became an issue when the Iraqi state was established in 1921.

3

FROM MESOPOTAMIA TO IRAQ: POLITICS DURING THE MANDATE (1921-1932)

We must recognize that we are fighting in Mesopotamia not a Constitutional question as to the future government of Mesopotamia, but for the very existence of civilization in the Middle East. If we are driven out, only anarchy can supervene.

N. W. E. Bray, British Intelligence Officer, August 26, 1920

You are flying in the face of four millenniums of history if you try to draw a line around Iraq and call it a political entity! Assyria always looked to the west and east and north and Babylonia to the south. They have never been an independent unit. . . . They have no conception of nationhood yet.

John Van Ess to Gertrude Bell in 1919

The adage "to the victors belong the spoils" proved its aptness at the conclusion of World War I. For one of the victors, the British, the downfall of the Ottoman Empire meant that now the British had a chance to acquire precious Mesopotamian antiquities along with assuming political control of the country itself. The citizens of the future state of Iraq essentially became British spoils of war and became subject to a political construct that was largely demarcated by British imperial interests.

In the Mandate period, between 1921 and 1932, the British government received a Mandate from the League of Nations to oversee the political development of Iraq. Ostensibly, the ultimate aim was to prepare Iraq for independence. At the same time, this goal was to be achieved fully in line with British interests. Nowhere were these concerns more manifest than in archaeology. While laying the groundwork for future archaeological institutions and practices in Iraq, this period also witnessed systematic attempts at ensuring that British or North American institutions and archaeologists would continue to enjoy considerable access to antiquities, even though new protocols and legislation were in place. During these years, the British were the predominant power and had the opportunity to determine the organization of most major political matters, including those related to archaeology.

This opportunity, however, was a double-edged sword. The commitment to control Iraq raised a range of difficult questions concerning the status of Iraq, in particular, and of the Middle East, in general. After having fought a ferocious, difficult war, resulting in enormous human casualties and material costs, the British were not willing, politically, psychologically, or financially, to spend the time, money, and energy needed to coerce and control the Middle East as they had aspired to in the past.

However, the war did not completely alter their attitude and philosophy concerning Britain's role in the non-Western world. As Bray's quotation above suggests, the British believed that they had an important "civilizing" mission in the former provinces of the Ottoman Empire. Instead of the openly exploitive imperialism of yesteryear, however, the modus operandi had evolved into a softer, gentler, and more subtle form of imperialism—a "benevolent" imperialism. An important aspect of such a civilizing mission was an effort to organize archaeological matters and to restore important monuments, since such affairs were, for the most part, in disarray. Indeed, in Iraq, considered the very cradle of civilization, the British pursued this mission energetically. As the epitome of British imperialism, Lord Curzon, an antiquities enthusiast, stated in the context of India, "it is . . . equally our duty to dig and discover [the antiquities], to classify, reproduce and describe, to copy and decipher, and to cherish and conserve."[1]

In the Middle East this sense of duty was particularly urgent, since Middle Eastern antiquities played an even larger role in Western popular imagination than those in other parts of the world. Yet, the presence of antiquities, which originally sparked some people's interest in the area, may actually have had the paradoxical effect of causing a negative image of and attitude toward the contemporary post–World War I situation. The antiquities served as reminders of a glorious, venerated past. By contrast, it seemed disconcerting to some that they were presently located amongst what was considered to be an unappreciative, almost hostile population. This attitude is seen in a remark by David Hogarth,

the Keeper of Oxford's Ashmolean Museum and T. E. Lawrence's mentor, who during the war served as the leading British intelligence officer
in the Middle East. He stated that the ancient monuments of the Middle
East "conspicuously exalt the past at the expense of the present."[2]
British politicians, who in most cases were more comfortable and familiar with the former civilizations of the Middle East than its present cultures, were susceptible to such persuasion. The quest to organize
archaeological matters, therefore, was closely aligned with the general
political mission to establish a new state in the cradle of civilization. This
new state would bring modernity to the lands that contained the
ancient civilizations—with relevant Western-style, modern educational,
military, and political institutions. Indeed a pivotal moment was coming
for Mesopotamia—one with immense political, economic, and cultural
consequences.

It is important to associate archaeological affairs with general political developments, because this illuminates the very character of the
early archaeological enterprise. All decisions concerning archaeology
were inherently tied to the overall political and administrative process.

In the formative years of the Iraqi state, the link between archaeology and politics is particularly strong. The main decisions concerning
archaeology were part of a general British political and philosophical
approach and attitude toward the country and its peoples. The early
decisions were formative in constructing a particular way of conducting
archaeology during the very archaeologically active decade of Mandate
Iraq (1921–1932). Yet these important decisions had far-reaching
effects beyond the Mandate years. The very nature of these early, critical British activities substantially determined and influenced later (particularly from the mid-1930s onward) Iraqi actions and reactions in
archaeological matters. Of particular importance in this context was the
fact that the Iraqi politicians actually *perceived* archaeology to be a
British enterprise—aimed primarily at the British, but also other
Western, concerns and interests. They developed this perception
because the main British actors in archaeology also had important roles
in other more visible aspects of the state-building process. Archaeology
was but one of the many hats that adorned the British politicians.
Therefore, in the subsequent Iraqi struggle for full political independence, archaeology was considered as part of the British political and
administrative program that either had to be rejected or radically
realigned in order to fulfill Iraqi political and cultural aspirations.

The view of Iraqi politicians that archaeology was an all-Western affair may have resulted eventually in a more determined approach to archaeology by the Iraqis. The Iraqis lamented the perceived plundering of their archaeological sites. They therefore sought to repair and restore lost opportunities and artifacts in their legislative and administrative reforms. But this emphasis and attitude did not appear immediately. During the years of Mandate Iraq, the British, primarily, made all the most influential archaeological determinations. In contrast, the Iraqis made a few ineffective attempts to sway archaeological policy. This initial lack of Iraqi success, as will be demonstrated herein, is a testimony to contemporaneous British power and stubbornness, suggesting that British officials' view of their "civilizing" mission was all-pervasive and indisputable.

The practicalities of the British "civilizing" mission were put to the test at the important crossroads that followed World War I. The British had to determine what to do with the landmass they had acquired and how to reconcile their current political views with the often cryptic and contradictory commitments they had made during the war. Their policy during World War I had been characterized by haste and improvisation, "out of whim and caprice, in deference to prejudices and abstract principles."[3] After having gained intimate knowledge of British and French views toward the Middle East during the Paris Peace Conference, President Woodrow Wilson of the United States confessed, "[I] gained impressions in Paris which I must frankly say were altogether unfavorable to the methods of both the French and the English in dealing with that part of the world."[4]

Mesopotamia was but one link in the chain with which Britain's overall Middle East policy was concerned. Britain had to formulate how much of a political and financial investment it would commit to that region after the war. Owing to the chaotic situation after the downfall of the Ottoman Empire, the British were actually in the unique and historic position to make fundamental decisions concerning the political future of Mesopotamia. Largely failing to consult—indeed choosing to ignore—the views of the local population, the British had the power and political will to decide, in close cooperation with the French, on the borders and form of governments in the former provinces of the Ottoman Empire.

As has been well documented, they decided to establish quasi-independent nation-states in what was the Ottoman Middle East. In that process, the modern state of Iraq was established in 1921. Because the status of archaeology was closely tied with the overall political situation, a closer look at the political formation of modern Iraq is necessary in order to appreciate the context in which Iraqi archaeological policy developed.

"IRAQ": FROM GEOGRAPHICAL TO POLITICAL TERM

U p until World War I, most Westerners, including the British, referred to the area that became Iraq as Mesopotamia, a classical Greek term. Yet with a new-nation state on the horizon that would be independent from the Ottoman Empire, composed of a predominantly Arab population, it was no longer appropriate to refer to this new country by its Greek name. The new entity needed a new name that would distinguish it from its Ottoman past and indicate its status as a new independent state. Therefore, the Arabic name *'Iraq*, a term that had a long tradition in the area, emerged to designate the area formerly known as Mesopotamia.[5]

The term Iraq was a common name amongst Arabs for the area that Westerners called Mesopotamia. Ever since the Arab conquest of the region in the seventh century, Arab geographers and scholars used primarily two names to refer to the area known today as Iraq: *al-'Iraq* and *al-Jazira*. There is some dispute and uncertainty as to what the name "Iraq" means.[6] According to E. W. Lane's *Arabic-English Lexicon* and Ibn Mansur's *Lisan al-'Arab*, it means generally the side or shore of water or of a sea. More specifically, it denotes the border of the rivulet (for irrigation) by which water enters a garden.[7] Since Iraq had long been an area of irrigated plains, it is conceivable that the region bore the name of its environmental characteristics. Both Lane and Ibn Mansur refer to several sources stating that "Iraq" is Arabized from a Persian appellation of which the meaning is said to be "having many palm trees and other trees."[8]

Specifically, by the term "Iraq," most Arab geographers, such as Ibn Hawkal and Al-Muqaddasi, meant only today's southern Iraq. The term did not encompass the regions north of the region of Tikrit on the Tigris and near Hit on the Euphrates. It applied only to the whole southern region to the Persian Gulf. Iraq was sometimes divided, particularly by later Arab geographers, into *'Iraq al-'Arab* and *'Iraq al-'Ajam*—meaning the Arab Iraq and the non-Arab (foreign), in this case specifically Persian, Iraq.[9] For example, when the Arab traveler Ibn Battuta reached the city of Isfahan in the fourteenth century, he considered it to be in *'Iraq al-'Ajam*.[10] Earlier, in the tenth century, the influential geographer Al-Muqaddasi did not employ that particular distinction but articulated a precise and thorough account of the territorial divisions of Iraq. He split Iraq into six regions named after their principal cities: Kufa, Basra, Wasit, Baghdad, Hulwan, and Samarra.[11] Al-Muqaddasi addressed the rhetorical question of why he places the town of Babil within the district of Baghdad when in "ancient times the whole province was called after it[.]"[12] Al-Muqaddasi recognized that one of his predecessors, al-Jaihani (ca. 907 C.E.), whose districting of Iraq al-Muqaddasi disagreed with, began his account by calling the country by the name of Babil (or Babylon). Al-Muqaddasi acknowledged, furthermore, that the name is mentioned both in the Hadith literature and in the Qur'an. Therefore, he conceded that the pre-Islamic name had some precedence. But al-Muqaddasi stated that he had "travelled the empire of Islam through its length and breadth and have not heard the people call this province by any other name than that of al-'Iraq; nay, most people do not know where Babil is."[13] Al-Muqaddasi, writing during the zenith of the Abbasid Caliphate, was eager to present a unified, Islamic empire. He therefore sought to minimize what he considered to be heterodox elements in the geography and culture of the empire, including place names such as Babil, which referred to pre-Islamic civilizations.

By the tenth century, according to the early Arab geographers, most people in the Arab Middle East referred to the area as Iraq. The consensual picture they present includes clear demarcations of what was considered to be Iraq. Ibn Hawkal, for example, considers Iraq to extend in length from Abadan to Tikrit and in breadth from Baghdad to Kufa, and from Qadissiya to Hulwan.[14] Therefore, in human and physical terms, Iraq already had a somewhat precise precedent that included both Arab and non-Arab populations in southern Iraq. Parameters of Iraq such as Ibn Hawkal's became paradigmatic for the next centuries. The British orientalist E. W. Lane, writing in the 1860s, states that the country known as Iraq extended from Abadan to Mosul in length and from Qadissiya to Hulwan in breadth and that it is said to be named so because of its "side" shore of the Tigris and Euphrates.[15]

The northern part of the territory between the Upper Tigris and Euphrates was known by most authors as *al-Jazira,* which normally means "island" or "peninsula." It was distinguished from *al-'Iraq* primarily in geographic, but also in political and human, terms.[16] Since the Arab conquests, al-Jazira, a region of relatively ample water and fertile lands, had been involuntarily, and often antagonistically, subject to political rule from Baghdad. The people in this region were often subject to either Khariji or Kurdish revolts in the Ummayyad and Abbasid periods and became a semi-independent province under the Hamdanid dynasty.

When the Ottomans gained control of both Iraq and al-Jazira early in the sixteenth century, they began to fight over certain key territories with the equally expanding Safavid Iran. These battles marked out the jurisdictions between the empires through various treaties such as the Treaty of Amasya in 1555 and the Peace of Zuhab in 1639 (and confirmed in 1746 after another round of fighting with Nadir Shah), which placed the provinces of Baghdad, Basra, and Shahrizor under Ottoman control, leaving Mehereban and its dependencies under Safavid rule.[17] Although the boundaries thus were placed under some sort of legal arrangement, in practice, however, the Ottomans and the Persians used their frontiers as buffer zones and no-man's-lands to ensure that neither gained a dangerous advantage or threatened vital regional cities. The boundary situation spurred regional imperial and religious rivalry, and from the Iraqi Ottoman perspective, was a major concern for the governors and military leaders. As Donald Pitcher observes, the frontiers of Iraq "fluctuated greatly and tended to advance or recoil as the central government grew strong or weak."[18] Yet defending the frontier from the imminent Persian invasions became a matter of active strategy, particularly in the early eighteenth century during and following the reigns of Vali Hasan Pasha (d. 1724) and his son Ahmad Pasha (d. 1747), whose reigns also coincided with the beginning of Mamluk rule in Iraq.[19] Because these battles were extensive and protracted, and the Persians most often held the military advantage, for example when they occupied Basra between 1775 and 1778 under Karim Khan, the Iraqi Mamluk Pashas could ill afford to wage a total war and seal off the border. Indeed, they were dependent on the economic, cultural, and religious interaction among the areas. For example, the provinces of Iraq were heavily dependent on Persian raw silk and the economic impact of the Persian pilgrim traffic to the Shi'i shrines in Iraq.[20]

Even though by the mid-nineteenth century the term *hudud* (frontiers) was present in the literature of Ottoman Iraq, referring primarily to its boundaries with Qajar Iran, the borders of Iraq were not solely defined by the various border agreements.[21] Rather, as historian Hala Fattah argues, the main demarcations were created by influential regional merchants, tribal leaders, and Mamluk military commanders. These influential men carved out economic and political zones based on their trade and migration.[22] The frontiers were flexible and fluid, functioning more as passages than barriers. It was a region that was "polythropic"—polyglot, polymeric, and polycentric. It was therefore not an insular area, but one of considerable exchange and travel lacking strong central political control. Prior to the twentieth century, therefore, the term Iraq was primarily a geographical name and did not become a political term until after World War I, when it came to refer to a new nation—a country that was semi-independent and part of the League of Nations.

FORGING A GOVERNMENT

The practice of archaeology was squarely placed within the overall British vision of Iraq. When the British started to analyze the geopolitical structure of Iraq during and immediately after the war, the scope and composition of the imminent state were far from clear-cut. In wartime treaties and agreements, the Western powers most often assumed that a new state would emerge in the region of Iraq. Whether one nation should emerge, or several, was very much open for debate. Consequently, the different wartime agreements had contradictory plans for Mesopotamia. When the British started to assess carefully the situation in the Middle East after World War I, however, they increasingly scrutinized the economic costs and benefits of a postwar settlement. Although they had been militarily victorious in the war, Britain's economy was in disarray, and tremendous reconstruction of the country's infrastructure was necessary. Consequently, when Winston Churchill became colonial secretary in 1921, he announced that "everything else that happens in the Middle East is secondary to the reduction in expense," testing all proposals and programs against that one overriding criterion.[23] Even though control of various provinces of the Middle East possibly could involve some material benefits—such as access to oil and antiquities—the political and fiscal mood of the time did not encourage further imperial expansion into the Middle East. The war brought an end to such political ambitions. The British were starting to feel the financial weight of the "white man's burden," to question its philosophical and political underpinnings.[24] Rather, a new political approach was deemed necessary. This entailed a mental shift for those who had been intimately tied to planning the political and administrative future of Iraq. For example, the seasoned diplomat Arthur Hirtzel wrote confidentially to his friend Arnold T. Wilson, then at Baghdad, "we must swim with the new tide which is set towards the education and not the government of what used to be subject peoples."[25]

Nevertheless, old views and habits were not easily eradicated. Seemingly unaffected by the ambivalence of most British citizens and politicians, there remained figures at the upper echelons of government who were convinced that the British still enjoyed a divine right to shape the future of the Middle East and its inhabitants. One pivotal figure who maintained this policy was Lord Curzon, the foreign secretary. Other figures in the British archaeological establishment, such as Kenyon at the BM, who lobbied energetically to influence archaeological policy in the Middle East, were also of the old school. At war's end, however, this brand of imperialism no longer seemed applicable. Britain could not possibly maintain this immense physical presence in the area as it had in the past. The soldiers were needed back home for other more pressing concerns, leading to large-scale movements of troops away from the Middle East. As a result, local British authorities in posts such as Egypt and Iraq had to improvise and figure out how to establish control and maintain security with minimal troops and arms at their disposal.

NEW VIEWS, OLD HABITS

The eventual governmental structure of Iraq, including that of archaeology, was thus based on Britain's imperial visions and its experience in the recent war. The military victory against the Ottoman armies gave the British the pretext and legitimacy to control this area. Though they had defeated the Ottomans militarily, an equally challenging battle was ahead: namely, how to convince the people of this region that British plans were legitimate and that the people should accept British authority. In some regards, the British concerns were similar to the views of the American and British governments in 2003, when the political future of Iraq was extensively discussed.

When the British occupied Baghdad in 1917, they issued a proclamation known as the Maude Declaration. In this "politically correct" statement, similar to the proclamation that Napoleon issued upon his invasion of Egypt in 1798, the British announced that they were coming as liberators rather than an occupying force. They stated that they had delivered the Baghdadis from "those alien rulers, the Turks who oppressed them." The British explained that they hoped that the "aspirations of your philosophers and writers shall be realized once again" and that the people of Iraq should "flourish and enjoy their wealth under institutions which are in consonance with their sacred laws and their racial ideal."[26] Although the British issued such tactfully worded and seemingly altruistic statements, they were primarily concerned with how they could most conveniently govern the area.

Yet Iraq was not a land without a people, and Iraqis resisted the foreign plans and occupation of their country. In June 1920, a large-scale popular rebellion broke out among certain tribes in the middle Euphrates region. The revolt was spurred by the people's belief that the British were refusing to grant the country its full independence. The British administrators in Iraq believed that the revolt stemmed from three primary categories: military, political, and socioeconomic.[27] Military, because the British felt that the Iraqis perceived a British military weakness;[28] political, because the Arabs felt betrayed by the Sykes-Picot Agreement and lack of progress in implementing Wilson's Fourteen Points and the Anglo-French Declaration; and finally socioeconomic, due to the difficult economic situation following the end of the war.[29]

Iraqi historians, by contrast, have primarily presented the rebellion as a popular nationalist uprising, suggesting that it was the beginning of Iraqi nationalism. In fact, it has become enshrined in Iraqi national mythology as the first symbol of Iraq's rejection of foreign rule.[30] While Western (particularly British) accounts focus primarily on the external or internal factors that provoked the rebellion (their concern is to analyze "what went wrong?" or "who failed?"), Iraqi accounts concentrate on the level of participation and who were the primary actors and initiators. Because this rebellion has become an important metaphor for anti-imperialist, anti-Western political activism, many different groups want to take credit for the success of the revolt. Therefore, different accounts present various interpretations, some labeling it as an example of full-fledged Iraqi nationalism (which at this point would technically not have been the case), while others declare that it is an example of local or regional unrest. Fariq al-Muzhir al-Fir'awn, for example, who belonged to one of the leading clans of the Fatla tribe that played a significant role in the rebellion, emphasizes how independent the tribes were in initiating the revolt with little or no contact with the people of Baghdad. Instead, the tribes relied more on the guidance of the Shi'i mujtahids in the shrine cities, who traditionally were opposed to, and independent from, political influence from Baghdad.[31] In contrast, Ali al-Bazirkan's account criticizes al-Fir'awn's portrayal, stressing instead the important role of various political circles in Baghdad and their close cooperation with the tribes.[32]

Although the sources, both Iraqi and Western, disagree on what caused the revolt and who the primary actors were, the ultimate result of the revolt is beyond dispute. Lasting for several months and characterized by anti-British sentiments, the rebellion could only be quelled by the British at considerable expenditure. It is estimated that 8,000 Iraqis may have died, and the British lost 450 of their soldiers. Furthermore, the rebellion cost the British treasury £40 million, which served as a direct reminder that new methods were required in Iraq. The result of the 1920 rebellion gave weight to Churchill's demand that a policy be formulated that would define the political objectives of the military occupation and relieve the WO of what he saw as an open-ended and embarrassing commitment. He even considered a complete withdrawal from Mesopotamia unless the country could be governed more cheaply.[33] Perhaps a more significant result of the rebellion was that, temporarily at least, the diverse segments of Iraqi society were united against a common cause—the political domination of the British. They were united against a common enemy and cast aside their immediate differences in battling the British troops on various fronts. Both urban Sunni Baghdadis and Shi'i mujtahids in the shrine cities displayed an unprecedented cooperative spirit.[34]

Although the Iraqis were not able to achieve full independence, they were able seriously to imperil British policy. Even if merely an outburst of local or regional unrest, the very act of rebellion fostered a communitarian spirit among various Iraqi groups and clearly identified the British as the opposing force. The uprising suggested, possibly for the first time, that all Iraqis had something in common, despite their ethnic and religious differences, which, in turn, indicated that political cooperation was possible, if not desirable. As a result of this outbreak, Britain had to abandon belligerence in favor of compromise. Now it became exceedingly clear that in order to maintain control of the area, the British had to cater to the local forces. The British politicians, therefore, had to reconsider their policy and approach to Iraq and realign it with what Bell and others had advocated. This reevaluation coincided with a 1920 League of Nations decision that recommended a particular form of government and administration in Iraq. This was the decision to award, or assign, Iraq as a Mandate to Britain.

THE MANDATE

By formally receiving the "Mandate" from the League of Nations for Iraq, the British became responsible to prepare Iraq for self-government. These arrangements were finalized in May 1920 by the Great Powers at San Remo without ever consulting any Middle Eastern opinions. Article 22 of the Covenant of the League of Nations established the Mandate system, based on the guiding principle that the well-being and development of the inhabitants of certain ex-colonies and territories constituted a "sacred trust for civilizations" under the tutelage of a Mandatory on behalf of the League. According to the patronizing language of the League's covenant, Mandates were not yet able to "stand alone." Therefore, they were to be placed under the tutelage of "advanced nations" until they were able to stand alone. The relationship between the Mandate power and its territory was the same as that of a guardian and child, since the covenant stated that the territory would be governed in the best interests of its subjects and accelerate their moral and political development.

Arab nationalists put little faith in this new brand of enlightened imperialism—"Mandate" was but a new word, which some thought to be a euphemism for an old-style colonialism that reduced them to orphaned minors who could not survive without a substitute parent. The Mandate proclamation rallied certain Iraqis to unite and protest this new proposal for the political future of Iraq under the banner of the Haras al-Istiqlal. During this protest, they focused on unifying both Sunnis and Shi'is into one political concern.[35] During Ramadan of 1920, which fell in June, the Shi'i and Sunni political leaders used the religiously charged atmosphere to emphasize the commonality of Iraqi

Muslims and encouraged their followers to work together, their internal differences notwithstanding.[36] However, as the Iraqi historians Muhammad Mahdi al-Bassir and 'Abd al-Razzaq al-Hassani emphasize, the different groups had little success in articulating a unified political platform.[37] Furthermore, several influential political groups and families, such as Baghdad's prominent Jewish community and the families of 'Abd al-Rahman al-Naqib, Jamil Zada, and 'Abd al-Majid Shawi, supported the general British designs.[38] Consequently, the British were able to exploit the sensitive political situation and greatly influence the course of events.

The British took their job as a Mandate power seriously and viewed themselves as undertaking an important pedagogical role. They were not aware that others viewed them as patronizing in their role as Mandatory power. As Bell wrote, "T. E. Lawrence says the Arab has character and needs intelligence. It's the exact contrary. He has plenty of intelligence. What he lacks is character. And that . . . is what a mandatory power is called on to supply."[39] Bell even amazed herself. "Truly we are remarkable people. We save from destruction remnants of oppressed nations, laboriously and expensively giving them sanitary accommodation, teaching their children and respecting their faiths."[40] Seemingly amnesic to the fact that they had themselves just engaged in a barbaric war, the Western powers still felt they could have a civilizing effect on the Arab Middle East.

Although the Mandates were presented as a new enlightened path of East-West relations, in actuality they were just a façade of indirect rule. As a memo to the American president Woodrow Wilson from William Linn Westermann, analyzing a secret French document that accidentally came into his hands, stated, "The old formulas 'zones' and 'zones of influence' is to be changed to 'mandates.'"[41] But there were some Westerners involved in Middle Eastern politics who did, at least momentarily, question their role. Despite her enthusiastic view of Britain's potential positive influence, Gertrude Bell at times suspected the Mandate idea, asking herself, "How can we, who have managed our affairs so badly, claim to teach others to manage theirs better?"[42]

The British set out to identify a ruler with whom they could work, who would both be sensitive to their interests and have broad-based appeal in this diverse country. Already in 1918, the British spoke openly about maintaining an "Arab façade." Percy Cox wrote in 1918 that the Naqib of Baghdad ('Abd al-Rahman al-Gaylani) "would form a suitable puppet and that he and his family carry necessary prestige both in Irak and India."[43] The British considered both Faysal and his brother Abdullah, the sons of Sharif Husayn of Mecca, as potential leaders of Iraq.[44] Both were competent politicians who, primarily due to their pro-Western sentiments, were considered ideal candidates by the British as well as the Americans.[45] The brothers were also appealing rulers, since as outsiders they would not have certain vested interests and were, therefore, more dependent upon Britain.[46]

In March 1920, a general Syrian congress in Damascus elected Faysal king of Syria. Although the tenure of Faysal's kingdom in Syria was short-lived (he was ousted by the French in July that same year), it was significant for Iraqi history, since many of his cabinet members were Iraqis who later played important roles in Iraqi politics. These included Nuri al-Sa'id and Yasin al-Hashimi, who both later served as prime ministers in Iraq. These politicians therefore gained invaluable insights into the practical aspects of running an administration, and, perhaps equally importantly, they learned from their failed rule how not to cooperate with a Mandate power.[47] At the same congress in which Faysal was elected king of Syria, thirty Iraqis also nominated Abdullah as king of Iraq. These Iraqis included Ja'far al-'Askari, Naji al-Suwaydi, and 'Ali Jawdat, all future prime ministers of Iraq.[48] However, partially owing to Arnold Wilson's stiff resistance, Abdullah never came close to sitting on a throne in Iraq. Instead, Faysal emerged as the ideal candidate, particularly after the French ousted him from Syria in July of 1920.

In March of 1921, Churchill summoned the leading British Middle East experts (such as Cox, Lawrence, Bell, and Wilson) to a conference in Cairo to discuss Middle Eastern policy.[49] Recent events in the region, such as the Iraqi rebellion and the troubles in Syria, convinced Churchill that it was impossible to reconcile the use of force with what they considered the more humane and benevolent ideals behind the Mandate system. A practical solution was necessary that would balance British strategic needs with the aspirations of local nationalists. Whether it was due to new political realities or an attempt to appease the conferees' guilt-ridden consciences for not having upheld some of the promises made to the Arabs during the war, one immediate result of the Cairo Conference was the renewal of the wartime alliance between the Hashemite family and the British. The conference recommended that a constitutional monarchy be established in Iraq with Faysal, who had been recently expelled from Syria as king, and that the British reduce their troops there and create a governmental structure that would include an Arab army.[50] The official plan abandoned direct British rule, as Wilson had advocated, in favor of indirect rule, through an ostensibly Iraqi government, backed by British "advisers."[51]

The British, therefore, finally moved forward and began to set up a government that would be agreeable to all. As Bell stated, "The drawback is that such a government doesn't exist. They [the Iraqis] haven't formulated what it is they really want and if one man did formulate it, the next would disagree."[52] In her discussions with Sassoon Hasqail, a prominent member of Baghdad's Jewish community, he explained that he felt sure that no local man would be acceptable as head of state "because every local man would be jealous of him."[53] The idea of bringing in an outsider to rule Iraq, therefore, became an increasingly attractive option for the British. Consequently, the sons of the Sharif Husayn of Mecca emerged as prime candidates. As Bell wrote to Lord Hardinge, "After all Egypt has an Albanian ruling family and we a German—why should not Mesopotamia have a Turkish?"[54]

Faysal's installation seemed like an ideal solution for the British. They believed that he had emerged as the leading political figure as the result of the Arab revolt; he had seemingly impeccable religious credentials, since he was a descendant of the Prophet and belonged to a family who were at this point protectors of the holy sites in Mecca and Medina. And finally, his installation would be reminiscent of the establishment of the glorious Abbasid Caliphate in Iraq, since Faysal would assume power in Baghdad via Mecca and Damascus. Yet the Iraqis, particularly the majority Shi'a population, were not particularly keen on his leadership. As the Naqib of Baghdad, 'Abd al-Rahman al-Gaylani, told Bell, "I would rather a thousand times have the Turks back in Iraq, than see the Sharif or his sons installed here."[55]

Despite these reservations, the British proceeded with their plans to crown Faysal. At his enthronement, Faysal announced plans for a Constituent Assembly, which would lay down the legal basis for relations between the British and the Iraqis. The Constituent Assembly eventually approved the treaty between the two countries and sanctioned a new electoral law and constitution. As important as constructing the theoretical and legal basis of the state was, a more pressing concern was to solidify and strengthen the state's legitimacy. In this endeavor, Faysal had at his disposal bombers from the British Royal Air Force, supported by armored car squadrons and detachments of locally recruited

levies, particularly Assyrian, who served under British officers. Any outbreak of truculence would be handled by the bombers.

When Faysal ascended to the throne in 1921, many details were yet
to be hammered out, and laws and regulations had to be written. As Bell
stated, "It's an immense business setting up a court and power."[56] Yet in
establishing Faysal as the king of Iraq, the British engineered one of
more bizarre episodes in modern Middle Eastern history. A native of the
Hijaz, a Sunni who had been educated in Istanbul and spoke with a distinct Hijazi accent, was brought to a predominantly Shi'i country that he
had never visited. He was unfamiliar with its dialects, geography, and history and had few immediate visions and plans for this new nation, which
was as unfamiliar to him as his subjects were to him. The irony and perhaps artificiality were not lost on Bell, who remarked in her now famous
words, "I'll never engage in creating kings again, it's too great a strain."[57]
These words also reflect her sense of empowerment and authority in the
Iraqi context, indicative of her later actions in archaeology.

At his enthronement speech in August of 1921, a careful and
ambivalent Faysal stated that "what we need for establishing this state is
assistance from another nation which will supply us capital and man-
power. The British are anxious to foster our interests. Therefore we
should rely on them to assist us in achieving our national goals."[58] Since
Faysal had previously learned the hard way in Syria not to be too
demanding toward a Great Power, he was cautious in his initial dealings
with the British. Yet he was also in a certain predicament, since he sincerely wanted to present himself as an independent ruler—a ruler that
would have Iraqi interests at heart. Consequently, he attempted in his
speech to appeal to the patriotic spirit of the Iraqis by stating, "Oh
noble Iraqis, this land has been in past generations the cradle of civilization and prosperity, and the center of science and knowledge,"[59]
hinting that equally glorious times would face the country's present and
future generations. He was, therefore, in the lonely, and somewhat contradictory, role of trying to be two things at once: unabashedly loyal to
the British, while also being sensitive to Iraqi nationalistic aspirations.
As Bell acknowledged, "Faysal has got a difficult task before him—what
amazes me is that he should want to be king of Iraq. However it's a
mercy that he does."[60]

Placing Faysal as king was ideal for the British, since they could
be viewed as presenting a leader who had a level of legitimacy.
Furthermore, given his lack of ties to the Iraqi population and power

groups, he would initially lean on the British for support and advice, which they were quite willing to give and offer. Yet Faysal was not the complete puppet who relied solely on the British. Much to the surprise of the British, Faysal actually adjusted quicker into Iraq than they anticipated and started to implement policies that were in direct contradiction to British wishes. For example, Faysal decided to build up a national army through universal conscription, whereas the British had preferred to rely on "martial races" such as the Assyrian levies. Furthermore, instead of appointing leading tribal shaykhs into key governmental positions, Faysal appointed his own friends, many of whom were not that familiar with the Iraqi political and cultural landscape. One such appointment was Sati' al-Husri to the Ministry of Education. Yet as we shall see regarding archaeology, in contrast to most other matters of government, he allotted the British, and in particular Bell, the power and opportunity to, somewhat independently, deal with and organize archaeological matters for the new Iraqi nation. It was a chance that the British relished, and they used the occasion to construct legislation in their favor.

For all intents and purposes, Iraq was designed to be a compliant country that would honor faithfully Britain's local strategic and economic interests. One of Britain's primary concerns was that its main oil supplier, Iran, might fall under hostile control, whether it was German or Bolshevik. Therefore, the British were interested in gaining exclusive control over potential alternative oil supplies, particularly in the north, in areas that were predominantly Kurdish, and ensuring that the oil could easily be exported out of the Persian Gulf. A unified, stable political structure that could guarantee ample and easily accessible oil was an important concern for the British that influenced the political and administrative boundaries of the country.

The British aimed to establish a governmental structure in Iraq that was best suited to their interests and would allow them to reap most of the potential political, strategic, and economic benefits. Yet, while doing so they also wanted to appear to be fulfilling the Mandate requirement and to appease the anti-imperialist concerns of the United States and its president Woodrow Wilson. This strategy, however, did not quite materialize in the tranquil manner the British had envisioned. First, there was a serious political contradiction between building an Iraqi state to represent the will of the inhabitants and, at the same time, compelling that state to acknowledge the authority of Britain.[61]

The different Iraqi political communities and ethnic groups, particularly the Kurds in the north and the Shi'is in the south, had serious reservations about the British-designed structure and were not as compliant as the British had hoped.[62] In the first years of the Mandate there were episodes of acrimony, distrust, and disharmony involving both the British and Iraqi sides.[63] The British were in the delicate position of not wanting to display too much influence or power, yet simultaneously wanting to make their presence felt in order to curtail any possible overthrow of Faysal's government. At the same time, Faysal and his cabinet wanted to appear independent and strong enough to oppose British influence without seriously jeopardizing Anglo-Iraqi relations. These complex, fragile, and contradictory positions led to a frustrating and tense political atmosphere in which the players involved were constantly accusing each other of making unacceptable demands.[64] A contemporary Iraqi poet, Ma'ruf al-Rasafi, captures the incongruities of the Iraqi state:

> **A flag, a Constitution, and a National Assembly**
>   **each one a distortion of the true meaning**
> **Names of which we have only utterances**
>   **but as to their true meaning we remain in ignorance**
> **He who reads the Constitution will learn**
>   **that it is composed according to the Mandate**
> **He who looks at the flapping banner will find**
>   **that it is billowing in the glory of aliens**
> **He who sees our National Assembly will know**
>   **that it is constituted by and for the interests of any**
>   **but the electors**
> **He who enters the Ministries will find**
>   **that they are shackled with the chains of foreign advisers.**[65]

Within this contradictory and complex milieu the politics and culture of Iraqi archaeology developed. To a certain extent, archaeological affairs followed in many ways the general trends of the political culture of the era. But at the same time, archaeological matters were also quite distinct. Although the British devised this seemingly ingenious indirect rule in Iraq, where the British would "advise" on all major policy issues, when it came to archaeology the British took full control of the matter by themselves and avoided any direct Iraqi participation.

When the role of the British in archaeology is examined, it raises questions about their objectivity in "advising" the Iraqi government in general, and demonstrates how they were eager, in certain issues, to even exclude the Iraqis from any significant participation. It is not entirely clear why the British took this stance in archaeological matters. Their position and rationale are never explicitly stated in official circles, yet they obviously viewed archaeology as their exclusive domain. However, one can assume that their view of the cultural sophistication and level of education of the Iraqi population was not particularly favorable. For example, an internal report by the Keepers at the British Museum stated that Iraq was not populated by "highly educated and intelligent classes," necessary for the creation of an indigenous archaeology. The Keepers argued that, in formulating antiquities legislation in Iraq, "science, fully as much as political consideration," demand that the legislation ensure Western interests and guarantee the export of antiquities from Iraq.[66] They did not deem the Iraqis capable of or interested in working on their own archaeological matters. To a certain extent, that was a realistic assessment, since there was not sufficient scientific knowledge in the country to independently organize archaeological matters adequately. At this point, no Iraqi had formally studied the science of archaeology. However, numerous Iraqis had extensive practical archaeological exposure, since many worked as laborers in the various Western archaeological expeditions in Iraq. This know-how, however, was not on par with that of the British and confined to the manual aspects of the enterprise.

Another more significant reason is that the British felt that archaeology was too important and valuable to allow the Iraqis any role in the decision-making process. Just as in other countries under their control, the British sought to limit as much as possible the amount of artifacts that would remain in the country. Instead of arranging for an Iraqi to be the primary decision-maker, with the British working as advisers, as with most other governmental portfolios such as in the Ministries of Education and Agriculture, the British tried to exclude any direct Iraqi involvement with archaeology. Given the value of Iraqi antiquities, they wanted to guarantee, as with Iraqi oil, that the British and other Western archaeologists and institutions would have an ample supply of antiquities and could easily facilitate their export. Although they pursued policies that tried to exclude any direct local input and were beneficial to Western interests, the British, and in particular Gertrude

Bell, were somewhat sensitive that Iraq should not be left out of the equation and that its interests, loosely defined, should be considered.

FORMULATING THE ANTIQUITIES LAW

F ew areas offer a more compelling view of the concern of the British to legitimize and protect their imperial actions and practice than the formulation of the antiquities law. Though it may seem like a rudimentary administrative and legal question, the spirit and letter of the law were critical to ensure British control and continuing access to Iraqi archaeological fields. The law enabled foreign archaeologists to continue legally exporting antiquities from Iraq, though in a much more restricted manner. Given the political realities and aims of the Mandate, however, the legislation also had to take into account Iraqi concerns. Nineteenth-century practices were no longer relevant or appropriate.

The ensuing legislation was thus a hybrid. It preserved some of the old and also incorporated elements of the new. The legislation devised by Gertrude Bell was an important intermediary phase to lay the groundwork for legislation and practices in Iraq that prevented large-scale exports of antiquities from Iraq. The development of the Iraqi Law of Antiquities suggests that the battle to control Iraqi antiquities was still very much a British concern, although there were traces of Iraqi resistance.

When the Iraqi state was established, with what the British deemed as requisite pomp and circumstance, it had to formulate legal instruments that emphasized sovereignty over its national wealth as well as its people. Given the tremendous potential of its archaeological sites, the Western nations' eagerness to start excavating anew in postwar Iraq, and both sides' desire to combat illicit traffic in antiquities, discussion about appropriate antiquities legislation took place among both British and Iraqi governmental officials. This discussion took on a level of urgency due to the immense archaeological potential of Iraq. Iraq's perceived archaeological wealth was exemplified by a comment by the American Assyriologist Albert T. Clay to a British official: "There is enough work to be done in the land to keep ten expeditions busy for 500 years."[67]

The future archaeological policy had been an issue during the war. The Samarra, Lisbon, and Hall/Campbell Thompson collections had made the relevance of archaeological legislation even more compelling.[68] As could be expected, British archaeologists were excited about the potential of having political control in Iraq, since such power could provide them with numerous and valuable opportunities for archaeological excavations and the accompanying gathering of antiquities. But it was not only the British who were optimistic about future archaeological prospects in the Middle East. For example, when Harry Pratt Judson, president of the University of Chicago, wrote to John D. Rockefeller seeking funds for the establishment for what would become the Oriental Institute at Chicago, he stated that he was confident that "as a result of the civilized control of the Near East large gains may come from archaeology."[69]

With these potential positive political circumstances on the horizon, many expeditions showed an interest in coming to Iraq. For example, the IO wrote to the Assyriologist Stephen Langdon at Oxford, who had written an enthusiastic letter seeking permission to go to Iraq in order to lay claim to a site, emphasizing that no excavations would be permitted until the new government brought into operation a new antiquities law.[70]

A memo recording a conversation between Kenyon at the BM and G. B. Gordon, director of the University Museum at the University of Pennsylvania, reflects this view that British political domination would allow archaeologists easy access and ample grazing at the green pastures of Iraqi archaeological sites. In the memo, they agreed that since Britain would have "jurisdiction over the archaeological interests of Mesopotamia, and as the authority is believed to be *highly beneficial to the cause of archaeological science,* . . . it is likely to afford opportunities for excavation and scholarly research that have not heretofore obtained in this region"[71] [emphasis added]. The men felt that it would be mutually beneficial if the two institutions would cooperate in pursuing archaeological excavation. Although this memo does not define what conditions would be so beneficial to the cause of archaeological science, it seems to indicate that whatever was beneficial for their respective institutions was beneficial for science as a whole. Given the American economic situation after the war, Penn would be able to supply the necessary capital, while the BM, because of its proximity to the British government, would seek beneficial political cooperation and most of the scientific know-how.

When the BM was asked by the British government for its input concerning future archaeological policy, the Museum promoted legislation that was favorable to its own interests, a law that would allow it easy access to Iraqi sites and antiquities. Even though the BM publicly stressed its role in the advancement of science, it clearly pursued and recommended a policy that would have most immediate material benefit for its own collection. Despite the universal goals of the scientific enterprise, the BM became quite nationalistic when advising on future archaeological policy. It considered various sites as "belonging" to the British and accepted French and American claims of other sites. These claims were made irrespective of the fact that an independent, sovereign nation was soon to be established in the area that would have jurisdiction over its resources and property within its borders. In this matter, the antiquities scramble of the nineteenth century, the "unedifying scramble," as archaeologist Seton Lloyd labeled it, was legitimized.

The sites claimed and the digs performed during that anarchic, questionable period ironically gained, in legal terms, a precedence status. Even though most archaeologists of the 1920s believed that the tactics of Botta, Place, Layard, and Rassam were crude and outdated, in actuality their allocation and determination of archaeological patrimony emerged as the BM's paradigm for future archaeological policy in Iraq. For example, in 1919, H. R. Hall wrote a letter to Arnold Wilson in response to a French request to obtain a general concession to excavate in the province of Mosul. Hall pointed out, however, that the BM had historic rights to the mounds of Kuyunjik (Nineveh). Therefore, Hall suggested that concessions be granted on a regular system that took into account historical claims of each nation. Hall submitted a memorandum that listed which nations had historic claims to which sites based on the random and treasure-seeking pursuits of the nineteenth century.[72]

Hall's list initially became a compass for the direction of policy and more importantly for archaeological proprietorship. This list became known in the archaeological community at large and caused some debate among the various institutions over who actually owned what site.[73] Even though the British were busy setting up a state that had all the appearances of being sovereign, they were simultaneously making plans to carve up some of its valuable cultural resources and divide them among institutions in the West. These plans cast doubt on British sincerity and undercut the political will to honor their rhetoric concerning an independent Iraq.

After British governmental officials sought his advice, Kenyon at the BM encouraged the establishment of a department of antiquities of Iraq and the introduction of a law promulgated along lines "generally recognized by civilized nations, which allow for the division of the proceeds of excavation between the country of origin and the excavators."[74] Kenyon did not mention, perhaps because it was self-evident, that in actuality there existed two different systems of archaeological legislation. Such a system was commonplace in non-Western countries where Western archaeologists conducted their excavations. In Western countries, however, this paradigm of sharing the proceeds between the excavator and the host country did not exist. Kenyon's selectivity should be viewed with the fact in mind that he was sensitive to the new, anti-imperialist climate that emerged after the war.

In an earlier correspondence with Mark Sykes, Kenyon revealed that he was worried that the British would "appear to be merely plundering the country [i.e., Iraq] in the interest of England." Therefore, Kenyon suggested that a policy be formulated that would foreshadow the future principle of archaeological legislation in Iraq, recommending that half of the excavated collection should remain in Mesopotamia while allowing the other half to be brought to England.[75]

Since the British were actively involved in creating new political nation-states in wake of the war in which, among numerous other things, they had to formulate archaeological legislation, Kenyon established the British Joint Archaeological Committee to serve as a neutral scientific entity to consult on archaeological matters (as previously stated, various British governmental officials were cynical about this new body).[76] This committee, which set forth several broad principles concerning archaeological organization, stated that in order to secure the adequate representation of a country's past, it was imperative that this past be restored to the country itself. However, the committee selectively applied this scientific principle, since it was quick to add, "The relative importance of this principle vary in different parts of the world, according to their nearness to the principal centres of modern civilization."[77] In other words, in its view, this principle applied primarily to Western nations that could appreciate and understand their own and other people's past. Nations, on the other hand, that were geographically distant from the "centres of modern civilization" did not necessarily need an adequate representation of their own past in their own country.

As discussed in Chapter 2, the question of Iraqi antiquities was raised on several occasions during the British occupation. Bell had written a memorandum on Iraqi antiquities and had as early as 1919 inquired of her friend George Hill at the British Museum about archaeological legislation in Palestine, clearly anticipating that she would eventually formulate a similar policy for Iraq.[78] Like other administrative and political matters, the question of archaeology was included in the 1922 Anglo-Iraqi treaty.[79]

Article 14 of the treaty, dealing with antiquities, enjoined the king to ensure the enactment of an antiquities law "within twelve months of the coming into force of this treaty, and to ensure the execution of a law of antiquities based on the contents of article 421 . . . of the Treaty of Peace with Turkey. This law shall replace the former Ottoman Law and shall ensure equality of treatment in the matter of archaeological research to the nationals of all states."[80] The Treaty of Peace with Turkey, or the Treaty of Sevres as it is more commonly known, had sought, as far as archaeology was concerned, to replace the previous Ottoman law; the Treaty was signed, but never ratified. The Treaty of Sevres stipulated that excavations should be mandatorily subject to the Ottoman government's approval. Even though the Treaty was never ratified, these provisions became binding on Iraq by virtue of the 1922 treaty between Britain and Iraq, which obliged Iraq to adopt a law based on the stipulations of the Treaty of Sevres. In due course, the archaeological articles in the Treaty of Sevres became the basis of the antiquities law in Iraq, as well as a precedent for other international instruments regarding archaeological excavations.[81]

The 1922 treaty formed the general basis of the relationship between Faysal and the British and guided his actions, along with Bell's advice and enthusiasm, toward his eventual interest in archaeology. After Faysal was installed as king of Iraq, he started to travel around the country to get to know its terrain, including its natural, as well as its cultural and political, landscapes. Despite what several commentators have suggested, Faysal took a keen interest in the ancient history of Iraq.[82] Bell reports that "Faysal was very eager to know about ancient monuments."[83] Bell and Faysal, two foreigners in Iraq, yet nevertheless at the epicenter of power, expressed a fascination and respect for the ancient history of their adopted country. The monuments were a reminder of a glorious past and put their own lives and rule of this new country in a certain perspective. The ancient history could be seen as an instructive paradigm of political and economic success, which Iraq would strive to achieve once again.

In order to show Faysal firsthand the magnitude and importance of Iraqi ancient history, Bell invited Faysal to a tour of Ctesiphon, the ancient winter capital of the Parthian and Sassanian Empires. By choosing Ctesiphon, an important seat of the Persian empires, Bell reminded Faysal of Iraq's historic vulnerability. During the tour, Bell reported that Faysal was an "inspiring tourist."[84] Yet, though he expressed an interest in history and had received an extensive education in the schools of the Ottoman Empire, Faysal still did not reveal an extensive knowledge of the local history. In a moving account, Bell described taking Faysal onto a hill from whence they could see the Tigris River. She used the opportunity to tell him about the Arab conquest as reported by al-Tabari. Bell recalled, "It was the tale of his own people—you can imagine what it was like reciting it to him. I don't know which of us was more thrilled."[85]

These travels may have convinced Faysal of the magnitude of Iraq's ancient history and the importance of exerting control and organization over these valuable monuments. Shortly after these excursions Faysal officially appointed Bell as the honorary director of antiquities in October 1922.[86] As previously stated, Faysal was also obliged by the Mandate Charter to enact within one year a new law of antiquities. It is a testimony to the importance of this legislation that Faysal asked Bell to formulate specific archaeological guidelines for the new Iraqi state. She was, at this stage, his most trusted liaison between his government and the British administration, and she had a plethora of political responsibilities. The king thus handed over to Bell a particularly appealing project to work on. Faysal owed his position to the British and surely felt that there were more pressing practical issues that needed his attention, such as establishing a comprehensive educational system and a national army. Archaeology was a luxury—a hobby—to which the young Iraqi state could not afford to pay too much attention. Faysal was probably relieved to be able to delegate to Bell, a person whose opinion he valued at this stage, the responsibilities to organize archaeological matters in the country.

As Bell reports in a letter in 1922 to her father, she was given carte blanche to formulate this legislation, without any seemingly local vested interests involved in the process:

**I got his [Faysal's] approval for *my* law of antiquities which I've com-
piled with the utmost care in consultation with the legal authorities. He
has undertaken to push it through Council—he's perfectly sound about
archaeology—having been trained by T. E. Lawrence and has agreed to
my suggestion that he should *appoint me,* if Sir Percy consents, provisional director of archaeology to his Government, in addition to my other
duties. I should then be able to run the whole thing in direct agreement
with him, which would be excellent.**[87] **(Emphasis added.)**

Even though Bell was officially appointed by the Iraqi government
and therefore subject to its desires and policies, she treated this legislation as her own private project and vigorously sought to imprint her
own views on how archaeological matters were to be conducted.

Bell was enthusiastic about the prospects of having sole control of
Iraqi archaeology and eagerly sought to implement a new policy. Yet the
law did not pass through as easily as she anticipated, despite the optimism of her letters. This optimism was not confined to her own personal correspondence but was also found among other members of the
British administration.[88] The archaeologist Leonard Woolley, who
recently had been commissioned by the University of Pennsylvania and
the British Museum for a joint expedition to Ur, also sensed this optimism. While he was in Baghdad in October 1922 obtaining the necessary permits, Bell promised Woolley that the proposed antiquities law
would go before the cabinet that next day and surely pass. Therefore,
he would soon receive the requisite permit for his planned excavations
at Ur.[89]

Contrary to Bell's prediction, however, the Iraqi cabinet did not pass
the law on the following day. Despite Bell's optimism and her wielding
influence in Iraqi politics, she unexpectedly ran into some resistance by
Iraqi nationalists such as Yasin al-Hashimi and Sati' al-Husri. Even
though archaeology was not an issue that was first and foremost on the
minds of the newly emerging group of Iraqi politicians, the influence of
al-Husri and his interest in an Arab perspective on history and education
largely prevented Bell from having the carte blanche that she had anticipated. As a result, the Ministry of Public Works issued Woolley only a
temporary permit, thereby yielding to some of al-Husri's pressure.

Until his expulsion from Iraq in 1941, al-Husri played a central role
in Iraqi's state-building process. He is primarily known as, if not the
leading, then one of the leading theoreticians and proponents of Arab
nationalism, although his role as director general of education in Iraq

is well established. Despite al-Husri's extensive discussion about his involvement in archaeology in his autobiography, those scholars who have studied his life and ideas have ignored his active and sincere interest in archaeology.[90] These scholars have hardly mentioned his important tenure as the first Iraqi director of antiquities from 1934 to 1941. However, as will be analyzed more fully in Chapter 4, al-Husri's involvement and interest in archaeology were natural extensions of his views on history and education.

Al-Husri was born to a prominent Syrian mercantile family in Yemen in 1882.[91] His father, Mehmed Hilal Effendi, was the chief Ottoman judge (qadi) in Yemen. Al-Husri received his education at the Mulkiye Mektebi, a prominent school for Ottoman bureaucrats, then studied in Paris on a governmental scholarship, where he immersed himself in the philosophies of Jean-Jacques Rousseau, Ernest Renan, and, more intensely, Johann Gottfried von Herder and Johann Gottlieb Fichte. During his studies abroad he had contacts with secret Arab national societies and with the Young Turks. Upon the completion of his studies, he became an influential educator in the Ottoman Empire and at an early age debated the influential Turkish nationalist Ziya Gokalp, in what has been called "one of the most exciting fights of the period," over the role of education in the Ottoman Empire.[92] In 1919, al-Husri left Istanbul to join Faysal's short-lived administration in Syria, where he served as minister of education. Two years later, Faysal appointed al-Husri director general of education in Iraq. As stated above, Faysal chose to appoint many of his friends in leading governmental positions, many of whom, like al-Husri, were new to Iraq, rather than promoting a local politician, which British policy recommended. It is plausible that by circumventing both British wishes and local Iraqi politics, Faysal sought to strengthen his own hold on the government in order to be more independent from both wings. Al-Husri's governmental position was unique and to a certain extent ideal for a committed individual like al-Husri, in that, as opposed to the position of minister of education, the director general was not subject to the frequent cabinet changes. Al-Husri's position in Iraq gave him the independence to pursue his pedagogical policies irrespective of the whims of party politics.[93]

By the time he became involved in education in Iraq, al-Husri had already established himself as a leading proponent of Arab nationalism. Heavily influenced by the German Romantics, filtered through his education in France, he believed that the Arabs constituted a nation and ought therefore to be united into a single state. For al-Husri, the fundamental criteria of nationhood were a shared language and a common history.[94] He states, "The strongest and most effective tie is the national tie, which derives from a common language and history."[95] Although the Arab nations were currently divided into several political states, al-Husri stressed that owing to the Arabic language and shared memories of their glorious past, the Arabs possessed all the critical ingredients for a single nationhood.[96] Al-Husri, whose primary language was Turkish and who spoke Arabic with a heavy Turkish accent, believed that political unification could only come as a result of a growing awareness of shared history.[97]

Given his pedagogical and intellectual interests, it is not surprising that he took an active interest in antiquities legislation. Furthermore, his commitment to the nationalist cause made him suspicious of any British attempts at introducing legislation that would allow for the export of historic artifacts from the country. Bell was obviously quite annoyed by what she considered interference when she described him as "a Syrian who was Faysal's Minister for Education in Damascus. I don't like him much, he's a dry little stick of a man and I think very prejudiced."[98] Bell's opinion was probably based on al-Husri's insistence that the legislation be more favorable to the Iraqi state than Bell believed was necessary.

In November 1922, several months after she first received the archaeology portfolio, Bell reported that she attended a meeting of the Iraqi cabinet for the first time to explain and defend her Antiquities law. She stated that "they labored clause by clause, for two hours. I got it passed in principle but certain verbal alterations are still to be made in the Arabic text."[99] She seemed to have reason to believe that the law as she envisioned it would soon come to fruition, especially after she attended another meeting of the cabinet in December. After that meeting, Bell still was optimistically describing the Iraqi ministers as "extraordinarily welcoming and sympathetic—it really warmed my heart—and we came to a very satisfactory conclusion. We agreed that anyway we would have a provisional law."[100] However, in the next months the matter stalled, and Bell made little progress in getting her bill passed. On a trip to Egypt in August the following year, Bell consulted with the French and British archaeologists there on how to frame the law in Iraq.[101]

On her return to Baghdad in September Bell continued "labouring at the Antiquities Law. We spent most of Sunday morning at it."[102] While she had been away in Egypt, Yasin al-Hashimi, with the help of al-Husri, had introduced a new law of their own that placed greater restrictions on what foreign excavators were allowed to export. However, Bell returned in time to thwart its progress. Once again, it is a testimony to her power and influence that she was still able to obstruct Yasin's efforts. Al-Husri described in his memoirs Bell's attempts to push through the antiquities legislation.[103] According to him, Bell argued that if the law was construed in such a way that all things excavated would belong to the state as al-Hashimi had recommended, no archaeologist would come to Iraq. When al-Husri pointed out that in Crete all antiquities discovered during excavations were given to the national museum, Bell bluntly replied, "Iraq is one thing and Crete is another thing altogether."[104]

This clash between Bell and al-Husri, two very influential figures in early Iraqi political history, is symbolic for the Anglo-Iraqi political and cultural struggle and represents a transitional phase in the history of archaeology in Iraq. Bell sought a law that would be favorable to Western archaeologists, because it allowed them to operate similarly, yet on a somewhat reduced scale, to the way nineteenth-century archaeologists did. They would be able to excavate without any governmental supervision and would be able to export significant portions of the fruit of their labor. Al-Husri, on the other hand, wanted legislation that resembled more a twentieth-century ethos and legislation in Western countries. Al-Husri's law also reflected the new political reality, namely, that a new sovereign state had been established in Iraq.

In a letter to Winston Churchill, Percy Cox summarized the difficulties in getting the antiquities legislation, which obviously surprised Cox, the veteran administrator. Cox specifically mentioned al-Husri's objections, stating that al-Husri felt that the Iraqi law should be modeled on legislation enacted in the Ottoman Empire rather than following the example of the Palestinian law, which was the British model.[105] Cox stated that the Turkish model would be "of course inadmissible as it would give the excavators little or no tangible return for their labors."[106] Cox mentioned how Bell convinced Faysal to try to persuade al-Husri to change his mind and the king promised that he would support Bell's original legislation.

Despite the king's support, the resistance of certain Iraqis delayed matters until, finally, almost two years after she initiated the process, Bell's law of antiquities passed in June of 1924.[107] It is a testimony to her power and influence and the ultimate British control of governmental decisions that she was able to push through her original legislation, as it was unfavorable to the Iraqi state and resisted by some influential Iraqi statesmen. It suggests, furthermore, that the Mandate period encompassed a mixture of the old and the new, which is indicative of the broader political realities following the war. The war brought an end to classical imperial designs and implementations, and the new Mandate states in the Middle East were supposed to reflect the new world order. General patterns of the nineteenth-century practices were incorporated into the twentieth-century political realities, yet the latter did not constitute a total break from the past. Rather, this was a transitional phase, which indeed was its ultimate purpose. It was therefore supposed to contain more elements of the new than the old. Yet, as this episode in Iraqi archaeology reveals, it actually contained more of the old than the new and sought rather to maintain the nineteenth-century legacy rather than adjusting to the contemporary reality.

The British Mandate period in Iraq thus marked a distinct transitional phase in Iraqi archaeology. It was an important preceding phase before the Iraqis took full control of their archaeological matters in 1936, a period during which Western archaeologists and institutions were able to capitalize on the relatively weak governmental institutions and the growing pains of the Iraqi state.

Through her determination, Bell was able to pass a law that gave her a monopoly in archaeological affairs in the country. When the law finally passed, she wrote jubilantly to her father, stating, "Congratulate me! Under its provisions the Dept. of Antiquities—*i.e., me*—has the right to give permission to any applicant to export antiquities and to charge a percentage of their value. This percentage . . . frees the exporter from export duty"[108] (emphasis added).

Although she couched the passage of the bill in positive terms and portrayed it as a victory (which to a large extent it was), Bell was surprised at how long the process took. It is not entirely clear what issue exactly caused the obstruction of Bell's antiquities legislation. In her letters and diaries, she does not cite specific reasons, which may indicate that some dirty politics had taken place. Al-Husri states in his autobiography, however, that it was due to her position that the foreign archaeologist be allotted a significant share of the excavated material. He maintained, furthermore, that he and other Iraqis attempted to impede the passage of the law, since they considered it to be too lenient.[109]

Al-Husri's position has probably some truth to it, considering the dialectical nature of Iraqi politics of the time. The British and the Iraqis each tried to prevent the other from gaining a favorable advantage, and it is, therefore, likely that the Iraqi cabinet members used the concessions and debates over archaeological legislation to negotiate on other administrative and political matters. An exhaustive search failed to uncover a single Iraqi historian who mentioned this debate in the cabinet; nor did it seem to attract much attention in the contemporary Iraqi newspapers.[110] In 1923 Woolley had told Gordon that the debate on the Antiquities Law in the Baghdad Chamber had been "acrimonious" and that he expected "some worry" over the details of the division of finds.[111]

Except for its provisions concerning the division of excavation finds, Bell's 1924 law followed standard antiquities legislation then prevalent in most countries of the world. Many of the provisions of the Iraqi law were based on the Treaty of Sevres, which itself followed the standard formulations present in most European countries. The first influential excavation agreement between nations was between Greece and Germany in 1874 concerning the excavation of Olympia.[112] This agreement served as a model for many later agreements because it included some important clauses necessary for mutually beneficial terms. These clauses include the stipulation that even if the excavations were financed by a foreign government all excavated material was property of the host country which could use its discretion to reward the excavators with duplicates or replicas.[113]

Yet, what set the Iraqi legislation apart from similar laws in countries outside the Middle East were the provisions concerning property division. These articles of the law, which were of most interest to the archaeological community at large and which would later become a source of contention between the Iraqis and Western archaeologists in the 1930s, were concerning the division and export of finds. Articles 22 and 23 stated:

At the close of excavations, the Director shall choose such objects from among those found as are in his opinion needed for the scientific completeness of the Iraq Museum. After separating these objects, the Director will assign [to the excavator] . . . such objects as will reward him adequately aiming as far as possible at giving such person a representative share of the whole result of excavations made by him. (Article 22)

Any antiquities received by a person as his share of the proceeds of excavations under the preceding article may be exported by him and he shall be given an export permit free of charge in respect thereof. (Article 23)[114]

These two articles raise important questions about the proprietorship of the antiquities in Iraq. They affiliate the Iraqi law with the liberal archaeological laws of Middle Eastern states that allowed for extensive exports of antiquities, in stark contrast to the more prohibitive enactments of Europe. Most European laws explicitly stated that all antiquities were the property of the state in which the excavation took place. For example, the 1909 Italian law, which can be traced back over four hundred years to a papal bull forbidding the export by anyone of cultural property from the Papal States, prohibited the sale or other transfer of cultural objects by public or private institutions. A French law of 1913, still in effect today, placed similar limitations on certain objects that the government classified as protected property. And in a law of 1918, the Soviet Union classified all cultural property as state property and prohibited any transfer or export thereof.[115] Finally, Cyprus issued a law in 1905 stating that all excavated antiquities belonged to the government and that the excavator would be allowed only to export duplicates of antiquities found.[116]

In these countries it is generally recognized that all undiscovered antiquities of a movable character are the absolute property of the government. Therefore, an archaeologist who works under such conditions is like a contractor in a capitalist system. The archaeologist, in a sense, is hired by the government to do the manual labor. The archaeologist cannot lay claim to any object but only receive as "wages" those duplicate objects that the government deems appropriate. Although the government, under these provisions, reaps the fruits of the archaeologist's labor, in terms of direct material benefits, duplicate antiquities are not the only reward the archaeologist receives. An excavation gives the archaeologist access to research sources and furthers scientific endeavor. One ultimate purpose of archaeology, after all, is not necessarily the amassing of antiquities, but the accumulation of knowledge.

In contrast, however, the various Middle Eastern countries, particularly those under Western supervision, had much more relaxed legislation that allowed for some discretion and flexibility in the export of antiquities. This feature was particularly true in countries that came under British influence, such as Palestine and Iraq. This fact may be because, since the war, the British archaeological establishment had been persistent in lobbying the British political authorities to implement more liberal laws of antiquities in countries falling under British dominion. These archaeologists emphasized that recent legislation in Cyprus and India prohibiting the export of antiquities, thereby preventing the British Museum from getting anything from those countries, was "parochial" and "shortsighted and ill-conceived."[117] They contested such prohibition, lest a "similar want of foresight may not render futile the plans made for the archaeological development of Mesopotamia," maintaining, furthermore, that "it would be an ironical result if, by the assumption of control of the country, the British Museum were to be debarred from adding to its collection."[118] The Keepers pointed out that since the BM was the archaeological museum of the "capital of the empire . . . its contents should represent the archaeology of the British possessions."[119] Therefore, whenever British archaeologists and Museum officials were asked to advise on archaeological legislation, they recommended that the law allow the excavator and his sponsoring institution a significant portion of his finds.

This self-serving view became influential when antiquities legislation was discussed in various regions of the Middle East. For example, an ordinance passed by the British in Mandate Palestine, stated that the director of antiquities should, after the close of the excavations, "make a fair division of all objects between the Museum and the person to whom the permit to excavate was granted aiming as far as possible at giving such person a representative share of the whole result of the excavation."[120]

Iraq had suffered, if not the most, one of the most extensive plunderings of antiquities in the nineteenth century in all of the Middle East. This rapine was primarily due to the isolation of archaeological activity from governmental supervision, Western imperial competition, and lack of organized local concerns.[121] The various Ottoman antiquities legislation (especially the 1874 and 1884 laws) utterly failed to oversee archaeological activities in the Empire, primarily because of the absence of any form of enforcement authority.[122] Most of the excavations in Ottoman times were hasty and ill-recorded, and the finds were not properly guarded. Despite the theretofore inauspicious history, though understandable given the scientific standards of the time, of archaeological excavations in Iraq, Bell's legislation, though well-intended, did not sufficiently safeguard the Iraqi interests. Bell's antiquities legislation was but a small step toward extensive control, conservation, and safekeeping of Iraqi antiquities. As far as it is possible to ascertain, it seems that the legislation did prevent, to some extent, illicit diggings and illegal exports from Iraq. During the Mandate years it seems that the price of Iraqi antiquities on the black market increased significantly, which indicates that there was a drop in overall supply. For example, Raymond Dougherty, a Yale Assyriologist, wrote his friend C. S. Knopf in 1928, "of course, the market price of these tablets is much higher since the war owing to the fact that it's more difficult to obtain antiquities from mounds in Iraq."[123] Yet Bell's legislation in Iraq did not take the full step and ensure that all antiquities, save duplicates, would become the property of the Iraqi government, according to the norm in most European and North American countries.

The legislation also lacked the necessary checks and balances that could prevent the director of antiquities from making arbitrary, illegal, or self-serving decisions. It allowed the director too much personal discretion in making critical decisions and included provisions, such as Article 20, which enabled the director to grant permission for "temporary" excavations that only lasted a month and were not subject to the regular rules and regulations. In essence, Bell wrote the law, executed it, and had full judicial authority. Bell's determination to have full and complete control in archaeological matters is evident in her success in placing the Department of Antiquities under the auspices of a ministry that Bell felt would be least intrusive.

According to Bell's legislation, the Department of Antiquities was placed under the Ministry of Public Works rather than the Ministry of Education, as in most countries, such as under the 1874 Law of Antiquities in the Ottoman Empire. Bell stated that "the department, to my great satisfaction has been placed under the Ministry of Public Works, so that I am directly under my friend Sabih Beg and shall have the help of the architect Major O. M. Wilson."[124] Al-Husri states that ostensibly Bell placed the department under the public works ministry because the Iraqi museum concerned itself with stone and architectural objects and thus with elements associated with engineering. The real reason, according to al-Husri, was that Bell wanted to avoid working under the Ministry of Education, which, from her perspective, contained too many fervent Iraqi nationalists.[125]

In the first years of the Iraqi state, a Shi'i was typically appointed minister of education. As her letters reveal, Bell was more comfortable with the Sunnis of Baghdad, who made up the majority of the cabinet, and who also tended to be more amenable to cooperating with the British. Since the Shi'is had received a paltry share of power in the British-designed government structure, the Shi'i ministers were more independent and less reliant on appeasing them. Hence, they often took an anti-British stance that the British interpreted as a fanatic, nationalist position. Although Bell never stated why she preferred the Ministry of Public Works over Education, apart from being able to work with her friend Sabih Beg, al-Husri's contention that Bell wanted a more politically neutral ministry is probably true.

In Egypt, as well, the Department of Antiquities was placed under the public works ministry rather than in its more natural abode, the Ministry of Education, which typically was responsible for cultural affairs. Bell, indeed, had visited Egypt in 1923 and consulted there with Western archaeological authorities. Given their experience with Egyptian ministers of education, who may have had more of a cultural mind-set and therefore were potentially more interested in archaeology than their engineering colleagues in the public works ministry, Bell may have inferred in Egypt from her Western counterparts' experience how she, too, could more easily avoid frictions in Iraq.[126] (In fact, a year after Bell died, her antiquities law was slightly amended, the only change being that the Department of Antiquities was placed under the Ministry of Education, which was what al-Husri and other Iraqi nationalists had demanded in the first place.[127] This change in the law indicates that the clause was very much bound to Bell's personal charisma and was therefore anachronistic once she passed away. It also suggests that the prevailing wisdom assumed that the Ministry of Education would be the most logical ministry to oversee archaeological matters.)

The Western archaeological establishment was generally pleased with Bell's Law of Antiquities. She received a letter from Kenyon of the BM, in which he stated that he considered her legislation "the model for the manner in which the division of finds is made between excavators and the local government" and that he would be satisfied as long as "things remained in her hands."[128] Since her actions were perceived as being potentially beneficial to them, Western archaeologists viewed favorably both Bell's legislation and her post as director of antiquities.

In a letter to Gordon, the director of the University Museum at Pennsylvania, Woolley was optimistic about the future of archaeology in Iraq and the potential benefits for their excavation, stating, "In Miss Bell we shall of course have a most sympathetic director."[129] Woolley was therefore positive about the general conditions in Iraq, even though Bell made it clear to him that she intended to establish a museum in Baghdad to house the nation's antiquities. She stated that she must ensure that the best artifacts remained in Iraq, since her primary duty was to preserve Iraq's heritage rather than to enrich Europe or America.[130]

In the case of archaeology, therefore, as in most other material relationships between the Middle East and the West during this period, the Middle East served primarily as a supplier of raw materials to the West—a relationship that was not advantageous in economic or cultural terms for the Middle Eastern states. This period was characterized by Western domination in archaeology. The history of archaeology during the Mandate years reflects the fact that archaeology was still primarily a Western affair—Westerners decided which sites should be excavated, how to interpret the artifacts, which antiquities should remain in Iraq, and how they should be displayed in a museum. The Western countries used their scientific know-how and institutional strength to pursue systematically the opportunities available to them. In contrast to the sometimes politically unpredictable Ottoman era in Iraq, the years of Mandate Iraq were particularly fruitful for the Western archaeological missions, or as one archaeologist has described this period, years of "great archaeological revival."[131] Reliable, pro-Western legislation and a British-supervised governmental structure that made peaceful and productive excavations possible were firmly in place. The number of missions sent to Iraq during this period indicates that the country was perceived as a very favorable working environment. Western museums and institutions were eager to send missions and personnel to Iraq and to establish archaeological schools and institutions in Iraq that would guarantee a long-term presence in the region.[132]

The Mandate years were characterized by productive missions which unearthed important and valuable artifacts that contributed to significant progress in the understanding of ancient civilizations. Yet this success was due not so much to the conducive political situation that enabled archaeological expeditions, as to the technical and scientific progress of archaeology as a science and method. Archaeologists were able to use this positive working environment to their advantage and had in general forsaken the trophy-hunting attitude of their nineteenth-century predecessors.

Whereas the antiquities legislation provided a basis for a comprehensive, controlled, and permanent approach to archaeology in Iraq, it also indicated the reach of British power. This was a period of transition where the British officials sought to safeguard their interests both informally and, as was the case with the antiquities legislation, formally. The paradigms were set for future archaeological research. The fact that Iraq would eventually enjoy a highly professional archaeological practice, with accompanying high standards, in the latter part of the twentieth century indicates that although the legislation was devised to preserve British interests, it also contributed to the eventual transition to Iraqi-controlled archaeology.

Yet because archaeology was associated with the British-backed administration and because it was a practice that initially largely barred Iraqis from participation on the decision-making level, another paradigm was set for archaeology. It was perceived as a British affair, a British practice, something that Iraqi nationalism should battle and question. Eventually, archaeology would become the fuel for nationalism and also the grounds on which nationalistic battles were fought. Iraqi nationalism, as evidenced in schoolbooks and general historiography, is largely critical of the British involvement in their nominally independent country. And archaeology was part of that parcel and thus was contested. Ultimately, though, archaeology entered the political sphere early on and held a central role in the political administration of the country and in the eventual definition of an Iraqi national identity. Initially, though, as Chapter 4 describes, it was primarily European and American scholars who practiced archaeology. But the idea had been introduced, through legislation and other mechanisms, that antiquities should by and large belong to the Iraqi state. The politics of archaeology during this hybrid stage was centered around control and proprietorship. And the excavations and the division of finds were points of many negotiations and much tension, which generally characterize periods of transition.

4

MANDATED ARCHAEOLOGY

The Creation of the Museum and the Vibrant Archaeological Scene (1921–1932)

The new political reality in Iraq was a boom for archaeologists. With sympathetic British administrators overseeing archaeological matters, the conditions were ripe for productive and fruitful research. During the years between 1921 and 1932 all major archaeological excavations were foreign, though antiquities were becoming more institutionalized on the Iraqi political and cultural landscape.

A new, more scientific methodical emphasis characterized archaeology during the Mandate years. This novel approach resulted in several long-running archaeological projects. During these years, the American, British, and Germans all invested considerable time and energy in extensive missions. Bell was careful to allow only those who had considerable experience and institutional support behind them to engage in archaeological activities in Iraq.[1]

The new legislation and the general scientific ethos prevented or discouraged random scrambles for specific trophies. Nevertheless, a different sort of race, or competition, emerged among archaeologists. This competition centered around who could find the oldest artifacts from the oldest civilizations or who could discover new, theretofore unknown cultures. Therefore, most sites that were excavated in this period were Sumerian sites, considered to represent the oldest civilization, such as Ur and Warka. Related to this quest was also a desire to unearth evidence of theretofore relatively unknown civilizations, such as those of the Amorites and the Hurrians, which became the preoccupation of several archaeologists and their missions. Hence, a different sort of scramble took place during the Mandate period, a more scientific and less destructive one, invigorated by the competitive spirit of institutions and the egos of the archaeologists in question.

Owing to their superior financial situation following World War I, American institutions played a prominent role in the ensuing interwar period.[2] During these years, several American institutions sought cooperation with British institutions, given their proximity to British politicians and thus, ultimately, to the Iraqi government. It was a mutually beneficial relationship: The Americans supplied the necessary capital, while the British in most cases contributed the primary personnel and goodwill among the authorities in Iraq. In fact, the first two excavation missions sent to Iraq after the war were both products of Anglo-American cooperation: the British Museum and the University of Pennsylvania at Ur and Oxford University and Chicago's Field Museum at Kish.[3]

The cooperation between the British and the Americans was particularly successful at the long-standing excavations at Ur. In May 1922, G. B. Gordon of the University Museum at the University of Pennsylvania (Penn) wrote to BM officials proposing a joint expedition to Iraq. Penn had already acquired some experience, albeit not very positive, in sending expeditions to Iraq, specifically to Nippur in the nineteenth century.[4] Perhaps because of Penn's prior misfortunes in the area, Gordon was seeking an experienced and well-connected ally, stating that Penn had at its disposal $2,500 and would be prepared to bear most of the expense "in return for the advantages to be derived from the prestige of the British Museum and its influence with local authorities."[5] The BM suggested an archaeological mission to Iraq headed by Leonard Woolley to "complete the excavation of Tell Obeid begun by Mr. Hall in 1919" and to "continue the excavation of Tell Muqayyar [Ur of the Chaldees] at which some work was done by Mr. Campbell Thompson"[6] Incidentally, Penn also had engaged in some minor work at Ur in the late nineteenth century and was therefore eager to return to that site. Among those accompanying Woolley was Sidney Smith, of the Department of Egyptian and Assyrian Antiquities at the BM, who later became honorary director of antiquities in Iraq.[7]

Once again, Penn's involvement in Mesopotamian archaeology did not begin fortuitously. An American named Hunter who was sent to London from Philadelphia to accompany Woolley to Iraq suffered a nervous breakdown while in London and was admitted to a mental hospital and eventually returned to the States.[8] As a result, during the first season at Ur, no Americans were present. Nevertheless, the first season was productive, or "eminently satisfactory,"[9] as the annual British Administrative Report labeled it. The archaeologists were able to uncover foundations of a temple, along with a headless statue of Ur-Nanshe and large quantities of jewelry of the Achaemenid period.[10]

The Penn-BM mission to Ur was hugely successful and was seen by many contemporaries as a model in terms of its thorough, scientific approach to excavation and its voluminous and meticulous publications. It benefited from generous funding from the American philanthropist John D. Rockefeller Jr., who, starting in 1925, contributed $15,000 a year to the Ur mission via the University Museum at Penn.[11] The long-lasting mission, which ran from 1922 to 1934, was also successful from a public relations point of view because the director of this mission, Woolley, had a flair for publicity and diligently capitalized on the spectacular finds he and his team unearthed. Like Layard's a century earlier, Woolley's discoveries and accessible writings captured the public imagination.

Woolley is indeed a legendary figure in the history of archaeology, and he played a very prominent role in Iraqi archaeology in the Mandate period. The son of an Anglican clergyman, Woolley considered becoming a minister himself. Instead of preaching about the Bible, however, Woolley chose instead to uncover some of its stories and figures, and was determined to prove the historicity of the Bible. Woolley wrote several accounts, characterized by his eloquent writing and vivid imagination, which, like Layard's, became best-sellers in England and the United States, probably due to their biblical connotations. Although most archaeologists working in Iraqi archaeology at this time were not as motivated by their religious beliefs, as, for instance, colleagues such as Albright, working in archaeology in Palestine, Woolley was clearly an exception to that general rule. As P. R. S. Moorey points out, "For analogies and comparisons, [Woolley] turned instinctively to the Bible as did many of the generations of readers for whom he was writing. His popular books were full of Biblical allusions and he was ever ready to bring the Old Testament to bear on his archaeological discoveries."[12]

Even though the archaeological evidence was scanty at best, Woolley devoted a full book, entitled *Abraham: Recent Discoveries and Hebrew Origins,* in 1936, to attempting to prove that Tell al-Muqayyar was identical to the "Ur of the Chaldees" mentioned in the Book of Genesis as the birthplace of Abraham. As Moorey points out, contrary to the view consistently argued by Woolley there is no proof the Sumerians Woolley wrote about were the same ones mentioned in the Bible.[13] When Woolley republished his *Excavations at Ur* in 1954, it was severely criticized by various reviewers who were struck by how little Woolley was influenced by subsequent evidence or changing perspectives that had challenged seriously his interpretation. As archaeologist Max Mallowan, who worked with Woolley at Ur, writes, Woolley was inclined to "play a lone hand and was reluctant to consult authority, particularly when he had built up a chronological framework which he considered to be satisfactory."[14]

Yet Woolley was a central character in the Mandate years and beyond, particularly due to his long-running and extensive excavations at Ur. Woolley's excavations there uncovered magnificent tombs containing valuable gold and lapis lazuli, along with remarkable evidence of funerary rituals.[15] According to the historian Glyn Daniel, these findings caused a sensation comparable only to the reactions to Schliemann's discoveries at Troy and those of Carnarvon and Carter of Tutankhamen's tomb in Egypt.[16]

From prehistoric times onward, Ur had been a great cultural and religious center of Sumerian civilization. The Sumerians were a non-Semitic people of southern Mesopotamia who, among their cultural achievements, created the world's earliest writing system, referred to as "cuneiform." Among nearly all surrounding cultures and peoples, both the Sumerian language and writing system were in use until the Hellenistic period. Sumerian culture was important in transmitting ideas and concepts, long after the language ceased to be spoken or independent kingdoms of Sumer flourished.[17] During its excavations at Nippur in the nineteenth century, the Penn expedition had uncovered large amounts of literary Sumerian documents that became the primary evidence for Sumerian literature.[18] In a more indirect way, Penn returned to the Sumerian scene as the primary financial contributor to Woolley's excavations at Ur.

At Ur, Woolley uncovered impressive remains of the Sumerian culture, which many scholars, including Woolley, believed had contributed largely to the various myths, stories, and ideas of the ancient Israelites. At a site called Muqayyar, Woolley found a large fortified city containing an extensive religious precinct, built by Nebuchadnezzar in the sixth century B.C.E. Within this site, in 1926, he found an early cemetery, dating from the Early Dynastic period, including a group of "Royal Tombs" whose accompanying display of contemporary riches astonished the world. These rectangular chambers built of stone rubble mostly had escaped the attention of ancient tomb-robbers. One of these tombs was of an unidentified female dignitary, who had been buried with four of her male servants, wearing a gold headdress. Woolley, in his typically detailed yet creative style, described this exciting find. The following account exemplifies the excitement and exhilaration that encouraged the archaeologist during mundane days and captured the imagination of the public as well:

The vault had been built of over a cent[e]ring of stout wooden beams, which ran right through the stonework, and their decay had left half a dozen holes, through which one could glimpse parts of the dim interior and by the light of electric torches, could even see on the floor below the shapes of green copper vessels and catch an occasional gleam of gold.[19]

Although Woolley's discoveries were well known and he became somewhat of a celebrity, less glamorous and, therefore, less well-known, but equally significant, contributions were made by the epigraphists who worked with Woolley, such as Leon Legrain and Cyril J. Gadd. Their study of the written documents found at Ur and their eventual publication resulted in significant advancement of knowledge of Sumerian literature, history, and culture.[20]

The British and the Americans also cooperated at Kish, near Babylon. Kish was considered to be the first seat of kingship after the Flood, and it was from Kish that Sargon set out to create the kingdom of Akkad. In the nineteenth century, the French had conducted sporadic diggings in the area. In 1923, Ernest Mackay initiated an expedition, on behalf of the Field Museum in Chicago and Oxford University, which was completed in 1933.[21] In the first season, it cleared the foundations of a ziggurat of an early Babylonian period.[22] In subsequent years, Steve Langdon directed this long-term excavation, and Mackay served as his field director. From 1926 onward Langdon worked primarily with Louis Watelin. Prior to his excavations at Kish, Langdon had worked extensively with the Nippur tablets at Penn and, like Woolley, was very concerned with discovering the biblical connection to some of the tablets.[23] The Kish site was not considered as rich archaeologically as Ur. But Langdon and his crew found at a site nearby, Jamdat Nasr, a large quantity of tablets from around 2500 B.C.E. in a quasi-pictographic script believed to have been in use before cuneiform.[24]

Most of the other expeditions that came to Iraq in the 1920s were similarly preoccupied with Sumerian remains.[25] For example, at Warka, the Deutsche Orient-Gesellschaft (DOG) obtained a concession for its excavation. Under the direction of Julius Jordan, who later became the director of antiquities in Iraq, the German team conducted extensive excavations at the site of Warka between 1928 and 1939.[26] At Warka, Jordan and Adam Falkenstein established for the first time a stratigraphic sequence of earliest Mesopotamian civilization. Furthermore, they also discovered a sequence of Sumer's oldest monumental buildings, dating from about 3000 B.C.E., and numerous small finds such as the "Uruk vase," a large alabaster vase decorated with cultic scenes that were valuable in the study of early Sumerian ritual.[27] Perhaps most significantly, they found thousands of tablets with valuable information about the Sumerian society and economy.[28]

American expeditions under the direction of James Henry Breasted and sponsored by the University of Chicago's Oriental Institute (OI) embarked on excavations in the Diyala area. Although Breasted is more noted for his involvement with Egyptology, he and his well-endowed OI also made significant contributions to Iraqi archaeology. The Tell Asmar and Khorsabad excavation sites sponsored by the OI were the envy of other archaeologists because they were equipped with modern photographic studios and laboratories. As the British archaeologist Seton Lloyd described it, Breasted's camps were not envisaged as "groups of intrepid explorers braving the perils and hardships of a savage country in the cause of science."[29]

In 1929, the OI began field excavations at Khorsabad, the capital city of the neo-Assyrian king Sargon II, under the direction of Edward Chiera. Like many other activities of the OI, Chiera's mission was generously funded by John D. Rockefeller. The OI carried out excavations at the site until 1935, initially under Edward Chiera and later under Gordon Loud, and unearthed important inscriptions and texts, such as a king list that lists the rulers of Assyria from earliest times to 748 B.C.E., along with various miscellaneous objects such as carved ivories and bronze door bands.[30]

In addition to the Sumerians, other cultures attracted interest in the Mandate period. Ephraim Speiser, an Assyriologist born in Poland in 1902 who taught at the University of Pennsylvania from 1931 till his death in 1965, was appointed the annual professor at the American School of Oriental Research (ASOR) at Baghdad in 1927.[31] Speiser was particularly interested in recovering information about Hurrian civilization, a people identified by their non-Semitic, non-Indo-European language. The Hurrians' main contribution to ancient history lies in the transmission of traditions they encountered before and during their migration across northern Mesopotamia to Syria and Asia Minor in the late third millennium B.C.E. In cooperation with Chiera, Speiser carefully studied the recently available tablets from Nuzi. His archaeological activities in Iraq focused on sites that would reveal the ethnic composition and cultural development of prehistoric northern Mesopotamia, which, in turn, could shed light on the Hurrians. For the next ten years he, in close cooperation with Charles Bache of Penn, conducted fairly extensive excavations at Tepe Gawra in northeastern Iraq and at nearby Tell Billa. These excavations were primarily funded by Dropsie College in the United States.[32] The sites were important, since they gave an almost continuous sequence of northern Mesopotamian occupations from the Late Halafian period through the end of the Late Uruk period. Still, the findings did not yield as much information about the Hurrians as Speiser had hoped.

The Yale Assyriologist Albert Clay was also concerned with finding material evidence of a Semitic people originally from northern Syria who emigrated to Mesopotamia in the early second millennium B.C.E. Clay was particularly interested in identifying the site of Mari, mentioned in a history of Mesopotamian kings as home to a royal dynasty, as he believed he would find there evidence for an ancient Amorite civilization in northern Syria and the Euphrates Valley. Driven by his religious beliefs and probably in response to the claims of the Pan-Babylonian school led by Delitzsch in Germany (see Chapter 1), Clay sought to demonstrate the importance of the northern Semitic empire of the Amorites.[33] This civilization, according to Clay, influenced both Mesopotamian and Israelite culture, such as inspiring the story of the Deluge. Therefore, the Mesopotamian legends also found in the Bible were derived from Israeli culture, rather than the biblical stories being derived from Mesopotamian sources.[34] His claims about the Amorite people did not receive a positive response from his colleagues. For example, Hogarth, the director of Oxford's Ashmolean Museum, wrote in a letter to a colleague in Baghdad that Clay "has a bee in his bonnet about Amorites, but if you haven't allowed him to go prowling about there, there's no harm done: for it's mostly moonshine—his Amorites."[35] Yet, Clay's theories were well received among conservative religious circles in the United States and contributed to the failure of the Pan-Babylonian school to spread in the United States.[36]

The first official Iraqi excavation also took place during this period. It was, however, Iraqi in name only, because it was on a site determined by Bell and directed by Chiera. Apart from the hired Iraqi manual laborers on site, there was no other Iraqi participation. Bell asked Chiera to conduct a small, yet fruitful, excavation in the spring of 1925 at Tarkalan, an Assyrian site near Kirkuk. This excavation was officially sponsored by the Iraq Museum in conjunction with the recently formed American school of archaeology in Baghdad.[37] Bell furnished Chiera with five hundred Iraqi rupees, which allowed him to employ twenty men at a time, and issued a temporary one-month permit, allowed under Article 20 of the antiquities law.[38] Such a permit did not follow the standard procedures of other excavations and allowed the excavator considerable more freedom and latitude. The expedition's partners decided that they would each get half of all objects found, but the American school would get the right of publication for all tablets found.[39]

Chiera was excited about this opportunity, since it legitimized the American school and himself as an excavator. Furthermore, he was able to reach an important agreement with Bell regarding the status of the American school. Chiera convinced Bell that since the school was stationed in Iraq, it was therefore an Iraqi institution. On that basis, it should be exempt from some of the legal restrictions on the export of antiquities. As a jubilant Chiera wrote to G. A. Barton, "This leaves the school perfectly free to do whatever it wants with her share of the finds. Tablets and objects can be exported to America, if so desired."[40]

Chiera's excavations near Kirkuk were continued later by four campaigns sponsored jointly by the Fogg Art Museum in Boston, Harvard's Semitic Museum, and the American School of Oriental Research, which collectively were known as the Nuzi expeditions. These excavations (under Chiera in 1927–1928, Robert H. Pfeiffer in 1928–1929, and Richard F. S. Starr in 1929–1931) unearthed more than five thousand tablets, which provided critical information about the economic, religious, and legal institutions of the Nuzians/Hurrians, who were believed to be the biblical Horites.

During the Mandate years, the Germans were also able to return to Babylon, where they had excavated before the war. As discussed above, they were forced to leave behind large quantities of antiquities at Babylon.[41] Upon the establishment of the Iraqi state, these antiquities became subject to Iraqi property laws and thus, strictly speaking, were the property of the government. The Iraqi government decided to keep, and guard, the antiquities as they found them in the excavators' house in Babylon. In 1926, a year after the death of Robert Koldewey, one of the original excavators at Babylon, the Deutsche Orient-Gesellschaft (DOG), wrote to the British ambassador in Berlin seeking permission to retain what it considered to be its rightful share of this collection. It stated that an important piece which had been left behind in Babylon, first under British and then later Iraqi supervision, somehow had appeared on the art market in London.[42] Fearing that the collection was being disseminated, the Germans were seeking to claim their share. They had been working under an arrangement with the Ottoman government that allotted half of the finds to Berlin and the other half to Istanbul.[43] The Iraqi government did not consider such agreements binding, but in May 1926, Bell was able convince the Iraqi cabinet that the German antiquities at Babylon should not be unilaterally confiscated by the Iraqi government. Instead, the remaining Babylon collection was to be treated as a new excavation and therefore subject to the "half-and-half" division of the new law.[44] Officially, she wrote to Bruno Guterbock of the DOG, inviting him and his colleagues to come to Iraq to participate in the division with the Iraqi government.[45] Privately, however, Bell wrote to her old friend Walter Andrae, one of the original excavators, proposing that he come to Iraq and arrange and catalogue the material before she made her division.[46] Eventually, Bell made her division, and the share that fell to the Iraq Museum comprised over ninety cases containing several thousands of objects.[47] This collection, therefore, contributed considerably to the slowly expanding collection in the Iraq Museum.

From an archaeological point of view, the Mandate years were prolific, and archaeological activities expanded to theretofore unknown dimensions. For example, in 1928–1929 there were eight large expeditions working in Iraq. These were:

(1) **Ur: joint expedition of the British Museum and the University of Pennsylvania (Leonard Woolley, director);**

(2) **Kish:** joint expedition of Oxford University and Chicago's Field Museum (Charles Watelin, director);
(3) **Nuzi (modern Yorghan Tepe):** Harvard–Baghdad School Expedition (Robert Pfeiffer, director);
(4) **Seleucia (Tell 'Umar):** Michigan–Baghdad School Expedition (Leroy Waterman, director);
(5) **Erech (Warka):** Deutsche Orient-Gesellschaft and Deutsche Not-Gemeinschaft (Julius Jordan, director);
(6) **Ctesiphon:** Deutsche Orient-Gesellschaft (Oscar Reuther, director);
(7) **Tallu':** Louvre and University of Kansas (l'Abbe de Genouillac, director);
(8) **Khorsabad:** University of Chicago (Edward Chiera, director).[48]

This list reveals the international interest in Iraqi archaeology and suggests the direction in which archaeology was headed. The missions had established and well-endowed institutions behind them, and an Iraqi government report estimates that these missions spent around forty thousand pounds sterling in Iraq, primarily on manual labor wages.[49] While the primary focus was on the earliest Sumerian periods (Ur, Kish, and Tallu'), an interest in later periods in Iraqi history was also starting to appear. The expedition at Khorsabad concentrated on the Assyrian period, particularly on the decorations of Sargon's palace from around 710–705 B.C.E.; the team at Warka found objects from a variety of periods, but its most important discovery that year was a small temple built around 1400 B.C.E. during the Kassite period. The work at Seleucia focused on a Hellenistic site and the German scholars at Ctesiphon examined remains of buildings from the Parthian, Sassanian, and early Islamic periods.[50]

The excavations of the 1920s had been sensational. They had resulted in spectacular finds and contributed to more systematic understanding of ancient Mesopotamian civilizations. This epistemological progress was not only due to the favorable political conditions in Iraq, but also to a more cooperative spirit among the archaeologists. The discipline demanded that results of the excavations be published, and the archaeologists themselves realized the importance of meeting and sharing information in order to better assess the state of scholarship. The significant accumulation of knowledge contributed to putting Mesopotamian archaeology on the agenda at the Eighteenth International Conference of Orientalists held in Leiden, the

Netherlands, in 1931. The conference reviewed the relevant Meso-potamian finds since the war and reached important conclusions concerning the chronology of early Mesopotamian history. Three dis-tinguishable periods were apparent: the Ubaid (4000–3500 B.C.E.), Uruk (3500–3200 B.C.E.), and Jamdat Nasr (3200–2800 B.C.E.). As Daniel points out, this scheme provided a vital systematization of south-ern Mesopotamian prehistory.[51] Although there were significant cases that did not easily fall into this scheme, it nevertheless enabled a more coherent comparative framework for interpretation. By 1940, various significant discoveries, such as Campbell Thompson's unearthing of Neolithic pottery at Kuyunjik, contributed to a new scheme that added two earlier stages to the Leiden plan.

DIVIDING THE FINDS

With the passing of Bell's archaeological legislation in 1924, a formal infrastructure to deal with archaeological missions was now in place in Iraq. Officially, the primary function of this infrastruc-ture was to safeguard the interests of the Iraqi state and people and to regulate archaeological activities in the country. Any prospective archaeologist now had to apply to the authorities in Baghdad and subject himself to national legislation. Although there was a growing understanding that more artifacts would remain in Iraq and that archaeologists would not have carte blanche to export the antiquities as they had in the past, the archaeological richness of Iraq was considered so ample that it was still worth the time, money, and effort to send archaeological missions to the country. Having a pro-Western govern-ment in place and Bell at the archaeological helm helped fuel Western archaeologists' optimism. As the director of the BM wrote to his American colleague at Penn, "Practically they [the Iraqi government] are not likely under present conditions to claim much but legally they are entitled to claim a good representative collection. Even so, there would almost certainly be an equally good and representative selection for us both."[52] Despite this optimism, there was, however, a potential source of tension in the system, since the Iraqi government could pos-sibly, via the director of antiquities, assert its rights and demand por-tions of the finds. While the parameters of the legal code were clear, the uncertainty concerning the outcome of the division left a cloud of unpredictability over each mission.

Given the circumstances, however, Western archaeological missions could not have asked for a more favorable environment. This was due primarily to the presence in Iraq of Bell, who had, in the early years of the Iraqi kingdom, strong political influence and basically a monopoly on archaeological matters. As previously demonstrated, Bell herself was interested in archaeology and was sympathetic to the work of the archaeologists and the desires of their sponsoring institutions. Naturally, each mission sought to claim as much as possible and leave behind in Iraq as little as possible. Since the archaeologist had spent time and energy to uncover the material and his sponsoring institution had invested considerable amounts of money in the expedition, they wanted to own artifacts to show for all their time and money. Like most other professions and academic disciplines, archaeology fuels competition among its practitioners. Archaeologists' reputations are not restricted to the soundness and brilliance of their scholarship; objects and finds that they uncover are in some cases just as important. Although the profession of archaeology has progressed methodologically and archaeologists have become increasingly careful in their scientific approach, the most stunning and famous archaeological discoveries, such as Schliemann's and Layard's, were by persons whose methods would be considered crude and unscientific by today's standards. The most famous archaeologists are not necessarily known for their rigorous method or brilliant exposition, but for the value and spectacle of their finds. And although these artifacts are not their property, they nevertheless extend a feeling of proprietorship over the properties, and an archaeologist's name sometimes becomes synonymous with an artifact. A lot is therefore at stake for the archaeologist to ensure the vitality of the antiquities he or she uncovers. Although these missions were scientific and for the advancement of knowledge, their material aspects were also important and were seen as the fruits of the participants' labor.

Lastly, these missions were most often sponsored by museums. By their very nature, museums demand that the actual artifacts be physically present in the museum as potential display items. If a museum has committed resources for an archaeological expedition, it is not sufficient to merely publish and illustrate the artifacts from the expedition. A museum is, after all, defined largely by its collection, and its public character requires visible and concrete materials. The archaeologist in Iraq, therefore, was caught between the desires of his sponsoring institution, his own feeling of proprietorship, and the Iraqi law, which required that a portion of the finds remain there.

In archaeological memoirs, the division of finds is often portrayed as a dramatic event. For example, in the memoirs of both Woolley and Max Mallowan these episodes were the climax of the excavation season and could easily make or break the expedition. The law required that the Directorate of Antiquities would come at the end of the season and allot to the excavator a "representative share." As previously noted, this provision allowed the director considerable leverage and freedom of interpretation; therefore, it was often the subject of considerable dispute what was in fact "representative."

The first division in Mandate Iraq occurred at Ur in 1923. Gertrude Bell arrived to inspect Woolley's finds. Bell describes this event: "It took us a whole day to do the division but it was extremely interesting and Mr. Woolley was an angel. We had to claim the best things for ourselves but we did our best to make it up to him and I don't think he was very much dissatisfied. We for our part were well pleased."[53]

In his letters and reports to his superiors at the BM and Penn, Woolley was in general quite satisfied with the results of the divisions. He writes in 1924, "Actually in the division we did very well and have no cause for complaint—though I would not say so to Miss Bell."[54] Woolley certainly played on Bell's sentiments and complained vigorously over each and every decision. In fact, after her 1924 division at Ur, Bell complained that it was an "agonizing job,"[55] and probably biased her verdicts somewhat to appease Woolley and to comply with his wishes. In 1925 Bell wrote to her parents, "The division was rather difficult but I . . . [was] fair and reasonable—I hope Mr. Woolley thinks the same in his heart, though he fussed a little, or rather declared himself to be very sad afterwards."[56] And she stated that in her last division at Ur in 1926 she had to take the "best thing they had got," which was a small statue of the Goddess Ba'u, but she also reluctantly relinquished "two very early plaques showing sacrificial scenes. I think I really ought to have taken one, but Mr. Woolley made a fuss and I thought after all that I had got a great deal for the Museum out of their labour, so I ended giving both."[57]

Woolley also called the division a "painful process,"[58] though for different reasons than Bell. He recognized, however, that the process was not "unfavorable to ourselves as I had feared."[59] In fact, it seems that

Woolley consistently gained the upper hand. In 1925 he reports that Bell was "convinced by my arguments and agreed to leave to the expedition all the great stela fragments in spite of the outstanding importance of that monument."[60] In a private letter to Kenyon at the BM, Woolley was more concerned with how to split up the finds with the chief financial sponsor, the University Museum at the University of Pennsylvania. He admitted to Kenyon that the division with Bell had been surprisingly easy: "I had expected a fight at least but Miss Bell was most reasonable and I hardly had to use argument to get the lot; and really she did not try to equalize things by taking much of the other stuff, so we came out remarkably well."[61] Woolley seems to have been so successful that when the results of the Ur exhibition were displayed in Oxford the following summer, which Bell, then on leave in England, visited, she remarked to Woolley, somewhat tongue in cheek, that she had been "much too lenient in the division when she saw what a fine show the things made!"[62] Bell's implicit threat, however, did not materialize the following season, since Woolley reports after the 1926 season that the division was "very fair and we have done very well out of it."[63]

With no Iraqi accompanying her (she was usually accompanied by another British official such as J. W. Wilson, Richard Cooke, who later became himself the honorary director of antiquities, or Lionel Smith, an official in the ministry of education), Bell had the ultimate authority on deciding what should be allotted to the Iraq Museum and what should be allowed to leave the country.[64] Because the community of Westerners in Iraq was a relatively small one and within that particular community those interested in archaeology and ancient history were even less numerous yet, it is likely that these individuals knew each other very well. The British officials working on behalf of the Iraqi government were in a position making it difficult to faithfully perform their duty and probably did not receive much support or sympathy from the archaeologists. For example, Leon Legrain an excavator with Woolley at Ur, wrote in 1925 to Lionel Smith, who often accompanied Bell in her divisions. In a mocking tone he wrote, "The 13th of March will be the end of the dig. It will probably bring you back to Ur on the painful duty of plundering the Joint Expedition for the love of the Iraqis. I hope you will forget your natural taste and appreciation of beautiful things and develop a real Arab sense for broken pots, metal objects and ugly Sumerian statues."[65]

A major rationale for claiming objects for Iraq was to build up a national collection in Iraq. Although it is difficult to discern who benefited more from this arrangement, it seems plausible that the Western institutions were, more often than not, on the receiving end. For example, a British Administration report from 1924 states that the Joint Archaeological Committee, which was the highest archaeological authority in England, was "satisfied with the manner in which the division has been made in this as well as in former seasons."[66] It is highly unlikely that an entity like the Joint Committee would express its satisfaction over current affairs unless it viewed the situation as beneficial for its members. Furthermore, in 1931, almost a decade after the existing arrangement was adopted, the archaeologist Edward Chiera complained to G. A. Barton, the president of ASOR, that it was difficult to pursue scholarly work in Iraq for lack of good libraries and "stranger yet, we have fewer tablets in Baghdad for practical study than we have in any of the big universities [in the United States]."[67] This remark by Chiera reveals that although numerous expeditions had been sent to Iraq and therefore numerous divisions had been performed, Iraq had not yet accumulated a plausible collection for local scholarly work.

While Bell typically appears to have seriously considered which objects should be kept in the country, she could also be unorthodox in her division. In an amusing account, she describes going to Kish in 1924 to do the division with Langdon:

"Who decides" said the professor, "if we disagree?" I replied that I did but he needn't be afraid for he would find me eager to oblige. At this he puffed, was this the law? Had it been shown to him? and so forth. So we turned to the necklaces. We spun a coin for the first pick, he won it and we picked, turn and turn about. . . . We put things into groups, spun for the first choice and picked—the professor grew more and more excited—he loved it. It is very amusing I must say. And isn't it fantastic to be selecting pots and things over six thousand years old?[68]

More typically, Bell was torn between her allegiance to England and her adopted country, Iraq, when deciding divisions. She had to remind herself that in her "capacity as Director of Antiquities I am an Iraqi official and bound by the term on which we gave the permit for excavation."[69] She was, as she stated herself, "eager to oblige" the archaeologist,[70] and often found the divisions to be very difficult, even though she felt she was "fair and reasonable."[71] She even seems to have had a bad conscience for doing her duty. When she received a letter from Kenyon, who complimented her work, she felt "relieved, for I feared they would never forgive me for taking the milking plaque which was by far the best thing they found. I could do no other and I am glad they recognized it."[72] It is admittedly impossible to assess exactly what was divided and how fair Bell was (1) to the archaeologists and (2) to Iraq, but anecdotal evidence suggests that she was initially more concerned with pleasing the Western archaeologists and their respective institutions than the Iraqi government.

Although she had a level of allegiance to both, Bell seems to have catered more to the former, often going out of her way not to offend or anger the Western institutions. From the Iraqi side, she had no one to report to but herself, and her actions were not systematically overseen by a local authority or board of directors.[73] Therefore, while a formal structure was in place to ensure Iraqi interests, it is debatable to what extent the governmental structures effectively sought to divide the result of the excavation. Various archaeologists complained officially about unfair treatment, but in their private correspondence they expressed satisfaction with the divisions and optimism about their prospects. For example, the British archaeologist Reginald Campbell Thompson wrote to the BM in 1927, when discussing the upcoming division, that he would strive to get "as many tablets as we can (all if possible)."[74] Campbell Thompson probably based this optimism on his prior experience, and indeed in the division he got most objects that he desired.

The optimism of institutions sponsoring archaeological excavations to Iraq was evidenced in the fact that more and more institutions were eager to send missions to Iraq.[75] In 1926, however, Bell, who had been so pivotal in Iraqi archaeology, committed suicide in Baghdad, only two years after she passed the antiquities legislation and organized and opened the first national museum.

It is generally difficult to ascertain why anyone commits suicide, and Bell did not leave a note. Her last letters indicate that she was becoming increasingly isolated in Iraqi political and social circles. Initially she was a critical player on the Iraqi political scene, especially as a liaison between King Faysal and the British government. She had confidently stated in 1920, "I have realized how prominent a place I have occupied in the public mind here as a pro-Arab member of the Administration,"[76] but by 1923–1924 that role was no longer as pivotal. As the Iraqis became more familiar with the governmental apparatus and the boundaries in British-Iraqi cooperation, they no longer had to rely on Bell as the liaison between themselves and the British.

Bell did not see a future for her considerable energies and experience in Iraq, nor did she envision any sort of career back in England. She was undoubtedly frustrated by her increasingly limited role in Iraqi politics, feeling that she was in a sense anachronistic in the Iraqi setting. Her prospects back home in England were bleak, especially for advancement in the British diplomatic corps or government, probably due to her gender.

As her direct political influence declined, Bell immersed herself more in archaeological matters. Bell found solace in the area's illustrious ancient history and its magnificent artifacts. In the last years of her life and before her eventual suicide in 1926, archaeology became her predominant concern. She conscientiously performed her duties as honorary director of antiquities, the role that she had so carefully laid out in her legislation. As someone who was one of the key players in establishing what is now Iraq and ensuring that archaeology be a central component in the administration, she was undoubtedly one of the most important players in the first years of the Iraqi state. Her contributions enabled archaeological excavations in Iraq in subsequent years to be unusually vibrant and successful, resulting in numerous important discoveries. She had been so dominant that she was almost synonymous with Iraqi archaeology.

Hence, after her death, significant changes began to appear on the horizon. However, Bell had carefully institutionalized archaeological affairs, and as a result, her immediate successors continued to operate in a similar fashion. For example, Campbell Thompson wrote in a letter to Kenyon at the BM that the "present conditions in Iraq appear to be most favourable and Mr. Cooke, the Director of Antiquities . . . is well disposed towards the project."[77]

Yet it was not the sudden death of Bell that resulted in certain changes in archaeological matters in Iraq; rather, the archaeologists actually became victims of their own success. In 1927, the Iraqi general public and politicians for the first time started paying increasing attention to the archaeological excavations when news emerged from the excavations at Ur that significant objects of gold had been uncovered. With the appearance of such obviously valuable pieces, as with the discovery of Tutankhamen in Egypt, Iraqi politicians started to pay closer attention to the divisions, and the foreign directors of antiquities had to be more sensitive and careful in the way they conducted their business. That year Woolley wrote to Kenyon: "Of course the finest things have been taken by Baghdad," including the gold dagger and vanity case. But Woolley was quick to point out that the "season has been so rich that what is left for us is an astonishingly rich collection."[78] The archaeologists were sensing a changed political climate.

In 1928 Woolley sought permission to send certain pieces of gold to London for treatment. In his discussion with Cooke, the honorary director of antiquities, Woolley pondered how he could possibly avoid frictions with the Iraq government. He stated, "They want to annoy, are excited by gold and quite suspect that the thing will never be sent back: we are bleeding the country white, and here is a flagrant illustration of the fact."[79] A British governmental report stated in 1929 that the Iraqi press "sometimes published, and private conversation continually employs, statements that the Iraq Museum contains objects of only inferior value and that the best objects are allotted in the divisions to foreign expeditions [and] it is commonly said that the gold objects in the Museum are not genuine."[80]

Accordingly, the archaeologists and the British director of antiquities, Sidney Smith, went out of their way to appease the Iraqis. As Woolley wrote that same year, "Certain of our best objects are kept here for temporary exhibition. [Sidney] Smith insisted on this for political reasons and I agreed (I could not do otherwise)."[81] The Iraqi political apparatus started slowly to include archaeological matters on its agenda, foreshadowing the politicized archaeology that emerged in the mid-1930s (to be discussed in Chapter 5).

In addition to sponsoring numerous archaeological expeditions in Iraq in the 1920s and early 1930s, foreign institutions also sought to make their presence more long-term in Iraq. Based on their view of the immense archaeological potential of Iraq, several institutions adopted a long-term view. In doing so, they sought to establish schools or institutes that would maintain a permanent presence in Iraq in order to facilitate their access to the archaeological fields of ancient civilizations and formalize their study of that history. Such schools of archaeology had been opened in Greece, Italy, Palestine, and Egypt—now Iraq was seen as a natural site for such an establishment.

In 1920 Albert Clay wrote to the British Foreign Office, informing it of his plans to establish an American school of archaeology in Iraq.[82] Clay, who was at the time a visiting professor at the ASOR in Jerusalem, agreed on behalf of the Archaeological Institute of America to visit Iraq and assess the feasibility of establishing an institution there. Clay's visit to Iraq brought intriguing reactions from the British officials that exemplified their current views of Americans. Although Bell and Wilson were both sympathetic toward him and his agenda, they were primarily impressed by his potential financial backing.[83] It is symptomatic of the times and of British cultural paternalism that the British were somewhat skeptical of the Americans' scholarly potential (Bell called Clay's plan to open an American School "silly business" in a letter to her parents).[84] Clay inaugurated the ASOR in Baghdad in 1923. In its first year, the school's program included public lectures, outreach among Iraqi educators, and archaeological surveys.[85]

Initially the school maintained close ties to the American consulate and was even housed there. The American School grew rapidly in importance. It helped coordinate, for example, the excavations of Chiera of the University of Chicago in 1925 at Yorghan Tepe near Kirkuk, four seasons at Nuzi (1927–1931) in cooperation with Harvard University, and excavations at Tell 'Umar with the University of Michigan. The establishment of the Baghdad School helped ensure and facilitate a continuous American presence in Iraq until 1990. Its activities encouraged and facilitated the study of ancient Mesopotamian civilizations in the United States. Its rich library, initially founded by Clay, is housed today in the Iraq Museum.

Because the British already had a formidable presence in Iraq, they perhaps did not feel the same urge to establish an archaeological institution there. Yet Bell guaranteed British access to Iraqi sites in more ways than one. In her will, she bequeathed a considerable sum, £6,000, for the establishment of a British School of Archaeology in Iraq (BSAI).[86] Her legacy in Iraqi archaeological matters, therefore, continued long after her death. Bell's gift was substantially supplemented by her brother and father and by a fund-raising drive in England in the early 1930s that was spearheaded by Sir Edgar Bonham-Carter.[87] In 1932, the BSAI became a reality. In its first decade it sponsored various expeditions, including those of Max Mallowan at Arpachiyah and later at Nimrud. The school has published since the 1930s the archaeological journal *Iraq.*[88] The inaugural issue of this journal contained articles by Henri Frankfort on gods and myths on Sargonid Seals, R. Campbell Thompson on the buildings on Kuyunjik (Nineveh), and Keith Cresswell on al-Mansur's great mosque at Baghdad.[89]

These foreign schools were not the only institutions that were being established in Iraq. At the same time, the Iraqis were planning a national museum, most fitting for the newly independent country. Furthermore, the massive amounts of artifacts that were being unearthed needed an appropriate venue to be displayed for the enrichment of public cultural life.

THE IRAQ MUSEUM

Any museum, through its collections, seeks to present the past, in all its forms, through the display of its remnants. A museum's ordered and unambiguous presentation of history most often stresses history's nativeness and continuity. Museums organize and visually present history in order to offer a distinct, simplified interpretation of the history and culture of a land and its peoples. Accordingly, museums seldom attempt to present the complexity of history or to accentuate differing interpretations of or debates over the data. Consequently, a national museum is bound to have potential in the state-building process in a recently established nation such as Iraq, with its numerous ethnic and religious groups.

In Europe, the creation of museums in the late eighteenth century succeeded an explosion of materials that the wider dissemination of ancient texts, increased travel, and more systematic forms of communication and exchange had produced and made available as empirical data. These factors contributed to the Europeans' increased curiosity toward other cultures. The establishment of museums also furthered the notion that Europe was the center of civilization and henceforth the natural abode of collected and valuable articles from around the world. In the eighteenth and nineteenth centuries, several significant European museums became state-sponsored. The British Museum and the Louvre, for example, were largely funded by their respective governments. In the United States, however, museums had closer ties to the private sector. The Metropolitan Museum of Art in New York, for example, which was established in 1870, was largely financed by private benefactors and to a lesser extent by the City of New York.[90] The Museum of Fine Arts in Boston and the Philadelphia Museum of Art, which were founded in the same decade, were each primarily supported by an individual philanthropist. As the sociologists Mark Lilla and Isabelle Frank point out, "Created, not inherited, the American museum was animated by an unabashedly bourgeois spirit, and was brought to fruition as a local, civic institution rather than as a nest for the national spirit."[91]

In Iraq, in contrast, the Iraqis inherited, but did not create, their national museum. Its establishment was not the result of wealthy patronage or philanthropy, as was the case with the British Museum and the Metropolitan Museum of Art in New York, or of conquest, as was the Louvre. Rather, initial efforts for creating the Museum were performed by non-Iraqis, particularly the British, who wanted the state to become the guardian of tradition and history.

The impetus for the establishment of the Iraq national museum originated primarily outside of Iraq. For example, several Western archaeologists wrote to the British authorities encouraging them to establish a museum in Iraq. As Clay pointed out in a letter to the British Foreign Office, many foreign expeditions had an interest in excavating in Iraq. Since half of the results of excavation would be retained by the Iraqi government, "a vast amount of material will have to be cared for by the government after these operations are under way." Therefore, it was desirable from Clay's point of view that "steps be taken to establish an archaeological museum for the preservation and exhibition of the antiquities now in storage in Iraq and elsewhere, besides those excavated during the war and temporarily loaned to the British Museum and especially for those antiquities which shall be retained hereafter from the results of excavations that will be conducted."[92] Furthermore, as was discussed in Chapter 3, during the war various British governmental officials discussed establishing a museum in Iraq in the near future to house its antiquities. The establishment of museums was seen as a natural development, even a duty of the British politicians in Iraq. In Iraq, the British administrators sensed the importance of conserving the country's past through its museum displays.

The British viewed themselves as having an important pedagogical role in Iraq, because they believed that as the Mandate power Britain was responsible for preparing Iraq to stand on its own. Because the

British were accustomed to modern, advanced states having national museums, it was important to consider establishing such an institution in Iraq. Few explicit statements, however, were made about the nation-building intent behind such an institution, nor was it clear whether the museum would serve as one of the primary instruments through which to effect a more national culture. One exception is found in a letter to Clay by Jerome Farrell, who worked in the Department of Education in Mosul, who stated, "I hold strongly that all 'show' objects be housed in the centre of Baghdad so as to be accessible to the native population."[93]

Yet those in official circles and those who were heavily involved in establishing the Museum did not offer any didactic statements on whether or how it could benefit the Iraqis. Its establishment was not an intentional attempt by the British to coerce and control the Iraqis. The Museum was not a deliberate instrument of power used to "reorder" Iraq and thus make Iraqis objectlike and legible in order to make them available to political and economic calculation.[94] Rather, it was initially envisioned primarily as a depository of antiquities that, as the result of the divisions with foreign excavations, were starting to pile up in Baghdad. It was a storage house that would ensure that the antiquities would not perish or leave the country. In its earliest stages, it did not display a metanarrative of the Iraqi nation. It recorded the results of the scientific archaeological mission in Iraq.

Initially the Iraq Museum was a humble creation of the British, in a nation of weak institutions and short, yet diverse, historical memory. As political scientist Eric Davis pointed out, rather than being the creation of a powerful Iraqi bourgeoisie, the first museums were established by a relatively weak state.[95] And unlike the national museums of Europe, it was not filled with war or imperial trophy, as was the Berlin Museum or Louvre. In contrast, the Iraq Museum housed objects, solely from Iraq, that had been unearthed in its immediate surroundings. The Museum did not pretend it had, nor did it attempt to display, a universal collection. It was a national museum in the precise sense of the word—a museum that housed domestic artifacts—although it was largely the result of foreign scientific know-how and interpretation.

Like many other facets of Iraqi political life at this time, the Museum and the history it represented were classified, studied, and controlled by the British. The British presented a history to the Iraqis that the British deemed most important and interesting. It was a visual memory of a certain past and perhaps implicitly indicated a sense of national continuity and a national genealogy. Although the Museum had a (minor) instructive role, a significant characteristic of the Iraq Museum was that its establishment and initial development were independent of, and far removed from, the Iraqi political struggle over the state's educational policies. As will be examined in Chapter 5, the Iraqis were vigorously establishing a comprehensive school system and curriculum in which the teaching of history was a central component. In that endeavor, the primary emphasis in the curriculum was Iraq's Islamic history and its role as the seat of the Abbasid Caliphate. And although the British advised the Iraqis on educational affairs, it was primarily through the influence of Sati' al-Husri that the curriculum put nearly exclusive emphasis on Arab and Islamic history, Iraq's ethnic and religious diversity notwithstanding. Yet the Museum had little to show of that chapter of Iraqi history. Instead, it emphasized pre-Islamic artifacts and history, those of a far, distant past rather than one nearer, and perhaps more relevant, at least to the nation's current inhabitants. Therefore, the Museum was certainly a state institution, but not of the Iraqi national government. Rather, it had the characteristics of a British institution. In essence, it was a state-within-the-state institution and initially had few formal or informal ties with the Iraqi politicians or to the population at large. It was a hybrid that made a distinct statement. Somewhat ironically, it was, for all intents and purposes, an apolitical establishment and aloof from the contemporary Iraqi political whirlpool.

Displaying the official Iraqi collections had modest, though commendable, beginnings. Bell was able to secure a small room in one of the government offices in the Sarai district to lodge the artifacts.[96] After having received various items from the first division at Ur in 1923, Bell, along with J. M. Wilson, a British official in Iraq who also was an architect, and Abdul Qadir Pachanji, a former employee of the Museum in Istanbul, laid out all the objects on tables. They identified each object with labels in English and Arabic and invited the king, the ministers, and other "notables," as Bell called them, to view the objects.[97] Bell was very happy with their reception and called this exhibition a "great success," with which the guests "were vastly impressed."[98] That same afternoon, the excavator at Ur, Leonard Woolley, gave a public lecture that was very well attended by both Iraqis and the British, and subsequently the Museum received many small gifts of antiquities.[99] Later that year, Bell organized another successful public lecture where Clay spoke on

Babylonian archaeology. According to Bell, "We had an enormous audience including lots of Baghdadis . . . there's a very genuine interest here in the ancient history of the country and people always flock to lectures."[100]

In October of 1923, Bell and other officials at the Ministry of Public Works started laying plans for the Iraq Museum to be in its own building. "It will be a modest beginning, but it will be a beginning."[101] In 1926, Bell was able to find appropriate housing for the Museum. She proudly stated, "It will be a real museum rather like the British Museum only a little smaller,"[102] noting further that she would take great pride in making it "something like a real museum."[103] In fact, she was so proud in her accomplishment that she said, "I burst with pride when I show people over the Museum. It is becoming such a wonderful place."[104]

In the summer of 1926 the Museum moved to its new location in the northern part of Baghdad. Bell arranged for King Faysal to officially open the Museum in June. Since much of the Museum was still under construction, Faysal actually only opened one room in the Museum. However, that one room, according to Bell, "looks extremely well and I hope it will impress the Ministers. It has indeed all the appearances of a Museum."[105]

After the opening ceremony, the Museum was open for a couple of hours two days a week. In addition to Bell, the staff consisted of "an old Arab curator, a very intelligent Jew clerk and an odd man."[106] On the first day that it was open to the public, Bell gratifyingly described that at any one time there were fifteen to twenty "ordinary Baghdadis going round it under the guidance of the old Arab curator."[107] At this point the Museum owned around three to four thousand objects, most of which needed to be classified and organized.[108] Many additions were made to the national collection from Ur, Kish, and Babylon later that year. By the end of the year, the number of objects in the Museum had almost tripled, exceeding ten thousand.[109]

Uncharacteristically for Bell, her descriptions indicate she was bewildered over how to organize the collection. Even though she had struck fear in archaeologists' hearts in her visit to their excavation sites and offered them advice and criticism (most often unsolicited) over their methods and interpretation, when she had to organize systematically the accumulated material herself, she was unsure of how to classify and present the material. Whenever an archaeologist would visit her she would seek out his advice on the collection. She worked long hours at the Museum preparing to systematically display the artifacts.

What emerged from Bell's efforts was a celebration of Iraq's pre-Islamic past, a most natural result, since most excavations in Iraq at this point had been at such sites. Unlike other national museums, it did little to venerate the current government and/or legitimize the current monarchy. Since Bell and the British had gone to great pains to establish the Hashemite monarchy in Iraq and surround it with a royal aura that the common Iraqi would respect, it is intriguing that Bell did not make any explicit political statements with the museum. Indeed, one reason the Hashemites had been so appealing to the British when they were considering who should lead Iraq was that they were descendants of the Prophet and therefore had prestigious Islamic credentials. Faysal was, in fact, presented to the population in such terms and his leading governmental role derived much of its legitimacy from that Prophetic connection. Yet despite the fact that Faysal needed any possible help in building up his own stature, Bell did not feel compelled to construct the Museum in a manner that would be useful for Faysal's political agenda. For her, the establishment and organization of the Museum were more of a hobby—a task that she could attend to outside her regular working hours. Its creation was therefore the result of leisurely activities of the British. In their spare time, Bell sought the cooperation of various British government officials to help her plan the Museum, clean and identify the artifacts, and finally arrange them in a coherent, systematic, and somewhat scientific way.

She and her like-minded British friends, perhaps frustrated with the current political realities, strove to re-create and document ancient Iraq within this modern kingdom. It was, after all, those ancient remnants that originally fostered their interest in the history and culture of the Middle East. And so in this small museum, they produced vestiges of that glorious past that they so admired and that had attracted many of them to the area. The Museum was created out of the artifacts available from recent excavations in Iraq. The sites and excavations had been chosen by Westerners, and therefore the artifacts available to Bell and her friends were replicas of historical antiquities that Westerners, primarily, found interesting and worth studying. Just like in the nineteenth century, in the early years of the Iraqi state, nearly all the excavated sites dated from pre-Islamic eras, and their selection was still predominantly guided by the notion of validating and shedding light on the Christian Bible. By producing the Museum from those artifacts, Bell created a mini-Iraq, portrayed and imagined through the Museum, so different from the new political state that she had just been instrumental in establishing.

Just as her political role started to diminish and her frustration with the current political process mounted, Bell found solace in the antiquities and the grand history and tradition that they represented. This British museum became the guardian of a generalized tradition, a home of regalia for British Iraq, a testament to Britain's Golden Age and glorious empire, with little connection to the current contemporary situation and inhabitants. For example, when al-Husri first visited the Museum in 1926, he was shocked to see how little emphasis was placed on Iraq's Islamic heritage.[110] Consequently, the Museum did not initially play a central role in Iraqi political and cultural life. In the construction of the Iraqi school curriculum, al-Husri did not incorporate visits to the Museum as part of his pedagogical agenda.

The Museum, though, continued to grow and prosper. The government allotted increasingly larger appropriations to the Museum between 1927–1931.[111] In 1928, the Museum received permission to hire three full-time staff members. It also acquired two impressive colossal winged bulls from Nimrud, which were placed in the front courtyard.[112] In subsequent years, the statues became quite famous and almost synonymous with the Museum. Through the efforts of Sidney Smith, the Museum remained open on Fridays to allow government officials and others to visit the collection. A short guide to the museum collection was printed, and uniformed police were on guard at all times.[113] Smith also regularly delivered lectures to teacher societies and arranged that tours would be offered in Arabic for school visitors and other groups. He also ensured that the leaders of the foreign expeditions offered summaries of their results in public appearances and that their reports were published in the local press.[114] These initiatives led to a marked increase in interest, seemingly among all classes of Iraqi society. In 1929, around one thousand Iraqis visited the Museum each week in addition to Western tourists.[115] In 1931, the staff of the museum had been increased to six in addition to the director of antiquities.[116] That year they also rearranged the principal exhibition rooms in the following manner:

First Floor:
**Rooms no. 1 and 2: Southern Iraq, prehistoric. Sumerian and
    Babylonian periods.**
Room 3: Northern Iraq, prehistoric. Hurritic, Assyrian periods.

Second Floor:
Room 4: Post-Babylonian period: Seleucid, Parthian, Sassanian.
Room 5: Islamic period.
Room 6: Hall of big sculptures.[117]

The Museum's collection had expanded to such an extent that it
was necessary to make arrangements for the construction of a new
Museum the following year. A German architect was hired to make
plans for this new building.

The early versions of the Iraqi national museum did not have characteristics similar to its counterparts in Europe and North America.[118] It
did not seek initially to map the universal evolution of the human
species and human historical development, nor was it intended to display imperial trophies. Though it originated as a British project, the
national museum subsequently became an important vehicle in Iraqi
political and cultural life and was eventually synonymous with local
governmental power.

THE COOKE AFFAIR

One of the primary purposes of the antiquities legislation was to
prevent illicit digging and to control the illegal traffic in and
export of antiquities. It is difficult, however, to estimate how successful
the legislation was in preventing such activities. It is impossible to find
direct evidence of the level of illicit digging due to its very nature. Yet
this sort of activity was a constant concern for Bell and her successor,
who often complained how powerless they were in controlling it. Bell,
for example, filed a report after her visit to Kish, Warka, Sunkara, and
Ur, probably in the year 1925.[119] At Warka she found a "large party of
men, women and children engaged in desultory excavation."[120] After
she had been informed that their activities were illegal, she purchased
from their leader several objects for the Iraq Museum and despaired
over the fact that a "considerable amount of harm is undoubtedly
being done."[121] At Sunkara, ancient Larsa, she also found evidence of
extensive illicit diggings. Given the inaccessibility of the site, the diggers

probably had a sure market for their finds, probably "some merchant in Baghdad."[122]

Several years later, in 1929, an Iraqi government report acknowledged that illegal digs had taken place over a considerable area in the northern part of the country between the Diyala and Nahrwan. The artifacts from these sites, primarily silver jewelry and lapis amulets, had surfaced on the market in Baghdad.[123] Similarly, a British Administration report from the same year stated that there had been a marked increase in "promiscuous digging, and it became clear that unless steps were taken to remedy this evil the country would continue to lose much of its archaeological wealth."[124] The Department of Antiquities therefore applied for funds to the parliament for three traveling inspectors, who would monitor any suspicious activities. In 1929, the current director of antiquities, Sidney Smith, complained almost helplessly in a letter to Woolley that "illicit digs are being conducted all over the country, to a greater extent in my opinion than ever before."[125] In 1931, Julius Jordan, who was then director of antiquities, wrote that illicit digs were so widespread that it was a "real catastrophe" and that they were the primary focus of his attention.[126] During the Mandate period, therefore, preventing illegal excavations was an important task for the antiquities department.

Yet the illicit digs were not the only concern of the authorities. Anecdotal evidence indicates that after the 1924 legislation passed, the antiquities market, both legal and illegal, continued to operate in Iraq. In the records of various archaeological missions, each institution seems to have nurtured relationships with local dealers who would sell them certain artifacts or just with people who came off the street. For example, Woolley related to Sidney Smith having bought several small antiquities from an anonymous Arab. The next day, however, he tried to sell Woolley a bad modern forgery, so Woolley notified the police and the seller was arrested.[127]

In Iraq in the 1920s there was a thriving antiquities market, which operated openly with permission from the government. An appendix to the 1924 antiquities law specified the conditions for traffic in antiquities, stating that each licensed dealer should keep a stock book recording all antiquities procured and the source from which they were obtained, and a register showing the daily sale of antiquities. Further, the dealer was obliged to report to the director of antiquities any object that he received that was more valuable than a specified price. Finally, it was made clear that the dealer was subject to the general rules concerning the export of antiquities.[128] Although it is not clear from the legislation how or whether the government actively supervised the legal antiquities market or how the antiquities dealers acquired their artifacts, anecdotal evidence indicates that this was a thriving market.

In 1930 Sidney Smith issued a memorandum to all expeditions in Iraq regarding the purchase of antiquities by expeditions. He noted in the memorandum that no regulation had previously been laid down on this subject. This memo stated that the expeditions were allowed to purchase objects "from any person whatever as best they can objects which they know . . . come from the immediate area in which their concession lies."[129] These objects would then be included in the objects subject to division.

The flourishing antiquities market was particularly attractive for Western institutions, archaeologists, and travelers who came to Iraq. For example, when Clay visited Iraq in 1919, primarily to explore the prospects of opening an American school of archaeology in Baghdad, another important task at hand was to acquire antiquities for Yale and to evaluate what was available in Iraq.[130] Eventually, however, the close relationship between some archaeologists and the illicit market in antiquities became a troubling issue.

As detailed above, one of the main tasks mandated by the antiquities legislation was to oversee the export and division of the finds. After Bell's death in 1926, various English officials served as director of antiquities on a year-to-year basis. Since there were several foreign archaeological expeditions in the country, there were significant tasks for the director in overseeing the export and division of finds. In 1926, Richard Cooke became director and served until 1928, when Sidney Smith, who had worked with Woolley at Ur, was appointed director.[131]

In general, the years between Bell's death in 1926 and the end of the Mandate in 1932 were relatively quiet, and archaeological matters became routine. One notable exception, however, was an episode that involved Cooke. He became involved in an embarrassing and serious scandal, which drew heavy criticism in the Iraqi papers and made various Iraqi politicians weary of the current state of archaeological affairs.

Richard Cooke was a prominent member of the British community in Baghdad. For several years, he served as an adviser to the Ministry of Awqaf (charitable endowments) and was also appointed, upon Gertrude Bell's death in 1926, as honorary director of antiquities. Although not a trained archaeologist, he had accompanied Bell on several divisions and inspection trips. After assuming the position of honorary director, he immersed himself in the subject and became "more or less an authority."[132] In 1928, he recommended to the Iraqi government that Sidney Smith of the BM replace him as director of antiquities, to which the Iraqi government agreed. In 1929 he lost his position in the awqaf ministry, and according to various reports, he then "executed many commissions for Americans who desired to purchase antiquities, Persian rugs or other articles of the country probably accepting a monetary recompense for his trouble."[133] He also was acting as a superintendent of construction on some buildings outside Baghdad on behalf of the University of Chicago's Oriental Institute.

According to American diplomatic dispatches, it had long been rumored that Cooke was using his position to enable the smuggling of antiquities out of Iraq.[134] Several objects allotted to the Iraq Museum from the division at Ur were missing from the Museum's catalogue. In a letter to Lionel Smith, Woolley speculated about the whereabouts of the objects and Cooke's name came up in that connection, although Woolley found that hard to believe.[135]

These rumors were confirmed in August 1930 when a package that Cooke had asked an Iraqi truck driver to deliver to Beirut was confiscated at the Syrian border. It contained a Gudea head, two ceremonial bronze weapons with gold handles, eight inscribed silver scrolls, three figurines in pottery, and a considerable quantity of cylinder seals and ornamental heads. Cooke had not applied for nor received the required export permits. Whether or not he had criminal intentions, all appearances indicated that he was illegally exporting antiquities.

According to American diplomatic records, Cooke was summoned before a committee of British officials, who investigated the matter and charged Cooke with illegal smuggling of antiquities.[136] Cooke made no defense and stated simply that he was a poor man and this act was a desperate measure to raise money. The committee of British officials recommended to the British high commissioner that Cooke be expelled from the country. Three days later he left Iraq. The Iraqi papers covered his departure extensively. This episode confirmed what they had long suspected—that the Westerners were plundering their country. Al-Husri recounted a parliamentary debate during this affair which demanded that funds be made available to increase the Iraqi governmental supervision of the foreign archaeological missions (Bell's law and the foreign directors of antiquities were clearly insufficient).[137] Perhaps because of this affair, the parliamentary education committee recommended that same year that archaeology be offered in Iraqi high schools and that the Museum be expanded.[138] This same committee added, "These are the treasures which the grandfathers left as a bequest to their grandsons, to serve as evidence of their brilliant civilization."[139] Iraqi political and educational leaders were starting to regard the didactic value of their antiquities. The Cooke affair, therefore, highlighted the neglected field of archaeology and forced the Iraqi leaders to address the issue of their antiquities. Yet, for the time being, this discussion was confined primarily within the halls of parliament. No drastic developments in general archaeological legislation or in the school curriculum occurred until several years later (to be discussed in Chapter 5).

The British in Iraq, however, were less worried, for the time being at least, about the ethical aspects of the Cooke affair. Rather, they were more concerned how this episode could damage their standing in the community. Yet this matter did not implicate the British alone. Upon his arrest in Syria, the Iraqi truck driver who carried the parcel for Cooke testified that he had been instructed to hand over the package in Beirut to an American who would call for it. Once he reached Beirut, he was told that the American had called three or four times to inquire whether he had arrived. He testified, furthermore, that upon meeting the American, he told him that the package had been confiscated. He stated that the American's name was Mr. Starr.

R. F. S. Starr was an eminent archaeologist who was the director of the Harvard expedition to Nuzi, which was financed in large part by Harvard's Fogg Art Museum. This expedition had been excavating in Iraq for several years. This mission would be greatly hurt, indeed Harvard's future archaeological pedigree in Iraq, and possibly elsewhere, was at stake, if Starr was connected with the illegal activity. When Sidney Smith, the director of antiquities in Iraq, wrote to the Harvard authorities, they expressed great indignation at the charges and called them "astounding." So great was their exasperation, they claimed, that it had taken them some time to recover sufficiently to answer Smith.[140]

In Harvard's letter to Smith, Starr stated that he had indeed known Cooke for some time and that Cooke had asked him to take a package from Iraq to the States. Starr maintained that he had not asked Cooke about the contents of the package. Yet he admitted that it had occurred to him that the package might contain smuggled antiquities. He quickly added, however, that he had dismissed the idea owing to Cooke's standing in the community. Smith was not satisfied with the explanations offered by Starr and Harvard, and he contacted the American Embassy in Baghdad. The Embassy, however, pointed out that Starr had little to gain from the risk of being involved in such an illicit operation, considering Harvard's continuing projects.[141]

Since he was never implicated in the Iraqi press nor officially mentioned in connection with this affair, Starr returned to Iraq the next season to resume his excavations at Nuzi. He reported in a letter to the director of the Harvard Semitic Museum that Sidney Smith did not view him particularly favorably and mentioned that Starr's name was unofficially associated with the Cooke affair.[142] Starr indicated during an interview with the American Consulate that he had been involved with Cooke in smuggling out the antiquities. Starr maintained, however, that he had merely been acting as an intermediary, since the ultimate recipient of the package was someone else. When the American consul asked why Starr had not contacted the authorities in Baghdad once it was discovered that the package contained smuggled goods, Starr replied that Cooke had been a very good friend and had been of great assistance not only to his expedition but to other American archaeologists. He, therefore, had hoped that if the authorities at Baghdad were not reminded of this matter they might allow it to drop. Starr also stated that he did not think that his role in this matter would become known, since he had received a promise from the Iraqi driver not to mention his name.[143]

Although the British authorities investigated the matter, they did not pursue it further, and Starr was allowed to proceed with his excavations. While it was being investigated, the *Baghdad Times* printed a list of archaeological expeditions currently working in Iraq. It mentioned the Harvard expedition but stated that it was uncertain who the director of the expedition was.[144] Shortly afterward, Richard Starr wrote a letter to the editor in which he stated, "I am not aware that there is any 'uncertainty' as to who the Director of the Harvard-Bagdad [sic] School Expedition is. Most Sincerely yours, Richard F. S. Starr, Director. Harvard-Bagdad School Expedition."[145] Although Smith and other British officials had considered not allowing Starr to lead the archaeological mission, in view of the press that the Cooke expulsion had received, it is likely that they felt it was in their own best interest to drop the matter.

Interestingly, Starr mentioned to the American consul that although Smith was not pleased with the situation, he remarked that if Starr was permitted to resume charge of the expedition it would solely be on monetary grounds. Smith was not alluding to possible bribes, but rather to the fact that Harvard had ample funds available to spend in Iraq, and "it would not be politic to offend that institution."[146] The British and the Americans were able to do some damage control over the Cooke affair, and no immediate effects of this scandal were felt. As will be discussed in Chapter 5, however, this episode became critical when the Iraqi government wanted to review the nation's archaeological legislation and introduce laws that limited exports of antiquities.

In 1931, Smith stepped down as director of antiquities, to be succeeded by Julius Jordan of Germany. Jordan steered the department through the last years of the Mandate. Prior to Jordan's assuming the position, C. J. Edmonds served as interim director for several months. The lack of checks and balances in Bell's law became even more evident with Jordan's appointment. Jordan served not only as director of antiquities, but also, as mentioned earlier, was the head of the German excavation team at Warka. Such a blatant conflict of interest reveals the potential number of loopholes in Bell's legislation, which suggests it was designed primarily for the benefit of archaeologists.

The years of Mandate Iraq were significant from an archaeological perspective. It was still primarily a Western choice which sites should be excavated, which artifacts were to remain in the country, and how the museum should be organized and displayed. These years were also a time of considerable progress from a scientific point of view, since a remarkable degree of new discoveries were established in this period. As previously stated, Mandate Iraq offered Western archaeologists ideal working conditions, since they were able to work under extremely favorable administrative and political conditions. They were also able to capitalize on this golden opportunity, since their science had progressed to such a level that long-running, thorough excavations were now the norm. Archaeologists also started paying increasing attention to their methods and publishing their results in order to accumulate greater knowledge on a regular basis. Archaeology was no longer solely concerned with acquiring more and more precious objects. Although that still remained an important component, the competition to find new peoples, cultures, and civilization became just as fierce.

But with the end of the Mandate, the Iraqis took archaeological matters increasingly into their own hands. From the British, they inherited institutions and legislation that were not particularly appealing to them. And as with any inheritance, they were able to do with it what they wanted and not necessarily what those who had bestowed it on them had wished. In particular, through the increasing influence of Sati' al-Husri and like-minded Iraqis, archaeology no longer operated as a foreign affair, but instead became a central component in the educational system and culture at large. Through al-Husri new trends emerged in Iraqi archaeology. Instead of maintaining an overarching emphasis on a non-Semitic pre-Islamic history, al-Husri would drive the discipline to stress the Semitic, Islamic history of Iraq. The end of the Mandate thus marked a new chapter in the history of archaeology in Iraq. No longer would Western institutions and archaeologists have such unbridled access to Iraqi archaeological sites. Instead, they found themselves subject to Iraqi laws and decisions made according to rules created on Iraqi terms—as was fit for the fully independent nation.

5

INDEPENDENT
NATION—INDEPENDENT
ARCHAEOLOGY (1932–1941)

The future of archaeology in Iraq is also extremely doubtful, and although the existing law is likely to continue in force and to be administered in the same spirit as in the past for another two years, there is strong probability that by that time the nationalist element in politics will insist on a change such as would make excavation in Iraq unprofitable from a Museum point of view; it seems advisable therefore to make hay while the sun shines.

British archaeologist Leonard Woolley, May 1932

May we throw a glance at our small museum and compare its contents with the objects unearthed in this country which have found their way into museums which have been sending expeditions into this country and find out whether our share has been a fair one or otherwise?

Editorial, *Sawt al-ʿIraq*, February 18, 1933

The 1920s had witnessed considerable changes in the Iraqi political landscape and significant institution-building. At the same time, a nascent Iraqi identity was in the early stages of its development. The end of the Mandate era, though, foreshadowed a time of political independence that would place a greater responsibility on Iraqi politicians. In the 1930s, archaeology increasingly entered the Iraqi political stage, and it was at this point that antiquities started to play a more significant role in Iraqi cultural life. The paradigmatic nationalism that would subsequently characterize Iraq had its roots in this decade—a time when Iraq was still forging a unified vision of itself and its political community.

In October 1932 Iraq was admitted to membership in the League of Nations as an independent country. At the same time, the League passed a resolution terminating the Mandate. Iraq was thereby officially raised from dependency to full-fledged international status. In practical terms, however, this new status did not necessarily entail complete independence. Britain still kept its military air bases in Iraq intact, and the British required that Iraq consult them in most significant matters of foreign policy. As historian Majid Khadduri points out, Iraq's official status was in fact the culmination of protracted negotiations between Iraq and Britain and "only one act in a larger movement of the challenge of Arab nationalism to European imperialism."[1] For the last years of Mandate Iraq, this act had already, to some extent, taken place in archaeology. During the years of independent Iraq, antiquities would likewise be a factor in the assertion of Iraqi independence and the continuing battle for fuller control of Iraqi resources. Eventually this led to an independent archaeology, in which Iraqis made all the most important decisions.

In the 1920s, Iraq had undergone an impressive state-building process in which it built, basically from scratch, some of the more obvious concomitants of a modern nation-state such as a nationwide school system and a national army. Accompanying this concrete institutional and political process was also an emotional and psychological development, perhaps not so explicit and systematic, in which the Iraqis, and in particular Iraqi politicians, discovered the limits of their own existence and their integral ties to one another. An active sense of belonging was emerging—to the new state and to its land. Within this attachment to the land also came a link to its history.

The perception of a common culture and common past is one way of learning that one is part of a community. The existence and awareness of a common heritage can make a powerful contribution to one's consciousness of the relationship between self and community. The very power of art and archaeological artifacts lies in their ability to use symbols and imagery to provide a sense of belonging to a group or community, a fundamental element of patriotism. In Iraq, in the course of this self-discovery, physical historical artifacts helped define who Iraqis were, and who they had been. These antiquities increasingly entered the political discourse. This sense of belonging to the past, developed during a restless and chaotic era immediately following independence, also tested the very foundation of the Iraqi state.

The achievement of independence infused a certain degree of radicalization into Iraq politics at a time many sources of authority were challenged and questioned. As historian Hanna Batatu has demonstrated, the predominately Sunni character of the government had always rendered it a usurpation in the eyes of the Shi'i majority and turned "popular enmity into an act of faith."[2] In fact, Batatu contends that in the first half of the twentieth century, "opposition to government became a matter of instinct" for the Iraqis.[3]

Yet by the early 1930s these feelings were starting to channel themselves into new, concrete, institutional forms. These years saw the emergence of organized labor in Iraq and the establishment of new political parties, such as the Iraqi Communist Party, which were determined to alter the political and cultural status quo.[4] At the same time, a prolonged debate ensued concerning the general design and structure of Iraq's domestic and foreign policies. In particular, Iraqi politicians did not agree to what extent the British presence should be maintained in the country.

This disagreement caused a polarization amongst the leading politicians, such as, on the one hand, the pro-British Nuri al-Said and Ja'far al-'Askari, and, on the other, politicians who questioned the need to cooperate further with the British, such as Yasin al-Hashimi and Rashid 'Ali al-Gaylani. The former favored a pragmatic cooperation with the British in economic and military affairs, whereas the latter rejected any such cooperation, which they believed would hinder Iraqi independence.[5]

This confrontation became a paradigm of sorts for Iraqi politics for the next thirty years,[6] and was compounded by the complicated issues concerning feudal relations within the tribal structure and the land tenure system. However, as we shall see, this confrontational paradigm does not easily apply to the politics of archaeology during the same period. In archaeology, the general approach favored noncooperation and assertion of Iraqi dominion over archaeological matters, rather than reliance on British or foreign advice. Therefore, in archaeological matters there was more agreement, at least in substance, among the Iraqi politicians that Iraq should take a more nationalist and proprietary approach in its dealings with foreign archaeologists than in other political, cultural, and economic matters. This was because of the inherent structure of the archaeological enterprise— it was a discrete sphere in which the British and other foreign archaeologists could more easily be challenged—and because the antiquities themselves were increasingly emerging as important objects, emotionally, politically, and pedagogically, for the politicians and the nation at large.

The Iraqi claim for greater independence in archaeological matters occurred during unusually tumultuous domestic political times. Internal divisions in Iraqi politics were further exacerbated in September 1933, when King Faysal died, only one year into Iraqi independence. Faysal had taken some interest in archaeological matters, but was generally willing to allow the British to handle that portfolio. Faysal was succeeded by his son, Ghazi, a young and inexperienced politician, who had received his education at military colleges in England. Ghazi did not show an inclination toward history and archaeology similar to his father's and was more interested in building up a modern army. Although the transition of leadership was smooth, it created nevertheless a political vacuum that the army and new political factions, such as the political party al-Ikha al-Watani, were ever so eager to fill. The laws and governmental institutions of the Iraqi state, including the Antiquities Law and the Department of Antiquities, were therefore put to a test as never before.

The gradual withdrawal of the British political presence and advisers brought Iraqi politicians face-to-face with a variety of internal problems that they had theretofore avoided and consequently had not sufficiently solved,[7] often simply blaming outsiders such as the British. But once independent, they could not so easily blame someone else. This situation was particularly difficult when the newly independent government was faced with the task of reconciling some of the serious concerns of the numerous ethnic and religious minorities of Iraq and the lingering tensions among the tribes and other rural communities.

The political tension came to the forefront, for example, in 1933, when the Assyrian community, which adhered to the Nestorian Christian Church and traced its lineage to the Assyrian Empire, attempted to capitalize on the perceived political vacuum by making claims of political autonomy. During the Mandate years, the British had afforded special protection to the Christian Assyrian population, particularly by relying on Assyrian levies in military affairs. Upon Iraqi independence, the fledgling Iraqi army became responsible for internal defense. The army resented the levies and considered them to be a threat to Iraqi security, since they were believed to be an entity controlled by the British.[8] When the Assyrians started making public and strident demands for autonomy, the Iraqi army, under the command of Bakr Sidqi, resisted these claims, and violent fighting ensued. As a result, several hundred Assyrians were killed, and their villages were plundered. This affair attracted worldwide attention, and questions were raised at the League of Nations about Iraq's capacity for self-government.

Most Iraqis, however, strongly supported the government's actions.[9] The Assyrians were perceived as traitors who had to be put in their rightful place. One important outcome of this affair was that it brought the army into national and political prominence. It introduced the idea that the military can be used to alleviate tensions and solve political problems in a certain manner.[10] Furthermore, this episode, as explained below, also occurred at a critical time in archaeological matters, as far as Western archaeologists were concerned.

In addition to the Assyrian affair, the 1930s also witnessed numerous tumultuous tribal uprisings and coups d'état. In 1936, for example, a military coup led by Bakr Sidqi installed a new administration, taken from the Jama'at al-Ahali party, under the leadership of Hikmat Suleyman. This alliance proved short-lived, and in 1937 Sidqi was assassinated by a group of his own officers. Yet his death did not bring an end to military intervention in politics. Instead, Sidqi laid down a pattern for a succession of military governments.

For the next few years, a half dozen military coups kept the country in a state of military turmoil, culminating in the 1941 coup led by the pro-German Rashid 'Ali al-Gaylani. However, Gaylani's government quickly collapsed, because the British army invaded and occupied Iraq and ousted Gaylani. The years between 1941 and 1958 were in great contrast to the dizzying 1930s, because they were characterized by relative calm and prosperity, at least for a certain segment of the population that benefited from the increasing oil production and more favorable oil prices. Yet a 1958 revolution brought this era to a dramatic halt.

Despite the uproarious nature of Iraqi politics in the 1930s, the various governments were able to make some progress in asserting their control over the country. In particular, systematic efforts were made to gain governmental command over the nation's natural resources. During the 1920s various agricultural goods, such as grain and dates, were the main export items. By 1934, however, oil had become one of the most important export commodities.[11] Yet the government had very little control over either oil production or prices, which were both determined by the Iraq Petroleum Company, an organization that was Iraqi in name only. This company was developed and controlled by international capital. Its revenue and organization were dictated by a 1925 international agreement among the French, Dutch, British, and Americans that explicitly formulated the company's structure and its relationship with Iraq. It was not until the 1950s that Iraq was able to renegotiate a new oil agreement, which granted the Iraqis half of the earned profits as well as higher royalties.[12]

The Iraqi politicians actually had considerable leverage in agricultural matters, in contrast to oil production. In the 1920s through to the 1940s, agriculture was the main economic preoccupation of the Iraqi government, involving the restructuring of irrigation projects and landholding in order to strengthen and build up the Iraqi economy. This led to the Iraqi politicians making certain decisions to ensure that these developments would benefit primarily themselves and their families. As several studies have demonstrated, most convincingly that of Batatu, the policies regarding the control of agriculture and its resources favored those tribal leaders who supported the government. The Iraqi parliament passed a series of laws under which arable lands were turned into freehold tenures, most of which went to the big landholders in the region. One outcome of these policies, among others, was a formidable concentration of landholdings. By 1958, two-thirds of the total agricultural land was held by only 2 percent of the landowning class.[13] The complex restructuring of landholding in the countryside and building of extensive irrigation projects created social and economic tensions in rural areas and a massive influx of population into urban areas. The political landscape of Iraq was drastically changing, and that transformation may have contributed to the violent revolution in 1958 that overthrew the Hashemite monarchy.

TURBULENT TIMES—
TURBULENT ARCHAEOLOGY

The new political status of Iraq in 1932 did not immediately bring changes to archaeology. In the first season in independent Iraq it was business as usual, with the number of excavations similar to earlier years. During the 1932–1933 season the following missions undertook excavations in Iraq:

(1) **at Uruk (Warka), Notgemeinschaft der Deutschen Wissenschaft (director, Nöldecke);**

(2) at Eshunna (Tell Asmar), Khafaji & Khorsabad (Dur
    Sharrukin); Chicago's Oriental Institute (director, Frankfort);
(3) at Tell Billa & Tepe Gawra, Penn and ASOR, Baghdad
    (director, Bache);
(4) at Ur, Penn and BM (director, Woolley);
(5) at Kish, Oxford and Chicago's Field Museum
    (director, Watelin);
(6) at Lagash (Tello), Louvre (director, Parrot);
(7) at Arpachiyah, BSAI (director, Mallowan).[14]

However, this status quo would soon be challenged.

In the wake of Iraqi independence, several Iraqi newspapers started an aggressive campaign concerning the state of archaeology in the country. The tone and direction of this discussion were unanimous and unequivocal: Iraq had been robbed and plundered by Western archaeologists; the government should take concrete measures to remedy that situation immediately.

An editorial in the newspaper *Sawt al-ʿIraq* (*The Voice of Iraq*) on February 18, 1933, exemplified this discussion. It called upon the government to take efficient steps for the protection and supervision of ancient sites where foreign archaeological missions were undertaking excavations.[15] It also urged the government to follow more carefully the division of archaeological finds between the government and the foreign missions, stating, "May we throw a glance at our small museum and compare its contents with the objects unearthed in this country which have found their way into the museums which have been sending excavation missions into this country and find out whether our share has been a fair one or otherwise?"[16] The editorial continued by bringing up the Cooke incident (see Chapter 4), about which it stated that the incident "opened their [the Iraqis] eyes and made them more watchful over the valuable ancient heritage of Iraq." Finally it urged the government to train more Iraqis in archaeology in order to take "precautions over this vital matter similar to the precautions adopted by the governments of Iran and Turkey, or at least those taken by Egypt."[17]

Several months later, a detailed and well-argued anonymous article in the newspaper *al-Ahali* (*The People*) also addressed the issue of archaeology.[18] That newspaper was the voice of the Jamaʿat al-Ahali, a political party that had been founded by a group of Iraqi students at the American University of Beirut in the late 1920s. The leaders of this group, such as Muhammad Hadid and 'Abd al-Fattah Ibrahim, had all vigorously opposed the government during the Mandate.[19] When the Jama'at al-Ahali started publishing *al-Ahali* in 1932, it soon became a well-known and popular forum for progressive, liberal ideas that stressed the total political and economic independence of Iraq and advocated social reformism and Iraqi uniqueness and nationalism (as opposed to pan-Arabism).[20]

The article in *al-Ahali* began by quoting an anonymous government official from the early 1920s, who stated, "Let them [i.e., the foreigners] take these images, for they are of use to none but idol-worshippers."[21] The author of the article stated that this apathetic view was typical for Iraqi politicians and displayed their "ignorance of the material and historical value of these antiquities."[22] This position, the author maintained, was in stark contrast to that of the rest of the world because "all the world's great museums and savants are deeply interested in *our* treasures"[23] (emphasis added). That the Iraqis easily used possessive pronouns when discussing the antiquities, thereby assuming and stressing that historical artifacts were restricted to the sovereign nation in which they were found, indicates the direction of the discourse. This suggests that the prevailing Iraqi view was that the antiquities might have universal appeal and relevance, but that they should be regarded in the same light as other resources discovered within the political borders of Iraq and therefore the property of Iraq.

The author then proceeds to analyze the 1924 antiquities legislation, which he associates with the "misguided person" Gertrude Bell, maintaining that it was designed to "provide facilities for scientific missions, to benefit museums connected therewith and to give opportunities to dealers and others for trading in antiquities rather than to secure any advantage for this country."[24] Instead of legislation that was designed to benefit the excavators and their institutions, as was presently the case, the author recommended new legislation that would protect the interests of the Iraqi government and people. Because a "kingdom like Iraq must regard its antiquities as among its most important assets," it was imperative that every antique should be regarded as the property of the Iraq Museum. The author argued, furthermore, that it did no harm to science if the excavator studied the object where he found it, and made pictures or models of the object. Science did not require the actual possession of the antiquities. Therefore, the original should remain the property of the museums of the country.[25]

Continuing his criticism in another article in *al-Ahali* the next day, the author focused his attention on the Iraq Museum. He was particularly critical of the Cooke episode, in which Cooke "trafficked in antiquities secretly with dealers and thieves and was well versed in the art of smuggling. It is painful that we do not know for certain what precious objects from the Iraq Museum were lost during the administration of this person, who for a long period abused his position."[26] Because of disadvantageous legislation, the Iraq Museum "contains nothing comparable to what was brought to light in past times, or what is discovered now by archaeological missions."[27] The author also brought up the issue of the German antiquities that were left behind at Babylon and, for the first time in the Iraqi press, raised the question of the Samarra antiquities, "which were sent to the museums of London for examination on the understanding that they would return later to the Iraq Museum. So far they have not returned. Has the Government surrendered its claim to them?"[28]

The author concluded that the current Antiquities Law should be abolished and a new act implemented that would repudiate the principle of sharing antiquities with archaeological missions, as well as prohibit the trading and export of antiquities.[29] Finally, the author admits that "the Iraqi people have to share the blame with the Government for the neglect of their antiquities but we feel sure that the enlightened section of the public will in the future become aware of this shortcoming."[30]

These discussions in the Iraqi press may have influenced actions by Julius Jordan, the director of antiquities. In order to be sensitive to the criticism in the press, in the upcoming division of finds with the British archaeologist Max Mallowan, Jordan insisted that Mallowan bring his finds from Tell Arpachiyah (mainly pottery vessels and fragments) to Baghdad, where the division would take place (all previous divisions in Iraq had occurred on the excavation site itself).[31] Jordan had actually carried out the division of most of the other foreign expeditions except Mallowan's that year.[32] But before he carried out the division with Mallowan, Jordan received new instructions from the Iraqi minister of education, 'Abbas Mahdi, that stipulated that the director of antiquities (Jordan) was in all future divisions to allot to the excavators only duplicates of objects already taken for the Iraq Museum; all unique objects were to stay in Iraq.[33] However, Jordan believed that these instructions did not supersede the antiquities legislation itself, which called for the excavator receiving "as far as possible . . . a representative share" (Article 22).

In most divisions in Iraq from 1921 onward, Article 22 typically meant a fifty-fifty division—although the law did not necessarily specify that half of the finds would be "representative." Obviously, Mahdi now felt that duplicate items were "representative" and that Iraq should receive all unique items. However, on May 24 and 25, Jordan conducted the Arpachiyah division in Baghdad following roughly the standard practice, and thereby, to some extent, ignoring the education minister's instructions. Jordan stated, however, that he had the interests of Iraq at heart, since he had made "a very 'strong' division, reserving all the best finds for Iraq."[34] At the end of the division, and as he was entitled to under Article 23 of the antiquities legislation, Mallowan made arrangements with a shipping company to transport his share of the finds out of the country.[35]

The next day, however, Mahdi, the Iraqi minister of education, demanded to see all the antiquities that had been allotted to Mallowan in order to ascertain whether Mallowan had only received "duplicates." Jordan refused this request, stating that it was a breach of standard practice and that he (Jordan) was complying with the law by allowing Mallowan to export his share of antiquities. Perhaps because of Jordan's actions, or lack thereof, the next day *Al-Ahali* published a vehement criticism of Jordan and severely repudiated his authority.[36] Finding himself in a difficult position, Jordan asked Mallowan to furnish an Arabic translation of the division list. He further stated that pending the minister's decision, Jordan could not issue an export permit for Mallowan's share, which Mallowan was expecting. Jordan was called before the minister and was met with the direct question "Did you or did you not make the division in accordance with the Minister's instructions?"[37] It was added that if he was unable to answer the question in the affirmative a new division would have to take place. Faced with such a categorical demand, Jordan defended himself by stating that it was impossible to execute the minister's demands, since the objects found at Tell Arpachiyah consisted almost entirely of painted pottery.[38] Because the hand painter never repeated himself exactly, Jordan had tried to pair off the objects and claimed that he had kept the better examples for Iraq.[39] Although Jordan was not able to get the export permit for Mallowan, he was able to stall the issue by keeping Mallowan's share at the national museum until the matter was resolved.

These actions in Iraq shocked the archaeological community in the West. The Arpachiyah division and the refusal to grant the export permit were clearly a violation of Iraq's own law and a breach of the common practice that had been established in Iraq. Western archaeologists had become accustomed to predictability and stability in Iraqi archaeology. Owing to this favorable situation, as discussed in Chapter 4, Western archaeological missions to Iraq had flourished. Now, for the first time since the establishment of Iraq, Iraqi politicians had interfered overtly and seemingly randomly in the division between the Iraq Museum and the excavator, a process that theretofore had been a routine archaeological matter.

This inhibiting action by Iraqi politicians indicated that the fruitful status quo could soon come to an end. As a British administration annual report stated, "Archaeology unfortunately came into politics in the course of the year."[40] The Western diplomatic community in Iraq speculated that the Iraqi politicians were attempting to emulate Egyptian politicians "who[,] some years ago, made a similar move against foreign archaeological expeditions in Egypt and who . . . have been successful in keeping most of the finds in that country."[41] The altered situation in Iraq brought a drastic response from the archaeological establishment in Europe and the United States.

Sir George Hill, the director of the BM, which had sponsored Mallowan's expedition in cooperation with the BSAI, coordinated a large-scale public relations effort in the British press in addition to applying pressure via diplomatic channels. By deploying such public pressure, both official and unofficial, Hill sought to convince the Iraqi government to reverse the course of events. He wrote numerous letters to the FO and to Sir Francis Humphrys, the British ambassador in Iraq, pleading with them to protest these violations of Iraqi law.[42] He also contacted all leading archaeologists and institutions with projects, past or present, in Iraq in order to coordinate their reaction and to present a unified front in the fight for any possible changes in Iraqi archaeology.

It was clear to Hill and other observers of the Mallowan episode that this was a purposeful political action aimed at embarrassing and weakening Jordan and thus by extension the Western archaeological community. As Woolley stated in a conversation with the FO, "The Minister of Education wants to elbow out the German Director of Antiquities in favour of his own creatures. He has acted illegally in this case endeavouring to upset the Director's decision."[43]

Over the course of the summer, and prior to sending archaeologi-cal missions to Iraq for the new season, the interested parties tried to evaluate the political climate and to receive some sort of assurance that the law would be upheld in the coming season.[44] Mallowan received a letter from Jordan in August informing him that the matter was still pending because the minister of education had objected to the division and wanted a special declaration that the principles that Jordan fol-lowed would correspond to "expert evidence recently given by the Ministry of Justice."[45] Jordan, who obviously was feeling remorse over these events, stated, "You may imagine how deeply I regret the unpleas-ant delay which affects your work and science likewise."[46]

The BM responded to Jordan by arguing that it was unfair discrim-ination that the Arpachiyah expedition was singled out to follow new principles based on "expert evidence."[47] The museum admitted that the Iraqi government was "perfectly justified in establishing a new interpre-tation in accordance with the advice of its Law officers," but pointed out that such advice should be "published and made clear to future excava-tors and [that] they cannot abrogate agreements already made on the basis of the old interpretation."[48]

Meanwhile, the British Embassy in Baghdad also became involved in this affair, stating in a letter to the FO that 'Abbas Mahdi, the minis-ter of education, who "is an obscurantist Shiah, very ill-disposed towards foreigners and us in particular," was planning to draft a new Antiquities Law.[49] It had seen a copy of his proposal and stated that it was "so one-sided and rabidly nationalistic that if passed in its present form no first class expedition would consent to work in Iraq."[50] The British Embassy agreed with Jordan in not seeing any reason to implement a new law, since the existing law had "worked well and fairly."[51] The only reason for its invalidation would be the "blind desire of a narrow nationalism to hamper foreign enterprise, which, by removing its share of the antiqui-ties discovered, is considered to be destroying a part of the national wealth."[52]

The Embassy also questioned Jordan directly about the Arpachiyah division. Jordan believed that the minister was not disputing the justice of the original division, but simply wished to make personal and politi-cal capital by bending the foreign director of antiquities to his will. In his conversation with the British Embassy, Jordan was pessimistic about the prospects of Iraqi archaeology because he long since had despaired of teaching any Iraqi to acquire "the outlook and enthusiasm of a true archaeologist; the only standard by which a discovery was judged in Iraq was that of cash value."[53]

The events in Iraq solidified the archaeological community around Hill in order to present a united front vis-à-vis the Iraqi government.[54] Toward the end of the summer, Jordan wrote a letter to Mallowan stating that the prevailing idea within the Iraqi government was not to renew excavation permits. This was because the Iraqi government felt there were not sufficient Iraqi officials fit for superintending the expeditions and also, interestingly, that there was no place for keeping more antiquities in the Iraq Museum.[55] Jordan, therefore, advised Mallowan and other archaeologists not to depart for Iraq until the new law had been passed.

Jordan indicated, furthermore, that the premise of the proposed law was similar to what had guided the minister's prior instructions to Jordan regarding the Arpachiyah division, namely, that the excavator would receive only duplicates of objects he found. This diminishing prospect was indeed troubling for the expeditions because it would entail a considerable decrease in material that they would be allowed to export from Iraq.

Iraqi archaeology seemed to be at a crossroads. It was not clear to Western archaeologists if they would, indeed, have any options in Iraq. The form this new wave of Iraqi interest would take was ambiguous and therefore subject to much speculation and even paranoia. It seemed imperative to act quickly and forcefully, and to attempt to sway the Iraqi government away from implementing a more restrictive law, like one that had been introduced in Egypt.

Because they believed that the Iraqis were interested only in the material aspects of archaeology, the Western archaeologists decided to present their arguments largely in economic terms. Such arguments were considered to be the most persuasive and best fitted to influence the Iraqi cabinet toward a favorable action. As historian Donald M. Reid has demonstrated, when faced with a comparable situation in Egypt, European and American archaeologists similarly presented their enterprise as one of selfless Western scientists against greedy Egyptian nationalists.[56]

They were not oblivious that such an approach was perhaps degrading the archaeological enterprise. As the American archaeologist James Breasted stated, "It is of course humiliating to Western scientists to present to the Iraqi Government arguments based so exclusively on purely material interests and material advantage. Nevertheless, my experience with Oriental cabinets, made up as they inevitably are of fanatical, nationalistic Orientals, would indicate that any consideration of the interest of science leaves them entirely indifferent."[57]

Hill worked closely with Breasted in the United States to formulate the right argument, and they sent back and forth long telegrams brainstorming over the exact wording of the impending representations.[58] As Hill wrote to the German archaeologist Walter Andrae, "the only effective reason we have for demanding a share of the antiquities from excavations [is] that unless we receive such a share, digs cannot be financed. Iraq will thus suffer material damage."[59] Therefore, the Western archaeologists put all of their energies into proving what positive economic impact Western archaeological expeditions had on the Iraqi economy as well as the adverse effects any change in legislation would have on material life in Iraq.

In the final draft of the memorandum that they planned to send to the British ambassador in Iraq to aid him in his representations to Iraqi politicians, the archaeologists stressed that the "ancient monuments of Iraq are the greatest reason why peoples of Europe and America are interested in the new nation of Iraq. . . . Anything done to hamper archaeological research in Iraq . . . would mean loss to Iraq of a very valuable interest of western peoples . . . and Iraq would not be able to stimulate tourist travel that brings money into Iraq such has long been the experience in Egypt."[60]

At the same time, however, Hill and his colleagues were concerned with disproving that the antiquities had any intrinsic material, as opposed to scientific, value. In addition, they strove to disprove that the 1924 law allowed for the removal from Iraq of valuable objects that formed a part of the national wealth. They maintained that it was a "fallacy that the 'value' of antiquities is intrinsic and can be measured in cash." Although they acknowledged the "cash value antiquities undoubtedly possess because museums in certain countries collect them," they stated that this was "an artificial value with no certain commercial significance." This claim was true because "there are hardly any private collectors of Babylonian antiquities."[61]

They stated, furthermore, that even though gold objects were valuable, it was not "for their intrinsic money value, but because, owing to the durable nature of gold in wet ground, they best preserve examples of good workmanship."[62] Finally, they maintained, "'Unique' applies to an object when it possesses features not otherwise found; many worthless objects are unique. . . . In cash, antiquities in public collection represent continual expenditure, not gain."[63]

In this somewhat twisted presentation, therefore, Hill and his colleagues argue that it was not the antiquity itself, i.e., the object, that brought value or material benefits to the country. Rather, the auxiliary activities surrounding the extraction of antiquities from the ground were more valuable in economic terms for Iraq than the objects that were actually leaving the country.

Therefore, according to the archaeologists, if Iraq passed a new law that materially altered the current legislation, "archaeological expeditions which are financed by foreign museums would not come to the country in the future. The Iraq Museum would no longer be supplied at no cost to itself the fruits of excavations. . . . The richest sites in Iraq would no longer be systematically worked and the *fellahin* [would lose] the regular winter employment which brings them good pay."[64] In this way, Hill and his colleagues were trying to deflect the attention away from the objects that were leaving the country onto what Iraq would lose if archaeological expeditions left the country.

The archaeologists' experience in Iraq may have led them to believe that Iraqis were solely interested in the material aspects and benefits of archaeology. However, their approach to influencing the Iraqi politicians was, in a sense, self-defeating. Because they sensed that the premise of the proposed legislation was to reduce the volume of antiquities leaving Iraq, and attributed this goal to an economic view of the antiquities, they actually fought the legislation on the very terms they were trying to avoid. The Western archaeologists misjudged the emotional and psychological impact that the antiquities had on the politicians and, to a lesser extent, on the general population. Furthermore, they failed to appreciate that this issue was not only bound to archaeology, but was also part of the prevailing Iraqi political climate, which demanded unimpeded access to all of the country's resources, both natural and cultural. And even though, from today's perspective, their views of Iraqis may seem condescending, what is equally striking is that they actually underrated the impact of their own activities in Iraq, believing them to have gone unnoticed, and their possible effects on the culture.

During the 1920s, the Western archaeologists had worked extensively in Iraq. The Iraqi population was becoming more accustomed to large-scale archaeological activities, and was perhaps beginning to sense that the antiquities being unearthed were deemed valuable enough to warrant such large, long-term missions. The archaeologists had been diligent in furthering their cause and educating the Iraqi public by giving public lectures at the museum about their excavations and recent trends in archaeology. Their excavations had considerably bolstered the collections of the Iraq Museum. The Western directors of antiquities, from Bell onward, had always sought to make the Museum more and more accessible to the public by having more tours and more convenient opening hours. The Iraqi newspapers often included small announcements or stories at the beginning of each archaeological season about which archaeologist was digging where. They also published similar announcements when an expedition came to an end.[65] As a result, the Western archaeologists had, directly and indirectly, contributed to a growing interest in ancient history and in the ancient artifacts. At the very least, through their extensive presence in Iraq, they, in a sense, institutionalized archaeology in the Iraqi cultural scene.

Although the collateral economic effects of large-scale archaeological expeditions were not lost on Iraqi politicians, the archaeologists mistook such benefits as being their sole interest. As the discussion in contemporary Iraqi newspapers reveals, the issue was not merely economic, but also one of pride and principle. The perception prevailed that Western archaeologists had in the past plundered the country and were continuing to do so. Therefore, it was natural for an independent country like Iraq to desire to control its property and thereby restrict and restructure activities that were seen to be detrimental.

The Western archaeologists failed to broaden their arguments to include the scientific and historic value of their enterprise. With the advantage of hindsight, it appears that Iraq approached archaeology in such a spirit. For example, the subsequent history of archaeology in Iraq, at least until 1980, indicates that once the Iraqis gained control of their own archaeological matters, they did not degenerate into a "miserable illicit traffic"[66] in antiquities or into the exploitation of "the archaeological treasures of their country in a spirit of true materialism,"[67] as the Western archaeologists predicted would happen if the Iraqis were left to themselves in archaeology.[68] The Western archaeologists in the 1930s did not anticipate that the Iraqis would fully use the systems, institutions, and knowledge that the Western archaeologists had helped to develop. They did not envision that the Iraqis would structure their archaeology, to a large extent, in accordance with the most scientific and professional archaeological standards. The Western archaeologists both underestimated the scientific and intellectual potential of the Iraqis and misjudged the extensive impact that their own activities had had on Iraqi society, which had helped foster a respect and interest in Iraqi ancient history among segments of the population.

LOBBYING AGAINST CHANGES

Resisting any change in the status quo was thus paramount for Western archaeologists and required a multipronged approach. The BM worked closely with the FO on how, or if, to present its arguments to the Iraqi government.[69] As with their dealings concerning archaeology during the British occupation of Iraq (see Chapter 2), the FO did not necessarily buy all of the BM's arguments and viewed the issue more from a strictly legalistic, impartial view. The FO pointed out that the BM did not know exactly the terms of the new law and was merely going on guesswork. It asserted that it was impossible to make official protests merely on suppositions. It also reminded the BM that "Iraq was now an independent country and, in the ultimate resort had the right to enact whatever antiquities legislation she desired,"[70] even though such "modifications may be considered injurious to Iraq's own interests."[71]

The FO viewed the situation comparatively by stating that even if Iraq should pass the law that it seemed to be contemplating, it would not "differ greatly from similar laws in force in other countries, e.g., Egypt, Persia, Syria, Greece."[72] Consequently, the FO doubted whether an official protest was justified. However, it did not discourage the BM from trying to influence the course of events through other channels, such as asking the British ambassador in Iraq to approach his personal contacts in the Iraqi government.

The FO was disappointed when it saw Hill's memo. An internal minute stated that the BM had obviously not followed the FO advice, and "it is clear that we cannot take action at Baghdad exactly as suggested by Hill, who makes no allowance for the fact that Iraq is now an independent country and that preaching is the last way of trying to induce the Iraqi Government to take a sensible line regarding the modifications of the Antiquities Law."[73] The FO officials did not agree with the tone and were not persuaded by the BM's economic arguments.

Upon receiving a memorandum from archaeologists at Oxford University containing their criticism of the possible change in legislation, an FO official wrote in an internal memo, "I am not favorably impressed by the tone of the memorandum—a typically donnish combination of sarcasm and acerbity which would be much resented by the Iraqi Government if they could indeed understand it."[74]

The FO letter to Humphrys, the British ambassador in Iraq, reiterated that the British government was not in a position to make a formal or official protest of the new law. But it did suggest that if the opportunity arose, that he could certainly inform the Iraqi government of the "uneasiness which exists over this matter."[75] The FO suggested pointing out that the law is "most ill-advised from Iraq's point of view." The FO diplomats took a more academic, and perhaps enlightened, approach than the archaeologists by suggesting that this law would "expose Iraq to justified accusations of putting obstacles in the way of the development of science and research."[76] Finally, the FO pointed out that the attitude which the Iraqi government adopted in this matter would "be regarded by many as a test of whether Iraq is really a modern and progressive state."[77]

Humphrys, the British ambassador, brought up the issue of the Arpachiyah division, as well as the possible new legislation, with the prime minister, Rashid 'Ali Gaylani. Gaylani belonged to that camp of Iraqi politicians who generally were less inclined to cooperate with the British. Even though the Assyrian affair, a serious international and domestic crisis facing the Iraqi government, was still raging, Gaylani promised to grant Mallowan at once the permit to export his share.[78] Perhaps it was, in fact, due to the Assyrian affair that Gaylani was more willing to facilitate the ambassador's request. As Breasted astutely noted in a letter to the U.S. State Department, the British representation was "well timed" in view of the Assyrian massacre, and "such personal, unofficial hints have always had great weight in the Near East."[79] More sensitive to Western scrutiny and criticism in the wake of the episode, the Iraqi Council of Ministers shortly thereafter invited Jordan to its session to explain his side of the matter. A week later, it voted to acknowledge Jordan's original division and subsequently granted Mallowan the permit to export.[80] Thus, after much ado, Mallowan and the BM finally received their share.

In a letter to Edgar Bonham-Carter, the president of BSAI, Humphrys explained that Rashid 'Ali Gaylani had come to visit him at the Embassy, at which time Gaylani stated that he had had great difficulty in inducing the Council of Ministers to pass a resolution to grant Mallowan the necessary permit. He stated that the difficulty was entirely due to the minister of education ('Abbas Mahdi), "an ignorant and bigoted Shia who threatened to resign."[81] Rashid 'Ali claimed that Mahdi was responsible for this whole business and was drafting a new antiquities law. He stated, further, that Mahdi was very unpopular with his colleagues and would shortly be dismissed if he did not resign. Gaylani maintained that if the minister were not a Shi'i, he would have been dismissed a long time ago. King Ghazi was hesitant to excite Shi'i resentment and therefore was proceeding with caution in this matter.[82]

Although 'Abbas Mahdi was seemingly acting alone in this particular matter, there appeared to be a widespread interest among governmental officials in adopting new archaeological legislation. Even though Gaylani generally preferred to diminish British influence in the country, he recognized that the law had not been followed at Arpachiyah. At the end of October 1933, Humphrys sent a memorandum to Gaylani, listing his concerns about possible changes in the archaeological legislation. Humphrys's letter to Gaylani basically followed word for word the arguments that he received from Hill. Humphrys's main emphasis, however, was to point out how detrimental it would be to the Iraqi economy to place restrictions on archaeological expeditions.[83] Gaylani promised to look into the matter and consult with Humphrys in the future.[84] Shortly thereafter, Humphrys received reassurances from the Iraqi government that any foreign missions that came to Iraq during the present season would work under the old Antiquities Law and "will not be obstructed in any way."[85]

Although they received top-level reassurances, many Western archaeologists decided not to venture to Iraq for the 1933–1934 season. The archaeologists' misgivings may have been compounded by the turmoil in the financial markets and the economic depression that most Western societies were experiencing, which dried up funds for expeditions. Whether it was the worldwide economic depression or Iraq's unstable domestic political situation, the number of expeditions declined from eight the year before to three.[86] Still bitter from his experience in Iraq the year before, Mallowan decided to stay in England and "write up the results of last season's work."[87] Woolley, on the other hand, was determined to return to Ur in order to continue his work there.

The 1933–1934 season, however, did not proceed entirely as planned. As Woolley wrote after the division, "The Director of Antiquities [Jordan] was more exacting than last season and far more so than previous holders of that office had been, and in every category of objects selected the best for Baghdad."[88] Once Woolley and Jordan had conducted the division, however, Woolley's application to export the antiquities was put on hold.[89] It seemed that the Arpachiyah affair was about to repeat itself. This time, however, Woolley was quick to react, "with such vigour,"[90] as a British memorandum described it, that Humphrys brought up the issue the next day with King Ghazi, stating that "the good name of Iraq was at stake in this matter."[91] His intervention was effective, because the next day Woolley received the export permit. Yet this minor episode served as a subtle reminder that archaeology was becoming more and more unpredictable, generating further uneasiness amongst the Western archaeological community.

THE POTENTIAL NEW ANTIQUITIES LEGISLATION

Western archaeologists' experience from the 1934 season only confirmed their belief that significant changes were around the corner in Iraqi archaeology. In Woolley's and Humphrys's conversations with leading Iraqi political leaders that year, it was made clear to them that a new draft of the Antiquities Law was being prepared for the upcoming parliamentary session.[92] That summer, Jordan sent Mallowan and Hill copies of the new proposal that had been scheduled to come before the Iraqi parliament in November 1934 so that it would be in force during the 1934–1935 season.[93]

The legislative changes that were of most concern to the Western archaeologists were the articles concerning the division of finds. The new draft stated that all unique objects would be assigned to the Iraq Museum. Expeditions would receive half of whatever was left of other objects. Only those objects that are "duplicate, i.e., objects of the same kind and type and of the same material historic and artistic value" would be allotted to the excavator.[94] The proposal was also explicit concerning objects of silver and gold, stating that they "may be allotted to the excavator only by special permit."[95] It stated, furthermore, that the division should take place in the presence of a committee of three people, the director of antiquities and two others. Should a disagreement arise among the members of this committee, the minister of education would have the final say.[96]

This proposal confirmed what Western archaeologists had feared; their potential share would be drastically reduced under the new legislation. They once again wrote frantic letters back and forth to each other discussing how to combat the proposed changes. Hill of the BM was particularly disturbed by the clause concerning gold and silver, which only seemed to confirm his suspicions that Iraqis had a treasure-hunt mentality concerning archaeology. He, therefore, suggested protesting that clause on the grounds that "the reservation of gold and silver objects is unscientific, since they have no more value, archaeologically, than objects in other materials."[97] However, Breasted warned Hill that he was battling windmills because "it is next to impossible to induce the average oriental to believe that Western archaeologists are present in their country for any other purpose than to dig for gold and silver."[98] Breasted therefore recommended keeping in mind the practical politics of the situation. Even though the "Iraq attitude on this point is barbarous . . . it would strengthen our position substantially if we could all agree that we are not making any claims for objects of gold."[99]

A group of Oxford professors stated that the section referring to articles of gold and silver "leads to the inevitable inference that the Iraq Government is solely interested in the bullion value of the objects."[100] The Oxford dons complained further of the proposed law's "entire lack of appreciation of scientific research displayed by these proposals which are conceived in so narrow a spirit of unintelligent nationalism that the Government is inevitably laying up for itself a legacy of universal condemnation from the learned world."[101]

Hill, once again in an attempt to convince British government officials to directly intervene in this matter, wrote a letter to the FO stating that the new law was "undesirable and obscurantist," pointing out that since 1922 the BM alone had expended over £65,000 sterling on expeditions in Iraq. Hill concluded that "this may furnish in a form intelligible to the Iraqi authorities some indication of the result of the attitude which they are adopting towards scientific exploration."[102]

And once again, the FO was not convinced by the BM's letter. Commenting on the BM's letter in internal memos, one FO official called it a "stupid letter"; another felt that the BM was "flogging a dead horse." The FO officials stated that the Iraqi government, like "other oriental governments, prefer[s] to decide for [itself] what is in [its] interest" and that archaeologists will have to learn that "in dealing with Oriental countries in their present state of development . . . nothing will be gained by adopting the irritating and condescending attitude that they are, from purely altruistic motives, conferring a benefit on the country, concerned by carrying out work which that the country is itself able neither to perform nor to appreciate."[103] They suggested that "at some stage we may have to make this clear as tactfully as possible to the BM and to Oxford."[104]

Despite the FO reservations, the British Embassy in Iraq wrote a letter to Tawfiq Beg al-Suwaydi, the Iraqi minister of foreign affairs, pointing out that the new law would cause foreign archaeological bodies to cease their activities in Iraq. Picking up on Hill's memorandum, it declared, further, that "foreign archaeological expeditions besides drawing attention to Iraq and thus adding to her prestige, bring a considerable amount of money into the country."[105]

Because of Iraqi national elections, the parliament did not meet that autumn. Indeed, Iraqi political life was going through a turbulent sequence of cabinet changes. Between October 1933, when the Ikha' coalition cabinet resigned, and early 1935, four different Iraqi cabinets were formed, and all failed to take sufficient control in the country. In August 1934, for example, 'Ali Jawdat formed a new cabinet and announced new elections for the fall. The Ikha', now in opposition to the new government, galvanized its supporters, particularly its tribal followers, to consider extraconstitutional measures to regain power.[106] The tribes, already restless due to a variety of economic and social grievances, especially questions concerning land ownership and settled agriculture, used the opportunity to revolt against the government in various southern provinces. With unrest reigning in the countryside, the Ikha' leaders petitioned King Ghazi to remove the cabinet and install a new cabinet under Ikha' leadership.[107] In March 1935, Ghazi complied with this request, and a new cabinet led by Yasin al-Hashimi was formed. Therefore, during these turbulent and uncertain political times, a new antiquities law did not get a chance to come before the parliament. Western archaeologists, as a result, were told that they could come to Iraq for the 1934–1935 season and work under the original legislation.[108]

In the meantime, the Iraqi government extended Jordan's contract for three more years. Yet instead of his old title "Director of Antiquities,"

Jordan was given the title "Technical Adviser to the Department of Antiquities." This new title did not carry with it any executive powers, because the Iraqi government was contemplating the appointment of an Iraqi director, who would hold the ultimate executive power.[109]

SATI' AL-HUSRI, DIRECTOR OF ANTIQUITIES

I n October 1934 the Iraqi government, then headed by 'Ali Jawdat, announced the appointment of Sati' al-Husri as director of antiquities. This was a historic event because al-Husri was the first Iraqi, albeit a naturalized one, to assume this position. Most other Middle Eastern countries still had a foreigner at the helm of archaeological matters. Even though al-Husri had had some dealings in archaeological matters, such as trying to influence Bell in formulating the antiquities law (see Chapter 3), he had not been actively involved in archaeology prior to his appointment. He had no training in archaeology but had a good educational background and was generally interested in history. As previously stated, he had worked extensively in the Ministry of Education between 1922 and 1927. He then took a position at the Teacher's Training College and had, since 1931, been teaching at the Law School at Baghdad University.[110] So in 1934, al-Husri, the former director general of education, returned to the Ministry of Education as director of a subdivision of that department.

Al-Husri took to his new job with enthusiasm and energy. He was critical of his predecessors and lamented the state of archaeology in his country. Always the educator, al-Husri initiated the publication of guide books and pamphlets on Iraqi antiquities aimed at the general public and sought to educate himself by attending international conferences on archaeology. He vigilantly tried to prevent several ambitious construction projects in Baghdad that would have jeopardized important historical sites. With al-Husri at the helm, and new antiquities legislation on the horizon, the British archaeological community decided not to send any missions to Iraq, ostensibly to protest the state of affairs. However, a British governmental report stated that this absence of British expeditions was more probably due to a lack of funds than anything else.[111] The British ambassador in Iraq called this boycott "idiotic."[112] For the 1934–1935 season there were three expeditions in Iraq, the same number as the year before, but this time two were American and one German.

Breasted, the American archaeologist, was fundamentally opposed to the boycott, though for self-interested reasons. He saw the potential boycott by British archaeological missions as beneficial to his Oriental Institute (OI) because it would allow the OI to fill the void that the boycott was causing. As Breasted explained to a State Department official, most excavations in Iraq had been sponsored by museums, "which operate to be sure with a desire to increase our knowledge and to advance science, but in order to increase their museum collections."[113] Breasted pointed out, however, that the OI was not bound by such considerations. Clarifying his position, Breasted explained that the OI is "to be sure exceedingly desirous of securing new monuments for scientific study and research . . . but the Institute's field work is not conditioned on a division of antiquities."[114] If the division of antiquities should actually be stopped, he believed that the OI would be the only institution in a position to continue its excavation. He emphasized, however, that he did not want this fact to be known to the Iraqi government. He did envision, perhaps only as the folly of wishful thinking, that the Iraqi government might actually be willing "for a time to depend on the excavations of the OI for the enlargement of its National Museum collections."[115]

Although Breasted interpreted the British boycott as having positive implications for his American OI, the British took this boycott seriously. When al-Husri wrote to several Western archaeologists to see if they were interested in contributing to a publication that the Iraq Museum was creating, the British archaeologist Campbell Thompson replied, "I find the attitude [as represented by the new law] at present adopted by the Iraq Museum towards British and other excavations so distasteful, and as a practical excavator so unreasonable, and if I may be allowed to say as one who served as a Captain in the British Army in Mesopotamia for more than three years of active service against the Turks in making Iraq a separate country, so ungrateful, that I must beg to decline the invitation of the Iraq Museum."[116]

The prospects of new, less generous legislation spurred Western archaeologists into some fancy reasoning to defend the old legislation. In a letter to *The Times*, Hill of the BM attempted to justify why the Iraqi legislation should not follow guidelines similar to those of Western European countries or Greece and Turkey. Hill wrote, "A law which denies the excavator a representative reward in the shape of material results of his work may be workable in Greece and Italy, which have gained by their literature such hold on Western civilization that the public are glad to subsidize research in those lands without hoping to see the results exhibited in their Museums." But, Hill maintained, the situation was different for countries "like Egypt and Mesopotamia which have no literary connection with Western civilization so that our interest in them must be fed by the export of their works of art to Western collections. Such export, judiciously regulated, is the best possible advertisement . . . for the country."[117]

Woolley similarly wrote a letter to the editor of *The Times,* published in December 1934, that vehemently criticized the proposed antiquities legislation. He stated that the "twelve years of foreign excavations have given to Baghdad one of the most important museums in the world for the study of Near Eastern antiquities and that because of, not in spite of, permission given to excavators to remove objects which were sometimes unique as well as precious."[118] The Iraqi newspapers and al-Husri were quick to criticize this article. Although Woolley had written with the intention of showing the Iraqis the error of their ways, in actuality, his article had the opposite effect.

Al-Husri gleefully used Woolley's article as an opportunity to give interviews in the Iraqi press where he could criticize Woolley's position and promote the government's position in amending the law. In an interview with the newspaper *al-Bilad,* he pointed out that he had been vehemently opposed to the legislation of 1924 and that Bell was able to place the Antiquities Department in a ministry that was dominated by the British, into which "no native influence could reach . . . and very soon the Directress managed to get that law proclaimed which is now in force."[119] Al-Husri admitted that the law may have suited the former conditions of Iraq, but argued that the present situation was entirely different. He maintained that "Iraq is no longer a land isolated from the civilized world and surrounded by a host of turbulent influences. . . . New communications have brought her amazingly close to the West. . . . We ought therefore to draw up new legislation appropriate to these new conditions."[120]

Another Iraqi newspaper, *al-Alam al-Arabi,* also raised the issue of the Woolley article, agreeing with Woolley that the foreign missions had rendered great service by bringing "*our* treasures to light"[121] (emphasis added). Furthermore, it pointed out that the foreign missions had similarly obtained an enormous reward for their expenditure of labor and capital. However, it declared that "anyone with a sense of justice who visits the great capitals of the West and compares the Iraqi treasures displayed there with those in the Baghdad Museum cannot but exclaim, 'Surely when one eats with a blind man, one should eat fair!'"[122] The writer ended on an positive note, proclaiming that "every patriotic Iraqi fervently hopes for the day when his people will be in a position without outside interference, to bring to light the buried treasures of their land for their own enrichment, both intellectual and economic."[123]

The FO and the British Embassy in Baghdad, which both monitored these events closely, did not feel that Woolley was doing his position any favors by wielding his pen in such a way. The FO called Woolley's correspondence "a mistake" that would only "draw fresh attention to the antiquities law."[124] Humphrys was even more critical, stating that it was "ungracious for Woolley to have a tilt in the Times against the Iraqi government who have always treated him with the greatest kindness and consideration and have loaned to him the whole of the Government share of the antiquities with which to illustrate his book."[125] Humphrys also informed the FO that the Iraqi government was planning on undertaking excavations on its own under the supervision of a foreign archaeologist. Humphrys, obviously frustrated with the antics and demands of the British archaeologists, claimed that this was a good idea because it would "provide a test of the claims of certain foreign institutions to indispensability in regard to Iraqi archaeology. If the Iraqis succeed on their own, so much better for them; if they fail, they may show a better appreciation of the efforts of foreign archaeologists."[126]

Even though legislative changes had been discussed for over a year, by the end of November 1935 the anticipated change in the Antiquities Law was still in its preliminary stages. Given the numerous difficulties and substantive issues facing the Iraqi politicians on other fronts, archaeology was probably not that high on their priority list.

Sir Clark Kerr, the new British ambassador in Iraq, met with Nuri Said, the Iraqi prime minister, in November 1935. During their meeting, Kerr stated, he "concentrated in the main on the points emphasized by Sir George Hill in his letter of July 12, 1934."[127] Hearing those economic arguments again, the pro-Western Said agreed that the proposed law would not be enforced until the next excavation season (1935–1936). He discussed some of the possible new clauses in the law, which were premised on the belief that all antiquities found would be the property of the Iraqi government. Nevertheless, as a reward for their labor, the archaeologists would be allowed to make castings of the antiquities and receive half of the duplicate items. In addition, the archaeologists would receive all antiquities that the Iraqi government could dispense with "in view of the existence of their perfect likes in kind, type, material, workmanship, historical significance and artistic value."[128] Clark Kerr then forwarded to the FO a draft of the new law.

In a meeting that the British Joint Archaeological Committee held to discuss the new law, it declared that it was quite impossible that the new law could be enacted, that it was not worth the Committee's while to examine or comment upon it in detail. It felt that "the only dignified line was to say so to the Iraqis and indicate that the law was unworkable."[129] An FO official attending the meeting pointed out that "however dignified this line might be it would not help either HM ambassador or archaeological interests. If constructive criticism were made, it might be possible to get the law modified in certain particulars."[130] Upon reading these minutes another FO official remarked, "Archaeologists are inclined to be like this and it is for us to guide them on rather more practical lines."[131]

AL-HUSRI'S FIRST DIVISION

The formal status of Iraq as an independent state in the political realm now was becoming translated into archaeology. Bell's legislation had left a great degree of latitude for the director of antiquities to interpret and execute the law. Now that an Iraqi was directing archaeological affairs, the Western archaeological community feared the worst. It watched with great anticipation how al-Husri would conduct his first division, which took place at Tell Asmar, where Henri Frankfort had been conducting excavations on behalf of the OI. On February 19, 1935, Breasted received a brief cable from Frankfort stating: "Seventeen best objects excluded and taken for museum according to letter of existing law rest divided."[132]

Even though Breasted did not have any further information, only the brief telegram from Frankfort, he was quick to jump to the conclusion that the "division is flagrantly unjust." Because this was the first division under al-Husri, Breasted believed that it was imperative that "such an obviously unfair division should not be accepted without action on our part or taken lying down."[133] Breasted's institution was the victim in this case. Therefore he seems to have forgotten, or have reconsidered, his earlier claims that the OI, being a nonmuseum entity, was not specifically interested in the division of finds. Now, having had the tables turned against him, Breasted urged the U.S. Department of State to pressure the Iraqi government. He stated further that all OI excavations would leave Iraq immediately if the division of finds at Tell Asmar were not satisfactorily adjusted.[134] Breasted therefore was threatening a boycott of Iraq, similar to British actions criticized by Breasted himself.

Frankfort wrote a detailed letter to Breasted describing this unusual, and in a sense historic, division, which rendered the Westerners helpless, virtually at the mercy of an Iraqi official. Frankfort describes how al-Husri came with Jordan, his technical adviser, to Tell Asmar and how they proceeded directly to the house where the antiquities were kept. They asked Frankfort to leave, and when he returned an hour later he sensed a tense atmosphere. It was obvious that al-Husri and Jordan had been arguing heatedly.[135] Frankfort immediately noticed that seventeen of the best objects had been put aside and he was told that the division of the remainder could now start. According to Frankfort, the ensuing conversation between him and al-Husri ran as follows:

Frankfort (F): *"What about those seventeen objects?"*[136]
Al-Husri (H): *"They are for the Iraq Museum."*
F: *"That seems to me illegal, since we are entitled to a representative share of our finds."*
H: *"Only as far as possible, only as far as possible. And the law states expressly that the Director must first select those objects which are needed for the Museum."*
F: *"The bull's head, for instance, is surely not needed in Baghdad— you have nine from Ur."*
H: *"There is a great difference with this one, not only a difference but a great difference."*
F: *"At this rate you will not see more than one or two expeditions in Iraq in the future, if they come at all."*
H: *"Oh no, they will come. They will come when the depression is over. You retain the honor of having discovered the object."*
F: *"I am legally powerless at the moment but I shall report at once to Chicago. I have warned you of the results. This division will be watched by all my colleagues."*[137]

As Frankfort realized, there was little he could do, since al-Husri was indeed following the letter of Bell's law, though perhaps not the spirit in which it had theretofore been observed. When dividing the finds, al-Husri was also more exacting than earlier directors and was not afraid to challenge the archaeologist, and did not give in to pressure. While al-Husri did fulfill the article of the law stating that he should choose those objects which are needed for the "scientific completeness" of the Iraq Museum, he did not "adequately" reward Frankfort, in accordance with the law, as far as Frankfort was concerned. Al-Husri, however, iterated that the article stated that the excavator should be rewarded adequately only "as far as possible."

When the American Embassy contacted the Iraqi government, Naji Beg al-Asli, a high-ranking official in the Ministry of Foreign Affairs, stated that the division had been fair, since the OI had received roughly half of the objects. The American diplomat pointed out that Frankfort's contention was not that he had received too few objects, but, rather, that all seventeen of the most valuable were taken for the Iraqi museum.[138] Al-Asli countered, however, that under the current law, the Iraq Museum was entitled to receive all unique objects. He stated, further, that the division was equitable and generous. When the American stated that the OI spent a lot of money in Iraq conducting its excavations, al-Asli replied that he was not interested in how much money archaeological expeditions spent.[139]

A few weeks later, Paul Knabenshue, the American Resident in Baghdad, met with Nuri Said, the foreign minister, to discuss the Tell Asmar division.[140] Said called al-Husri to his office to meet with Knabenshue, who asked al-Husri whether "he did not think it desireable, because of its moral effect for the Iraq Museum to make an effort to satisfy the Oriental Institute, even if it entailed a slight sacrifice."[141] As a result of that meeting, Said asked al-Husri to supply a report about his actions. In that report, al-Husri stated that the division was correct but, bowing to Said's pressure, offered a "promise of acceptable division next year to compensate for results of this year's division."[142] Al-Husri also proposed to insert a clause in the new law that would permit expeditions that were currently excavating in Iraq to operate under the old law for the next two years.[143] Finally, as an additional compromise, al-Husri generously suggested that the Iraq Museum exchange one of its Ur bull's heads for the Khafaje bull, which

Frankfort had just found. Therefore, the division stood, but the OI received certain concessions that same year and a promise for a more liberal division the next year.

Once this matter was resolved, after numerous high-level meetings among Frankfort, al-Husri, Jordan, Knabenshue, and Said, a curious twist in the saga ensued that raises questions about the sincerity and responsibility of Frankfort and, to a certain extent, of the archaeological community at large. In a confidential conversation with Knabenshue that Frankfort stressed should not be passed onto Breasted, Frankfort admitted that in his opinion only five of the seventeen objects should properly be given serious consideration, since only those were in any way first-class. And those five objects, with perhaps one or two exceptions, should, properly speaking, under the Iraqi law, go to the Iraq Museum.[144] Because the expedition had been granted an Ur bull in lieu of the Khafaje bull, it was about the most that could be expected "even from an impartial archaeological jury."[145]

The extent to which Frankfort's overreaction to al-Husri's act was typical of contemporary Western archaeologists is difficult to ascertain. However, if Frankfort's reaction and insincerity were standard, they may suggest that Western archaeologists abused their superior scientific knowledge and used political pressure to gain an upper hand in the divisions. The more complaints lodged and the more fuss stirred, the more likely it was that an archaeologist would receive more than he should have according to the letter of the law.

Because he was not aware of the full picture, Breasted was taken aback by al-Husri and complained to the U.S. Department of State. As usual, Breasted was quick to jump to conclusions, maintaining that it was "puzzlingly difficult to deal with this type of Oriental."[146] He stated nevertheless that he was going to make an effort to "cultivate Nuri Pasha [Said], who seems both friendly and intelligent. It is evident that an important item in our job is to educate a small group of these ignorant and fanatical Iraqis, and I propose to undertake it."[147] Eventually, however, Frankfort wrote Breasted a long letter in which he described how the seventeen objects were not unique, as he had earlier indicated. He also pointed out that the wording of the law "justifies the actions taken by Saty."[148]

Moreover, Frankfort admitted that al-Husri had a "watertight case" and that foreign archaeologists were not in a strong position, since their position had been spoilt by "Cooke's smuggling, and there is no denying that we are extremely unpopular with the public and the press."[149] He stated that al-Husri is a man of "undoubted integrity . . . much travelled, well educated and possesses the biggest private library which I have seen so far in this country."[150] He did not doubt that al-Husri would stick to his promise and would accord the OI a more favorable division the next year. Frankfort therefore urged Breasted to reconsider his threat of stopping excavating in Iraq, in view of the favorable compromise reached with al-Husri. Once Breasted had heard the whole story, he changed his mind. The next year, the OI sent its mission to Iraq, again under the direction of Frankfort.

As Frankfort predicted, al-Husri stood by his word. In the division, al-Husri made up for the seventeen objects the year before. Frankfort said that they had an "excellent division . . . even of the exceptional objects we got a fair share."[151] Frankfort's contention was that the more experience al-Husri gained in archaeology, the more he showed a "sympathetic understanding of the difficulties of the expedition,"[152] and was therefore more inclined to surrender to the foreign excavator a satisfactory share. Breasted, who died the following year, did not live long enough to witness the emergence of an independent Iraqi archaeology.

FINALLY, THE NEW LEGISLATION

In May 1936, after almost three years of planning and discussion, the Iraqi parliament passed new antiquities legislation. The most important amendment was Article 49, which dealt with the question of the division of objects. Article 49 stated:

All antiquities found by excavators shall be the property of the Government. Nevertheless as a reward for his labors the excavator shall be given (firstly) the right to make castings of antiquities found by him, (secondly) half of the duplicate antiquities and (thirdly) certain antiquities already in the possession of the Iraq Government or included among the articles discovered by an archaeological expedition which the Iraq Government can dispense with in view of the existence in the Iraq Museum of other articles sufficiently similar in respect to kind, type, material, workmanship, historical significance and artistic value.[153]

Instead of the "representative share," the excavator would receive half of the duplicate antiquities and those antiquities with which the Iraq government could dispense.

The new law also introduced a novel approach to facilitating the division. It allowed the director of antiquities to create a "suspense account." To this he would allot certain unique objects that would be carried over to the next year. If the following year's excavation found a similar object, it would enable one to be retained by the Museum and one by the expedition.[154] This provision was unique and was based on an idea by Knabenshue. This article made the Iraqi law more favorable to foreign archaeologists than, for example, the law in Greece or Turkey, because the expedition could obtain a number of duplicate objects for its labor.

The premise of the law was that all objects belong to the Iraqi government. It, therefore, reduced considerably the share that foreign archaeological teams would be able to export from the country. Even though Western archaeologists working in Iraq vehemently fought against implementing these changes, as if the strictures were extremely novel and rigorous, in actuality the Iraqi law followed closely the prevalent trends and ideas in the international scientific community. For example, the Sixth Committee of the League of Nations agreed on a resolution in 1937, entitled the "International Statute for Antiquities and Excavations," which stated that it was essential that the "objects found in the course of excavations should be set apart, in the first place, for the formation, in the museums of the country where the excavations are carried out, of complete collections fully representative of the civilization, history, and art of that country."[155] Furthermore, the declaration proclaimed that the national authorities "may present the excavator with a share of his finds. This share shall consist of duplicates or, generally, of objects or groups of objects which the authorities are able to relinquish because of their similarity to those already in the possession of the national museums."[156]

As al-Husri explained in his conversations with Knabenshue, the new Iraqi law was closely modeled on the statutes of Egypt, Iran, and Greece, which also restricted the partitions of finds with the foreign excavator.[157] Al-Husri realized that Iraq's new law could turn foreign archaeologists away from Iraq for a while, but he predicted that they would return before long, particularly those who are interested "primarily in the scientific side more than in the feature of securing exhibits for museums."[158] Moreover, he maintained that he was more interested in having the former in Iraq than the latter.

For almost four years, Western archaeologists and their diplomats in Iraq had been resisting changes in the antiquities law. Their canvassing was to a certain extent successful, because they were able to convince the Iraqis to introduce certain articles that were not totally restrictive. For example, the debate to change the law had taken almost four years, which gave the archaeologists more time to work under the old agreement. Yet this delay was not only because of the effective lobbying by the archaeological establishment. Rather, the turbulent times in Iraqi politics generated an unpredictable atmosphere that caused a level of inefficiency in the governmental machinery. The mid-1930s were so tumultuous that any long-term planning or efforts to design concrete administrative features, such as new antiquities legislation, were practically futile, or at the very least very unlikely to be implemented.

Despite the valiant and sustained efforts by the Western archaeological establishment, there was very little that could have been done to stem the inroads of Iraqi proprietorship into archaeology. With new political realities in the Middle East, the Western "moment" in Iraqi archaeology in particular, and in Middle Eastern archaeology in general, was coming to an end—or at least entering a new phase. No amount of diplomatic pressure or convincing argument could have helped persuade the Iraqis to keep the old structure in place. That arrangement, as far as the Iraqis were concerned, belonged to a bygone era of overt Western imperialism and thus did not reflect the new, modern Iraq, which was an independent, progressive nation.

The dawning progressive era in archaeology should be seen in the context of Iraq's asserting its independence and trying to break free from British control. The developments in archaeology closely followed similar trends in other aspects of Iraqi political and cultural life, in which the Iraqis sought to assert government control over the land and its resources. Because some aspects of the British-Iraqi economic and political relationship were still "untouchable," such as certain military affairs or the general arrangement in the oil industry, archaeology was a convenient, reasonable fight for the Iraqis to choose. Furthermore, the Iraqis knew that the current archaeological arrangement was not modeled on archaeological practices in the rest of the world. Neither the West nor Iraq's neighbors had liberal antiquities laws in place in their own countries. As the FO officials had pointed out, it was quite natural for an independent country to introduce more restrictive legislation. In this sense, Iraq was merely following the example set in other Western and Middle Eastern countries.

Whether it was a result of the new legislation or, what is more likely, worldwide economic depression, the number of foreign expeditions in Iraq decreased significantly in 1936. The new legislation also came at a time when some significant long-running missions, such as Ur and Khorsabad, were already coming to an end and probably would not have continued much longer even if the legislation had not changed. The newspaper *al-Akhbar* ran a series of articles in December 1938 and January 1939 discussing the lack of interest of foreign excavators in Iraq. The series pointed out that the law "does not deprive the foreign archaeological expeditions of their rights" and, at the same time, "protects the intrinsic and natural rights of Iraq of its relics." It also maintained that the drop in missions was due to world economic factors rather than domestic Iraqi politics, and predicted that the expeditions would return once the world recovered fully from the depression.[159] However, for one reason or another, the years leading up to 1958 were not as archaeologically active as the years of the Mandate. Fewer foreign missions came to Iraq, and their emphasis and organization were different. Nevertheless, this reduction did not mean that all was quiet on the archaeological front. On the contrary, as could be expected, al-Husri used his new position to energetically work toward his own goals.

A MEANS TO AN END

Just as in his prior tenure in the Department of Education, when al-Husri became antiquities director, he sought to make Iraqis aware of their Arab identity and its implications. For al-Husri, one primary reason for the study of a nation's past was to inculcate an Arab national feeling.[160] Archaeology was a means to that end. Al-Husri did not hesitate to use the immense pedagogical potential of archaeology.

In his post as the director of antiquities, al-Husri remained very much an educator, and his archaeological policies reflected his educational and political philosophy. Al-Husri had introduced a specific scheme of history into the Iraqi public schools. Once he became antiquities director, he viewed his department to be an extension of the education ministry, just as he had argued with Bell in 1923. His tenure as director is best viewed in the context of, and as a continuation of, his prior work in the Ministry of Education. An investigation into his lasting and important role in creating the Iraqi public school system is instructive in order to evaluate fully his tenure and philosophy in archaeology.

Initiating a comprehensive educational system was no easy task for al-Husri and his colleagues at the Ministry of Education in the early 1920s. The expansion of the Iraqi educational system was one of the more important developments in the consolidation of the Iraqi state. In 1920 Iraq had around eight thousand students in two hundred state primary schools; by 1930 there were thirty-four thousand students in two thousand schools.[161]

The newly founded state of Iraq had inherited an insufficient educational infrastructure from the Ottoman Empire. A 1919 report by Major H. E. Bowman, who had been appointed director of education during the British Occupation, depicted a bleak state of educational affairs. He stated that the educational "fabric possessed a fine façade, but the foundations were weak and the interior a hollow shell." He maintained that "almost without exception the youth of the country are without education in the true sense of the term . . . they are as a rule unable to write a letter without grammatical and orthographical mistakes . . . of the history and geography of the ancient and modern world . . . they know nothing."[162]

Once Faysal had appointed al-Husri to the Ministry of Education in 1922, al-Husri was quick to incorporate his ideas about the role and content of education in Iraq. Al-Husri viewed the curriculum of the schools as a mechanism of social change. As he stated, "I will employ every means to strengthen the feeling of nationalism among the sons of Iraq to spread the belief in the unity of the Arab nation."[163] This theme is prevalent in a patriotic song that was frequently sung in Iraqi schools during al-Husri's tenure:

From Baghdad's towers to Syria's strand
My land is every Arab land
From shore to shore its boundaries run
Egypt, Yemen, Fitwan are one!

No barrier can between us rise;
No differing faiths can break the ties

Which link all Arabs each to each
with sacred bonds of Arab speech.

Awake, our kinsmen near and far!
with science as our guiding-star
March forward, singing hand in hand—
"Our land is every Arab land." [164]

The initial school curriculum in the new state of Iraq was designed by al-Husri to be closely aligned with his nationalistic policies and his practical pedagogical experience in the Ottoman Empire. Heavily influenced by the French academic primary school curriculum of the late nineteenth century, the new Iraqi curriculum emphasized the instruction of a standardized Arabic language and a new national history. [165] These two subjects accounted for approximately half the hours the Iraqi child spent in primary school. [166] Even though al-Husri had grown up speaking Turkish, he believed that a common Arabic language and history constituted the basis of nation formation and Arab nationalism. He believed that "neither religion nor the state nor a shared economic life are the basic elements of a nation, and nor is common territory . . . [however] language is the soul and the life of the nation, but history is its memory and its consciousness." [167]

As was evident in al-Husri's curriculum, Iraq's history was Arab history, which was not solely confined to Islamic history, but was supposed to transcend religious and community-level ties. Consequently, when the first primary curriculum was introduced in 1923, there was little attention given to the various religious, ethnic, or linguistic cleavages of Iraq. Rather, since the school, for al-Husri, was not only a place of study but also an instrument to promulgate social change, the fundamental concern was establishing a unified national consciousness based on al-Husri's concept of Arab unity. [168] He was adamant that his historical perspectives and philosophy be followed.

In his instruction to primary-school teachers, he declared that "the primary purpose of teaching history in elementary schools is to teach the history of the nation and the past of the nation, and the ultimate aim intended by this is to strengthen patriotic and nationalistic feelings in the hearts of the students." [169] As al-Husri states in his memoirs, "what the Arab needs above all else, is 'social education' which will strengthen and develop in him a spirit of mutual cooperation and obedience."[170] The purpose of this approach is to "bring out clearly" the idea of unity of the Arab nation and the "Arabness of Iraq."[171]

In the initial years, al-Husri was compelled to work within a requirement from the League of Nations that stressed the inclusion of Iraq's ethnic and religious diversity within the national educational curriculum. On this point, al-Husri vigorously battled the various British advisers in the Ministry of Education to implement his own plan, which was not congruent with the League's instructions. Al-Husri describes in his memoirs how the British adviser Jerome Farrell resigned in 1922 after a conflict with him over the philosophy of education in Iraq. Farrell sought to incorporate in Iraq a system similar to that in various British boarding schools, which stressed group solidarity through sports and other outdoor activities.[172] However, al-Husri maintained that such a system might work for Britain, but historical conditions in Iraq would not allow such a plan.[173]

Given al-Husri's determination to diminish sectarian loyalties in Iraq, he also came into conflict with fellow Iraqis such as Fadil al-Jamali, a Shi'i, who eventually succeeded al-Husri as the director general within the Ministry of Education. Perhaps because he took his pedagogical mission so seriously, al-Husri had always remained aloof from local Iraqi politics and did not make many friends by being consistent and adamant in his outlook. Even though, certainly, he deliberately constructed the educational system to serve what he considered to be the betterment of Iraqi society, that, in and of itself, was not his ultimate purpose. Rather, educating the Iraqi public was but a means to an end, namely, the eventual political unity of the Arab nation. He therefore had a more universal view of politics and education, one which transcended the local Iraqi situation. As he declared, "I will employ every means to strengthen the feeling of nationalism among the sons of Iraq to spread the belief in the unity of the Arab nation. And I shall do this without joining any of the political parties which will eventually be formed."[174]

Al-Husri believed that, to achieve this goal, the schools had to become the cultural and social educators. In the schools, the future citizens of Iraq would learn to love the fatherland and the Arab nation, discipline and communal cooperation. Consequently, al-Husri, through the curriculum, emphasized the study of history and language. Therefore, Arabic, history (both Middle Eastern and to a lesser extent

European), and civics comprised half of what the Iraqi child learned in primary school in the 1920s and 1930s.[175] Instead of learning about a history that was specifically Iraqi or local, the school curriculum of this period emphasized the commonality of the histories of Iraq and its Arab neighbors. In such a construction, there was little room for various non-Arab, non-Islamic civilizations such as the Babylonian or Sumerian, peoples and history to which the other Arab countries did not necessarily trace their lineage.

Al-Husri may have been too apolitical in domestic politics or too idealistic to function effectively in the Iraqi political structure. He was eventually succeeded in 1928 by the more politically connected al-Jamali. Although al-Jamali generally was firmly committed to an al-Husri brand of Arab nationalism, he nevertheless favored a school system that took local circumstances more into account. Therefore al-Jamali established in all rural provinces secondary schools whose access to resources was similar to the schools in urban settings such as Baghdad. This extended into provincial areas more opportunities for Shi'i and Kurds to receive an education than under al-Husri's plan.[176]

The didactic approach to the teaching and studying of history continued in the Ministry of Education up through al-Jamali's tenure. In a well-known quotation, Sami Shawkat, who became minister of education in 1937, stated at a meeting of history teachers in Baghdad, "History for history's sake has no place in our present society; it is a matter for the specialist and for those who devote themselves to learning alone. The histories which are written with this aim in view are buried and nobody reads them."[177] Rather, the aim in teaching history was to present an unambiguous past of the nation that would strengthen the feelings of national unity. For example, when the British traveler Freya Stark attended an Iraqi government school for girls in 1931 to improve her Arabic she was amused to note in the history lessons "how the doings of the early Caliphs could be made to teach modern nationalism."[178]

ARAB HISTORY AND ARCHAEOLOGY

To what extent this view of history influenced the approach to archaeology is difficult to determine. Nevertheless, it is important to keep the didactic goal of Iraqi history in mind and consider whether or not such a view leads to a more politicized view of archaeology. What is clear, however, is that al-Husri and his successors in the Ministry of

Education had a definite purpose for the school's curriculum. Similar trends are discernible in his tenure as director of antiquities.

During al-Husri's tenure practically all the department's funds and energies were directed toward the restoration of Islamic monuments. He was instrumental in 1937 in the establishment of the Museum of Arab Antiquities, which contained objects solely from Iraq's Islamic era, in a famous covered market in Baghdad, the Khan Murjan.[179] Consequently, there was some change in the displays of the Iraq Museum. A museum guide from 1937 shows that instead of displaying antiquities from the Islamic period, Room V now had a wide selection of objects from the Sassanian period.[180]

The Iraq Museum thus became a museum solely for the pre-Islamic civilizations of Iraq, whereas the new Islamic museum housed the regalia for al-Husri's Iraq, so different from the interpretation of Iraq's history that Bell had presented. As Amatzia Baram points out, al-Husri's creation of the Islamic museum and the pride he took in it were "strangely reminiscent of Gertrude Bell's affection for and pride in her own creation."[181] Al-Husri did not see much need for studying those ancient civilizations of Iraq, which had theretofore been the primary focus of nearly all archaeological excavations in the country. Those civilizations, according to al-Husri, had been "buried under the sands of time for thousands of years . . . to revert to those lost epochs was an attempt to revive that which is dead and mummified."[182] Therefore, that ancient history was irrelevant for the present population, according to al-Husri.

In February 1936, the Iraqi press announced that the Iraqi Department of Antiquities was about to embark on the first official Iraqi excavation. As mentioned in Chapter 4, Chiera had conducted some minor soundings for Bell on behalf of the Iraq Museum, which technically was the first Iraqi excavation. The site that was chosen by al-Husri was Wasit, the capital of the Iraqi province during the Ummayyad dynasty and an important regional city during the Abbasid Caliphate. Given al-Husri's devotion to pan-Arab nationalism, the choice of Wasit made a clear political and philosophical statement.

Prior to al-Husri's decision, the newspaper *al-Bilad* had published several articles praising certain ruins and recommending that they be excavated and restored. During the month of December (around the time of the controversy surrounding the article by Woolley in *The Times*, discussed above) the articles in *al-Bilad* specifically stated that the

Department of Antiquities, in cooperation with the Department of Waqf (Special Endowments), should undertake excavations or restorations of the following sites: Ukhaidar, Wasit, the citadel of Baghdad, the minaret of Suq al-Ghazl, Bab al-Wastani, and the Abbasid bridge of Zakho.[183] The decision to excavate Wasit came as a logical choice, given the preceding discussions in the Iraqi press.

Most foreign contemporaries did not interpret the choice of Wasit as a particularly political move. Kerr, the British ambassador, stated that the Iraqis had chosen this site because an Islamic site was relatively easier to excavate than a Sumerian, Babylonian, or Assyrian city.[184] In fact, al-Husri stated in his autobiography that Wasit was chosen because of its relative simplicity.[185] Knabenshue, the American Resident in Baghdad, acknowledged that al-Husri wanted to attract "patriotic and nationalistic support to his scheme," yet stressed that this choice of an Islamic site was to "avoid competing with the foreign archaeological expeditions."[186] Because the Iraqis were planning their first independent expedition, Kerr also inquired whether the BSAI wouldn't be willing to offer unconditional support to this pioneering enterprise. He pointed out that "Gertrude Bell would have been the first to have helped them in every way she could" and such help would "dispel the clouds of suspicion and ill-will which have so unfortunately gathered over archaeology in this country."[187] Despite Kerr's pleading, the BSAI did not offer funds for this excavation.

Although the practical concern of excavating a comparatively easy Islamic site may have been the determining factor in the decision, al-Husri undoubtedly had more than such practical methodological concerns when choosing that site. Even though an Islamic site might not require going through as many layers, the science and methodology of an archaeological site from an Islamic era were just as difficult as with sites from other eras. Rather, for al-Husri, archaeology was but one means toward his pan-Arab end. His commitment to this cause was recognized by a parliamentary committee in 1940, which commended al-Husri's Department of Antiquities for its interest in Arab and Islamic antiquities and its efforts to build Arab museums.[188]

RECLAIMING THE SAMARRA COLLECTION

O nce al-Husri had become the director of antiquities, the issue of reclaiming Iraqi antiquities from abroad came to the fore.

Because Islamic and Arab history was of utmost importance to al-Husri, the various sites from Iraq's Ummayyad and Abbasid Caliphates gained increasing importance. While making plans to excavate some of these sites, such as Wasit, al-Husri also started to reclaim some of the antiquities that had left Iraq in one way or another. For example, in 1935 he took deliberate steps to seek the return of the Samarra antiquities, which had been an issue primarily between the British and the Germans during World War I.[189]

The return of cultural property is becoming at the beginning of the twenty-first century one of the more pressing issues facing governments, museums, and universities alike. Particularly in the wake of the discussion surrounding the claims of Holocaust survivors and their descendants for their art and gold, plundered by the Nazis and stored by the Swiss and others, the controversy and debate over returning cultural property have reached new heights and intensity.

The issue of returning cultural property raises numerous complicated legal and moral questions. In general, the debate is characterized by two contrasting points of view.[190] On the one hand, there are those that identify with the "source" nation and believe that cultural objects belong within the boundaries of the nation of origin and should stay there.[191] If such objects are found abroad, they should be returned. On the other side, people take the position that distinctions should be made among different kinds of cultural objects, between theft and legal export. They take into account the possibility that in some cases the demand for the return of cultural objects, whatever its nationalist justification, could serve no universal interest.[192]

The issue of returning cultural property is made all the more difficult because of the radically different interests of "naturally" antiquities-rich countries, such as Mexico, Egypt, and Iraq, as compared to antiquity-importing countries. A related controversy has emerged over whether there is indeed a significant relationship between modern nations and the ancient civilizations that once occupied the same lands. It is not entirely clear whether such ancient remnants should adhere to the modern borders and therefore become the property of a particular nation or whether such artifacts have such universal appeal and relevance that they become the property of humanity at large.

Returning cultural objects has become an ever-increasing concern for the current governments in the Middle East, such as those of Iraq and Egypt. For example, the main newspaper of the ruling Ba'th party in Iraq, *al-Thawra*, stated in 1980 that previous Iraqi governments did not grasp the importance of antiquities and expressed no interest in the "stolen treasures" that adorn museums in the West. That they were not returned to "the homeland from which they emerged is a cultural calamity and a major crime." The newspaper declared, however, that the current government was "determined to restore the treasures which are the symbol of the first and greatest civilizations in human history."[193] Given the changing nature of the discussion and corresponding sympathy, and more political pressure to return cultural objects, this may indeed become an even more important issue in the new millennium.

These postmodern ethical concerns were not the guiding principle regarding the Samarra collection. The Iraqis were merely requesting a collection that they knew was earmarked for them, and the British Museum, which was keeping the collection, was not persuaded by high moral grounds to return the antiquities, but only grudgingly agreed to do so after it had been pressured by the FO.

In April of 1935, after Iraqis had gained more control of their archaeological affairs, the Iraqi Ministry of Foreign Affairs wrote to the British ambassador raising the issue of the Samarra antiquities, stating that it was not fair that "such antiquities, discovered in and rightly belonging to Iraq, should be distributed among various museums in Europe and America to the deprivation of Iraq thereof."[194] As described in Chapter 2, this was a collection resulting from German excavations at Samarra before World War I. The British took the objects as war booty and surreptitiously exported them from Iraq under orders from Winston Churchill and Percy Cox in direct opposition to FO orders. Once the collection was in England, T. E. Lawrence and Ernst Herzfeld divided the collection, allotting certain segments to Western institutions and setting apart a "representative" share for the soon-to-be-established Iraq Museum.

Since 1927, the Iraqi media had on occasion raised the question of the Samarra antiquities. But in 1935, following al-Husri's directions, the Iraqi Ministry of Foreign Affairs requested that the Samarra antiquities be restored to the Iraq Museum.[195] The FO, which at this point was not familiar with this decade-old affair, questioned the BM about the status of Iraq's share. It seems to have lapsed from the BM consciousness that the Iraq Museum had been established for over a decade. The BM sheepishly responded that it would send a collection of antiquities to

Baghdad "now that a Museum exists."[196] An enclosed report from Sidney Smith, the keeper of the Western Asiatic antiquities at the British Museum, who had several years earlier served as the director of antiquities in Iraq, stated that the remaining collection included shreds of pottery and fragments of architectural decoration which were in bad condition and concerning which "it was doubtful whether the cost of transport to Baghdad is worthwhile."[197]

Smith had conveniently forgotten that under the original agreement between the FO and the BM, the BM was to keep a collection packed and send it free of charge to Baghdad once the Iraq Museum was able to receive it. It had also been agreed that Iraq would have first claim, and thereby, before any sets of fragments were sent to other museums, acquire the best objects, not just the odds and ends that remained. Therefore, in this matter, the Museum authorities violated a British governmental dictum. An internal British Museum memo is particularly revealing, stating that Iraq's portion was "archaeological junk and no serious purpose can be served in shipping it to Baghdad."[198] George Hill, the director of the BM, admitted in a private letter to a friend named Hobson that "we are a little in the wrong, because we have kept the things long after Baghdad Museum became competent to receive its share."[199] Despite that private recognition and contrary to the original agreement, the BM tried to convince the FO that the Iraqi government should pay for the shipment.

The FO finally persuaded the BM to send, free of charge, a share of the collection to Baghdad, where it was received in September 1936—almost a year after the matter was first raised—a shipment that was hardly "representative," as had been agreed upon in 1922.

Despite the archaeological insignificance of the eventual shipment to Iraq, reclaiming historical Samarran fragments from the Abbasid Caliphate from Britain was a major political victory for al-Husri and the Department of Antiquities. The Iraqi press covered the return extensively, thereby bolstering the department's presence on the political scene. Al-Husri was diligent in promoting his interpretation of the artifacts and how they related to the current political situation. Furthermore, because the return of the Samarran antiquities came in the wake of new antiquities legislation that had been passed in the face of intense foreign diplomatic pressure, archaeology in Iraq was perceived as becoming increasingly independent. In stark contrast to the insignificance of the objects from an archaeological point of view, reclaiming the remnants of the Samarra collection was politically symbolic. The independent nation now had full control of its archaeology and its ancient history and was taking steps to repatriate objects from abroad. This episode, however, is one of the very few successful attempts of the Iraqi government to reclaim antiquities.

The remaining years of al-Husri's tenure in the Department of Antiquities proved to be relatively quiet. In 1936–1937 there were three expeditions: Penn, OI, and Michigan (at Seleucia). The next year, the Americans sent none, and the only foreign presence was the German expedition at Warka. The Germans continued their work in 1938 and were very happy with their treatment. In fact, Dr. Grobba, the German ambassador, indicated to the British ambassador in Baghdad that the Iraqis would welcome more expeditions to Iraq.[200]

By the mid-1930s, more and more Iraqis became involved in archaeology. Around the time that al-Husri became director of antiquities, the first Iraqis went abroad specifically to study archaeology. In 1934, Fuad Safar and Taha Baqir went to the OI at Chicago and received their master's degrees there in 1938.[201]

Just prior to the outbreak of World War II, two American institutions (Harvard's Peabody Museum and the Mary-Helen Warden Schmidt Foundation) conducted some minor surveys in order to assess possible future projects. Harvard's Lauriston Ward reported to Knabenshue that he and his associates were very pleased with the treatment they had received from al-Husri. He had "leaned over backwards" to accommodate them, and Ward felt that the new Antiquities Law was fair and would make it possible for Harvard to consider an extensive archaeological mission to Iraq.[202] Due to World War II, these missions did not come to fruition. The Iraqis, however, continued their work at Samarra, Wasit, and Khorsabad to some extent until 1941.

Yet as in the twilight of Bell's career a decade earlier, al-Husri was slowly drifting to the edge of Iraqi politics and society. Like Bell, he was an erudite, energetic foreigner in Iraq who was extremely interested in preserving and studying Iraq's ancient past. During Faysal's reign they both had important roles in establishing long-lasting and influential institutions, thus ensuring Iraq's future. In fact, they were so successful in that endeavor that they made themselves expendable. But both ended up working with Iraq's ancient history. In 1941, as a result of his support of the anti-British, pro-German al-Gaylani coup d'état, al-Husri was forced to leave Iraq, to which he never returned.

Despite his rather hurried exit from Iraq, his legacy nevertheless remained. His idealistic enthusiasm and his determination to restructure the governmental institutions of education and archaeology had a lasting impact. His didactic view of archaeology influenced future generations of archaeologists and politicians. During his tenure archaeology became politicized in Iraq. In subsequent decades, there was a close and intricate relationship between the governmental authorities and the Antiquities Department, a relationship that was established during al-Husri's term of office. Furthermore, given his pedagogical mind-set, al-Husri's policies helped ensure that archaeology did not become a concern primarily of the bourgeois Westernized elite, as was often the case in other Middle Eastern countries such as Egypt, but instead shaped the general school-going public.

EGYPT AND IRAQ

I t is instructive to compare the developments in archaeology and politics in Iraq and Egypt.[203] In the latter, the spectacular discovery of the tomb of Tutankhamen by the English archaeologist Howard Carter came only a few months after Britain's unilateral declaration of limited Egyptian independence in 1922.[204] The intense foreign interest and the dramatic nature of the finds were bound to cause tensions between the newly independent Egyptians and the British excavators. The Egyptians, still in a nationalistic, even euphoric, mood, were not willing to see these valuable treasures leave the country as the English patron of this expedition, Lord Carnarvon, had demanded.[205]

The Egyptian government, through the Frenchman Pierre Lacau, who was the director general of the Egyptian Antiquities Service, put certain restrictions on Carter and his crew.[206] Because Carter had earlier experienced less rigorous methods by the Antiquities Service, he decided to sue the government in the so-called Mixed Courts of Egypt. In response, the new Wafdist government under Sa'd Zaghlul canceled Carter's concession, and eventually the court ruled that the contents of Tutankhamen's tomb should be allotted to the Egyptian Museum.[207] Subsequently, the Egyptian parliament passed a new antiquities law, with the assistance of Lacau, which, according to historian Donald M. Reid, was "so draconian that it largely dried up foreign excavation in Egypt for a generation."[208]

Although the result of the new law may have led to fewer foreign excavations in Egypt, it should not be seen as the sole reason. To maintain that the Egyptian law was "draconian" is also a bit of an overstatement. Although the new Egyptian antiquities law created slightly more restrictions than the prior legislation, it still offered certain benefits to the archaeologist. As Breasted, who had conducted extensive work in Egypt, noted, "The amazing fact is that the Egyptian law still calls for a fifty-fifty division and has never been repealed. Our French colleague [Lacau] simply ignores the law with the support of the native Cabinet, and substitutes ministerial regulation in place of the law. The law and the actual practice, therefore, are diametrically opposed."[209]

The introduction of the new law in Egypt also coincided with the opening up of other archaeologically rich sites, such as Iraq and Palestine, which were emerging as new Mandates under British tutelage. The British and the Americans were probably more willing to excavate at those sites, because they were away from French control. In Egypt, Lacau still maintained oversight of archaeology. Therefore the relatively pristine sites of Iraq and Palestine, where archaeology was still firmly under British dominion, were more feasible options.

The discovery of Tutankhamen's tomb could not have entered the Egyptian political process in a more spectacular way and/or at a more sensitive time. The Egyptian example was viewed closely by other Middle Eastern states, since Egypt was the country with the most experience and the most active archaeological scene. In Iraq, the incorporation of archaeology into politics was more gradual. Archaeology was not as closely associated with Western imperialism as in Egypt, and eventually archaeology became more closely affiliated with the general governmental apparatus than in Egypt. In Egypt, Egyptology primarily became the preoccupation among certain intellectuals who in the 1920s and 1930s advocated an image of Egypt that was based exclusively on Egyptian elements, thus deemphasizing the Arab influence. Intellectuals such as Taha Husayn and Tawfiq al-Hakim argued that Egypt's true national personality was based on the unique Golden Age of Egypt represented by the Pharaonic era.[210] However, by the 1940s and 1950s, Islam and Arabic history became the primary influences in Egyptian intellectual discourse and public life. This contributed to the rise of Gamal Abd-al Nasir's (Nasser) popular brand of Pan-Arabism and the development of the organization of the Muslim Brotherhood, which continued at least until the death of Abd-al Nasir in 1970.

Regarding their relationship to and emphasis on ancient history, Iraq and Egypt are almost mirror images of each other. In Iraq, the 1920s–1930s Pan-Arabism was the command of the day, eventually leading to various interpretations of Iraqi particularism and a resistance to Pan-Arabism in the 1940s–1960s. Furthermore, in Iraq, the role of intellectuals in using archaeology and ancient history had not been so drastic and problematic as in Egypt. This may be because Iraq gained control of its archaeological matters at a much earlier period and that did not coincide with sensitive and dramatic events as in Egypt. Therefore archaeology in Iraq has not been as polarized as in Egypt and fit more seamlessly into the political and cultural system.

Between 1932 and 1941, archaeology entered the main stage of Iraqi politics and has remained there till today. During this decade, Iraqi archaeology, just like most other aspects of the general life of the country, became increasingly independent. For the first time, archaeology in Iraq was not controlled by outsiders, whether "foreign Iraqis," such as Bell and al-Husri, or foreign institutions and archaeologists. In subsequent decades Iraqis made all the major decisions in archaeological matters and, up until 1990, were active participants in the international scholarly community. In a matter of a few years, archaeology and the national museum transformed from being a part-time hobby of British administrators and politicians into a well-established, centralized operation under the purview of Iraqi politicians and scholars. In the latter half of the twentieth century, archaeology thus became a critical component in the construction of Iraqi national identity. The foundation for this incorporation of archaeology in the national narrative was laid in the interwar years. History, archaeology, and politics all became intertwined as Iraqis sought paradigms from the past to confront and understand the dilemmas and the contradictions of the present.

CONCLUSION

The decades after 1941 witnessed a tremendous degree of archaeological activity in Iraq. Iraqi archaeology, like so many features of Iraqi political life, was under the close control of the central government. During these years, the thrust of Iraqi national identity was in flux, in that different historical paradigms and periods were emphasized to legitimize the state and the nation and took their turns in characterizing Iraqi political life. In this time period, archaeology and Iraqi archaeologists played a significant role.

In 1940–1941, in close cooperation with Seton Lloyd, Fuad Safar excavated Tell 'Uqair and found materials belonging to the Uruk and Jamdat Nasr periods.[1] That year, following the coup d'état by Rashid Ali al-Gaylani, al-Husri fell out of favor and was forced to leave Iraq in 1941. Yusuf Ghanima became the director general of antiquities in his place. Ghanima initiated the rearrangement of the Iraq Museum, which would be "representative of the successive cultural phases in the history of Iraq."[2] He stated, further, that because the "most important function of a modern Museum is an educational one," it was important to organize the objects in a chronological sequence according to their approximate dating, "thereby giving some impression of the gradual development of Mesopotamian culture from the earliest times onwards."[3] As before, the Iraq Museum only displayed objects from the pre-Islamic period, leaving the Islamic objects to the Islamic museum.

Shortly after World War II, Dr. Naji al-Asli became the director of antiquities and along, with the two recent Iraqi graduates from foreign universities, Safar and Taha Baqir, organized the department along apolitical and scientific lines. Their efforts to build a first-class scientific institution from within came at about the time that concerted attempts were made by the Iraqi government to become a modern state. Just prior to and during World War II, at the time the first Iraqi archaeologists were conducting their excavations, several notable cultural institutions were established to promote Western culture, such as the Institute of Music (established in 1937), the Iraq School of Fine Arts (1939), and the state-sponsored Museum of Modern Art (1943).[4]

In 1952, Safar and Baqir were two of the founders of the Faculty of Archaeology at the University of Baghdad, organized along the lines of similar departments in Western universities, which in subsequent years would be the main department educating Iraqi archaeologists.[5]

Their first major archaeological projects in the post–al-Husri era, when the fervor of Pan-Arabism had somewhat subsided in Iraq, were primarily directed toward Sumerian remains. In 1942–1943, Baqir conducted excavations at 'Aqar Quf, a ruined ziggurat near Baghdad identified with the Kassite city of Dur Kurigalzu, which was first identified by Rawlinson in the 1860s. In the first excavation report, Baqir stated that in addition to the archaeological importance of the site there were several other reasons why this site was chosen. The first was economic; owing to the war, it was important to excavate in the vicinity of Baghdad.[6] Second, the proximity to Baghdad also allowed people in Baghdad, both Iraqis and the many Allied troops stationed in the area, to witness an archaeological project in progress. Baqir maintained that many hundreds of Allied troops and many parties of Iraqi schoolteachers and students visited the site.[7] Assisting Baqir in these excavations were Seton Lloyd, the technical adviser to the department of antiquities, the architect Muhammad Ali Mustafa, Ata Sabri, Sabri Shukri, and Izeddin Sanduq. The excavations, which lasted until January 1945, found numerous works of art, including gold ornaments and jewelry, and contributed to a better understanding of the Kassite dynasty.[8]

During the 1940s, Safar and Baqir, most often in cooperation with Seton Lloyd, conducted extensive excavations at Tell 'Uqair, where they unearthed the first known Sumerian painted temple, with colored frescoes covering the inside walls and the altar. At Tell Harmal, near Baghdad, Baqir found two thousand tablets—including letters and lexical, literary, and mathematical texts—and a temple. And at Eridu, Safar discovered the earliest Ubaid pottery, an Ubaid cemetery, and two palaces from the middle of the third millennium B.C.E. Samuel Kramer, the father of Sumerian literary studies, positively notes these Iraqi efforts, stating that they were of "particular relevance and importance" to Sumerian studies and that they had "surprised the scholarly world."[9] The archaeologist Seton Lloyd maintains that the standard of competence of the Iraqi expeditions of the 1940s "could be considered equal to that of most Western expeditions."[10]

The Iraqis, the inheritors of a legacy of rich archaeological research in their country, which had been carefully planned and executed by Bell, Sidney Smith, Jordan, Lloyd, and others, were systematically using their position and were making positive steps toward creating a professional and scientific ethos in archaeological matters. Once the dust had settled concerning the new antiquities legislation, the transition from foreign-controlled archaeology to an independent Iraqi archaeology was a relatively smooth one.

The Western-educated Iraqi archaeologists did not overtly emphasize Islamic archaeology as had been the norm during al-Husri's tenure. In 1945 the Iraqi Department of Antiquities started an excellent annual archaeological publication entitled *Sumer*, which indicated the thrust of interest in the department. The history of the Sumerian civilization was what these archaeologists wanted to emphasize both to the Iraqis and to the world at large. (It is interesting to note that the BSAI journal is entitled *Iraq*).

The 1950s were a transitional decade in Iraq. This time period saw a considerable rise in the national revenue due to a new agreement between the government and the Iraq Petroleum Company that resulted in almost a sixfold increase of state income. The Iraqi government established the Iraqi Development Board (IDB), which sought, as its name indicates, to enhance the development of Iraq into a modern nation. The Board sought to further centralize landholdings in the country and also had ambitious plans to change the urban landscape of Baghdad. For that purpose, the IDB invited some of the world's leading architects, such as Alvar Aalto, Walter Gropius, Le Corbusier, and Frank Lloyd Wright. Wright in particular proposed and designed fantastic plans (which were never built), for an opera house, national museum, theme park, and university, that were inspired by Iraq's glorious history, especially the legacy of Haroun al-Rashid and stories of the *1001 Nights*.[11]

At the same time that the government had ambitious and creative plans for Baghdad's architecture, Iraqi artists were also exhibiting exciting creative instincts whether in literature, architecture, or the visual arts. The Iraqi Pioneers (al-Ruwaad) Movement was experimenting with forms inspired by Iraq's ancient history. Jawad Salim, in particular, who had worked at the national museum during the war, was very concerned with establishing an Iraqi national tradition in the visual arts. He was one of the founders of the Baghdad Association of Modern Art in 1952. Similarly, the Iraqi poets Abd al-Wahhab al-Bayati and Badr Shakir al-Sayyab were proponents of new trends in Arabic literature, and Baghdad was home to the influential Free Verse movement. Iraqi artists and intellectuals all along the political spectrum were thus starting to use Iraq's rich ancient history to further enrich the nation's cultural production.

During the 1958 revolution, the pro-British Hashemite Kingdom was overthrown, and the leader of this revolution, Brigadier Abd al-Karim Qasim, declared Iraq to be a republic.[12] He established close ties with the Soviet Union and the rest of the Eastern bloc and, more importantly, opposed the current pan-Arab trends advocated by Egypt's Gamal Abd al-Nasir. Qasim's resolute independence marked the end of the Arab "age of innocence" regarding pan-Arab unity. Therefore, the aftermath of the revolution led to conflict between the particular nationalism in Iraq and the regional nationalism of Abd al-Nasir. Qasim concentrated on building a sovereign Iraq, politically isolated from the rest of the Arab world.

Whether or not it was due to the extensive work by Iraqi archaeologists on pre-Islamic civilizations in the 1940s–1950s, Iraq unveiled a new emblem and a new national flag with symbols from pre-Islamic Iraq. It is also possible that this pre-Islamic emphasis may have stemmed from the extensive Iraqi Communist Party participation in the 1958 revolution, Communists typically preferring Iraqi particularism to the pan-Arab emphasis of the preceding decades. During Qasim's reign, Iraqi archaeologists played prominent roles. Large floats and displays based on Mesopotamian history were featured prominently in the celebration for the first anniversary of the revolution.[13] Qasim also incorporated into the national flag and emblem Akkadian and Babylonian symbols, which portrayed and asserted Iraq's affiliation with those civilizations. When Qasim was overthrown in 1963 by dissident factions within the military led by Colonel Abd al-Salam Arif, and Iraq once again entered into the pan-Arab dialogue and sought full union with Egypt, some of the Iraqi archaeologists, such as Taha Baqir, who had enthusiastically supported Qasim's government, were exiled.

The 1950s–1960s also witnessed a resurgence of Western missions. Mallowan returned to Iraq and along with David Oates excavated at Nimrud, while American excavators returned to Nippur. There was also a new emphasis, particularly among American archaeologists such as Robert Adams and Robert J. Braidwood, on the environment and the origins of agriculture and of village and city life.[14]

With the ascension to power of the Ba'th Party in 1968, there was a renewed Iraqi interest in archaeology. The government announced in 1969 that all graduates from the Department of Archaeology at Baghdad University would find full-time employment in the Department of Antiquities.[15] The Antiquities Law of 1936 was amended in 1974 and 1975 and broadened the definition of "antiquities." The amendments also put a total prohibition on the export of antiquities, even of duplicates, and omitted the clause concerning the "suspense" account.[16]

During the presidency of Saddam Husayn (between 1979 and 2003), an emphasis on and appreciation of Iraq's pre-Islamic history resurfaced. Ironically, Husayn came to power through the ruling Ba'th Party, which was defined, in the romantic and stirring language of its cofounder Michel Aflaq, as an instrument to bring about Arab unity. A main feature in the party's platform was the belief in the existence of a single Arab nation defined by its language and the religion of Islam.[17]

However, Husayn often looked far beyond the traditional Ba'thi historical view. Because the Iraqi Shi'is and Kurds were generally ambivalent about the Ba'thi pan-Arab doctrine, Husayn strove to find a neutral plane to unite the country's disparate elements. Therefore, the history of ancient Mesopotamia once again emerged as a useful political tool because it contained civilizations, figureheads, and myths of nonsectarian appeal. Furthermore, the general public was not too familiar with the basic facts of that history, as it was with Islamic history, and the Mesopotamian stories were not enmeshed in popular culture. Hence, they provided a convenient basis for the implementation of a new national identity.

Husayn realized the political potential of archaeology. For example, in a 1979 speech before a convention of Iraqi archaeologists, President Saddam Husayn maintained, "Antiquities are the most precious relics the Iraqis possess, showing the world that our country . . . is the legitimate offspring of previous civilizations which offered a great contribution to humanity."[18] In order to prove his point, Husayn initiated the

rebuilding of archaeological sites and vigorously incorporated archaeological themes into his cult of personality. As aptly described by Amatzia
Baram, Husayn, and his loyal cadre of poets, historians, and archaeologists went to great lengths to depict Husayn as the direct heir to
Nebuchadnezzar, Hammurabi, Sennacherib, and other ancient historical figures.[19] Thus, he legitimized his own rule and positioned it as the
culmination of glorious, powerful empires that ruled most areas around
the Persian Gulf. By presenting his government as a successor to these
earlier empires, Husayn found historical precedent for his expansionist
policies. Relatively speaking, the government expended large amounts
each year on archaeological projects and hosted lavish festivals to cele-
brate Iraq's ancient past and its contribution to world civilization.

Nevertheless, despite this strong governmental support and interest, the archaeology in the late 1990s Iraq was in a chaotic and destructive state. There is compelling evidence that the extensive bombings
during the Persian Gulf War destroyed various archaeological sites in
southern Iraq. Furthermore, the various futile uprisings against Saddam
Husayn in 1991, which were encouraged by the Western powers, did not
have the intended effect of overthrowing Husayn. Instead, they wrought
havoc on the various museums, both in the north and south. These
museums were perceived as symbols of government power. One form of
rebelling against that power, therefore, was to destroy the museums,
resulting in loss and irreparable damage to numerous valuable artifacts.

The strict economic embargo placed on Iraq after the invasion of
Kuwait in 1990 has led to a calamity in Iraqi society and in the economy, with immense human and environmental consequences. The sorry
state of affairs has been clearly felt in archaeology, because the desperate economic situation has caused people to find any means possible to
survive. In such conditions, the respect and protection of antiquities has
been easily disregarded. During the decade of sanctions, immense
smuggling of antiquities out of the country took place in order to raise
valuable currency, an enterprise often sanctioned and organized by
members of the government.[20] Delicate archaeological sites were also
being bulldozed, literally and figuratively, in order to create more agricultural lands and also to hasten the process of finding desirable artifacts.[21] In desperate economic situations, people are not that patient,
nor are they interested in the careful, exact scientific excavations dictated by modern archaeology. In fact, archaeology in Iraq plummeted
to a new level of destructive operations, probably even more ruinous

than the reckless diggings of various nineteenth-century excavators such as Layard or Rassam.

The extensive, illegal, and unsupervised digs at archaeological sites all over Iraq in the aftermath of the 2003 war resemble and even pale in comparison with the "unedifying scramble" of yesteryear. The looting of the Iraqi national and regional museums after the war in 2003 and the destruction of many Iraqi libraries and educational facilities were a tragic culmination of sanctions on Iraq. The calamity represented an end to a period and a woeful indictment of the cultural priorities of the current age.

After the war and civil strife of 2003 the task for the Iraqi nation is daunting. In addition to confronting the numerous civil and health care issues facing the country, Iraqis will need to reclaim—physically, politically, psychologically—their plundered past. It will be a slow and painful process and sad reminder of this nation's tragic political history.

Seventy years after it was first institutionalized by the British, Iraqi archaeology essentially began to come to an end with the Iraqi invasion of Kuwait in 1990, which culminated in the irreparable destruction in 2003. However, the study of the ancient civilizations of Iraq continues in universities and museums around the world, using materials that came as the result of the various divisions in the twentieth century or through other channels, both legal and illegal. It is an ironic twist that some of the predictions by Hill, Breasted, and others from the 1930s have sadly come to pass. We can see, with the advantage of hindsight, that legislation allowing more antiquities to leave Iraq with the excavator would have been, as the situation now stands, more fruitful from the scientific and academic point of view, since the artifacts probably would have been better preserved in Western museums and universities. However, at the time, that was not a political option, nor has it been since then. The Western archaeologists of 1920–1940 certainly made self-serving arguments and may have abused their position in one way or another, but in the end, at least as it seems in the last years of the twentieth century in Saddam's Iraq, their activities were more beneficial to archaeology as a science and their recommendations, in the long run, could have preserved more artifacts. However, the presence of the archaeological artifacts in Iraq was a major contributor to its cultural enrichment. For most years of Iraq's existence, its governments and archaeologists had high professional standards and were active participants in the international scientific cooperation.

Yet the artifacts that could possibly have been saved by a more liberal legislation are trivial in number compared to the immense potential of the many unexcavated, or only partially excavated, sites remaining in Iraq that could yield countless artifacts and new epistemological discoveries. Yet given the extensive and recent destruction of archaeological sites in Iraq, the potential for new discoveries has now been severely limited. It is now questionable whether the declaration made in 1921 by the Yale Assyriologist Albert T. Clay, "there is enough work to be done in the land to keep ten expeditions busy for 500 years,"[22] is still applicable, even after only seventy years.

Now that the Iraqi nation has the opportunity to reestablish some of its institutions, in a nation-building process perhaps similar to that of the 1920s, it will undoubtedly turn once again to its ancient history and archaeology. Given the tradition of paradigmatic nationalism, Iraqis will find ample paradigms in their history to inspire a unified and peaceful future, particularly if the lessons of the past are not overlooked but confronted in a constructive manner. Given the obliteration of Iraqi society, reclaiming the plundered past will face difficult obstacles, perhaps even more difficult than the problems facing the nation at the start of the Mandate era. Again, archaeological activities will need to be organized and brought under control. In the next years many unresolved issues will need to be addressed. The Iraqi-born poet Fadel Jabr, who now lives in the United States, has written a poem entitled "Archaeologists." Its final stanzas capture the ambiguous and uncertain future that archaeology has in Iraq:

> **Those archaeologists!**
> **They are busy**
> **With things outside our attention**
> **Those invisible creatures**
> **Digging for incomplete joys!**
> **If only**
> **They could find**
> **The missing halves**
> **Of the facts**
> **In the puzzle of crossed fates!**
>
> ∼
>
> **Archaeologists!** [23]

This book has explored the integral ties between politics and archaeology in Iraq. It has demonstrated how the politics of archaeology in Iraq has followed hand in hand with the politics of nationalism and imperialism.

After a stage of limited Iraqi interest, which was dominated by extensive Western archaeological excavations, archaeology became an issue in the overall struggle for control and power. Whereas the British and other Western powers still had ultimate command over Iraq's oil resources and to a certain extent directed its military maneuvers, the issue of archaeology became a convenient battleground for Iraqis to question Western control in the region. Eventually, the Iraqis were able to assert their dominion in archaeological matters and produced legislation that sought to prevent any antiquities found in Iraqi soil from leaving the country.

Many of the subsequent Iraqi decisions in archaeological matters were framed by the perception that the Westerners had conducted matters in a manner that was detrimental to Iraq. As an independent, sovereign state, Iraq vigorously asserted its independence in archaeology, stressing that this new state should have ultimate control over its historical artifacts. Therefore, when Iraq was being ushered into a new stage, that of a nation-state, archaeology entered the political discourse early, making the two realms at times indistinguishable. In fact, archaeology was a very important contributing factor in the production of national culture.

Archaeology has been a useful tool in the construction of national identity in Iraq, promulgating not only a sense of belonging to a particular history, but also proprietorship over specific artifacts. Under the impetus of nationalism, archaeology in Iraq has been less concerned with answering universal, all-engrossing questions. Rather, official archaeology has concentrated on interpreting the archaeological record as the history of specific peoples and an explanation of how contemporary Iraqis are the inheritors and descendants of certain ancient peoples and their civilizations. This construction has been deliberate, because it was largely undertaken by individuals and institutions with political purposes in mind. The standardization of education and the establishment of museums sought to appeal to the citizens nationwide and thus be suggestive of how Iraq's history is genealogical and linear and not multidimensional. Iraq developed its paraphernalia, such as flags, patriotic songs, and stamps, to verify its authenticity. Archaeology would contribute to this paraphernalia by supplying materials and motifs for public monuments and displays.

In such an atmosphere, archaeologists are under much pressure to produce specific results that can be easily articulated in political discourse. This narrowly determines the parameters of research, since the questions that are allowed to be asked about the past are limited. Nevertheless, such interpretation is a powerful tool that has promoted group identity in Iraq and provided meaning for countless Iraqis during periods of intense political and social change.

In the time period under consideration, archaeology—as a science, philosophy, business, and even a certain outlook—was an important feature in making "Iraq" an Iraq. It was one of the many underlying features that complicated Iraq's relations with the Mandate power, Britain. Yet at the same time, the motifs of this story are not limited to the Iraqi experience. Rather, as the general history of postindependence states in Africa, the Middle East, South Asia, and Southeast Asia suggests, many newly created states, often with nascent governmental institutions, aggressively sought to have control over their own history and historical artifacts in order to help legitimize and consolidate the nation. As an academic discipline, history was part of the nationalist enterprise. As an economic and emotional resource, archaeological artifacts became symbols of the embryonic state. And as the nation-states grew in their ambition and internal scope and were faced with the numerous, complicated practical challenges of developing in the modern world, antiquities were employed, both literally and figuratively, to produce paradigms of nationhood. In Iraq, this paradigmatic nationalism has been a central feature of national identity, conveying to and then imposing on its citizens a logical historical sequence that has culminated in the modern state of Iraq.

On a more symbolic level, the looting and destruction of heritage removed vestiges of Iraq's past, perhaps indicating that a new reality was in place. The recent experience and memory of a repressive and ruthless government and crippling economic sanctions may have necessitated a clean break with the past. Yet if the Iraqi nation is to fully recover from the trauma of its past, it will need to come to terms with that past and seek motivation and guidance in its history. This inspiration and common ground can be found in Iraq's ancient history, symbolized most vividly in the unique archaeological heritage of the country.

Throughout Iraqi history, the national narrative has emphasized unity of Iraq's disparate ethnic and religious groups and thus presented a distinct political reading and presentation of the nation's past.

NOTES

INTRODUCTION

1. The Web sites of the Middle East Librarians Association Committee on the Iraqi Library, hosted at the Oriental Institute at the University of Chicago, and the Middle East Library Committee at the University of Exeter contain useful links pertaining to Iraq's library collections. A group of Middle East specialists (Keith Watenpaugh, Edouard Méténier, Jens Hanssen, and Hala Fattah) formed the Iraqi Observatory and visited Iraq in June of 2003 to survey the damage and issued a report entitled *Opening the Doors: Intellectual Life and Academic Conditions in Post-War Baghdad*, which also is available online (http://www.h-net/org/about/press/ opening_doors/).

2. The first news stories suggested that over two hundred thousand pieces had been taken. Subsequently, with more information and research, it became clear that Iraqi museum officials had removed many important museum pieces for storage in the country's central bank, among other places. See newspaper article by Eric Rich in the *Hartford Courant*, "A Treasure beneath the Rubble," June 3, 2003.

3. The Internet site http://www2.h-net.msu.edu/~museum/iraq .html contains an exhaustive digest of news relating to the looting of Iraqi museums. Of the many articles on this topic, see, for example, Jonathan Steele, "Museum's Treasures Left to the Mercy of Looters" in *The Guardian*, April 14, 2003. The Oriental Institute at the University of Chicago also initiated an Internet-based project that tracked developments regarding Iraqi archaeology (http://listhost.uchicago.edu/pipermail/iraqcrisis/).

4. "Pentagon Was Told of Risk to Museums. U.S. Urged to Save Iraq's Historic Artifacts" in *Washington Post*, April 14, 2003, p. A19.

5. Although a term that is laden with problems, in this book the term "Western" will be used to designate European and North American nationals or countries. Most often, it suggests the British, but American, German, and French nationals also played important roles.

6. The events of 2003 indicate what happens to artifacts when there is an absence of power.

7. In this study, the terms "Iraq" and "Mesopotamia" will be used interchangeably. In general, the former will only be used to denote the modern state that was established in 1921. Therefore, if the discussion is centered before that date, the term Mesopotamia will be used to describe the area which today is known as Iraq.

8. On the formation of modern Iraq and its early political history see Peter Sluglett, *Britain in Iraq 1914–1932* (London: Ithaca Press, 1976); Stephen Longrigg, *Iraq 1900–1950* (Oxford: Oxford University Press, 1953); 'Abbas al-'Azzawi, *Ta'rikh al-'iraq bayna al-ihtilalayn,* 8 vols. (Baghdad: Matba al-Baghdad, 1955); 'Abd al-Razzaq al-Hasani, *Ta'rikh al-wizarat al-'iraqiyyah,* 10 vols. (Sidon, Lebanon: Matba'at al-Irfan, 1933–1967). For an excellent article on nationalism in interwar Iraq see Reeva Simon, "The Imposition of Nationalism on a Non-Nation State: The Case of Iraq during the Interwar Period, 1921–1941," in *Rethinking Arab Nationalism,* ed. James Jankowski and Israel Gershoni (New York: Columbia University Press, 1997), pp. 87–105.

9. In 1921 there were numerous religious and ethnic groups in Iraq. In addition to Arabs (both Sunni and Shi'i), Iraq was also home to Kurds, Turkomans, Assyrians, Sabeans, Persians, Armenians, Chaldeans, Jews, and Yazidis. For the best and most detailed discussion on the diversity of Iraqis see Hanna Batatu, *The Old Social Classes and the Revolutionary Movements of Iraq* (Princeton, N.J.: Princeton University Press, 1978), especially Chapters 2 and 3. For population estimates see R. I. Lawless, "Iraq: Changing Population Patterns," in *Populations of the Middle East and North Africa,* ed. J. I. Clarke and W. F. Fisher (London: London University Press, 1972), pp. 97–127.

10. Eric Davis, *Memories of State: Politics, History and Collective Identity in Modern Iraq* (Berkeley: University of California Press, 2004), p. 2.

11. Quoted in Batatu, *The Old Social Classes,* pp. 25–26.

12. Samir al-Khalil (pseud.), *Republic of Fear: The Inside Story of Saddam's Iraq* (New York: Pantheon Books, 1990), p. 152. This work was subsequently published under the author's real name, Kenan Makiyeh.

13. Sami Shawkat, *Hadhihi ahdafuna* (Baghdad: n.p., 1939), p. 81.

14. See for example, Philip L. Kohl and Clare Fawcett, eds., *Nationalism, Politics and the Practice of Archaeology* (Cambridge: Cambridge University Press, 1995) and Margarita Diaz-Andreu and Timothy Champion, eds., *Nationalism and Archaeology in Europe* (London: University College of London Press, 1996). For the Middle East, see Neil Asher Silberman, *Between Past and Present: Archaeology, Ideology, and Nationalism in the Modern Middle East* (New York: Henry Holt & Company, 1989); Nadia Abu El-Haj, *Facts on the Ground: Archaeological Practice and Territorial Self-Fashioning in*

Israeli Society (Chicago: University of Chicago Press, 2001); and Donald Malcolm Reid, *Whose Pharaohs? Archaeology, Museums, and Egyptian National Identity from Napoleon to World War I* (Berkeley: University of California Press, 2002).

15. For Lebanon see Michelle Hartman and Alessandro Olsaretti, "'The First Boat and the First Oar': Inventions of Lebanon in the Writings of Michel Chiha," *Radical History Review* 86 (2003): 37–65. See also Paul Salem's *Bitter Legacy: Ideology and Politics in the Arab World* (Syracuse, N.Y.: Syracuse University Press, 1994), especially Chapter 5.

16. Linda Colley, *The Britons: Forging the Nation, 1707–1838* (New Haven, Conn.: Yale University Press, 1992), p. 6.

17. Peter Sahlins, *Boundaries: The Making of France and Spain in the Pyrenees* (Berkeley and Los Angeles: University of California Press, 1989), p. 271.

18. The best accounts covering the pan-Arab period are found in Majid Khadduri, *Independent Iraq, 1932–1958* (London: Oxford University Press, 1960); Batatu, *The Old Social Classes;* and Reeva Simon, *Iraq between the Two World Wars: The Creation and Implementation of a Nationalist Ideology* (New York: Columbia University Press, 1986). For the stages of Iraqi particularism see Uriel Dann, *Iraq under Qassem: A Political History 1958–63* (New York: Praeger, 1969); Amatzia Baram, *Culture, History and Ideology in the Formation of Ba'thist Iraq, 1968–89* (New York: St. Martin's Press, 1991). See also Amatzia Baram's "A Case of Imported Identity: The Modernizing Secular Ruling Elites of Iraq and the Concept of Mesopotamian-Inspired Territorial Nationalism, 1922–1992," *Poetics Today* 15 (2): 279–319. For a very good discussion of this clash of paradigms, see Davis, *Memories of State,* especially Chapters 1 and 2. Charles Tripp's *The History of Iraq* (Cambridge: Cambridge University Press, 2002) is an excellent political history of Iraq.

19. Quoted in Baram, *Culture, History,* p. 49.

20. For the third stage, see Baram, *Culture, History.* Because of the political and economic situation in Iraq, gaining access to primary source materials in Iraqi archives is impossible. Therefore, this book focused on the first two stages because the sources for the period under consideration (1810–1941) were more available outside Iraq. Baram in his impressive *Culture, History* collected and analyzed numerous Iraqi newspapers and political tracts in a study that is more concerned with explaining the cultural policies of the Ba'athi Iraq than the political history of archaeology.

21. *Illustrated London News* (London, July 27, 1850), p. 3.

22. C. M. Hinsley, "Revising and Revisioning the History of Archaeology: Reflections on Region and Context," in *Tracing Archaeology's Past: The Historiography of Archaeology,* ed. Andrew L. Christianson (Carbondale: Southern Illinois University Press, 1989), p. 88.

23. *Al-Thawra* (Baghdad), August 6, 1980. Quoted in Baram, *Culture, History,* p. 43.

24. Baram, *Culture, History,* p. 43.

25. Hinsley, "Revising and Revisioning," pp. 89–90.

26. Ibid.

CHAPTER ONE

1. By the 1760s, for example, Enlightenment writers such as Adam Smith were conceptualizing the development of human society as a progression through a series of stages characterized by different modes of subsistence.

2. One historian has argued that the idea of progress was of central importance because it offered a compromise between the old creationism and the more extreme manifestations of the new materialism. See Peter J. Bowler, *The Invention of Progress: The Victorians and the Past* (Oxford: Basil Blackwell, 1989), pp. 4–5.

3. Herbert Butterfield, *The Origins of History* (London: Basic Books, 1981), p. 214.

4. Ian Jenkins, *Archaeologists and Aesthetes in the Sculpture Galleries of the British Museum 1800–1939* (London: British Museum Press, 1992), p. 10.

5. Frank M. Turner, *The Greek Heritage in Victorian Britain* (New Haven, Conn.: Yale University Press, 1981), p. 213. This theme of reflection is also discussed in Dwight A. Culler, *The Victorian Mirror of History* (New Haven, Conn.: Yale University Press, 1985), which focuses on the habit of the Victorian British of drawing analogies between their own age and various historical periods of the past in attempting to understand their own problems.

6. Hugh Honour, *Romanticism* (New York: Harper & Row, 1979), p. 18; see also George W. Stocking, *Victorian Anthropology* (New York: Free Press, 1987).

7. See Robert Drews, *The Greek Accounts of Eastern History* (Cambridge, Mass.: Harvard University Press, 1973).

8. In the nineteenth century many painters turned to the ancient world as a source of mythological fantasy and imagination. These painters often portrayed the leisure class of the ancients very much in their own image, or, as Peter Bowler has argued, as "'Victorians in Togas[,]' and thus promoted an almost cyclic vision of history." Bowler, *Invention of Progress,* p. 46.

9. Arnaldo Momigliano, *Studies in Historiography* (London: Harper & Row, 1966), p. 2.

10. As Momigliano points out, it is noteworthy that most great antiquarians of the seventeenth century were physicians, as interpretation of individual objects or inscriptions was the favorite exercise of these men.

Arnaldo Momigliano, *The Classical Foundations of Modern Historiography* (Berkeley: University of California Press, 1990), p. 58.

11. Richard Stoneman, *Land of Lost Gods: The Search for Classical Greece* (Norman: University of Oklahoma Press, 1987), pp. 56–83.

12. Edward Tylor, *Anthropology: An Introduction to the Study of Man and Civilization* (New York: D. Appleton and Co., 1881).

13. See Marjorie Caygill, *The Story of the British Museum,* 2nd ed. (London: British Museum Press, 1992); Francis Haskell, *Rediscoveries in Art: Some Aspects of Taste, Fashion and Collecting in England and France* (Ithaca, N.Y.: Cornell University Press, 1976).

14. For an extensive history of art collecting see Joseph Alsop, *The Rare Art Traditions: The History of Art Collecting and Its Linked Phenomena Wherever These Have Appeared* (Princeton, N.J.: Princeton University Press, 1982).

15. Douglas Newton, "Old Wine in New Bottles, and the Reverse," in *Museums and the Making of "Ourselves": The Role of Objects in National Identity,* ed. Flora E. S. Kaplan (London: Leicester University Press, 1994), pp. 269–271.

16. Austen Henry Layard, *The Monuments of Nineveh* (London: John Murray, 1849), p. 3.

17. For this literature see Jean Delumeau, *History of Paradise: The Garden of Eden in Myth and Tradition* (New York: Continuum, 1995); A. B. Giamatti, *The Earthly Paradise and the Renaissance Epic* (Princeton, N.J.: Princeton University Press, 1966); and J. E. Duncan, *Milton's Earthly Paradise: A Historical Study of Eden* (Minneapolis: University of Minnesota Press, 1972).

18. G. H. T. Kimble, *Geography in the Middle Ages* (London: Methuen & Co., Ltd., 1938), p. 31. See also F. Plaut, "Where Is Paradise? The Mapping of a Myth," *Map Collector* 24 (1984): 24–36. As Kimble, and later Delumeau, discuss, sacred history often determined geographical conceptions. Up until the twelfth century, most European maps usually put the East at the top. However, by the end of the twelfth century, the Arab model, which placed either the North or the South at the top of maps, became predominant. Such a configuration placed Jerusalem as the focal point of the map, which further epitomized its role for the faithful Christian. Delumeau, *History of Paradise,* p. 56.

19. For such paradigms and configurations see Max F. Schulz, *Paradise Preserved: Recreations of Eden in Eighteenth- and Nineteenth-Century England* (Cambridge: Cambridge University Press, 1985), especially pp. 1–5.

20. No monograph exists specifically on the role of Babylon or Nineveh in Western apocalyptic thought. For general studies see Christopher Hill, *Antichrist in Seventeenth-Century England* (London: Oxford University Press, 1971); Steven Goldsmith, *Unbuilding Jerusalem: Apocalypse and Romantic Representation* (Ithaca, N.Y.: Cornell University Press, 1993); J. F. C. Harrison, *The Second Coming: Popular Millenarianism, 1780–1850* (New Brunswick, N.J.: Rutgers University Press, 1979); Bernard McGinn, *Visions*

of the End: Apocalyptic Traditions in the Middle Ages (New York: Columbia University Press, 1979). In David Bjelajac's *Millennial Desire and the Apocalyptic Vision of Washington Allston* (Washington, D.C.: Smithsonian Institution Press, 1988), he analyzes how Allston's millennial beliefs were integral in some of his paintings.

21. See, for example, Paul Boyer, *When Time Shall Be No More: Prophecy Belief in Modern American Culture* (Cambridge, Mass.: Harvard University Press, 1992), especially Chapters 9 and 10.

22. Karl H. Dannenfeldt, *Leonhard Rauwolf: Sixteenth-Century Physician, Botanist, and Traveller* (Cambridge, Mass.: Harvard University Press, 1968), p. 110.

23. See Christopher Hill, *Puritanism and Revolution* (London: Mercury Books, 1958), especially Chapter 12.

24. Marilyn Butler, "John Bull's Other Kingdom: Byron's Intellectual Comedy," *Studies in Romanticism* 31 (3): 284.

25. Richard Philips, *The Picture of London for 1806,* p. 301, as quoted in William Feaver, *The Art of John Martin* (Oxford: Clarendon Press, 1975), p. 9.

26. For a study on the mid-nineteenth century see Kenneth Paul Bendiner, "The Portrayal of the Middle East in British Painting" (Ph.D. diss., Columbia University, 1979), which focuses primarily on David Roberts, David Wilkie, John Frederick Lewis, and William Holman Hunt.

27. See Morton D. Paley, *The Apocalyptic Sublime* (New Haven, Conn.: Yale University Press, 1986).

28. Robert Rosenblum, *Modern Painting and the Northern Romantic Tradition* (New York: Harper & Row, 1975), pp. 10–40.

29. John Davis, *The Landscape of Belief: Encountering the Holy Land in Nineteenth-Century American Art and Culture* (Princeton, N.J.: Princeton University Press, 1996).

30. *New Monthly Magazine,* no. 2, p. 171, as quoted in Feaver, *Art of John Martin,* p. 42.

31. Feaver, *Art of John Martin,* pp. 40–43.

32. Kermode, Frank, *The Sense of an Ending: Studies in the Theory of Fiction* (New York: Oxford University Press, 1967).

33. Lynn Robert Matteson, "Apocalyptic Themes in British Romantic Landscape Painting" (Ph.D. diss., University of California, Berkeley, 1975), p. 72.

34. Interestingly, in the same year, John Martin published a pamphlet, *Mr. John Martin's Plan for Supplying with Pure Water the Cities of London and Westminster,* which was entirely in keeping with the gargantuan scale of the Oriental cities of his paintings. As Balston suggests, Martin was inspired by the cities of his imagination, as he envisaged two colonnades of several miles' length on either side of the Thames, which were to be illuminated, like his Oriental palaces, by gas lamps. Thomas Balston, "John Martin and Metropolitical Improvements," in *Architectural Review* 102 (1947): 51–54.

35. Matteson, "Apocalyptic Themes," pp. 133–134. For example, in 1819 Sir John Soane, in a lecture at the Royal Academy of Art, reminded his audience that the vestiges of the ancient cities such as Nineveh, Babylon, Palmyra, and Balbeck form a "melancholy memento of the instability of human grandeur." Quoted in Matteson, "Apocalyptic Themes," p. 138.

36. Feaver, *Art of John Martin*, p. 40. The emphasis is mine.

37. Norah Monkton, "Architectural Backgrounds in John Martin" *Architectural Review* 104 (1948): 81–84. As Martin's biographer Thomas Balston relates, Martin's library contained a number of histories in which descriptions of ancient cities could be found, such as Diodorus, Herodotus, Josephus and Plutarch, as well as Thomas Maurice's *The History of Hindustan*. Thomas Balston, *John Martin: His Life and Works* (London: G. Duckworth, 1947), pp. 267–268. Another source Martin may have relied on was Fischer von Erlach's "Spectacula Babylonica," included in his *Entwurff für Historisches Architektur* (1721), which emphasized Babylon's wide embankments and streets going in right lines, intersecting each other at right angles.

38. Paley, *Apocalyptic Sublime*, p. 132.

39. Ibid.

40. Jerrold Cooper, "From Mosul to Manila: Early Approaches to Funding Ancient Near Eastern Studies Research in the United States," in *Culture and History* 7 (1992): 131–134.

41. See, for example, A. J. Wensinck and G. Vadja, "Fir'awn" in *Encyclopedia of Islam* (Leiden, the Netherlands: Brill, 1965), 2:917–918.

42. The Qur'anic verse is Surah II:95. "When there has come to them a Messenger from God confirming what was with them, a party of them that were given the Book reject the Book of God behind their backs, as though they knew not, and they follow what the Satans recited over Solomon's kingdom. Solomon disbelieved not, but the Satans disbelieved, teaching the people sorcery, and that which was sent down upon Babylon's two angels, Harut and Marut; they taught not any man, without they said, 'We are but a temptation; do not disbelieve.'"

43. Based on A. J. Wensinck's entry "Harut and Marut" in *Shorter Encyclopedia of Islam* (Leiden, the Netherlands: Brill, 1995), pp. 134–135. According to Enoch 8:8 and 9:7, Harut and Marut remained in Babil and taught sorcery. In the thirteenth century, al-Qazwini, when describing the ruins of Babil, stated that the village was visited by Jews and Christians on certain festivals, particularly to see the "Dungeon of Danyal," believed by most of the population to be the well of Harut and Marut. See Georges Awad, "Babil" in *Encyclopedia of Islam* (Leiden, the Netherlands: Brill, 1974), p. 846.

44. For example, verses 22:1; 22:7; 40:59–61; 42:17; and 54:1.

45. Tarif Khalidi, *Islamic Historiography: The Histories of Mas'udi* (Albany: State University of New York Press, 1975), p. 82.

46. In his history *Ta'rikh; al-rusul wa'l-muluk (The History of Prophets and Kings)*, Tabari states that Babil was the first city to be built on earth (see *The History of al-Tabari*, vol. 1 trans. Franz Rosenthal [Albany: State University of New York Press, 1989], p. 341), whose first ruler, Tahmurath, was given so much power by God that *Iblis* and his satans were submissive to him (1:345).

47. As Khalidi points out Tabari's extensive treatment of Persian history also stemmed from his belief that the Islamic empire was heir to the Persian empire. Khalidi, *Islamic Historiography*, p. 83, n. 3.

48. See al-Tabari, *The History of al-Tabari*, vol. 4 trans. by Moshe Perlman (Albany: State University of New York Press, 1987), pp. 1, 6, and 17.

49. al-Tabari, *The History of al-Tabari*, 4:36–38, 40, 48–55, 60–71.

50. Ibn Haykal in *The Oriental Geography of Ebn Haukal*, trans. William Ouseley (Frankfurt: Institute for the History of Arabic-Islamic Science, 1992), p. 70. See also Awad, "Babil," p. 846. Other Arab writers would refer to Ibn Haykal's account in their own summaries of the area. For instance, Abu al-Fida' and al-Qazwini, writing in the thirteenth century, described the ruins of Babil and mentioned how the current inhabitants would quarry its bricks for their own houses (a practice that would continue well into the twentieth century). The Danish scholar Carsten Niebuhr, during his visit in the seventeenth century, would make similar observations.

51. Ibn Khaldun, *The Muqaddimah*, trans. Franz Rosenthal (New York: Pantheon Books, 1958), 1:58.

52. Ibn Khaldun, *The Muqaddimah*, 2:287–288.

53. For similar ideas among American missionaries in Syria see Ussama Makdisi, "Reclaiming the Land of the Bible: Missionaries, Secularism, and Evangelical Modernity," *American Historical Review* 102 (3): 680–713.

54. On Egyptology and its origins see Rosalie A. David, *Discovering Ancient Egypt* (New York: Facts on File, 1994); Margaret Alice Murray, *The Splendour That Was Egypt* (New York: Philosophical Library, 1949); Nancy Thomas, ed., *The American Discovery of Ancient Egypt* (Los Angeles: Los Angeles County Museum of Art, 1996); Werner Kaiser, *75 Jahre Deutsches Archäologisches Institut Kairo, 1907–1982* (Mainz, Germany: P. von Zabein, 1982). For a history of archaeological activities in Egypt see Brian Fagan's *The Rape of the Nile: Tomb Robbers, Tourists and Archaeologists in Egypt* (New York: Scribner, 1975). On the influence of Egypt on Western art and thought see Richard Carrot, *The Egyptian Revival: Its Sources, Monuments, and Meaning, 1808–1858* (Berkeley: University of California Press, 1978); James Stevens Curl, *Egyptomania: The Egyptian Revival; A Recurring Theme in the History of Taste* (New York: St. Martin's Press, 1994).

55. For technical archaeological histories of Iraq see Charles Keith Maisels, *The Near East: Archaeology in the "Cradle of Civilization"* (London: Routledge, 1993); David Oates, *Studies in the Ancient History of Northern Iraq*

(London: Oxford University Press, 1968); Stoneman, *Land of Lost Gods;* Nicholas Postgate, *The First Empires* (Oxford: Elsevier-Phaidon, 1977); Joan Oates, *The Rise of Civilization* (Oxford: Elsevier-Phaidon, 1976). Svend Pallis has an excellent and exhaustive survey in his *The Antiquity of Iraq: A Handbook of Assyriology* (Copenhagen: E. Munksgaard, 1956).

56. Frederick N. Bohrer, "A New Antiquity: The English Reception of Assyria" (Ph.D. diss., University of Chicago, 1989), p. 1. The fascination with Egypt continues up to the present day, as the vibrant tourist industry of Egypt suggests. However, Iraq has never through its history been a popular destination for tourists. Although people clearly identify ancient Egypt with the modern state of Egypt, such an association is much more vague for many Westerners when it comes to Babylonia or Assyria and its geographical links to modern Iraq.

57. For example, Thomas Maurice, a librarian at the British Museum writing in 1816, starts his discussion on the history of Babylon by quoting St. Jerome's commentary on Isaiah 13 as proof of the utter decay of Babylon. Thomas Maurice, *Observations Connected with Astronomy and Ancient History, Sacred and Profane on the Ruins of Babylon, as Recently Visited and Described by Claudius James Rich* (London: J. Murray, 1816), p. 27. While commenting on the fauna of Mesopotamia, Maurice states on p. 191 that "various parts of scripture confirm this account of the swampy nature of Babylonian territory," such as Isaiah, which states, "I will dry the sea of Babylon and make her springs dry." The inescapable destiny of Babylon was clear for Maurice: "That Babylon should become a desolation was recorded among the high and irrevocable decrees of that providence, which generally employs secondary causes for the execution of them" (p. 202).

58. Glyn Daniel, *A Hundred Years of Archaeology* (London: Duckworth, 1950), p. 70.

59. Thomas Maurice, *Observations on the Remains of Ancient Egyptian Grandeur and Superstition as Connected with Those of Assyria: Forming the Appendix to the Observations on the Ruins of Babylon* (London: J. Murray, 1818), p. 27. Even though he relies entirely on secondary accounts for his discussion, Maurice goes to great lengths to emphasize how barren and desolate the area around Babylon is. He states, "the abundance and fertility induced by the Euphrates and Tigris . . . which had been the labor of so many kings . . . made it [the land] a chosen seat of princely domination . . . [but] is now for the most part a barren desert and inhabited by savage Arabian hordes" (p. 3).

60. John M. Lundquist, "Babylon in European Thought," in *Civilizations of the Ancient Near East,* ed. Jack Sasson (New York: Scribner, 1996), 1:68.

61. Layard, *The Monuments of Nineveh,* pp. 2–3.

62. Pallis, *The Antiquity of Iraq,* p. 42.

63. Lundquist, *Babylon in European Thought,* p. 68. Not all travelers were concerned with the ruins of Mesopotamia during their travels. For exam-

ple, Marco Polo's and "John Mandeville's" journeys through Asia, in 1271–1295 and 1322–1356, respectively, do not mention the ruins despite their visits to Mosul and Baghdad.

64. Lundquist, *Babylon in European Thought*, p. 69.

65. Leonhard Rauwolf, *Aigentliche Beschreibung der Raisz so er vor dieser zeit gegen Auffgang inn die Morgenländer . . . selbs volbract* (Laugingen, Germany: Verlag G. Willers, 1583). For an early English account of his travels see John Ray, ed., *A Collection of Curious Travels and Voyages in Two Tomes: The First Containing Dr. Leonhart Rauwolff's Itinerary into the Eastern Countries . . .* (London: Royal Society at the Princes Arms, 1693). For a more recent study on Rauwolf see Dannenfeldt, *Leonhard Rauwolf.* According to Dannenfeldt, Rauwolf was the first European to describe the preparation and drinking of coffee and the routine of a Turkish bath.

66. Dannenfeldt, *Leonhart Rauwolf,* p. 107.

67. For the writings of these early travelers see Richard Haklyut, *The Principal Navigations, Voyages, Traffiques and Discoveries of the English Nation,* 10 vols. (London: J. M. Dent and Sons Ltd., 1927–1928); 3:201–202 (Federici), 3:283 (Fitch), and 3:324–325 (Eldred).

68. Della Valle's travel account has recently been republished in *The Pilgrim: The Travels of Pietro Della Valle,* translated, abridged, and introduced by George Bull (London: Hutchinson, 1989). On Della Valle's travels to Babylon see pp. 106–107.

69. Carsten Niebuhr, *Reisebeschreibung nach Arabien und andern umliegenden Ländern* (Copenhagen: N. Möller, 1778), 2:353.

70. Pallis, *The Antiquity of Iraq,* p. 45.

71. Maurice de Beauchamp, "An Account of Some of the Antiquities of Babylon Found in the Neighbourhood of Baghdad: Also of What Is to Have Been the Tower of Babel, and of the Yezidis," in *European Magazine* 5 (1792): 340.

72. John Ruskin complained in the early decades of the nineteenth century that "the endeavours at representation of Oriental character or costume which accompany the travels of even the best educated English traveller are without exception the clumsiest, most vulgar and most ludicrous pieces of work." In John Ruskin, *The Works of John Ruskin,* ed. Cook and Wedderburn (London: George Allen, 1903–1912), 35:405.

73. Dannenfeldt, *Leonhart Rauwolff,* p. 95.

74. Quoted in Bendiner, "Portrayal of the Middle East," p. 41.

75. Edward Said, *Orientalism* (New York: Vintage Books, 1978); Henri Baudet, *Paradise on Earth: Some Thoughts on European Images of Non-European Man* (New Haven, Conn.: Yale University Press, 1965); Samuel Chew, *The Crescent and the Rose* (New York: Oxford University Press, 1937); Norman Daniel, *Islam and the West: The Making of an Image* (Edinburgh: Edinburgh University Press, 1960); Rana Kabbani, *Europe's Myths of Orient* (Bloomington: Indiana University Press, 1986); Dorothee Metlitzki, *The*

Matter of Araby in Medieval England (New Haven, Conn.: Yale University Press, 1977); Raymond Schwab, *La Renaissance Orientale* (Paris: Payot, 1950); R. W. Southern, *Western Views of Islam in the Middle Ages* (Cambridge, Mass.: Harvard University Press, 1962).

76. The role of the Orient in this endeavor has been well documented in Said's *Orientalism*.

77. Benjamin Kedar, *Crusade and Mission: European Approaches to the Muslims* (Princeton, N.J.: Princeton University Press, 1984); James Field, *America and the Mediterranean World 1776–1882* (Princeton, N.J.: Princeton University Press, 1969); L. Carl Brown, *International Politics and the Middle East* (Princeton, N.J.: Princeton University Press, 1984); Roger Owen, *The Middle East in the World Economy 1800–1914* (London: Methuen, 1981); Albert Hourani, *Europe and the Middle East* (Berkeley: University of California Press, 1980).

78. A valuable study on the politics of nineteenth-century Mesopotamia is Tom Nieuwenhuis's *Politics and Society in Early Modern Iraq: Mamluk Pashas, Tribal Shayks and Local Rule between 1802 and 1931* (The Hague: M. Nijhoff, 1982).

79. See, for example, Mogens Trolle Larsen, *The Conquest of Assyria* (London: Routledge, 1996), p. 27.

80. For an excellent discussion on the Ottoman Antiquities legislation and museums in the empire, see Wendy M. K. Shaw, *Possessors and Possessed: Museums, Archaeology, and the Visualization of History in the Late Ottoman Empire* (Berkeley: University of California Press, 2003).

81. Stanford Shaw and E. K. Shaw, *History of the Ottoman Empire and Modern Turkey* (Cambridge: Cambridge University Press, 1977), 2:111.

82. Claudius J. Rich, *Memoir on the Ruins of Babylon* (London: Longman, Hurst, Reese, Orme & Brown, 1815). Posthumously another memoir was published, edited by his wife: *Narrative of a Residence in Kooridstan, and on the Site of Ancient Nineveh, with a Journal of a Voyage down the Tigris to Baghdad etc.* (London: Duncan and Malcolm, 1836). Rich's memoirs stimulated considerable academic discussion and public excitement and even made their way into the poem *Don Juan* by Lord Byron: ". . . some infidels, who don't / because they can't, find out the very spot. / Of that same Babel, or because they won't / (Though Claudius Rich, Esquire, some bricks has got, / and written lately two memoirs upon't)."

83. Rich, *Narrative.*

84. Quoted in Balston, *John Martin,* p. 107.

85. On French imperial ambitions in the area see William Shorrock's *French Imperialism in the Middle East: The Failure of Policy in Syria and Lebanon, 1900–1914* (Madison: University of Wisconsin Press, 1976).

86. Seton Lloyd, *Foundations in the Dust* (London: Oxford University Press, 1947), p. 103.

87. Botta has not received extensive attention. See Charles Levavasseur, "Notice sur Paul-Emile Botta," in Paul Emile Botta, *Relation d'un Voyage Dans l'Yemen* (Paris: B. Duprat, 1880), pp. 1–34. Botta's own account was only published in English translation: *M. Botta's Letters on the Discoveries at Nineveh* (London: Longman, Brown, Green, 1850).

88. Larsen, *Conquest of Assyria,* p. 24. Botta also communicated with Layard in Constantinople. Austen Henry Layard, whose voluminous collection of private papers is housed in the British Library, followed Botta's achievement closely and in a letter from July 3, 1843 (Papers of Austen Henry Layard [AHL], BL Add. MS. 58161, 11–13) to Botta he expressed his excitement over the findings and offered enthusiastic suggestions for interpretation.

89. Jenkins, *Archaeologists and Aesthetes,* p. 154.

90. Paul-Emile Botta, *Monument de Ninive découvert et décrit par M. P. E. Botta, mesuré et dessiné par M. E. Flandin. Ouvrage publié par ordre du gouvernement sous les auspices de M. le Ministre de l'Intérieur et sous la direction d'une commission de l'Institut* (Paris: Imprimerie Nationale, 1849).

91. A considerable amount of literature exists on early oriental museum exhibitions and ethnographic displays, such as Richard D. Altick, *The Shows of London* (Cambridge, Mass.: Harvard University Press, 1978); Annie Coombes, *Reinventing Africa: Museums, Material Culture, and Popular Imagination in Late Victorian and Edwardian England* (New Haven, Conn.: Yale University Press, 1994); William Schneider, *An Empire for the Masses: The French Popular Image of Africa, 1870–1900* (Westport, Conn.: Greenwood Press, 1982); John M. Mackenzie, *Propaganda and Empire: The Manipulation of British Public Opinion, 1880–1960* (Manchester: Manchester University Press, 1964).

92. Emile Zola, *L'Assommoir,* Eng. transl. A. Symons (New York: A. A. Knopf, 1924), p. 77. See also Daniel Sherman, "The Bourgeoisie, Cultural Appropriation and the Art Museum in Nineteenth-Century France," *Radical History Review* 38 (1987), p. 50, and Bohrer, "New Antiquity," p. 7.

93. His illustrious career has been adequately documented. Apart from his own writings, which include *Autobiography and Letters* (London: John Murray, 1903), *Nineveh and Its Remains* (London: John Murray, 1849), and *Discoveries in the Ruins of Nineveh and Babylon* (London: John Murray, 1853), an excellent synthesis of Layard's archaeological career is found in the recent study by Mogens Trolle Larsen, written in Danish, placing Layard within the origins of Assyriology and early archaeological activities in Mesopotamia and Asia Minor. His sources include Layard's private papers at the British Library. This book, *Sunkne Paladser: Historien om Orientens Opdagelse* (Copenhagen: Gyldendalske Bokforlag, 1994), was subsequently translated into English under the title *The Conquest of Assyria.* The standard biography is Gordon Waterfield's *Layard of Nineveh* (London: J. Murray,

1963). See also Arnold Brackman, *The Luck of Nineveh* (New York: McGraw-Hill, 1978). A good essay on Layard's archaeological career can also be found in a monograph on various aspects of Layard's life. See Julian Reade, "Reflections on Layard's Archaeological Career," in *Austen Henry Layard Tra L'Oriente e Venezia*, ed. Frederick Fales and B. J. Hickey (Rome: L'Erma di Bretschneider, 1987), pp. 47–53.

94. Layard, *Autobiography*, pp. 306–307.

95. See Larsen, *Conquest of Assyria*, pp. 108–109, 113.

96. For Layard's views on local culture in Iraq see Frederick Mario Fales, "Layard's Observation of Iraq," in *Austen Henry Layard Tra L'Oriente e Venezia*, ed. Frederick Fales and B. J. Hickey (Rome: L'Erma di Bretschneider, 1987), pp. 55–77.

97. Layard, *The Monuments of Nineveh* (London: J. Murray, 1849), 1:40–41.

98. Quoted in Bohrer, "New Antiquity," p. 46.

99. Apart from the laudatory biography of Rawlinson by his brother George, *Memoir of Major-General Sir Henry Creswicke Rawlinson* (London: Longmans, Green & Co., 1898), no biography exists on this remarkable and boisterous figure who, due to his importance in the decipherment of cuneiform, merits a serious academic study. Useful assessments of his works are found in Lloyd's *Foundations in the Dust* and in the standard histories by Ceram and Daniel. For an account of Rawlinson's diplomatic activities in Iran see Abbas Amanat, *Pivot of the Universe: Nasir al-din Shah and the Iranian Monarchy* (Berkeley: University of California Press, 1996).

100. Glyn Daniel, *Short History of Archaeology* (London: Thames & Hudson, 1981), p. 76.

101. AHL, BL Add. MS. 38977, 25–27, August 5, 1846.

102. Ibid.

103. Quoted in Larsen, *Conquest of Assyria*, p. 113.

104. This process was vividly described with illuminating illustrations in the *Illustrated London News* in various issues, such as July 27, 1850, October 26, 1850, February 8, 1851, and February 28, 1852.

105. Quoted in John Malcolm Russell, *From Nineveh to New York: The Strange Story of the Assyrian Reliefs in the Metropolitan Museum and the Hidden Masterpiece at Canford School* (New Haven, Conn.: Yale University Press, 1997), pp. 37–38.

106. See Jenkins, *Archaeologists and Aesthetes*, pp. 56–74.

107. Quoted in H. W. F. Saggs's preface to A. H. Layard, *Nineveh and Its Remains* (reprint, New York: Praeger, 1970), p. 19. See also Frederick Bohrer's illuminating article "Assyria as Art: A Perspective on the Early Reception of Ancient Near Eastern Artifacts," in *Culture and History* 4 (1989): 7–29. This quote is found in a letter sent to Layard from Rawlinson, AHL, BL Add. MS. 38976, 255–256, November 26, 1845.

108. Quoted in Edward Miller, *That Noble Cabinet: A History of the British Museum* (London: Andre Deutsch, 1973), p. 192. On these debates see also Jenkins, *Archaeologists and Aesthetes*, pp. 153–167.

109. Quoted in Bohrer, "Assyria as Art," p. 20. The Museum keepers refused to admit the Danish three-age system into the arrangement of the halls and divided the halls into "sculpture" and "smaller remains, of whatever nation or period."

110. AHL, BL Add. MS. 38977, 373–376, May 24, 1846. For Layard and Kellogg see Larsen, *Conquest of Assyria*, pp. 154–165, and Waterfield, *Layard of Nineveh*, pp. 181–183.

111. Quoted in Waterfield, *Layard of Nineveh*, p. 171.

112. Waterfield, *Layard of Nineveh*, p. 180.

113. Richard Barnett, "Layard's Influence on British Orientalism in the Nineteenth Century," in *Austen Henry Layard Tra l'Oriente E Venezia*, ed. Frederick Fales and B. J. Hickey (Rome: L'Erma di Bretschneider, 1987), pp. 177–181.

114. *The Times*, February 9, 1849.

115. See, for example, D. K. Grayson, *The Establishment of Human Antiquity* (New York: Academic Press, 1983).

116. As Larsen describes, the engineer Ainsworth, who lived in Mosul, had theretofore ridiculed the efforts at finding the exact location of Nineveh, pointing out that it had first been located at Mosul, then Botta had moved it to Khorsabad, and then the British wanted to move it to Nimrud. Larsen quotes him as writing, "There will be a native Nineveh, a French Nineveh and an English Nineveh." Larsen, *Conquest of Assyria*, p. 222.

117. A good history of decipherment is Holger Petersen, *The Discovery of Language: Linguistic Science in the Nineteenth Century* (Bloomington: Indiana University Press, 1931).

118. As Maurice Olender points out, many of the earliest philologists looked for the presumed first tongue that humans spoke and where those people had lived. One theory assuming a primal language, from which all others stem, was based on the story of the tower of Babel. Maurice Olender, *Languages of Paradise: Race, Religion, and Philology in the Nineteenth Century* (Cambridge, Mass.: Harvard University Press, 1992), especially Chapter 1.

119. BL Add. MS. 38978, 63–66, March 28, 1848.

120. Pallis, *The Antiquity of Iraq*, p. 95.

121. Grotefend's significant scientific achievements have not received the credit or attention that they deserve. For standard accounts on Grotefend see C. W. Ceram, *Gods, Graves, and Scholars* (New York: Knopf, 1967), pp. 254–267; Pallis, *Antiquity of Iraq*, pp. 99–103.

122. William Stiebing, *Uncovering the Past* (Buffalo, N.Y.: Prometheus Books, 1993), p. 96.

123. Larsen, *Conquest of Assyria*, p. 308.

124. Lloyd, *Foundations in the Dust*, p. 109.

125. Larsen, *Conquest of Assyria*, p. 309.

126. The interesting and somewhat unappreciated life of Hormuzd Rassam is dealt with briefly in an article by Julian Reade, "Hormuzd Rassam and His Discoveries," *Iraq* 54–55 (1993): 39–60. According to Reade, the family papers of Rassam, including his diaries and unpublished autobiography, appear to have perished. The sources for Rassam's life consist, therefore, largely of his own published writings, such as his *Asshur and the Land of Nimrod* . . . (New York: Eaton & Mains, 1897) and the letters and reports in the archives of the British Museum and British Library.

127. Waterfield, *Layard of Nineveh*, pp. 197–198.

128. Stiebing, *Uncovering the Past*, p. 107.

129. Quoted in Stanley Lane-Poole, *The Life of the Right Honourable Stratford Canning* . . . (London: Longmans, Green, 1888), 2:149.

130. Quoted in Brackman, *Luck of Nineveh*, p. 121.

131. Reginald Campbell Thompson and R. W. Hutchinson, *A Century of Exploration at Nineveh* (London: Luzac & Co., 1929), pp. 47–58.

132. The most important feature of Wellhausen's study was his dismissal of the notion of a singular author of the Old Testament books. Wellhausen stated that Moses was not the author of the Pentateuch. Rather, Wellhausen argued, the books were composed from four different sources. He also maintained that the Old Testament had begun as a body of oral tradition passed from generation to generation until it was collected and canonized into a single account.

133. For French excavations from this period see Ernest de Sarzec, *Découvertes en Chaldée* (Paris: E. Leroux, 1884–1912).

134. The story of German activities is well documented in Johannes Renger, "Die Geschichte der Altorientalistik und der voderasiatischen Archaologie in Berlin von 1875 bis 1945," in *Berlin und die Antike*, ed. Willmuth Arenhövel and Christa Schreiber (Berlin: Deutsches Archäologisches Institut, 1979), pp. 151–192. See also Edward Meyer's "25 Jahre Deutsche Orient-Gesellschaft," in *Mitteilungen der Deutchen Orient-Gesellschaft*, no. 62 (Berlin: Deutsche Orient-Gesellschaft, 1923), pp. 1–25, and Susan Marchand's excellent *Down from Olympus: Archaeology and Philhellenism in Germany, 1750–1970* (Princeton, N.J.: Princeton University Press, 1996).

135. American archaeological activities in general have been adequately covered in Gordon Willey and Jeremy Sabloff's *A History of American Archaeology* (San Francisco: W. H. Freeman, 1993). For an interpretive history see Thomas C. Patterson's *Toward a Social History of Archaeology in the United States* (Fort Worth, Tex.: Harcourt Brace, 1995). For American expeditions in the Middle East see Philip King, *American Archaeology in the Mideast* (Philadelphia: American Schools of Oriental Research, 1983); C. W.

Meade, *Road to Babylon: The Development of U.S. Assyriology* (Leiden, the Netherlands: Brill, 1974); H. V. Hilprecht, *Explorations in Bible Lands during the Nineteenth Century* (Philadelphia: A. J. Holman, 1903); Bruce Kuklick, *Puritans in Babylon: The Ancient Near East and American Intellectual Life, 1880–1930* (Princeton, N.J.: Princeton University Press, 1996).

136. Such as Eli Smith and H. G. O. Dwight, *Researches of the Rev. E. Smith and the Rev. H. G. O. Dwight in Armenia; Including a Journey through Asia Minor and into Georgia and Persia, with a Visit to the Nestorian and Chaldean Christians of Oormiah and Salmas* (Boston: Crocker & Brewster, 1833).

137. On Robinson's career see G. Ernest Wright, "The Phenomenon of American Archaeology in the Near East," in *Near Eastern Archaeology in the Twentieth Century: Essays in Honor of Nelson Glueck*, ed. James A. Sanders (Garden City, N.Y.: Doubleday, 1970), pp. 3–40.

138. Robinson was accompanied on his travels by the missionary Eli Smith, who was fluent in Arabic and could speak to the local population to ascertain the location of specific biblical sites.

139. Edward Robinson, *Biblical Researches in Palestine, Mount Sinai and Arabia Petraea in 1838* (New York: Crocker & Brewster, 1841).

140. Quoted in King, *American Archaeology*, p. 7. Echoing this spirit, William Thompson published his *The Land and the Book; or Biblical Illustrations Drawn from the Manners and Customs, the Scenes and Scenery, of the Holy Land* (New York: Harper & Brothers, 1859) at close to the same time. The Palestine Exploration Fund's projects included the first scientific mapping of Jerusalem, as well as a exhaustive geographical survey of Palestine between 1872 and 1878, in which ten thousand sites were mapped. One of the surveyors in this project was Horatio H. Kitchener, who later embarked on a successful military career in India and Sudan, culminating in his position as the British secretary of state of war during World War I.

141. Its history is covered by Ernest Saunders, *Searching the Scriptures: A History of the Society of Biblical Literature, 1880–1980* (Chicago: Scholars Press, 1982).

142. Kuklick, *Puritans in Babylon*, p. 5.

143. Hilprecht, *Explorations in Bible Lands*, p. 290.

144. Kuklick, *Puritans in Babylon*, p. 26.

145. For the story of Peters, the Babylonian Exploration Fund, and subsequent excavations in Mesopotamia, see Kuklick, *Puritans in Babylon*, especially Chapters 1–4. The primary sources for these expeditions are found at the University Museum at the University of Pennsylvania.

146. For this dispute see Kuklick, *Puritans in Babylon*, Chapter 6.

147. Two expeditions were sent to Nippur under the direction of Peters between 1888 and 1890. The third expedition between 1893 and 1896 was under the direction of J. H. Haynes, later U.S. consul in Baghdad, and the fourth in 1898–1900 directed by Hilprecht.

148. Wright, "The Phenomenon of American Archaeology," p. 12. Samuel Noah Kramer would subsequently make these discoveries known and accessible in his *History Begins at Sumer* (Garden City, N.Y.: Doubleday, 1959).

149. Kuklick, *Puritans in Babylon*, p. 7.

150. See E. M. Earle, *Turkey, the Great Powers and the Baghdad Railway: A Study in Imperialism* (New York: Macmillan, 1923); Lothar Rathmann, *Berlin-Baghdad: Die imperialistische Nahostpolitik der kaiserlichen Deutschlands* (Berlin: Dietz, 1962). For German-Ottoman relations in general see Gregor Schöllgen, *Imperialismus und Gleichgewicht: Deutschland, England und die orientalishe Frage, 1871–1914* (Munich: R. Oldenburg, 1984); Ulrich Trumpener, "Germany and the End of the Ottoman Empire," in *The Great Powers and the End of the Ottoman Empire,* ed. Marian Kent (London: G. Allen & Unwin, 1984), pp. 111–140; Ulrich Trumpener, *Germany and the Ottoman Empire, 1914–1918* (Princeton, N.J.: Princeton University Press, 1968).

151. For a useful study of the diplomatic history of the railroad see John Wolf, *The Diplomatic History of the Bagdad Railroad* (Columbia: University of Missouri Press, 1936).

152. Marian Kent, ed., *The Great Powers and The End of the Ottoman Empire* (London: G. Allen & Unwin, 1984), p. 3. The other great powers, especially Britain, felt threatened by this new German initiative. As will be discussed later, they followed this project closely, often deploying archaeologists on expeditions close to the project to follow its progress. The most famous example of this intelligence work was that of T. E. Lawrence and Leonard Woolley, who were excavating at Carchemish in Syria prior to World War I. Their archaeological endeavors seem to have been secondary and even perhaps a cover for more covert activities.

153. For this rivalry see Paul Kennedy, *The Rise and Fall of British Naval Mastery* (London: Ashfield Press, 1976); Paul Kennedy, *The Rise of the Anglo-German Antagonism, 1860–1914* (London: G. Allen & Unwin, 1980).

154. Renger, "Die Geschichte der Altorientalistik," p. 159.

155. Quoted in Marchand, *Down from Olympus*, p. 194.

156. Friedrich Delitzsch, *Babel and Bible: Three Lectures on the Significance of Assyrological Research for Religion* (Chicago: Open Court Publishing, 1906). Delitzsch was a very energetic spokesman for Assyriology. With the patronage and even partial collaboration of the Kaiser, Delitzsch wrote a play entitled *Sardanapal*, which took place in the ancient Near East. The sets and costumes were designed after sketches by the archaeologist Walter Andrae. According to Bohrer, this play was performed four times in the Royal Opera House in Berlin in September 1908, and was well attended and received good reviews. Bohrer, "New Antiquity," p. 17.

157. On this controversy see Jacob Finkelstein, "Bible and Babel: A Comparative Study of the Hebrew and Babylonian Religious Spirit," *Commentary* 26 (1958): 431–444; Herbert B. Huffman, "Babel und Bible:

The Encounter between Babylon and the Bible," *Michigan Quarterly Review* 22 (1983): 309–320.

158. Marchand, *Down from Olympus*, p. 191.

159. For a good discussion of these efforts see Schöllgen, *Imperialismus und Gleichgewicht*, and Marchand, *Down from Olympus*, especially Chapter 7.

160. Marchand, *Down from Olympus*, p. 196.

161. Koldewey's own account can be found in his *Das wiedererstehende Babylon* (Leipzig, Germany: J. C. Hinrichs, 1913). See also Walter Andrae, *Babylon: Die versunkene Welstadt und ihr Ausgräber Robert Koldewey* (Berlin: W. de Gruyter, 1952).

162. Said, *Orientalism*, p. 1.

CHAPTER TWO

1. See, for example, Stephen Longrigg, *Iraq 1900–1950* (Oxford: Oxford University Press, 1953), and Philip W. Ireland, *Iraq: A Study in Political Development* (London: J. Cape, 1937). Longrigg states, for example, that despite vast potential, Iraq had not been developed because of "the impediments of sheer poverty, governmental ignorance, and pervading insecurity" (p. 2). "The tempo of life was that of earlier ages, traditional manners held the field and life in every relationship was based on Islam. No restless progressiveness had appeared and the evils of the times were accepted to all by submissive fatalism" (p. 17). "The level of enlightenment was low by any standards, gross superstition was rife . . . security was uncertain even in town . . . and malnutrition was the lot of four-fifths of the population" (p. 18).

2. Hanna Batatu, *The Old Social Classes and the Revolutionary Movements of Iraq* (Princeton, N.J.: Princeton University Press, 1978), p. 13.

3. Ibid., pp. 16–17.

4. For a good study on the policies of the Ottoman government in the Arab-populated parts of the empire, particularly in the early twentieth century, see Hasan Kayali's *Arabs and Young Turks: Ottomanism, Arabism and Islamism in the Ottoman Empire, 1908–1918* (Berkeley: University of California Press, 1997).

5. For general discussions of the Tanzimat see Stanford and E. K. Shaw, *History of the Ottoman Empire and Modern Turkey*, 2 vols. (Cambridge: Cambridge University Press, 1977); Bernard Lewis, *The Emergence of Modern Turkey* (Oxford: Oxford University Press, 1968). For a discussion on Tanzimat in Iraq see 'Abbas al-'Azzawi, *Ta'rikh al-'iraq bayna al-ihtilalayn* (Baghdad: Matba'at Baghdad, 1935), especially vol. 8.

6. See al-'Azzawi's *Ta'rikh al-'iraq*, especially vol. 8.

7. For a discussion of this period see Kayali, *Arabs and Young Turks;* Sukru Hanioglu, *The Young Turks in Opposition* (New York: Oxford University Press, 1995); Feroz Ahmed, *The Young Turks: The Committee of Union and*

Progress in Turkish Politics, 1908–1914 (Oxford: Oxford University Press, 1969).

8.   For more about this increase see 'Abd al-Razzaq al-Hasani, *Ta'rikh al-sihafa al-'iraqiyya* (Sidon, Lebanon: Matba'at al-Irfan, 1971), especially Chapters 1 and 2. Yitzhak Nakash, *Shi'is of Iraq* (Princeton, N.J.: Princeton University Press, 1994), pp. 52–55, demonstrates that in the shrine cities of Najaf and Karbala this new freedom of expression not only brought forth new publications, but also, more significantly, gave the mujtahids an opportunity to develop their self-image as the leaders of Muslim opposition. This image had begun to ferment during Iran's Constitutional Revolution, but the freedom of publication enabled the mujtahids to reach a wider audience and thus transformed political life in the shrine cities.

9.   Gertrude Bell, *Amurath to Amurath* (London: W. Heinemann, 1911), p. viii.

10.   Ibid.

11.   Gertrude Bell was a prolific writer and has also been the subject of various biographies and studies. Some of her own writings include *Safar Nameh, Persian Pictures* (London: Bentley, 1894); *Poems from the Divan of Hafiz* (London: W. Heinemann, 1897); *The Desert and the Sown* (London: W. Heinemann, 1907); *Amurath;* and *Palace and Mosque at Ukhaidar* (Oxford: Clarendon Press, 1914). Her letters to her parents were published by her stepmother (Florence Bell) in 1927 and entitled *Letters of Gertrude Bell,* 2 vols. (London: E. Benn, 1927). Biographies of Bell include Elizabeth Burgoyne, *Gertrude Bell* (London: E. Benn, 1961); H. V. F. Winstone, *Gertrude Bell* (New York: J. Cape, 1978); and Janet Wallach, *Desert Queen. The Extraordinary Life of Gertrude Bell: Adventurer, Adviser to Kings, Ally of Lawrence of Arabia* (New York: Anchor Books, 1996).

12.   On these women, such as Amelia Edwards, Hester Lucy Stanhope, and Margaret Gibson Dunlop, see Billie Melman, *Women's Orients: English Women and the Middle East, 1718–1918* (London: Macmillan, 1992). Melman considers Bell to be "atypical," since she was an exception to the patriarchal culture of exploration (p. 25).

13.   Bell was an accomplished mountaineer. She tackled and succeeded in climbing some of the most difficult peaks in the French and Swiss Alps. She even climbed peaks that had not yet been scaled, both on Engelhorn (one of its peaks is named Gertrude's Peak in her honor) near Chamonix and on the Finsteraarhorn glacier. These achievements are a testimony to Bell's athletic stamina, physical strength, and determination that would serve her well in her travels in the Middle East.

14.   Bell's travel account to Iran, entitled *Safar Nameh,* was published in 1894. Her uncle, Frank Lascelles, had recently been appointed the British envoy to Nasir al-Din Shah.

15.   Bell, *The Desert and the Sown,* p. 5. Bell often alluded to how the Middle East, and in particular the desert, was liberating. In a letter to her

father, where she complains of stress and the burden of her work, she stated that she "had the wildest desire to escape into the desert." Gertrude Bell Collection (GBC), Robinson Library, Special Collections, University of Newcastle-upon-Tyne, Letter to Father, January 18, 1918.

16. GBC, Letter to Mother, March 6, 1909. Similarly, in a book that Bell published in 1911, she describes Arabs at Nineveh: "At dusk the villagers assembled under the mound, which marks the spot as some small suburb of Nineveh, and watered their flocks at the pool; I watched them from my tent door and thought that the scene must have changed but little in the past three thousand years." Bell, *Amurath*, p. 263.

17. GBC, Letter to Father, April 18, 1918.

18. For these reviews, see Wallach, *Desert Queen*, pp. 78–80.

19. David Fromkin, *A Peace to End All Peace: The Fall of the Ottoman Empire and the Creation of the Modern Middle East* (New York: H. Holt, 1989), p. 449.

20. Bell, *Amurath*, pp. v–vii.

21. Ibid., p. 3.

22. Ibid., p. 4.

23. Ibid., p. 11.

24. GBC, Letter to Mother, March 18, 1909.

25. See, for example, her articles "The Excavations at Babylon," *The Times*, June 4, 1909, and "The First Capital of Assyria," *The Times*, August 23, 1910.

26. Bell's willingness to express her opinions and dominating personality did not always win her friends. Mark Sykes, a Member of Parliament who later became influential in Middle Eastern politics, disdainfully wrote a letter to his wife after he met Bell in Jerusalem wishing "10000 of my worst bad words on the head of that damned fool" and characterized her as a "silly chattering windbag of conceited, gushing, flat-chested, man-woman, globe-trotting, rump-wagging, blathering ass." Quoted in Wallach, *Desert Queen*, p. 73.

27. Jeremy Wilson, *Lawrence of Arabia: The Authorized Biography of T. E. Lawrence* (New York: Atheneum, 1990), p. 88. Bell did not seem too impressed by their archaeology, although she enjoyed their company and conversation and thus gained a favorable initial impression of Lawrence, or, as she said, "He is going to make a traveller." This in her vocabulary was high praise indeed, since she was comparing him to herself. GBC, Letter to Father, May 18, 1911.

28. GBC, Letter to Mother, April 18, 1909.

29. Bell, *Amurath*, p. 229.

30. Bell, "The First Capital of Assyria," in *The Times*, August 23, 1910.

31. Bell, *Amurath*, p. 229. For these German excavations see below.

32. Bell, "The First Capital of Assyria," in *The Times*, August 23, 1910.

33. GBC, Gertrude Bell Diary, March 10, 1911.

34. GBC, Letter to Mother, March 6, 1909.

35. GBC, unpublished manuscript, Item 20.

36. Bell, *Amurath*, p. 169.

37. Ibid.

38. GBC, unpublished manuscript, Item 20.

39. For example, commenting on current transportation links between Damascus and Baghdad, Bell wrote in *Amurath* that by traveling that road, she had the "opportunity to study the oldest problem of government" (p. 94). When she observed bitumen furnaces in the village of Hit, she observed, "The first under the troughs of molten bitumen sent up their black smoke columns between the trees; half naked Arabs fed the flames with the same bitumen, and the Euphrates bore along the product of their labors as it had done for the Babylonians before them. So it must have looked . . . for the last 5000 years and all the generations of Hit have not altered by a shade the processes taught by their first forefathers" (p. 108).

40. Bell, *Amurath*, pp. 115–116.

41. Susan Marchand, *Down from Olympus: Archaeology and Philhellinism in Germany, 1750–1970* (Princeton, N.J.: Princeton University Press, 1996), p. 192. Marchand contends, however, that this arrangement ironically had the effect that the archaeologists were more at the mercy of their politicians and diplomats, not less.

42. Conrad Preusser, *Nordmesopotamische Baudenkmaler Altchristlischer und Islamischer Zeit* (Leipzig, Germany: Druck von A. Pries, 1911).

43. Friedrich Sarre and Ernst Herzfeld, *Archaeologische Reise im Euphrat- und Tigris-Gebeit*, 4 vols. (Berlin: D. Reimer, 1911–1920).

44. Marchand, *Down from Olympus*, p. 209.

45. For these excavations at Babylon see Robert Koldewey, *The Excavations at Babylon* (London: MacMillan & Co., 1914). See also Walter Andrae, *Lebenserinnerungen eines Ausgräbers* (Berlin: W. de Gruyter, 1961), and his *Babylon: Die versunkene Weltstadt und ihr Ausgräber, Robert Koldewey* (Berlin: W. de Gruyter, 1952).

46. Koldewey, *Excavations at Babylon*, p. v.

47. Svend Pallis, *The Antiquity of Iraq: A Handbook of Assyriology* (Copenhagen: E. Munksgaard, 1956), p. 308.

48. GBC, Letter to Mother, April 18, 1909. Bell also describes visiting Assur in *Amurath*, pp. 221–226.

49. GBC, April 26, 1909.

50. See Marchand, *Down from Olympus*, pp. 214–220.

51. A voluminous literature deals with the Eastern Question mainly from the viewpoint of Western diplomatic history. See M. S. Anderson's thorough *The Eastern Question, 1774–1923* (London: Macmillan, 1966); George Lenczowski, *The Middle East in World Affairs* (Ithaca, N.Y.: Cornell University Press, 1980); David Gillard, *The Struggle for Asia: A Study in British and Russian Imperialism* (London: Methuen, 1977). L. Carl Brown's *International Politics and the Middle East* offers a more nuanced study of the

Question and takes into account some of the internal Middle Eastern political realities instead of focusing solely on European ones.

52.   For this report see Aaron S. Klieman, "Britain's War Aims in the Middle East in 1915," *Journal of Contemporary History* 3 (3): 237–253.

53.   For a good critical biography see Roger Adelson's *Mark Sykes: Portrait of an Amateur* (London: Cape, 1975).

54.   Douglas Goold, "Lord Hardinge and the Mesopotamian Expedition and Inquiry," *Historical Journal* 19 (4): 929.

55.   Ibid., p. 930.

56.   Mark Sykes, "Notes on the Arab Question" (n.d.) in Papers of Mark Sykes, Brynmor Jones Library, The University, Kingston-upon-Hull. DDSY (2) 11/68.

57.   Ireland, *Iraq*, p. 47.

58.   Ibid., pp. 60–61.

59.   Of the numerous studies on Kitchener, some of the most relevant ones are Philip Warner, *Kitchener: The Man behind the Legend* (New York: Atheneum, 1986), and Philip Magnus, *Kitchener: Portrait of an Imperialist* (New York: E. P. Dutton, 1959). Kitchener's extensive activities in the Middle East, including his work in Palestine as well as his campaigns in the Sudan, have not received much attention. For the latter see Robin Neillands, *The Dervish Wars: Gordon and Kitchener in the Sudan, 1880–1898* (London: J. Murray, 1996). For the former, see Samuel Daiches, *Lord Kitchener and His Work in Palestine* (London: Luzac & Co., 1915). For a good, yet brief, discussion of Kitchener's archaeological surveys, see Neil Asher Silberman, *Digging for God and Country: Exploration, Archaeology, and the Secret Struggles for the Holy Land, 1799–1917* (New York: Knopf, 1982), pp. 119–124. Kitchener's own publication covering this subject is his *Book of Photographs of Biblical Sites* (London: The Society's Office, 1876).

60.   See H. V. F. Winstone's biography on Woolley entitled *Woolley of Ur: The Life of Sir Leonard Woolley* (London: Secker & Warburg, 1990), pp. 41–43. In a letter to her parents, Gertrude Bell states that she was doing intelligence work in Cairo and met Woolley, "ex-digger at Carchemish and now in the Intelligence Department . . . and Mr. Hogarth and Mr. Lawrence (you don't know him, he is also of Carchemish, exceedingly intelligent)." GBC, Letter to Mother, November 30, 1915.

61.   The available sources on T. E. Lawrence are extensive. In fact, in the Western world, probably no other figure in Middle Eastern history has been the subject of as many studies as Lawrence. *The Letters of T. E. Lawrence* (edited by David Garnett) was published in 1938. Lawrence also wrote a memoir in confessional form, the well-known *Seven Pillars of Wisdom*, originally published in 1926, on his role in the Arab Revolt of 1916–1918. His epic-like reputation, originally due to a documentary by the American filmmaker Lowell Thomas and his subsequent best-selling biography *With*

Lawrence in Arabia (1924), has contributed to over sixty biographies on Lawrence. Needless to say, given Lawrence's superstar status, these biographies are of varying quality. The best studies that critically use the available sources include Jeremy Wilson, *Lawrence of Arabia*. A more alternative interpretation is found in Lawrence James, *Golden Warrior: The Life and Legend of Lawrence of Arabia* (London: Weidenfeld & Nicolson, 1990). An excellent analysis is also found in Konrad Morsey's *T. E. Lawrence und der arabische Aufstand 1916–18* (Osnabruck, Germany: Biblio-Verlag, 1976). Using unpublished sources, Morsey compares Lawrence's own account of the Arab Revolt in *Seven Pillars* with the evidence of contemporary documents. To the best of my knowledge, no study exists focusing on Lawrence's career as an archaeologist. A brief summary is found in Stephen E. Tabachnick, "Lawrence of Arabia as Archaeologist," *Biblical Archaeology Review* 23 (5): 40–47, 70–71.

62. Hogarth was a prominent archaeologist and a well-known authority on the ancient history of the Middle East. His publications include *A History of Arabia* (Oxford: Clarendon Press, 1922) and *The Ancient East* (New York: H. Holt and Company, 1914). For a somewhat speculative general overview of British intelligence work in the Middle East that focuses on many archaeologists see H. V. F. Winstone, *The Illicit Adventure: The Story of Political and Military Intelligence in the Middle East from 1898 to 1926* (London: J. Cape, 1982). Jeremy Wilson challenges some of Winstone's assumptions (Wilson, *Lawrence of Arabia*, p. 1009 n. 96) and denies that Hogarth had close ties to the intelligence community. Fromkin, *A Peace to End All Peace*, p. 171, however, claims that Hogarth worked with intelligence agencies before the war. For a study on the relationship between academe and intelligence in the American context see Robin Winks's *Cloak and Gown: Scholars in the Secret War, 1939–1961* (New York: Morrow, 1987). The activities of the Arab Bureau during the war have been extensively covered due to its role in the Arab Revolt, the Sykes-Picot Agreement, and the Husayn-McMahon Correspondence. The only study focusing solely on the Bureau itself is Bruce Westrate, *The Arab Bureau: British Policy in the Middle East, 1916–1920* (University Park: Pennsylvania State University Press, 1992). Numerous other studies discuss the work of the Bureau, including Elisabeth Monroe, *Britain's Moment in the Middle East* (Baltimore: Johns Hopkins Press, 1956); Briton C. Busch, *Britain, India and the Arabs* (Berkeley: University of California Press, 1971); Elie Kedourie, *In the Anglo-Arab Labyrinth* (Cambridge: Cambridge University Press, 1976).

63. The results of the excavations were published in C. Leonard Woolley, T. E. Lawrence, and P. L. O. Guy, *Carchemish: Report on the Excavations at Djerabis on Behalf of the British Museum*, 3 vols. (London: British Museum, 1914, 1921, 1952). See also P. R. S. Moorey, *Cemeteries of the First Millennium B.C. at Deve Huyuk, near Carchemish, Salvaged by T. E. Lawrence and*

C. L. Woolley in 1913, British Archaeological Reports Series #87 (Oxford: Archaeopress, 1980).

64. Hogarth wrote to Frederick Kenyon at the British Museum in 1911, "there is no important primitive stratum here," and expressed doubts about future work at the site, "I should not advise you to go on here." British Museum, Central Archives (BMCA), Hogarth to Kenyon, April 1, 1911.

65. Winstone, *Woolley of Ur,* p. 28, claims that "the role of the British Museum seems at best to have been one of giving respectability to an archaeological expedition which had shadowy undertones." Wilson, *Lawrence of Arabia,* pp. 125–134 and 1000, disagrees vehemently, while Tabachnick, "Lawrence of Arabia as Archaeologist," sides with Winstone. In subsequent seasons, the excavations at Carchemish became more fruitful. The British Museum secured an extensive private grant, and when Woolley arrived in 1912, he was able to have around a hundred workers at his disposal. They were even able to employ the services of the railway construction equipment to clear away spoils and assist in the digging of trenches.

66. Leonard Woolley, *As I Seem to Remember* (London: Allen and Unwin, 1962), p. 93.

67. Tabachnick, "Lawrence of Arabia as Archaeologist," p. 46. Lawrence and Woolley, to their credit, did publish an archaeological report to the members of the Palestine Exploration Fund entitled *The Wilderness of Zin* (London: Order of the Committee, 1915). The area that Woolley and Lawrence surveyed would later be General Edmund Allenby's first conquest in his Palestine campaign during World War I. During this mission, Lawrence also explored Aqaba, which would become the site of Lawrence's most important military victory during World War I.

68. Westrate, *Arab Bureau,* p. xiii.

69. For the siege at Kut see Russell Braddon's *The Siege* (New York: Cape, 1969).

70. British Library, India Office (BLIO), L/P&S/10/689, India Office Departmental Minute, December 21, 1918. This question is a critical one for the archaeological enterprise as a whole. Although it assumes an apolitical world of scholarship, it highlights the complexity of who owns the past and its artifacts.

71. For a history of war plundering see Russell Chamberlain, *Loot! The Heritage of Plunder* (New York: Facts on File, 1983). See also Cecil Gould, *Trophy of Conquest: The Musée Napoleon and the Creation of the Louvre* (London: Faber and Faber, 1965); Karl E. Meyer, *The Plundered Past* (New York: Atheneum, 1973); Barbara Hoffman, "The Spoils of War," *Archaeology* 46 (3): 37–40.

72. Jeremiah 52:19.

73. Joseph Alsop, *The Rare Art Tradition: The History of Art Collecting and Its Linked Phenomena Wherever These Have Appeared* (New York: Harper & Row,

1982), p. 172. In recent years, increasing attention has been paid to the plundering of art objects during World War II. See, for example, Lynn H. Nicholas, *The Rape of Europa: The Fate of Europe's Treasures in the Third Reich and the Second World War* (New York: Knopf, 1994).

74. Cited in Alan Marchisotto, "The Protection of Art in International Law," *Vanderbilt Journal of Transnational Law* 7 (1974): 693.

75. For these agreements see Sharon A. Williams, *The International and National Protection of Movable Cultural Property: A Comparative Study* (New York: Dobbs Ferry, 1978), pp. 15–19.

76. The Hague Convention is reprinted in *The Spoils of War: World War II and Its Aftermath: The Loss, Reappearance, and Recovery of Cultural Property*, ed. Elisabeth Simpson (New York: H. N. Abrams, 1997), pp. 278–279.

77. Lawrence M. Kaye, "Laws in Force at the Dawn of World War II: International Conventions and National Laws," in *The Spoils of War: World War II and Its Aftermath: The Loss, Reappearance, and Recovery of Cultural Property*, ed. Elisabeth Simpson (New York: H. N. Abrams, 1997), pp. 100–105.

78. Michael Posner, "Public Records under Military Occupation," *American Historical Review* 49 (1944): 213.

79. British Museum, Central Archives (BMCA), CE 32/392, *Report from the Keepers* (H. Read, A. H. Smith, G. J. Hill, and L. D. Barnett), London, October 28, 1918, p. 3. Similar sentiments were expressed in postrevolutionary France when seizure of the spoils of war by Napoleon were rationalized on the premise that France, as the center of liberty and enlightened political thought and the pivot of Europe, should be the most suitable and natural repository for the world's artistic heritage. D. M. Quynn, "The Art Confiscations of the Napoleonic Wars," *American Historical Review* 50 (1945): 437–439.

80. BLIO, L/P&S/10/689, Letter from Cecil Harcourt Smith, Victoria & Albert Museum, to Sir Reginald Brade, War Office, June 28th, 1917.

81. Ibid.

82. For a good history of the India Office see Arnold P. Kaminsky's *The India Office, 1880–1910* (New York: Greenwood Press, 1986).

83. BLIO, L/P&S/10/689, Telegram from Percy Cox, Baghdad, to IO, July 8, 1917.

84. Ibid.

85. BLIO, L/P&S/10/689, Letter from B. B. Cubitt, Army Council, to General Officer Commanding, British Forces, Mesopotamia, May 3, 1918.

86. BLIO, L/P&S/10/689 Telegram, from Arnold T. Wilson, Baghdad, to IO, June 23, 1918.

87. Shuckburgh was a veteran in the India Office, having worked there since 1900. In 1921 he was appointed by Winston Churchill to head the newly formed Middle East Department at the Colonial Office.

88. BLIO, L/P&S/10/689, Mr. Shuckburgh's notes accompanying Cox's cable from June 23, 1918.

89. Hirtzel was a veteran IO diplomat who worked there since 1894. Montagu was an influential politician who was the secretary of state for India. He was also a leading figure in the British Jewish community. S. D. Waley has written an adequate biography entitled *Edwin Montagu: A Memoir* (New York: Asian Publishing House, 1964).

90. BLIO, L/P&S/10/689, Inter-Office IO memo, June 23–24, 1918.

91. BLIO, L/P&S/10/689, IO Office Memo, June 23–24, 1918.

92. BLIO, L/P&S/10/689, Letter from FO to IO, July 25, 1918.

93. BLIO, L/P&S/10/689, Inner-Office Memorandum by Edwin Montagu, n.d.

94. Ibid.

95. BLIO, L/P&S/10/689, Inner-Office Memorandum by Arthur Hirtzel, August 12, 1918. Hirtzel is referring to Article 56 of the Hague Convention, which stated, "Any seizure or destruction of, or willful damage to historic monuments and works of art is forbidden and should be made the subject of legal proceedings."

96. BLIO, L/P&S/10/689, Minutes from Eastern Committee Meeting, August 20, 1918.

97. Ibid.

98. BLIO, L/P&S/10/689, Memorandum #85, "The Safeguarding of Antiquities in the 'Iraq," by Gertrude Bell, October 22, 1918. Note that GB uses the term "'Iraq" in her title, not a common usage for the area then. In her own letters to her parents she did not start using the term consistently until 1920.

99. There is no record of what happened to the three cases between Samarra and Basra. They may have been damaged in transit, lost, or stolen.

100. BLIO, L/P&S/10/689, Memorandum #85, "The Safeguarding of Antiquities in the 'Iraq," by Gertrude Bell, October 22, 1918.

101. Ibid.

102. BLIO, L/P&S/10/689, IO Departmental Minute, December 21, 1918.

103. Ibid.

104. BLIO, L/P&S/10/689, IO Memorandum by Thomas Holderness, February 17, 1919.

105. BLIO, L/P&S/10/689, Letter from Tilley, FO, to Kenyon, BM, January 27, 1919. Lord Curzon was an influential politician in the first decades of the twentieth century and was Britain's foreign secretary between 1919 and 1925. He was interested in Middle Eastern affairs and was the author of such books as *Persia and the Persian Question* (1892) and *Russia in Central Asia* (1899). He was the viceroy of India 1898–1905, the chancellor of Oxford University in 1907, and a Member of Parliament,

both in the House of Commons and House of Lords. Numerous studies of Curzon are available, such as Kenneth Rose, *Superior Person: A Portrait of Curzon and His Circle in Late Victorian England* (London: Weidenfeld & Nicolson, 1969), and the Earl of Ronaldshay's standard *The Life of Lord Curzon*, 3 vols. (London: E. Benn, 1928).

106.   Hall even suggested that the government of India be allotted a portion of the finds in view of the important part that India has played in the conquest and administration of Mesopotamia. He was quick to point out that the Indians should not receive any of the Assyrian or Babylonian antiquities. They could be of no interest whatever to India except as curiosities, since there was no connection between the ancient civilizations of Mesopotamia and India. The two countries knew nothing of each other until the end of the Persian period, when the old Babylonian civilization was coming to an end. Curiously, Hall did not apply that yardstick when considering whether the antiquities should go to England.

107.   BLIO, L/P&S/10/689, Report from H. R. Hall, June 7, 1919.

108.   BLIO, L/P&S/10/689, Telegram from IO to Political, Baghdad, August 25, 1919.

109.   BLIO, L/P&S/10/689, Letter from A. T. Wilson to IO, August 29, 1919.

110.   BLIO, L/P&S/10/689, Letter from Lord Curzon, FO, to IO, November 4th, 1919.

111.   BLIO, L/P&S/10/742, Letter from Kenyon, BM, to IO, November 29, 1919.

112.   BLIO, L/P&S/10/689, Telegram from Percy Cox to FO, February 2, 1921.

113.   BLIO, L/P&S/10/689, Letter from Winston Churchill (CO) to FO, February 25, 1921.

114.   Public Records Office (PRO), Kew, FO 371/2883/E2883, Letter from CO to FO, March 14, 1922.

115.   BLIO, L/P&S/10/689, Letter from T. E. Lawrence to Frederick Kenyon (BM), February 25, 1921. The Colonial Office later wrote to the BM stating for the record that in order to avoid all misunderstanding it wanted to make clear that the dispatch of the antiquities to England was purely a provisional measure designed to facilitate their preservation until their ultimate disposal (in PRO, Kew, FO 371/384/E2642, Letter from CO to Kenyon, March 15, 1921).

116.   PRO, Kew, FO 371/384/E2642, Letter from Lancelot Oliphant (FO) to Churchill (CO), March 8, 1921.

117.   PRO, Kew, FO 371/2883/E2883, Letter from Cox to CO, February 13, 1922.

118.   Particularly Cox—it is unclear how much Bell was involved in the decision-making process.

119. PRO, Kew, FO 371/384/E8460, Letter from BM to CO, July 29, 1921. They stated, furthermore, that some boxes had evidently been broken in transit and that it was therefore unfortunate they were not brought home earlier under proper supervision.

120. On the Lisbon Collection, see below.

121. British Museum, Department of Oriental Arts (BMOA), Samarra Collection Folder, Report from Herzfeld, September 12, 1921.

122. Ibid.

123. PRO, Kew, FO 371/384/E8460, Letter from BM to CO, July 29, 1921.

124. BMOA, Report from Herzfeld, September 12, 1921.

125. These institutions were: The Victoria & Albert Museum, London; The Louvre; The Danish Museum; National Museum, Stockholm; Gravenhagen Art Museum, the Netherlands; Ethnology Museum, Vienna; Kaiser Friedrich Museum, Berlin; Musée Arabe, Cairo; Istitut Français, Damascus; Royal Ontario Museum, Toronto; Museum of Fine Arts, Boston; Metropolitan Museum of Art, New York; University Museum, Ann Arbor, Michigan; The Cleveland Museum of Art; Art Institute of Chicago; The Museum, New Delhi.

126. BMOA, Samarra Collection Folder.

127. BMOA, Letter to E. W. Morgan, September 23, 1921.

128. PRO, Kew, FO 371/2883/E2883, Letter from CO to FO, March 14, 1922.

129. Ibid.

130. PRO, Kew, FO 371/2883/E2883, Letter from CO to BM, April 1, 1922.

131. BLIO, L/P&S/10/689, Telegram from Paris Peace Delegation to IO, January 31, 1919.

132. BLIO, L/P&S/10/845, Report by Dr. A. S. Yahuda to Edwin Montagu, April 20, 1920.

133. The status of the Lisbon Collection raises an interesting legal question—Portugal had never formally declared war against Turkey, although it had entered the war on the Allied side in 1915. However, as British diplomats would realize, current Portuguese law would stipulate that they be governed by a Portuguese Prize Court, which would undoubtedly rule them to be Portuguese property.

134. Yahuda claims that the Germans through their secret agents offered the Portuguese ten to twelve thousand pounds to facilitate the transfer. However, British Intelligence heard about the matter. Since the money amount offered by the Germans was so high, the British suspected that the cases contained some important war material. They were able to prevent the matter from proceeding further, opened several cases and found them to contain only antiquities.

135. According to Walter Andrae's memoirs, Kaiser Wilhelm II recommended sending a warship to Porto, where the antiquities were kept, to bombard the city until the artifacts were released. Andrae, *Lebenserinnerungen eines Ausgräbers,* p. 258.

136. These suggestions ranged from presenting the antiquities as a gift to Belgium as compensation for Belgian art destroyed by the Germans during the war or returning them to Mesopotamia. The Portuguese themselves had ideas of their own on what to do with the collection, such as establishing a Museum of Near Eastern Antiquities, selling it to the highest bidder, forwarding it to the Germans, or returning it to Mesopotamia. From Yahuda's Report to Edwin Montagu, April 20, 1920.

137. BLIO, L/P&S/10/845, Proceedings of Conference on the Lisbon Antiquities held at the IO, May 10, 1920.

138. Ibid. It is unclear from the proceedings of this conference whether the British were aware of the secret 1899 agreement between the Germans and the Ottomans.

139. BLIO, L/P&S/10/845, Report by Dr. A. S. Yahuda to Edwin Montagu, April 20, 1920.

140. BLIO, L/P&S/10/845, Letter from W. Andrae to Gertrude Bell, January 31, 1920.

141. GBC, Letter to Mother, April 14, 1911.

142. GBC, Letter to Herzfeld, February 13, 1915. In this card she stated that she often thought of her German friends and longed for news of Koldewey and Andrae.

143. BLIO, L/P&S/10/845, Letter from Gertrude Bell to Walter Andrae, March 12, 1920.

144. Ibid.

145. Those present included Arthur Hirtzel, J. Shuckburgh, and C. Garbett (all IO), H. W. Young (FO), A. Jerrold (Treasury), E. Budge (BM), and A. S. Yahuda (University of Madrid and special British envoy in this matter).

146. BLIO, L/P&S/10/845, Proceedings of Conference on the Lisbon Antiquities held at the IO, May 10, 1920. Although Yahuda, who had previously been in communication with the Portuguese, doubted whether this approach would be successful, he had in previous reports suggested that the British appeal to the Portuguese "as the noblest representative of the higher traditions of chivalry and generosity of the Portuguese People in order that Mesopotamia might regain possession of its ravished property." BLIO, L/P&S/10/845, Report by Dr. A. S. Yahuda to Edwin Montagu, April 20, 1920.

147. Not all British officials were happy with this approach. In a letter of October 28, 1919, from an anonymous Treasury official to W. Robinson ESQ (PRO, T 161/5), he states that he did not know why the FO was so "anxious to agitate our ancient allies, the Portuguese not apparently in the interests of Mesopotamia."

148. BLIO, L/P&S/10/845, Letter from J. A. C. Tilley at FO to Lancelot D. Carnegie, Lisbon, June 22, 1920.

149. BLIO, L/P&S/10/845, Letter from Carnegie to FO, June 22, 1920. The BM, however, contacted in February 1921, since it had been informed by French dealers that the Portuguese authorities had no desire to retain the antiquities themselves and only sought to make a profit off them. The Museum had also been in contact with German agents who were actively seeking the cases. The BM believed that the collection could easily be bought for twelve to fifteen thousand pounds and asked whether the FO was going to take any further steps to "secure the interests of Mesopotamia." Letter from Kenyon, BM to FO, February 2, 1921.

150. T 161/5, Letter from William Seeds, British Ambassador in Portugal, to Lord Curzon, September 24, 1919.

151. BLIO, L/P&S/10/845, Internal IO memorandum, November 23, 1920.

152. *The Times,* July 26, 1926, "Seized Antiquities to Be Restored."

153. BLIO, L/P&S/10/742, Letter from F. G. Kenyon, British Museum, to Mark Sykes, September 25, 1918.

154. Ibid.

155. Ibid.

156. BLIO, L/P&S/10/751, Proclamation no. 13, signed at Baghdad, May 22, 1917, by Lieut.-General F. S. Maude. This detailed proclamation includes articles prohibiting unauthorized archaeological excavations, the selling of antiquities, or the defacing of ancient monuments.

157. BMCA, CE 32/352, Letter from WO to Kenyon, February 20, 1918. See also BLIO, L/P&S/10/742, Letter from Kenyon to Holderness (IO), February 11, 1919.

158. BMCA, CE 32/352, Letter from Kenyon to WO, September 11, 1918.

159. BLIO, L/P&S/10/742, Preliminary Report on British Museum Excavations in Southern Babylonia, May 1919, by H. R. Hall.

160. BMCA, CE 32/352, Letter from Hall to Kenyon, April 15, 1919.

161. BLIO, L/P&S/10/742, Internal IO Memo, September 25, 1919.

162. BLIO, L/P&S/10/742, Internal IO Notes, May 17–19, 1919. The IO officials contacted Wilson and asked why the shipment was allowed. He blamed it all on the military authorities, since he did not have power over their actions, yet seemed also to suggest that he was sympathetic to their removal.

163. BLIO, L/P&S/10/742, Curzon's minute is included in a letter from Young (FO) to Hirtzel (IO), October 27, 1919. See also PRO, Kew, FO 371/113, General Correspondence, FO Memo, March 1920.

164. BLIO, L/P&S/10/742, Letter from Kenyon (BM) to Wakeley (IO), November 6, 1919.

165. BLIO, L/P&S/10/742, Report on the Hall/Campbell Thompson Collection by T. E. Lawrence, November 12, 1919.

166. Ibid.

167. BLIO, L/P&S/10/742, Letter from IO to FO, January 8, 1920.

168. BLIO, L/P&S/10/742, Letter from IO to Kenyon, BM, January 15, 1920.

169. BLIO, L/P&S/10/742, Letter from Kenyon to IO, February 25, 1920.

170. Ibid.

171. BLIO, L/P&S/10/742, Letter from IO to Kenyon, April 10, 1920.

172. BLIO, L/P&S/10/845, Letter to IO from FO, November 11, 1920.

173. BLIO, L/P&S/10/742, Memorandum no. 2070-1, September 13, 1917.

174. BLIO, L/P&S/10/742, Letter from Foreign and Political Department, Government for India, to Edwin Montagu, Secretary of State for India, April 26, 1918.

175. Ibid.

176. BLIO, L/P&S/10/742, Minute no. 2447, June 6th, 1918.

177. BLIO, L/P&S/10/742, Telegram from Political Officer, Baghdad to IO, September 6, 1918.

178. BLIO, L/P&S/10/751, Proclamation no. 13, signed at Baghdad, May 22, 1917, by Lieut.-General F. S. Maude.

179. BLIO, L/P&S/10/845, Letter to IO from FO, November 11, 1920.

CHAPTER THREE: FROM MESOPOTAMIA TO IRAQ

The epigraph was taken from the British Library, India Office (BLIO), L/P&S/10/866, N. W. E. Bray, Note on the Causes of the Outbreak in Mesopotamia, August 26, 1920, p. 2.

1. Quoted in Benedict Andersen, *Imagined Communities* (London: Verso, 1983), p. 179.

2. David Hogarth, *Accidents of an Antiquary's Life* (London: Macmillan, 1911), p. 1.

3. Elie Kedourie, *England and the Middle East: The Destruction of the Ottoman Empire 1914–1921* (London: Mansell Publisher, 1987), p. 175.

4. Letter to Bainbridge Colby, March 29, 1920, in Arthur S. Link et al., eds., *Papers of Woodrow Wilson* (Princeton, N.J.: Princeton University Press, 1991), 65:141.

5. It is difficult to pinpoint exactly when the term "Iraq" was first used by the British in the modern, political sense. During the British occupation the term was widely used in British diplomatic circles. Gertrude Bell, for example, used it interchangeably with Mesopotamia between 1914 and 1921, but used Iraq consistently after 1921. Although Iraq was officially established in August of 1921, there apparently was some confusion in official diplomatic circles.

6. See, for example, Maximilian Streck, *Die Alte Landschaft Babylon-ien nach den Arabischen Geographen* (orig. 1900–1901; Frankfurt: Institut für Geschichte der Arabisch-Islamischen Wissenschaften, 1986), pp. 2–3, who states that the evidence from Arab dictionaries, lexicons, and geographical and travel accounts are inconclusive.

7. E. W. Lane, *An Arabic-English Lexicon*, bk. 1, pt. 5 (London: Williams and Norgate, 1863), p. 2021. See also Muhammad ibn Mukarram Ibn Mansur, *Lisan al-'arab*, vol. 3 (Cairo: Dar al-Marif, 1981).

8. Lane, *Arabic-English Lexicon*, p. 2021. Hans Wehr's Arabic-English dictionary indicates that the word Iraq derives from words that mean "noble" or "ancient," which could therefore refer to the ancient civilization that once flourished in the lands of Iraq. Hans Wehr, *A Dictionary of Modern Written Arabic* (Ithaca, N.Y.: Cornell University Press, 1976), p. 607. Streck, *Alte Landschaft*, p. 2, doubts that it has Persian origins and states that the name means "plain" or "valley."

9. The name "Iraq Ajami" was given to the ancient region known as Mah, or Media, to distinguish it from Arabian Iraq. Some Arab geographers, such as Ibn Hawkal, also refer to this area as "Jibal," due to its mountainous terrain. Although the boundaries are never well defined in Ibn Hawkal or al-Muqaddasi, for example, it was generally bounded to the east by the deserts of Khurasan and to the south by Khuzistan and in the north by the Alburz mountain range, which is in the southwestern region of modern Iran.

10. Ibn Battuta, *Travels in Asia and Africa 1325–1354*, trans. H. A. R. Gibb (Cambridge: Cambridge University Press, 1958), p. 91.

11. Abu 'Abduallah Muhammad ibn Ahmad ibn Abi Bakr al-Banna, Al-Bashshari, more commonly known as al-Muqaddasi, *Ahsan al-taqasim fi ma'rifat al-aqalim* transl. by G. S. A. Ranking and R. F. Azoo (orig. 1897; Frankfurt: Institut für Geschichte der Arabisch-Islamischen Wissenschaften, 1989), pp. 171–172. Al-Muqaddasi states that his divisions of Iraq are not what they were in the "olden days," but that he follows the current state of affairs among the contemporary inhabitants. For a study on al-Muqaddasi from a geographical point of view, see Basil Anthony Collins, *Al-Muqaddasi: The Man and His Work* (Ann Arbor: University of Michigan, 1974).

12. Al-Muqaddasi, *Ahsan al-taqasim*, p. 175.

13. Ibid., p. 176.

14. Istakhri, *Kitab al-masalik al-mamalik* (Frankfurt: Institute for the History of Arabic-Islamic Science, 1992), p. 61. Al-Muqaddasi, *Ahsan al-taqasim*, p. 104, has similar demarcation, stating it extends from the gulf on the south to the province of Aqur (al-Jazira) in the north, then extends to the "country of the Greeks" (i.e., Byzantium), to the west by the Euphrates and to the east by Khuzistan and al-Jibal.

15. Lane, *Arabic-English Lexicon*, p. 2021.

16. Istakhri, *Kitab al-masalik*, pp. 54–60. Al-Muqaddasi, *Ahsan al-taqasim*, more often employs the term "Aqur."

17. Richard Schofield, ed., *The Iraq-Iran Border, 1840–1958* (Farnam, England: Archive Editions, 1979), 1:311.

18. Donald Edgar Pitcher, *An Historical Geography of the Ottoman Empire* (Leiden, the Netherlands: Brill, 1972), p. 141. See also Tariq Ismael *Iraq and Iran: Roots of Conflict* (Syracuse, N.Y.: Syracuse University Press, 1982), pp. 1–5.

19. For their rule and their military actions against Iran see Rasul Al-Karkuli, *Dawhat al-wuzara fi ta'rikh waqa'i baghdad al-zawra* (Beirut: Maktabat al-Nahda, 1963), particularly pp. 19–92. See also Tom Nieuwenhuis, *Politics and Society in Early Modern Iraq: Mamluk Pashas, Tribal Shayks and Local Rule between 1802 and 1931* (The Hague: M. Nijhoff, 1982).

20. See Yitzhak Nakash, *Shi'is of Iraq* (Princeton, N.J.: Princeton University Press, 1994), pp. 164–173; Hala Fattah, *The Politics of Regional Trade in Iraq, Arabia and the Gulf, 1745–1900* (Albany: State University of New York, 1997), pp. 32–35.

21. See, for example, Ibrahim Fasih ibn Sabghattullah Al-Haidari, *Kitab unwan al-majd fi bayan ahwal baghdad wa al-basra wa al-najd* (Basra: Manshurat al-Basri, n.d.), pp. 179–180, 190–193. Although one could expect al-Haidari to use the term to refer to a distinct military-strategic zone, he has a fairly fluid, all-encompassing view of the region that transcends the modern borders of Iran and Iraq.

22. Fattah, *Politics of Regional Trade*, pp. 19–22.

23. Martin Gilbert, *Winston S. Churchill, 1916–1922* (Boston: Houghton Mifflin, 1975), p. 638. See also David Fromkin, *A Peace to End All Peace: The Fall of the Ottoman Empire and the Creation of the Modern Middle East* (New York: H. Holt, 1989), pp. 499–501.

24. For this change in British views of imperial expansion and control see Lawrence James, *The Rise and Fall of the British Empire* (New York: Little, Brown, 1994), especially pp. 335–467. See also Correlli Barnett's *The Collapse of British Power* (Gloucester, UK: Eyre Methuen, 1984); E. J. Hobsbawm, *The Age of Empire* (New York: Vintage, 1987); and Derek Hopwood, *Tales of Empire: The British and the Middle East, 1880–1952* (London: I. B. Tauris, 1989). James quotes a British MP who said in 1922 that it was preposterous to assume that "we have specific gifts from God to shape the destiny of Orientals." James, *Rise and Fall*, p. 395.

25. British Library, London, Papers of Arnold T. Wilson (BLAW), Letter from Arthur Hirtzel to Arnold Wilson, September 17, 1919.

26. For the Maude Declaration, see Stephen Longrigg, *Iraq 1900–1950* (Oxford: Oxford University Press, 1953), p. 93.

27. In Western accounts of this revolt, the focus has primarily been on what caused the rebellion. See Aylmer L. Haldane, *The Insurrection in Mesopotamia, 1920* (Edinburgh: Allborough Publisher, 1922); Eliezer Tauber, *The Formation of Modern Syria and Iraq* (London: Frank Cass, 1995), especially pp. 306–317; and Amal Viongradov, "The 1920 Revolt in Iraq

Reconsidered: The Role of Tribes in National Politics," *International Journal of Middle East Studies* 3 (2): 123–139.

28. Tauber, *Formation of Modern Syria and Iraq*, p. 308.

29. Public Records Office (PRO), Kew, FO 371/5230, "Mesopotamia —Preliminary Report on Causes of Unrest," September 14, 1920; WO 33/969, "An Examination of the Cause of the Outbreak in Mesopotamia," October 1920. See also Haldane, *Insurrection*, pp. 73–76; and Tauber, *Formation of Modern Syria and Iraq*, 308–309.

30. See, for example, 'Abdallah Al-Fayyad, *Al-Thawra al-'iraqqiya al-kubra sanat 1920* (Baghdad: Matba'at Irshad, 1963). The most informative account, however, is found in 'Abd al-Razzaq al-Hasani's *Al-Thawra al-'iraqqiyya al-kubra* (Sidon, Lebanon: 'Abd al-Razzaq al-Hasani, 1965).

31. Fariq al-Muzhir Al-Fir'awn, *Al-Haqaiq al-nasi'a fil-thawra al-'iraqiyya sanat 1920 wa-nata'ijiha* (Baghdad: Al-Najan Press, 1954), especially pp. 3–16.

32. Ali Al-Bazirkan, *Al-Waqa'i al-haqiqiyya fil-thawra al-'iraqiyya* (Baghdad: n.p., 1954).

33. Gilbert, *Winston S. Churchill*, p. 511.

34. Despite Fir'awn's reservations (discussed above), most other Iraqi historians, such as Al-Bazirkan and al-Hasani, have emphasized this point. British governmental sources also stress the close cooperation between the urban centers and the countryside and between people of different backgrounds. This cooperation made the revolt so much more difficult to contain for the British. See PRO, Kew, FO 371/5230, "Mesopotamia—Preliminary Report on the Causes of Unrest" by N. W. E. Bray, September 1920.

35. Muhammad Mahdi Al-Basir, *Ta'rikh al-qadhiya al-'iraqiyya* (Baghdad: Matba'at al-Fallah, 1924), 1:136–137.

36. This episode is covered in Ali Al-Wardi's *Lamahat 'ijtima'iyya min ta'rikh al-'iraq al-hadith* (Baghdad: Matba'at al-Irshad, 1969–1978), vol. 5, pt. 1: 172–176, 188–193.

37. See al-Hasani, *Al-Thawra al-'iraqiyya al-kubra*, pp. 55–64; Al-Basir, *Ta'rikh al-qadhiya*, 1:136–144.

38. Muhammad Al-'Umari, *Ta'rikh muqadarat* (Baghdad: Matba'at al-Fallah, 1925), 3:3–4; Ghassan Attiyah, *Iraq, 1908–1921: A Socio-Political Study* (Beirut: Arab Institute for Research & Publication, 1973), pp. 280–283. The Naqib was the leading protagonist of the British administration. His family were the guardians of the Qadiri Shrine and enjoyed wide religious influence among the Sunnis of Baghdad.

39. Gertrude Bell Collection (GBC), Robinson Library, Special Collections, University of Newcastle-upon-Tyne, Letter to Father, September 5, 1920.

40. GBC, Letter to Father, November 10, 1922.

41. Link, *Papers of Woodrow Wilson*, 57:443.

42. GBC, Letter to Father, September 5, 1920.

43. BLAW, Telegram from Percy Cox to Political Office, Baghdad, May 16, 1918. A later letter from Hirtzel to Wilson stated that everyone at the IO would prefer an Arab emir because an Arab emir presided over by a British high commissioner does not really constitute an Arab state. "Can't you possibly find a member of some local family to put in if only for the first few years?" BLAW, Letter from Hirtzel to Wilson, April 15, 1920.

44. For an excellent study on Abdullah see Mary C. Wilson, *King Abdullah, Britain and the Making of Jordan* (Cambridge: Cambridge University Press, 1987). A good critical study of Faysal has yet to be written. For a somewhat useful summary of his life and times see (Mrs.) Steuart Erskine, *King Faysal of Iraq* (London: Hutchinson, 1933). A collection of Faysal's speeches and writings was published in 1945 and entitled *Faysal Ibn al-Husayn fi kutabihi wa aqwalahi* (Baghdad: Matba'at al-Hukumah, 1945).

45. Bell called Abdullah a "gentleman who likes a copy of the Figaro every morning at breakfast time." GBC, Letter to Father, June 14, 1920. In a letter to Woodrow Wilson, Charles Crane (of the King/Crane Commission) wrote that "Faysal, despite limitations of education had become a unique outstanding figure capable of rendering greatest service for world peace . . . confirmed believer in Anglo-Saxon race, really great lover of Christianity. Could do more than any other to reconcile Christianity and Islam and longs to do so. Even talks seriously of American College for Women at Mecca." *Papers of Woodrow Wilson*, 61:442–444.

46. Marion Farouk-Sluglett and Peter Sluglett, *Iraq since 1958: From Revolution to Dictatorship* (London: I. B. Tauris, 1990), p. 11.

47. For this short, yet significant, reign see Zeine N. Zeine, *The Struggle for Arab Independence: Western Diplomacy and the Rise and Fall of Faysal's Kingdom in Syria* (Beirut: Khayat's, 1960).

48. PRO, Kew, FO 371/5040, Letter from Ernest Scott to FO, September 24, 1920.

49. For a detailed history of the Cairo Conference and the events preceding and resulting from it, see Aaron S. Klieman, *Foundations of British Policy in the Arab World: The Cairo Conference of 1921* (Baltimore: Johns Hopkins Press, 1970).

50. Abdullah was sponsored for the throne of the emirate of Trans-jordan. While this policy aimed at expediency, particularly to reduce their military commitments and thus their financial burden in the region, the British seem to have overestimated the practical aspects of the calls for Arab unity as well as the appeal of the Hashemite dynasty as political leaders to the rest of the Arab world.

51. Farouk-Sluglett and Sluglett, *Iraq since 1958*, p. 11.

52. GBC, Letter to Parents, October 10, 1920.

53. Ibid.

54. GBC, Letter to Baron Hardinge, February 8, 1921.

55. Quoted in Arnold T. Wilson, *Mesopotamia: A Clash of Loyalties* (London: Oxford University Press, 1931), 2:340.

56. GBC, Letter to Father, November 28, 1918.

57. GBC, Letter to Father, July 7, 1921.

58. Portions of speech appear in 'Abdul Razzaq al-Hasani's *Ta'rikh al-'iraq al-siyasi al-hadith* (Sidon, Lebanon: Dar al-Kutub, 1948), pp. 194–195. It also appears in Faysal Ibn al-Hussein, *Faysal Ibn al-Hussein,* pp. 261–264.

59. Ibn al-Hussein, *Faysal Ibn al-Hussein,* p. 263.

60. GBC, Letter to Mother, July 10, 1921.

61. Matthew Elliot, *"Independent Iraq": The Monarchy and British Influence, 1941–58* (London: I. B. Tauris, 1996), p. 7.

62. For an informative contemporary account see Al-Basir *Ta'rikh al-qadhiya.* See also 'Abdallah Al-Nafisi, *Dawr al-shi'a fi tatawwur al-'iraq al-siyasi al-hadith* (Beirut: Dar al-Nahar, 1973), especially pp. 155–189; and *Al-Haraka al-islamiyya fi al-'iraq* (Beirut: Muassaset al-Jihad, 1985), pp. 3–93.

63. The early political history of Iraq and the often tenuous relations between the Iraqis and the British is well documented in Peter Sluglett, *Britain in Iraq 1914–1932* (London: Ithaca Press, 1976); Philip W. Ireland's *Iraq: A Study in Political Development* (New York: J. Cape, 1937) is a valuable sourcebook, along with Longrigg's *Iraq 1900–1950.* Several Iraqi politicians who were active during this period have written their memoirs, such as Ali Jawdat Al-Ayyubi's *Dhikrayati* (Beirut: Matba'at al-Wafa, 1967); Tawfiq Al-Suwaydi's *Mudhakkirati* (Beirut: Dar al-Katib al-Arabi, 1969); and Taha Hashimi's *Mudhakkirat Taha al-Hashimi, 1919–1943* (Beirut: Dar al-Taliah, 1967).

64. The most potent issues concerned the determination of Iraq's frontiers, oil concessions, and the development of an Iraqi army. See Sluglett, *Britain in Iraq,* pp. 67–89, 141–170.

65. Quoted in Mohammad Tarbush, *The Role of the Military in Politics: The Case Study of Iraq to 1941* (London: KPI, 1982), p. 40.

66. BMCA, Report from Keepers at the British Museum (H. Read, A. H. Smith, G. J. Hill, L. D. Barnett), October 28, 1918.

67. Yale Babylonian Collection (YBC), Letter from Albert T. Clay to Clyde Garbett, December 16, 1921.

68. See Chapter 4.

69. Rockefeller Center Archives (RCA), Box 111, Education, Letter from Harry Pratt Judson to John D. Rockefeller, Jr., May 7, 1919.

70. PRO, Kew, FO 371/113/15437, Letter from IO to Langdon, December 7, 1920.

71. University Museum Archives (UMA), University of Pennsylvania, Philadelphia, Letter to Kenyon from G. B. Gordon, June 2nd, 1919. Kenyon reminded Gordon in his reply that "definite assurances can . . . be given until the question of the future government of Mesopotamia has been

settled." However, there was "good ground to hope that an Administration of antiquities will be setup, which will act in accordance with the principles laid down by the Archaeological Committee founded by the British Academy." UMA, Letter to Gordon from Kenyon, June 11, 1919.

72. BLIO, L/P&S/10/742, Memorandum on Sites for Excavations in Mesopotamia to which various nations have prior rights or which can be appropriately granted to them, or to others if they waive them, by H. R. Hall. Hall recommended that any French concession would be dependent on France's abandonment of its "unscientific exclusive claim" to excavate in Persia. He argued that French prior claims, although considerable, were in no way as great as those of England. He also maintained that the Americans had dug very little on the whole and therefore had no prior rights compared to the British or even the French.

73. G. B. Gordon of Penn stated in a letter to Kenyon in 1919 that his institution had a prior claim on Ur, not the BM. UMA, Letter to Kenyon, June 2nd, 1919. This list still had relevance two years later when Albert Clay wrote to Garbett at the FO, "When I was in Baghdad I asked for the reservation of two sites. Fortunately Senkereh happens to be the site that Dr. Hall seems to think should be reserved for Americans." YBC, Letter from Clay to Garbett, December 16, 1921. See also a letter from S. Langdon to A. T. Clay. "I told you that we had resigned Senkereh after I found that you had prior claims." YBC, Letter from Langdon to Clay, May 30, 1922.

74. BLIO, L/P&S/10/742, Letter from Kenyon to IO, February 25, 1920.

75. BLIO, L/P&S/10/742, Letter from Frederick Kenyon, BM, to Mark Sykes, September 25, 1918.

76. See Chapter 4.

77. BLIO, L/P&S/10/742, Joint Archaeological Committee Report.

78. GBC, Letter from George Hill to Bell, April 8, 1919.

79. Bell felt that the Anglo-Iraqi treaty was the first open and decis-ive step in the evolution of new relationships between nations. She also believed that it was an experiment conducted under highly favorable conditions, in a country where there was no tradition of direct British authority to recast. It was an experiment in mutual confidence that could turn into a valuable example, with, "as we believe[,] enduringly beneficial effect on our intercourse with the East" GBC, Memorandum on Great Britain and the Iraq, n.d., p. 20.

80. PRO, Kew, FO 371/33/E7241.

81. The role of the Sevres provisions in influencing later archaeological legislation will be discussed below.

82. See, for example, Amatzia Baram's article "A Case of Imported Identity: The Modernizing Secular Ruling Elites of Iraq and the Concept of Mesopotamian-Inspired Territorial Nationalism, 1922–1992," *Poetics Today* 15 (2): 281–283.

83. GBC, Letter to Father, July 31, 1921.

84. GBC, Letter to Father, August 6, 1921.

85. Ibid.

86. PRO, Kew, FO 371/10095, Report on Iraq Administration, April 1922–March 1923, pp. 161–162.

87. GBC, Letter to Father, July 22, 1922. It is unclear what Bell means by stating that Faysal had been trained by Lawrence in archaeology. There is no evidence that Faysal ever visited Lawrence during his archaeological excavations.

88. For example, the British official J. M. Wilson wrote to Albert Clay in November 1922, that the Antiquities Law would be passed "soon." YBC, Wilson to Clay, November 29, 1922.

89. H. V. F. Winstone, *Woolley of Ur: The Life of Sir Leonard Woolley* (London: Secker & Warburg, 1990), pp. 119–120.

90. See, for example, William Cleveland, *The Making of an Arab Nationalist: Ottomanism and Arabism in the Life and Thought of Sati' al-Husri* (Princeton, N.J.: Princeton University Press, 1971); Bassam Tibi, *Arab Nationalism: Between Islam and Nation-State* (New York: St. Martin's Press, 1997); Elias Murqus, *Naqd al-fikr al-qawmi: Sati' al-Husri* (Beirut: Dar al-Taliah, 1966), which all deal extensively with his ideas and his tenure in the Ministry of Education, yet overlook his post in the Department of Antiquities.

91. Due to al-Husri's literary output a fairly accurate picture is available about his life and thought. The most important work concerning his tenure in Iraq is his *Mudhakkirati fi al-'iraq, 1921–1941*, 2 vols. (Beirut: Dar al-Taliah, 1967–1968). His *Yawm maysalun: safhah min ta'rikh al-'arab al-hadith* (Beirut: Maktabat al-Kashshaf, n.d.) is an excellent narrative on the last days of Faysal's kingdom in Syria, in which al-Husri participated. During his tenure as director general of education in Iraq, al-Husri was the editor of an educational journal, *Majallah al-tarbiyah wa al-ta'lim*, 5 vols. (Baghdad, 1928–1932). Al-Husri also authored several influential writings on Arab nationalism, including *Ma hiya al-qawmiyyah?* (Beirut: Dar al-Ilm lil Malayin, 1959) and a comprehensive collection of his essays, *Abhath mukhtarah fi al-qawmiyyah al-'arabiyyah* (Beirut: Markaz Dirasat al-Wahdah al-Arabiya, 1959). An excellent study on al-Husri's ideas, based not only on al-Husri's writings but also on several personal interviews with him, is William L. Cleveland's *The Making of an Arab Nationalist*. For a sympathetic biography also concentrating on al-Husri's Arab nationalist thought, see Muhammad 'Abd al-Rahman Burj, *Sati' al-Husri* (Cairo: Dar al-Katib al-Arabi, 1969).

92. Niyazi Berkes, *The Development of Secularism in Turkey* (Montreal: McGill University Press, 1964), p. 409. For this debate see also L. M. Kenny, "Sati' al-Husri's Views on Nationalism," *Middle East Journal* 17 (1963): 232; Reeva Simon, *Iraq between the Two World Wars: The Creation and Implementation*

of a Nationalist Ideology (New York: Columbia University Press, 1986), p. 76; and Cleveland, *Making of an Arab Nationalist,* pp. 32–33.

93. Simon, *Iraq between the Two World Wars,* p. 75.

94. In the 1940s–1950s al-Husri republished his articles and speeches written between 1920 and 1940. These include *Ara' wa ahadith fi al-tarbiyya wa al-ta'lim* (Cairo: Matba'at al-Risalah, 1944); *Ara' wa ahadith fi al-wataniyya wa al-qawmiyya,* 4th ed. (Beirut: Dar al-Ilm lil Malayin, 1961); and *Ara' wa ahadith fi al-qawmiyya al-'arabiyya,* 4th ed. (Beirut: Dar al-Ilm lil Malayin, 1964).

95. Al-Husri, *Ara' wa ahadith fi al-wataniyya,* pp. 20–21.

96. For these ideas see al-Husri's writings cited above. See also Tibi, *Arab Nationalism,* part 3.

97. An American diplomat stated that al-Husri "speaks Arabic badly and scarcely writes it at all." National Archives (NA), Records of the Department of State Relating to the Internal Affairs of Iraq, 890g.927/90, Letter from Knabenshue to U.S. Secretary of State, January 29, 1935.

98. GBC, Letter to Father, July 31, 1921.

99. GBC, Letter to Father, November 1, 1922.

100. GBC, Letter to Father, December 16, 1922.

101. GBC, Letter to Father, August 30, 1923.

102. GBC, Letter to Mother, September 11, 1923.

103. Al-Husri, *Mudhakkirati,* 1:177–182.

104. Ibid., 1:180.

105. BMCA, WY1, Letter from Cox to Churchill September 1, 1924.

106. Ibid.

107. *Iraqi Government Gazette,* September 15, 1924, p. 2. See also PRO, Kew, FO 371/9004, Report by His Britannic Majesty's Government on the Administration of Iraq for the period April 1923–December 1924, pp. 53–54.

108. GBC, Letter to Father, June 25, 1924. Bell stated further that she had fixed and gotten her minister's consent for a percentage that she considered reasonable.

109. Al-Husri, *Mudhakkirati,* 2:413

110. American and British diplomatic records do not offer any clues nor do any letters, private correspondences, or memoirs of the various archaeologists that were consulted for this study. Iraqi archival material, presently inaccessible, may provide clues.

111. UMA, Ur Archives, Woolley to Gordon, November 15, 1923.

112. Lyndel Prott and P. J. O'Keefe, *Law and the Cultural Heritage* (Abingdon, Oxon: Professional Books, 1984), 1:72.

113. Ibid. See also C. W. Ceram, ed., *Hands on the Past* (New York: A. A. Knopf, 1966), p. 34.

114. *Antiquities Law* (Baghdad: Iraqi Government Press, 1924), p. 9.

115. Lawrence M. Kaye, "Laws in Force at the Dawn of World War II: International Conventions and National Laws," in *The Spoils of War: World War II and Its Aftermath: The Loss, Reappearance, and Recovery of Cultural Property,* ed. Elisabeth Simpson (New York: H. N. Abrams, 1997), p. 102.

116. *Cyprus Gazette Supplement,* no. 3, May 19, 1905, pp. 5626, 5631.

117. BMCA, Report from Keepers at the British Museum (H. Read, A. H. Smith, G. J. Hill, L. D. Barnett), October 28, 1918, pp. 2–3.

118. Ibid., p. 2.

119. Ibid., p. 3.

120. YBC, *Official Gazette of the Government of Palestine,* October 15, 1920, p. 4.

121. Even archaeologists who were involved in archaeology in Iraq later in the twentieth century acknowledged their predecessors' amateurish and questionable activities. See, for example, Seton Lloyd, *Foundations in the Dust* (London: Oxford University Press, 1947), pp. 130–153.

122. For a good discussion on the development of the Ottoman legislation, see Wendy M. K. Shaw, *Possessors and Possessed: Museums, Archaeology, and the Visualization of History in the Late Ottoman Empire* (Berkeley: University of California Press, 2003), especially Chapter 4.

123. YBC, Robert Dougherty to C. S. Knopf, September 20, 1928.

124. GBC, Letter to Father, October 22, 1922.

125. Al-Husri, *Mudhakkirati,* 1:181.

126. PRO, Kew, FO 371/10095, *Iraq,* Report on Iraq Administration, April 1922–March 1923, p. 162.

127. BL, *Iraqi Government Gazette,* no. 4, January 22, 1927.

128. GBC, Letter to Father, August 20, 1924.

129. UMA, Letter from Woolley to Gordon, February 12, 1925.

130. Winstone, *Woolley of Ur,* p. 120.

131. Lloyd, *Foundations in the Dust,* p. 206.

132. For discussions on who excavated where and when, see the standard histories by Daniel, Lloyd (1947), Pallis, and Hawkes discussed above. See also Samuel Noah Kramer, *The Sumerians: Their History, Culture and Character* (Chicago: University of Chicago Press, 1963), pp. 18–32; Seton Lloyd, *Mesopotamia: Excavations on Sumerian Sites* (London: L. Dickson, 1936).

CHAPTER FOUR

1. Bell was judgmental in her evaluation of prospective archaeologists. For example, when Mackey from Oxford University came to Iraq she stated that she did not like him and did not think he could possibly conduct the excavation of so important a site with success. She wrote a letter of protest to Oxford and the Joint Archaeological Committee and insisted that he take on a local English foreman for his mission. Gertrude Bell Collection

(GBC), Robinson Library, Special Collections, University of Newcastle-upon-Tyne, Letter to Father, March 11, 1923.

2. The view that Americans were rich and had access to seemingly unlimited funds was prevalent among British officials in Iraq. For example, Bell describes a trip to Kish in 1926 where she was accompanied by a Yale professor (Dougherty?). She writes, "We took with us an American professor. I am very polite to American professors, hoping they may suggest to someone that we are promising recipients when you are thinking of giving 2,000,000 for a museum." GBC, Letter to Mother, March 31, 1926.

3. Public Records Office (PRO), Kew, FO 371/10095, *Iraq*, Report on Iraq Administration, April 1922–March 1923, p. 162.

4. The leaders of this excavation, John Punnett Peters and Hermann V. Hilprecht, both wrote popular accounts on this mission. Although they planned a multiseries report, only one volume appeared in this series. For the popular accounts, see John Punnett Peters, *Nippur, or Explorations and Adventures on the Euphrates,* 2 vols. (New York: Putnam, 1897–1898); H. V. Hilprecht, *Explorations in Bible Lands during the Nineteenth Century* (Philadelphia: A. J. Holman, 1903), pp. 289–577. On the institutional politics and some of the difficulties of the Nippur mission see Bruce Kuklick, *Puritans in Babylon: The Ancient Near East and American Intellectual Life, 1880–1930* (Princeton, N.J.: Princeton University Press, 1996).

5. British Museum, Central Archives (BMCA), Minutes of the Com-mit-tee of the Board of Trustees, June 10, 1922. At the University Museum at the University of Pennsylvania, correspondence between Penn and the BM concerning this mission can also be found.

6. BMCA, Minutes of the Committee of the Board of Trustees, October 14, 1922.

7. Woolley is a legendary figure in the history of archaeology. His memoirs are entitled *Spadework: Adventures in Archaeology* (London: Lutterworth Press, 1953) and *As I Seem to Remember* (London: Allen & Unwin, 1962). H. V. F. Winstone has also written an informative biography entitled *Woolley of Ur: The Life of Sir Leonard Woolley* (London: Secker & Warburg, 1990). The scene and characters of Agatha Christie's famous novel *Murder in Mesopotamia* are widely regarded as being based on Woolley's mission to Ur. Sidney Smith was also an influential figure in British archaeological circles. He served as honorary director of antiquities in Iraq between 1929 and 1931.

8. BMCA, Minutes of the Committee of the Board of Trustees, October 14, 1922.

9. PRO, Kew, FO 371/10095, *Iraq*, Report on Iraq Administration, April 1922–March 1923, p. 162.

10. Ibid.

11. Rockefeller Center Archives (RCA), Box 117, JDR, Jr., Educational Interests, Letter from Fosdick to Adams, January 4, 1928.

12. P. R. S. Moorey, *Ur "of the Chaldees": A Revised and Updated Edition of Sir Leonard Woolley's Excavations at Ur* (Ithaca, N.Y.: Cornell University Press, 1982), p. 8.

13. Ibid., p. 9.

14. Max Mallowan, *Mallowan's Memoirs: The Autobiography of Max Mallowan* (London: Collins, 1977), p. 25. Also quoted in Moorey, *Ur "of the Chaldees,"* p. 10.

15. PRO, Kew, FO 371/9004, Report by His Britannic Majesty's Government on the Administration of Iraq for the period April 1923 –December 1924, p. 54.

16. Glyn Daniel, *A Hundred Years of Archaeology* (London: Duckworth, 1950), p. 201.

17. Samuel Noah Kramer, "Sumerian Literature: A General Survey," in *The Bible and the Ancient Near East: Essays in Honor of William Foxwell Albright*, ed. G. Ernest Wright (Garden City, N.Y.: Doubleday, 1961), especially pp. 257–259; and "Sumerian Literature: A Preliminary Survey of the Oldest Literature in the World," *Proceedings of the American Philosophical Society* 85 (1942), especially pp. 240–243.

18. Kuklick, *Puritans in Babylon*, p. 167.

19. C. L. Woolley, *Ur of the Chaldees* (London: E. Benn, 1929), p. 70.

20. The scholar who was most diligent in promoting Sumerian civilization is Samuel Noah Kramer, as in his famous *History Begins at Sumer* (Garden City, N.Y.: Doubleday, 1959).

21. The archaeologists themselves published extensively on these excavations. Some examples of publications include: Stephen Langdon, *Excavations at Kish I, 1923-4* (Paris: P. Guenther, 1924); Louis Watelin and Stephen Langdon, *Excavations at Kish III, 1925–1927* (Paris: P. Guenther, 1930); Louis Watelin and Stephen Langdon, *Excavations at Kish IV, 1925–1930* (Paris: P. Guenther, 1934); and Ernest Mackay, *A Sumerian Palace and the "A" Cemetery at Kish, Mesopotamia* (Chicago: Field Museum, 1929). Important syntheses on Kish include McGuire Gibson, *The City and the Area of Kish* (Miami: Field Research Projects, 1972); and P. R. S. Moorey, *Kish Excavations, 1923–1933* (Oxford: Clarendon Press, 1978).

22. PRO, Kew, FO 371/10095, *Iraq*, Report on Iraq Administration, April 1922–March 1923, p. 162.

23. In 1915, he published *Sumerian Epic of Paradise, the Flood, and the Fall of Man* (Philadelphia: University Museum, 1915), which sought to prove that the Sumerian documents referred to, and therefore corroborated, the same biblical accounts. When later scholars evaluated the evidence it became clear that Langdon had aggressively overinterpreted the data and that the texts that Langdon referred to did indeed not correlate to the biblical stories. See Samuel Noah Kramer, "Langdon's Historical and Religious Texts from the Temple Library of Nippur—Additions and Corrections," in *Journal of the American Oriental Society* 60 (1940): 234–257.

24. BL, *Report by His Britannic Majesty's Government to the Council of the League of Nations on the Administration of Iraq for the Year 1926* (London, 1927), p. 40.

25. Seton Lloyd, *Foundations in the Dust* (London: Oxford University Press, 1947), p. 212.

26. For an impressive overview of the significant discoveries at Warka see Adam Falkenstein, *Die neusumerische Gerichtsurkunden*, 3 vols. (Munich: Verlag der Bayerischen Akademie der Wissenschaften, 1956–1957).

27. Henri Frankfort, *Art and Architecture in the Ancient Orient* (orig. 1954; New Haven, Conn.: Yale University Press, 1996).

28. They were first published in Adam Falkenstein's *Archaische Texte aus Uruk* (Leipzig, Germany: O. Harrasowitz, 1936), which remained for half a century the most important contribution to the study of archaic Mesopotamian writing of documents. The early Uruk tablets have been studied and published in various studies by a team at the University of Berlin, including Hans Nissen, Robert Englund, and Peter Damerow. See, for example, *Archaic Bookkeeping: Early Writing and Techniques of the Economic Administration in the Ancient Near East* (Chicago: University of Chicago Press, 1993).

29. Lloyd, *Foundations in the Dust*, p. 217.

30. Gordon Loud, *Khorsabad: Excavation in the Palace and at a City Gate* (Chicago: University of Chicago Press, 1936); and Gordon Loud and Charles Altman, *Khorsabad: The Citadel and the Town* (Chicago: University of Chicago Press, 1938).

31. Speiser, who for many years was the chair of the Department of Oriental Studies at Pennsylvania, was a prolific writer and editor. Among his numerous publications: *Introduction to Hurrian* (New Haven, Conn.: American Schools of Oriental Research, 1941); *At the Dawn of Civilization: A Background of Biblical History* (New Brunswick, N.J.: Rutgers University Press, 1964). During World War II, he was a member of the Office of Strategic Services and issued numerous reports concerning the contemporary Middle East. After the war he issued *The United States and the Near East* (Cambridge, Mass.: Harvard University Press, 1950), which describes the role of the region's historical background in some of the current political debates and problems.

32. BL, *Report by His Britannic Majesty's Government to the Council of the League of Nations on the Administration of Iraq for the Year 1927* (London, 1928), p. 48.

33. See his *Amurru, the Home of the Northern Semites: A Study Showing that the Religion and Culture of Israel Were Not of Babylonian Origin* (Philadelphia: Sunday School Times, 1909), which argues that Hebrew literature and religious views were derived from the Amorites, a Semitic culture as well.

34. Benjamin R. Foster, "Clay, Albert Tobias," in *American National Biography* (New York: Oxford University Press, 1999), p. 18.

35. Oxford University, St. Anthony's College, Papers of Lionel Smith (OULS), Letter from David Hogarth to Smith, May 17, 1920.

36. Foster, "Clay," p. 18.

37. BL, *Report by His Britannic Majesty's Government to the Council of the League of Nations on the Administration of Iraq for the Year 1925* (London, 1926), p. 32. See also Yale Babylonian Collection (YBC), Letter to Barton from Chiera, January 25, 1925. The formal name of this expedition was "The Joint Expedition of the Iraq Museum and the American School of Oriental Research."

38. YBC, Letter to Dougherty from Chiera, March 14, 1925.

39. Ibid.

40. YBC, Letter to Barton from Chiera, April 1, 1925.

41. See Chapter 4.

42. PRO, Kew, FO 371/2337, Letter from Deutsche Orient-Gesellschaft to British Ambassador, Berlin, April 3, 1926. Instead of taking this matter up with the Iraqi government directly, the Germans instead chose to go through British diplomatic channels—an indication of where decisions in archaeology were considered to be made.

43. PRO, Kew, FO 371/2337, Letter from Deutsche Orient-Gesellschaft to British Ambassador, Berlin, April 3, 1926.

44. GBC, Letter to Father, May 26, 1926. See also BL, *Report by His Britannic Majesty's Government to the Council of the League of Nations on the Administration of Iraq for the Year 1926* (London, 1927) p. 40.

45. PRO, Kew, FO 371/2337, Letter from Gertrude Bell to Bruno Guterbock, June 16, 1926.

46. GBC, Letter to Father, May 26, 1926.

47. BL, *Report by His Britannic Majesty's Government to the Council of the League of Nations on the Administration of Iraq for the Year 1926* (London, 1927), p. 40.

48. Government of Iraq, *Takrir'in al-hafariyat fi 'Iraq mu'sim 1928-9 (Report on Excavations in 'Iraq during the Season 1928-9)* (Baghdad: Department of Antiquities, 1929), pp. 1-7. The number of missions to Iraq increased in the next years. During the 1930-1931 season there were eleven long-term expeditions in Iraq and a number of shorter expeditions.

49. Ibid., p. 1. The expeditions seem to have generally paid each worker one pound sterling every three weeks. A letter from Campbell Thompson to Kenyon in 1927 states, "I estimate [from information about wages from an office at Mosul last year] that the wages of a hundred diggers for three weeks would be a 100 pounds. The actual bill for wages would be, for say fifteen to eighteen weeks, about 500-600 pounds." BMCA, 1690, Letter from Campbell Thompson to Kenyon, January 18, 1927. For the same period

Campbell Thompson would receive three hundred pounds in salary, or half of the combined salaries of a hundred workers. For sake of comparison, Leonard Woolley, the director of the Ur expedition, received six hundred pounds for one season at Ur in 1922, or the equivalent of the combined salary of a hundred Iraqi workers working for four months. For the budget of the BM missions see BMCA, Minutes of the Committee of the Board of Trustees, October 14, 1922.

50. Government of Iraq, *Report on Excavations in 'Iraq during the Season 1928–9*, pp. 1–7.

51. Glyn Daniel, *Short History of Archaeology* (London: Thames & Hudson), p. 202. For a newer scheme, see Robert Ehrich, ed., *Chronologies in Old World Archaeology* (Chicago: University of Chicago Press, 1993).

52. University Museum Archives (UMA), University of Pennsylvania, Philadelphia, Kenyon to Woolley, August 26, 1922.

53. GBC, Letter to Father, March 1, 1923.

54. UMA, Woolley to Gordon, May 24, 1924.

55. GBC, Letter to Father, March 6, 1924.

56. GBC, Letter to Parents, March 13, 1925.

57. GBC, Letter to Father, March 16, 1926.

58. UMA, Annual Report by Leonard Woolley, March 8, 1924.

59. Ibid.

60. UMA, Annual Report by Leonard Woolley, March 3, 1925.

61. British Museum (BM), miscellaneous correspondence, WY1/1/13, Letter to Kenyon from Woolley, March 9, 1925.

62. UMA, Woolley to Gordon, July 18, 1925.

63. UMA, Annual Report by Leonard Woolley, March 28, 1926.

64. Al-Husri admits that until he became director of antiquities in 1934, no Iraqi official or supervisor from the Ministry of Education or Public Works ever officially visited an excavation site. Sati' Al-Husri, *Mudhakkirati fi al-'iraq, 1921–1941*, 2 vols. (Beirut: Dar al-Taliah, 1967–1968), 2:414. See also Amatzia Baram, "A Case of Imported Identity: The Modernizing Secular Ruling Elites of Iraq and the Concept of Mesopotamian-Inspired Territorial Nationalism, 1922–1992," *Poetics Today* 15 (2): 283.

65. OULS, Letter from Leon Legrain to Lionel Smith, February 21, 1925.

66. PRO, Kew, FO 371/9004, Report by His Britannic Majesty's Government on the Administration of Iraq for the period April 1923–December 1924, p. 5.

67. YBC, Letter from Chiera to Barton, November 25, 1931.

68. GBC, Letter to Parents, March 24, 1924.

69. GBC, Letter to Father, March 6, 1924.

70. GBC, Letter to Parents, March 24, 1924.

71. GBC, Letter to Parents, March 15, 1925.

72. GBC, Letter to Father, August 20, 1924.

73. GBC, Letter to Father, May 26, 1926. In this letter, Bell states, "The Iraq Government has complete confidence in me as a Director and would not question anything I did."

74. BMCA, 1690, Letter from Campbell Thompson to Kenyon, December 20, 1927.

75. For example, in 1929 there were eight foreign expeditions in Iraq: Ur, Kish, Lagash, Khorsabad, Seleucia, Kuyunjik, Tarkalan, and Ctesiphon. A year later eleven expeditions conducted excavations. In 1923 there had been two (Ur and Kish).

76. GBC, Letter to Father, September 29, 1920.

77. BMCA, 32/3/21, Campbell Thomson to Kenyon, September 29, 1938.

78. BMCA, 715/2, Woolley to Kenyon, February 23, 1927.

79. BMCA, 768/1, Woolley to Kenyon, January 31, 1928.

80. BL, *Report by His Britannic Majesty's Government to the Council of the League of Nations on the Administration of Iraq for the Year 1929* (London, 1930), p. 147.

81. BMCA, 827, Woolley to Kenyon, March 6, 1929.

82. PRO, Kew, FO 371/113/E5138, Letter to from Clay (Yale) to Wakeley (FO), April 18, 1920.

83. Wilson wrote to the IO, "I have got an interesting archaeologist staying with us, an American named Clay, full of enthusiasm and very likely to be helpful as he appears to have money behind him." British Library, London, Papers of Arnold T. Wilson (BLAW), Letter from Wilson to Stephenson (IO), March 1, 1920.

84. GBC, Letter to Parents, November 7, 1923.

85. PRO, Kew, FO 371/9004, Report by His Britannic Majesty's Government on the Administration of Iraq for the period April 1923–December 1924, pp. 53–54. For the history of this school and the ASOR in general, see Philip King, *American Archaeology in the Mideast* (Philadelphia: 1983). The Baghdad School initiated the publication of a leading Assyriological journal, *The Journal of Cuneiform Studies*, in 1947.

86. BMCA, Minutes of the Committee of the Board of Trustees, November 27, 1926.

87. BMCA, Minutes of the Committee of the Board of Trustees, April 11, 1932; November 12, 1932.

88. For detail of the archaeological fieldwork conduced by the BSAI see Max Mallowan, *Twenty-Five Years of Mesopotamian Discovery, 1932–1956* (London: British School of Archaeology in Iraq, 1956); and John E. Curtis, ed., *Fifty Years of Mesopotamian Discovery: The Work of the British School of Archaeology in Iraq, 1932–1982* (London: British School of Archaeology in Iraq, 1982).

89. *Iraq*, vol. 1 (London: British School of Archaeology in Iraq, 1934).

90. On the establishment of the Metropolitan and its close ties with private benefactors see Calvin Tomkins, *Merchants and Masterpieces: The Story of the Metropolitan Museum of Art* (London: E. P. Dutton, 1970). See also Nancy Einreinhofer, *The American Art Museum: Elitism and Democracy* (London: Leicester University Press, 1997), especially Chapters 2 and 3; and Victoria D. Alexander, *Museums and Money: The Impact of Funding on Exhibitions, Scholarship, and Management* (Bloomington: Indiana University Press, 1996), Chapter 3.

91. Mark Lilla and Isabelle Frank, "The Medici and the Multinationals," *Museum News* 66 (3): 34.

92. PRO, Kew, FO 371/113/E5138, Letter from Clay (Yale) to Wakeley (FO), April 18, 1920. It is interesting to note that Clay, an American, was fully aware of the various collections that the British had acquired during the occupation, such as the Campbell Thompson and the Samarra collections, and that some of them, such as the Samarra artifacts, were merely on loan from the Iraqi government.

93. YBC, Forrell to Clay, March 12, 1920.

94. In recent years several studies in Middle Eastern cultural history have been premised on this idea including Timothy Mitchell's *Colonising Egypt* (Berkeley: University of California Press, 1991) and Edward Said's *Orientalism* (New York: Vintage Books, 1978).

95. Eric Davis, "The Museum and the Politics of Social Control in Modern Iraq," in *Commemorations: The Politics of National Identity*, ed. John R. Gillis (Princeton, N.J.: Princeton University Press, 1994), p. 91.

96. PRO, Kew, FO 371/9004, Report by His Britannic Majesty's Government on the Administration of Iraq for the Period April 1923–December 1924, p. 54.

97. GBC, Letter to Parents, March 11, 1923.

98. Ibid.

99. PRO, Kew, FO 371/9004, Report by His Britannic Majesty's Government on the Administration of Iraq for the period April 1923–December 1924, pp. 53–54.

100. GBC, Letter to Father, October 30, 1923.

101. GBC, Letter to Parents, October 13, 1923. Uncharacteristically for Bell when she discussed organizing and establishing the Museum, she felt daunted and overwhelmed by the task. She wrote to her father in February 1926, "Still busy with plans for my museum. . . . I wish I knew more about arranging museums." In a letter on March 23, 1926, to her mother she wrote, "I have been spending the afternoon today trying to learn a little about arranging a museum. Oh dear! There's such a lot to be learnt that my heart sinks." And in a May 18th letter that same year she states, "In the evening if I am alone I read Babylonian history or books about seals and things so that I may know a little better how to arrange the Museum." This

burden and seeming lack of energy in tackling the task is surprising, especially when compared to her earlier, more complex projects. A few months
after Bell wrote these lines, though, she committed suicide. Her uncharac-
teristic modesty, indecision, and hesitance with the museum project indicate that she may have been feeling depressed and drained.

102. GBC, Letter to Mother, March 3, 1926.

103. GBC, Letter to Father, March 3, 1926.

104. GBC, Letter to Father, May 4, 1924.

105. GBC, Letter to Father, June 9, 1926.

106. GBC, Letter to Mother, June 16, 1926.

107. Ibid.

108. Ibid.

109. BL, *Report by His Britannic Majesty's Government to the Council of the League of Nations on the Administration of Iraq for the Year 1926* (London, 1927), p. 40.

110. Al-Husri, *Mudhakkirati,* 2:409.

111. For example, in 1926 the Museum and the Antiquities Depart-ment received 0.15 lakhs of rupees, whereas the total budget amounted to 556.50 lakhs of rupees. The Department therefore received 0.02 percent of the overall budget. In 1927 Antiquities received 0.42 lakhs, or 0.08 percent. In 1930 it received 0.64 lakhs, or 0.11 percent of the overall budget. Cal-cula-tions based on Final Expenditure Statements in British Administration Reports.

112. BL, *Report by His Britannic Majesty's Government to the Council of the League of Nations on the Administration of Iraq for the Year 1928* (London, 1929), p. 136.

113. Ibid.

114. BL, *Report by His Britannic Majesty's Government to the Council of the League of Nations on the Administration of Iraq for the Year 1929* (London, 1930), p. 147.

115. Ibid.

116. Iraq Government, Ministry of Education, Department of Antiquities, *Report on the Excavations in Iraq during the Seasons 1929–30, 1930–1, and 1931–32. Report on the Activity of the Department of Antiquities from 1st October, 1931 until 30th September, 1932* (Baghdad, 1933), p. 44.

117. Ibid., p. 44.

118. For the characteristics of European and American national muse-ums see Tony Bennett's *The Birth of the Museum* (New York: Routledge, 1995).

119. BMCA, WY1/2/83, Report on Kish, Warka, Sunkara, and Ur by Gertrude Bell, January 19 (no year given—probably 1925).

120. Ibid.

121. Ibid.

122. Ibid.

123. Iraq Government, Ministry of Education, Department of Antiquities, *Report on Excavations in Iraq during the Season 1928–9* (Baghdad, 1929), p. 7.

124. BL, *Report for the Year 1928*, p. 1.

125. BMCA, WY1/2/51, Letter from Sidney Smith to Leonard Woolley, December 5, 1929.

126. OULS, Letter from Julius Jordan to Lionel Smith, April 25, 1931.

127. BMCA, WY1/2/65, Letter from Woolley to Smith, December 4, 1920.

128. *Antiquities Law* (Baghdad: Iraq Government Press, 1924), p. 12.

129. BMCA, WY1/2/69, Memorandum from Sidney Smith, December 10, 1930.

130. YBC, Clay to President and Fellows of Yale, February 17, 1919. Another Assyriologist, Edward Chiera, while in Baghdad in 1924, wrote to Clay, "I have had a very large number of people come and offer me tablets. Besides all the big dealers, I have explored the cellars of a good many houses. . . . If I had money of my own, you can be certain that I would buy the tablets right away in full confidence that I could realize a good profit on them." YBC, Chiera to Clay, November 10, 1924.

131. BL, *Report for the Year 1926*, p. 40.

132. National Archives of the United States (NA), Records of the Department of State Relating to Internal Affairs of Iraq, 1930–1944, Decimal File, 890g.927/31, Letter from American Consulate in Baghdad to U.S. Secretary of State, Washington, August 20, 1930.

133. Ibid.

134. OULS, Letter from Lionel Smith to Frederick Kenyon, November 20, 1930.

135. BMCA, WY1/2/40, Letter from Woolley to Lionel Smith, December 27, 1928.

136. It is interesting that Sidney Smith only appointed British officials to this committee and therefore treated it as a matter confined to the British community in Iraq, although Cooke's alleged offense was in violation of Iraqi law. Although one can find references to this episode in the various BM materials, no documents were found that covered it explicitly. Furthermore, the British government archives did not contain specific references to the matter. All information is therefore taken from American diplomatic records and archives at Harvard University.

137. Al-Husri, *Mudhakkirati*, pp. 398–400.

138. Ibid., p. 401.

139. Ibid., p. 403. See also Baram, "Imported Identity," p. 285.

140. NA, 890g.927/31, Letter from American Consulate in Baghdad to U.S. Secretary of State, August 20, 1930.

141. Ibid.

142. Harvard Semitic Museum, Nuzi Excavation Papers, Letter from R. F. S. Starr to David Lyon, November 2, 1930.

143. NA, 890g.927/32, Letter from American Consulate in Baghdad to U.S. Secretary of State, January 3, 1931.

144. *Baghdad Times,* November 28, 1930, p. 4.

145. *Baghdad Times,* December 5, 1930, p. 5.

146. NA, 890g.927/32, Letter from American Consulate in Baghdad to U.S. Secretary of State, January 3, 1931.

CHAPTER FIVE

The epigraph is taken from the British Museum, Central Archives (BMCA), 941/2, Memo from Leonard Woolley, "Political Future of Iraq and Its Repercussions on Archaeology," May 1932.

1. Majid Khadduri, *Independent Iraq, 1932–1958* (London: Oxford University Press, 1960), p. 2.

2. Hanna Batatu, *The Old Social Classes and the Revolutionary Movements of Iraq* (Princeton, N.J.: Princeton University Press, 1978), p. 466.

3. Ibid., p. 468. Batatu quotes an Arab poet, whose dictum Batatu believes applies with special force to Iraqis, that "Half the people are enemies to the holder of power and this if he is just."

4. On the labor movement see Marion Farouk-Sluglett and Peter Sluglett, "Labor and National Liberation: The Trade Union Movement in Iraq, 1920–1958," *Arab Studies Quarterly* 5 (1983): especially pp. 146–150. On the Communist Party, see Batatu, *The Old Social Classes,* especially pp. 389–439.

5. For this polarization see Liora Lukitz, *Iraq: The Search for National Unity* (London: F. Cass, 1995), pp. 75–77.

6. See, for example, the following memoirs by Iraqi politicians: Taha Al-Hashimi, *Mudhakkirat Taha al-Hashimi 1919–1943* (Beirut: Dar al-Taliah, 1967), pp. 140–148; Tawfiq al-Suwaydi, *Mudhakkirati* (Beirut: Dar al-Katib al-Arabi, 1969).

7. Phebe Marr, *History of Modern Iraq* (Boulder, Colo: Westview, 1985), pp. 55–59. Marr labels the years between 1932 and 1945 "an era of instability."

8. See Khaldun Husry, "The Assyrian Affair of 1933 (I)," *Interna-tional Journal of Middle East Studies* 5 (2): 161–176; and "The Assyrian Affair of 1933 (II)," *International Journal of Middle East Studies* 5 (3): 344–360. (Khaldun is the son of Sati' al-Husri.) Marr, *History of Modern Iraq,* p. 57; and Mohammad Tarbush, *The Role of the Military in Politics: The Case Study of Iraq to 1941* (London: KPI, 1982), pp. 95–101.

9. Husry, *Assyrian Affair* (II), pp. 351–352.

10. Marr, *History of Modern Iraq,* p. 59.

11. Peter Sluglett, *Britain in Iraq 1914–1932* (London: Ithaca Press, 1976), pp. 198–199.

12. Samira Haj, *The Making of Iraq 1900–1963: Capital, Power and Ideology* (Albany: State University of New York Press, 1997), p. 71.

13. See Batatu, *The Old Social Classes,* pp. 108–131. See also Haj, *The Making of Iraq,* pp. 33–34.

14. National Archives (NA), Records of the Department of State Relating to the Internal Affairs of Iraq, 890g.927/38, Note from American Embassy, December 2, 1932.

15. *Sawt al-'iraq,* February 18, 1933, p. 1.

16. Ibid.

17. Ibid.

18. All articles in *al-Ahali* were anonymous. The series of articles in *al-Ahali* about archaeology was well-written, obviously by someone who took an active interest in the subject and had observed developments in archaeology for the last decade. According to my interviews with several Iraqis, such as Abd al-Rahman al-Alawi and Najdat Safwat, it is very unlikely that Sati' al-Husri wrote these articles, since he never wrote in *al-Ahali.* Rather, they all agreed that in all likelihood it was 'Abd al-Fattah Ibrahim who penned these articles.

19. For a good study on the al-Ahali group, see Mudhaffar Amin, "Jama'at al-Ahali: Its Origin, Ideology and Role in Iraqi Politics, 1932–46" (Ph.D. diss., Durham University, 1980).

20. Marion Farouk-Sluglett and Peter Sluglett, *Iraq since 1958: From Revolution to Dictatorship* (London: I. B. Tauris, 1990), pp. 18–19.

21. *Al-Ahali,* May 13, 1933. This statement is reminiscent of the famous quotation by the Ottoman Sultan Abdul Hamid II who commented on the Western interest in archaeological remains, "Look at these stupid foreigners! I pacify them with broken stones." Quoted in Susan Marchand, *Down from Olympus: Archaeology and Philhellenism in Germany, 1750–1970* (Princeton, N.J.: Princeton University Press, 1996), p. 188.

22. *Al-Ahali,* May 13, 1933.

23. Ibid.

24. Ibid.

25. Ibid.

26. Ibid., May 14, 1933.

27. Ibid.

28. Ibid. The issue of the Samarra antiquities was discussed in Chapter 2.

29. The author once again emphasized the importance of developing native knowledge in archaeology, so that Iraqi officials with archaeological knowledge could accompany each mission to take part in the work and keep strict watch. For this purpose, the author urged the government to send students to European and American universities to acquire the necessary skills.

30. *Al-Ahali,* May 14, 1933.

31. BMCA, CE 32/1910, "Memorandum on the Action of the Minister of Education in Iraq with Respect to Mr. Mallowan's Finds at Tell Arpachiyah," by George Hill, June 24, 1933. The reason that this unusual

procedure was adopted was an attempt to dispel any suspicions as to the justice of the division.

32. Public Records Office (PRO), Kew, FO 371/3744/5523, Letter from Sir Francis Humphrys, British Embassy, Baghdad, to FO, September 14, 1933. See also BMCA, CE 32/1936/2/2.

33. Ibid.

34. PRO, Kew, FO 371/3755/E5058, Letter from Oglivie-Forbes (Baghdad) to Rendel (FO), August 13, 1933.

35. BMCA, CE 32/1910, "Memorandum on the Action of the Minister of Education in Iraq with Respect to Mr. Mallowan's Finds at Tell Arpachiyah," by George Hill, June 24, 1933.

36. *Al-Ahali,* May 27, 1933.

37. PRO, Kew, FO 371/3744/5523, Letter from Sir Francis Humphrys, British Embassy, Baghdad, to FO, September 14, 1933. See also BMCA, CE 32/1936/2/2; and NA, 890g.927/64, Letter from U.S. Embassy, Baghdad, to U.S. Secretary of State, October 26, 1933, p. 5.

38. A report of this expedition is found in M. E. L. Mallowan and J. Cruikshank Rose, "Excavations at Tall Arpachiyah, 1933," *Iraq* 2 (1935): 1–178.

39. PRO, Kew, FO 371/3744/5523, Letter from Sir Francis Humphrys, British Embassy, Baghdad, to FO, September 14, 1933. See also BMCA, CE 32/1936/2/2.

40. PRO, Kew, FO 371/2204/E2204, "Iraq. Annual Report," March 1934, p. 7.

41. NA, 890g.927/64, Letter from U.S. Embassy, Baghdad, to U.S. Secretary of State, October 26, 1933. In none of the Iraqi newspapers consulted was the Egyptian example cited by the Iraqis.

42. For this correspondence see PRO, Kew, FO 371/3755/E3755; E4343; E4876; and E5058, containing letters and minutes between Hill and the FO between June and August 1933. Copies of this correspondence are also found in the BMCA, CE 32, as well as in the BMCA, Papers of Max Mallowan (BMCA, MM), which contains extensive documents covering this episode.

43. PRO, Kew, FO 371/3755/E3755, Minutes of a meeting at the FO with Leonard Woolley, July 10, 1933.

44. PRO, Kew, FO 371/3755/E4345, Letter from Hill to FO, August 2, 1933.

45. BMCA, MM, Letter from Jordan to Mallowan, August 3, 1933. Jordan was vague about what were the criteria of this "expert evidence." Presumably, it was the minister's directions that only duplicates leave the country.

46. Ibid.

47. Mallowan's expedition was the only one singled out for this treatment. That year, the finds from Woolley's Ur expedition were divided

according to the standard practice. PRO, Kew, FO 371/3744/5523, Letter from Sir Francis Humphrys, British Embassy, Baghdad, to FO, September 14, 1933. See also BMCA, CE 32/1936/2/2.

48. PRO, Kew, FO 371/3755/E4876, Letter from Hill to Jordan, August 18, 1933. See also BMCA, CE 32.

49. PRO, Kew, FO 371/3755/E5058, Letter from Oglivie-Forbes (Baghdad) to Rendel (FO), August 13, 1933. Some British archaeologists seemed to believe that this action was due to Julius Jordan. Leeds, the director of Oxford Ashmolean, stated, "It is obvious that the spirit of the whole thing is due to German interference. How the British Government ever allowed a German to be put there passes my comprehension." BMCA, CE 32, 2006, Letter from Leeds to Hill, July 16, 1934. The Oxford professor Stephen Langdon interpreted this affair and other developments in Iraqi archaeology similarly and stated, "For heavens sake keep Iraq out of German intrigue." BMCA CE 32, 2007, Letter from Langdon to Hill, July 18, 1934. Based on the evidence now at our disposal, these criticisms are unwarranted.

50. PRO, Kew, FO 371/3755/E5058, Letter from Oglivie-Forbes (Baghdad) to Rendel (FO), August 13, 1933.

51. PRO, Kew, FO 371/3744/5523, Letter from Sir Francis Humphrys, British Embassy, Baghdad, to FO, September 14, 1933. See also BMCA, CE 32/1936/2/2.

52. Ibid.

53. PRO, Kew, FO 371/3755/E5058, Letter from Oglivie-Forbes (Baghdad) to Rendel (FO), August 13, 1933.

54. Those archaeologists and Assyriologists who were in contact with Hill regarding this matter were: Walter Andrae (Berlin), Rene Dussaud (Louvre), Henri Frankfort (Chicago), James Breasted (Chicago), Guiseppe Furlani (Florence), H. H. Jayne (Penn), Steve Langdon (Oxford), and Leroy Waterman (Michigan).

55. BMCA, MM, Letter from Jordan to Mallowan, September 24, 1933. See also NA, 890g.927/64, Letter from U.S. Embassy, Baghdad, to U.S. Secretary of State, October 26, 1933. The American ambassador did not put as much blame on the minister of education as the British did. Rather, the Americans believed that the instigator for these developments was Abdul Razzaq Lufti, a curator in the Iraq Museum, who they thought was intriguing to oust Jordan and become the director of antiquities himself.

56. Donald M. Reid, "Nationalizing the Pharaonic Past: Egypt 1922–1952," in *Rethinking Nationalism in the Arab Middle East,* ed. Israel Gershoni and James Jankowski (New York: Columbia University Press, 1997), pp. 133–134.

57. BMCA, CE 32, 1952/1, Letter from Breasted to Hill, September 27, 1933. It should be pointed out that Breasted was not altogether heedless

that Iraqis could develop an interest in archaeology that was not purely economic. In his letter to Hill, he pointed to the example of Hermann Hilprecht, who, according to Breasted, "gained his large influence with the Turkish Government by showing really tangible evidence of an interest in the Constantinople Museum and contributing a good deal of his time to the development of that museum. The Turks used to say that he was the only representative of a Western nation who had ever shown any such interest and it had a great influence on them. With this experience in mind I have stressed the possibilities of cooperation between the Iraq Government and the foreign archaeologist working in Iraq as a means of developing the Baghdad Museum into a great national institution." BMCA, CE 32, 1952/1, Letter from Breasted to Hill, September 27, 1933. It is not clear why Breasted did not decide to follow Hilprecht's example in Iraq in this particular case.

58. One of Breasted's telegrams to Hill contained over six hundred words. This was at a time when each word in a telegram was expensive, showing how important Breasted viewed this matter. See BMCA, CE 32/1945G, Telegram from Breasted to Hill, September 30, 1933. In a letter to the U.S. Department of State explaining the Iraq situation, Breasted included Hill's memorandum. Breasted pointed out, "You will note, perhaps with some amusement, that this document contains only very materialistic and obvious considerations. A long experience with Oriental politicians has, however, demonstrated to me the fact that any mention of science whatsoever leaves the Oriental politician altogether uninterested." NA, 890g.927/49, Letter from Breasted to Murray, September 27, 1933.

59. BMCA, CE 32, 1925, Letter from Hill to Andrae, September 7, 1933. In his correspondence with Hill, Breasted, who represented the United States on the Committee of the League of Nations for International Intellectual Cooperation, offered to raise this issue before the League of Nations. Given Iraq's recent admission and eagerness to participate in the League, it was plausible that the Iraqis would respond favorably in that venue. BMCA, CE 32, 1931, Letter from Breasted to Hill, September 15, 1933.

60. BMCA, CE 32, 1945G, Telegram from Breasted to Hill, September 30, 1933. See also BMCA, CE 32, 1950a, Letter from Hill to FO, October 2, 1933. This correspondence led to the Memorandum on Foreign Archaeological Expeditions in Iraq, BMCA, CE 32, 1981/2. This memorandum, which was eventually sent to the British ambassador in Iraq, was supposed to arm him with appropriate arguments so that he could "protest on reasoned grounds" to the members of the Iraqi cabinet.

61. BMCA, CE 32, 1981/2, Memorandum on Foreign Archaeolog-ical Expeditions in Iraq.

62. BMCA, CE 32, 1950a, Letter from Hill to FO, October 2, 1933.

63. Ibid.

64. BMCA, CE 32, 1981/2, Memorandum on Foreign Archaeolog-ical Expeditions in Iraq.

65. These announcements or stories were by no means large, front-page news items, but were present nevertheless.

66. BMCA, CE 32, 1950a, Letter from Hill to FO, October 2, 1933.

67. PRO, Kew, FO 371/3755/E5058, Letter from Oglivie-Forbes (Baghdad) to Rendel (FO), August 13, 1933, quoting Julius Jordan.

68. Unfortunately these predictions came to fruition during the recent government of Saddam Husayn, particularly after the Persian Gulf War. Due to a variety of reasons, including the UN economic embargo on Iraq, the antiquities markets in the West have been flooded with artifacts that were once housed in the Iraq Museum. See *New York Times,* "Ancient, Priceless and Gone with the War," December 8, 1996, and "Thieves Methodically Strip Iraq of Treasures from a Storied Past," March 15, 1998.

69. The BM officials had several meetings with the FO to discuss this issue. See BMCA, CE 32 1947/2, Memo from Sidney Smith to Hill, September 30, 1933; and PRO, Kew, FO 371/3755/E5840, FO Memo from September 29, 1933. The American ambassador in Britain, Mr. Atherton, also wrote to the FO stating that the U.S. Department of State would be glad to join Britain and other interested powers in representations to the Iraqi government. See PRO, Kew, FO 371/3755/E588, Letter from Atherton to FO, October 2, 1933.

70. PRO, Kew, FO 371/3755/E5840, FO Memo from meeting with Sidney Smith (BM), September 29, 1933.

71. BMCA, CE 32, 1959/2, Letter from FO to Humphrys (Baghdad), October 5, 1933. See also PRO, Kew, FO 371/3744/E5833.

72. PRO, Kew, FO 371/3755/E5840, FO Memo from meeting with Sidney Smith (BM), September 29, 1933.

73. PRO, Kew, FO 371/3755/E5883, FO Minutes, October 3, 1933.

74. PRO, Kew, FO 371/1831/E4933, Internal FO comments on "Memorandum on the Antiquities Law in Iraq" from the members of the faculty at Oxford University (Leeds, Langdon, Margliouth, Campbell Thompson), July 15, 1934.

75. PRO, Kew, FO 371/3755/E5883, Letter from FO to Humphrys, October 5, 1933.

76. Ibid.

77. Ibid.

78. PRO, Kew, FO 371/3755/E5931, Telegram from Humphrys to FO, October 8, 1933.

79. NA, 890g.927/70, Letter from Breasted to Murray, December 8, 1933.

80. BMCA, CE 32, 1980, Letter from Jordan to Hill, October 19, 1933.

81. PRO, Kew, FO 371/3755/E6541, Letter from Humphrys to Bonham-Carter, October 13, 1933.

82. Ibid.

83. In his private representation to the Iraqi prime minister, the American Minister Resident in Baghdad also used the arguments presented in Hill's memorandum. See NA 890g.927/69, Letter from Knabenshue to Humphrys, November 10, 1933.

84. PRO, Kew, FO 371/412/21, Letter from Humphrys to FO, October 30, 1933.

85. BMCA, CE 32, 1985/2, Telegram from Humphrys to FO, November 18, 1933.

86. PRO, Kew, FO 371/1831/E2116, Letter from Humphrys to FO, March 17, 1934.

87. BMCA, CE 32, 1987, Letter from Bonham-Carter to Hill, November 20, 1933.

88. BMCA, 983, Letter from Woolley to Kenyon, March 1, 1934.

89. PRO, Kew, FO 371/1831/E1831, Minute by Rendel, March 20, 1934. See also FO 371/1831/E2116, Letter from Humphrys to FO, March 17, 1934.

90. PRO, Kew, FO 371/1831/E1831, Minute by Rendel, March 20, 1934.

91. PRO, Kew, FO 371/1831/E2116, Letter from Humphrys to FO, March 17, 1934.

92. Ibid.

93. PRO, Kew, FO 371/1831/E4751, Letter from Jordan to Mallowan, July 1, 1934.

94. Ibid.

95. Ibid.

96. Ibid.

97. BMCA, CE 32, 2006, Notes by Hill concerning new Antiquities legislation in Iraq.

98. BMCA, CE 32, 2010, Letter from Breasted to Hill, July 24, 1934.

99.Ibid.

100. PRO, Kew, FO 371/1831/E4933, "Memorandum on the Antiquities Law in Iraq" from members of the faculty of Oxford, July 1934.

101. Ibid.

102. PRO, Kew, FO 371/1831/E5371, Letter from Hill to FO, August 22, 1934.

103. PRO, Kew, FO 371/1831/E5371, Internal FO minutes commenting on Hill's letter, August 22, 1934.

104. Ibid.

105. PRO, Kew, FO 371/1831/E5556, Letter from Oglivie-Forbes to al-Suwaydi, August 17, 1934.

106. 'Abd al-Razzaq al-Hasani, *Ta'rikh al-wizarat al-'iraqiyyah* (Sidon, Lebanon: Matba'at al-Irfan, 1933–1967), 4:31–34.

107. Ibid., 4:48–49.

108. PRO, Kew, FO 371/1831/E5969, Letter from British Embassy to FO, September 10, 1934.

109. PRO, Kew, FO 371/1831/E6096, Letter from Oglivie-Forbes to FO, September 20, 1934.

110. BMCA, CE 32, 2026, Letter from Oglivie-Forbes to FO, October 18, 1934.

111. PRO, Kew, FO 371/940/940E, *Annual Report on Iraq for 1934* (London, 1935), p. 7.

112. PRO, Kew, FO 371/337/E1298, Letter from Humphrys to FO, February 14, 1935. Humphrys stated further, once he heard that Mallowan was instead thinking of taking his expedition to Syria on a mission sponsored by the BSAI, that "the fact that Mallowan's expedition has gone to Syria and is partly financed from the Gertrude Bell Memorial Fund is enough, in the opinion of her friends, to make Miss Bell turn in her grave. There can be little doubt that this expedition could have had a very successful season at Arpachiyah this year and I deprecate the faint heart that took it elsewhere."

113. NA 890g.927/66, Letter from Breasted to Murray, November 8, 1933.

114. Ibid.

115. Ibid.

116. BMCA, CE 32, 2034/2/2, Letter from Campbell Thompson to al-Husri, March 27, 1935.

117. BMCA, CE 32, Copy of Hill's Letter to *The Times,* published in August 1933. Hill uses the old term "Mesopotamia" to refer to the political state of Iraq, thereby not fully acknowledging that a new, fully independent sovereign state existed in that area.

118. Leonard Woolley, "Letter to the Editor," *The Times,* December 12, 1934.

119. *Al-Bilad* (Baghdad), December 29, 1934, "A Law That Neglects the Antiquities of Iraq. Refutation of Dr. Woolley, the Archaeologist. Statement by the Iraqi Director of Antiquities."

120. Ibid.

121. *Al-Alam al-'arabi* (Baghdad), December 30, 1934, "Our Historical Treasures. The Antiquities Act." Note the pronoun "our," which indicates that the writer felt that these objects properly belonged to Iraq.

122. Ibid. Like many similar articles, this article also touched on the Cooke affair (see Chapter 4) as evidence of Westerners abusing their position in Iraq to bolster their own collections.

123. Ibid.

124. PRO, Kew, FO 371/337/E337, FO minute, January 14, 1935.

125. PRO, Kew, FO 371/337/E1298, Letter from Humphrys, February 14, 1935.

126. Ibid.

127. PRO, Kew, FO 371/337/E6901, Letter from Clark Kerr to FO, November 13, 1935.

128. Ibid.

129. PRO, Kew, FO 371/337/E6901, FO Minutes of Joint Archaeological Committee meeting, December 16, 1935.

130. Ibid.

131. Ibid.

132. NA, 890g.927/98, Letter from Breasted to Murray, February 19, 1935.

133. Ibid.

134. Ibid.

135. NA, 890g.927/112, Letter from Frankfort to Breasted, February 22, 1935.

136. Those seventeen objects included a bull's head, cylinder seals, and terra cotta plaques.

137. NA, 890g.927/112, Letter from Frankfort to Breasted, February 22, 1935. The papers of Henri Frankfort, consisting of extensive field notes, drafts of articles, and private correspondence, are housed at the Warburg Institute in London. They did not contain any materials relevant to this study.

138. NA, 890g.927/107, Enclosure no. 1 to Confidential Diplomatic Despatch no. 457, dated March 7, 1935, from the American Legation at Baghdad.

139. Ibid.

140. Knabenshue seems to have had a close personal relationship with Said. They played tennis together regularly, and Knabenshue had taught him to swim. Therefore, Knabenshue probably felt he could speak frankly and openly with Said about the division. See NA, 890g.927/113, Letter from Knabenshue to U.S. Secretary of State, April 8, 1935.

141. Ibid.

142. NA, 890g.927/107, Telegram from Knabenshue to U.S. Secretary of State, March 6, 1935.

143. Ibid.

144. NA, 890g.927/113, Letter from Knabenshue to U.S. Secretary of State, April 8, 1935.

145. Ibid.

146. NA, 890g.927/112, Letter from Breasted to Murray, March 22, 1935.

147. Ibid.

148. NA, 890g.927/115, Letter from Frankfort to Breasted, March 29, 1935.

149. Ibid.

150. Ibid.

151. PRO, Kew, FO 371/1030/E1167, Letter from Clark Kerr to FO, February 20, 1936.

152. PRO, Kew, FO 371/1030/E1176, Letter from Clark Kerr to FO, February 26, 1936.

153. *Iraqi Government Gazette,* June 7 (Baghdad, 1936).

154. Ibid.

155. PRO, Kew, FO 371/654/98, League of Nations, "International Statute for Antiquities and Excavations," September 30, 1937.

156. Ibid.

157. NA, 890.g927/116, Letter from Knabenshue to Murray, April 3, 1935.

158. Ibid.

159. *Al-Akhbar,* January 1, 1939, p. 3.

160. Sati' al-Husri, *Mudhakkirati fi al-'iraq, 1921–1941* (Beirut: Dar al-Taliah, 1967–1968), 1:211–219, 2:277–280.

161. M. E. Yapp, *The Near East Since the First World War* (London: Longman, 1991), p. 76.

162. PRO, Kew, FO 371/4183, H. E. Bowman, Memorandum on Educational Policy, Baghdad, August 12, 1919.

163. Al-Husri, *Mudhakkirati,* 1:38.

164. Taken from Fakhri al-Barudi, ed., *Al-Anashid al-wataniyya* (Beirut, 1937).

165. An excellent source on school curriculums in Iraq is Matta Akrawi's *Curriculum Construction in the Public Primary Schools of Iraq* (New York: Columbia University, 1943). Reeva Simon has carefully studied education in interwar Iraq. See her *Iraq between the Two World Wars: The Creation and Implementation of a Nationalist Ideology* (New York: Columbia University Press, 1986) and her article "The Teaching of History in Iraq before the Rashid Ali Coup of 1941," *Middle Eastern Studies* 22 (1986): 37–51.

166. Akrawi, *Curriculum Construction,* p. 180.

167. Quoted in Bassam Tibi, *Arab Nationalism: Between Islam and Nation-State* (New York: St. Martin's Press, 1997), p. 122.

168. Naim 'Attiyah, "Ma'alim al-fikr al-tarbawi fi al-bilad al-'arabiyyah fi al-mi'at al-sanah al-akhirah," in *al-Fikr al-'arabi fi mi'at sanah,* ed. Fu'ad Sarruf and Nabih Amin Faris (Beirut: American University of Beirut, 1967), pp. 527–528.

169. Al-Husri, *Mudhakkirati,* 2:239.

170. Ibid., 2:278.

171. Ibid.

172. Ibid., 1:65–71.

173. Simon, *Iraq between the Two World Wars,* p. 83.

174. Al-Husri, *Mudhakkirati,* 1:38.

175. Akrawi, *Curriculum Construction*, p. 180.

176. Phebe Marr, "The Development of a Nationalist Ideology in Iraq, 1920–1941," *Muslim World* 75 (2): 98–99.

177. Sami Shawkat, *Hadhahi ahdafuna* (Baghdad: n.p., 1939), p. 43. See also Simon, *Iraq between the Two World Wars*, p. 96.

178. Freya Stark, *Baghdad Sketches* (Evanston, Ill.: Northwestern, 1992), p. 65.

179. For Iraqi museum guides see *Dalil al-mathaf al-'iraqi* (Baghdad, 1937). See also *Dalil mathaf al-athar al-'arabiyyah fi khan marjan bi baghdad* (Baghdad, 1938).

180. *Dalil al-mathaf al-'iraqi* (Baghdad, 1937), p. 74.

181. Amatzia Baram, "A Case of Imported Identity: The Modernizing Secular Ruling Elites of Iraq and the Concept of Mesopotamian-Inspired Territorial Nationalism, 1922–1992," *Poetics Today* 15 (2): 290.

182. Quoted in Amatzia Baram, *Culture, History and Ideology in the Formation of Ba'thist Iraq, 1968–1989* (New York: St. Martin's Press, 1991), p. 26.

183. See, for example, *Al-Bilad*, December 13 and 18, 1934.

184. PRO, Kew, FO 371/1030/E1030, Letter from Clark Kerr to FO, February 8, 1936. It was his contention that the decision was primarily that of Jordan, who wanted to keep the Iraqis out of the more ancient ruins.

185. Al-Husri, *Mudhakkirati*, 2:434–444.

186. NA, 890g.927/90, Letter from Knabenshue to U.S. Secretary of State, February 20, 1935.

187. PRO, Kew, FO 371/1030/E1030, Letter from Clark Kerr to FO, February 8, 1936.

188. Al-Husri, *Mudhakkirati*, 2:499.

189. Concurrently, the Iraqi Department of Antiquities also conducted some excavations at Samarra. See their *Excavations at Samarra, 1936–1939* (Baghdad, 1940).

190. A useful collection of essays that highlights the disagreements and to a certain extent the complexities of this debate is found in Phyllis Mauch Messenger, ed., *The Ethics of Collecting Cultural Property: Whose Culture? Whose Property?* (Albuquerque: University of New Mexico Press, 1989).

191. For advocates of this position, see, for example, Jeanette Greenfield, *The Return of Cultural Treasures* (New York: Cambridge University Press, 1989); and Lyndel Prott and P. J. O'Keefe, *Law and the Cultural Heritage* (Abingdon, Oxon: Professional Books, 1984).

192. See Paul Bator, *The International Trade in Art* (Chicago: University of Chicago Press, 1982) and the various publications by John Henry Merryman. See also interview with Philippe de Montebello, Director of New York's Metropolitan Museum of Art, in Garry Wills "Athens of Fifth Avenue" in *New York Review of Books*, June 10, 1999, pp. 38–40.

193. *Al-Thawra,* August 6, 1980. See also Baram, *Culture, History,* p. 43.

194. PRO, Kew, FO 371/337/E3735, Letter from Iraqi Ministry of Foreign Affairs to British Embassy, Baghdad, April 9, 1935.

195. Ibid.

196. PRO, Kew, FO 371/337/E4394, Letter from BM to FO, July 16, 1935.

197. PRO, Kew, FO 371/337/E4392, Letter from BM to FO, July 15, 1935.

198. BMCA, CE 32/2085, Memo from Sidney Smith to George Hill, August 21, 1935.

199. BMCA, CE 32/2087, Letter from Hill to Hobson, September 23, 1935.

200. PRO, Kew, FO 624/14, Letter from Newton (Baghdad) to Keeling, British School of Archaeology, June 20th, 1939.

201. Lamia al-Gailani Werr, "Safar, Fuad" in *Oxford Encyclopedia of Archaeology in the Near East,* ed. Eric M. Meyers (New York: Oxford University Press, 1998), p. 448. See also Bahnam Abu al-Suf, "Dawr al-tanqibat al-athariyya fi al-kashf 'an hadarat al-'iraq al-qadim," in *Hadarat al-Iraq* (Baghdad: n.p., 1985,) pp. 71–72. For the life of Taha Baqir see Fawzi Rashid, *Taha Baqir: Hayatuhu wa-atharu* (Baghdad: Wizarat al-Thaqafah, 1987). See also their journal, *Al-Murshid ila mawatin al-athar wa al-hadarah,* (Baghdad, 1962–1966) on Iraqi archaeology.

202. NA, 890.g927/144, Letter from Knabenshue to U.S. Secretary of State, February 7, 1939.

203. For an excellent overview of the politics of archaeology in Egypt see Donald M. Reid, *Whose Pharaohs? Archaeology, Museums, and Egyptian National Identity from Napoleon to World War I* (Berkeley: University of California Press, 2002).

204. For this discovery see Thomas Hoving, *Tutankhamun: The Untold Story* (New York: Simon & Schuster, 1978); Nicholas Reeves, *The Complete Tutankhamun: The King, the Tomb, the Royal Treasure* (London: Thames & Hudson, 1990). For the political history of this period see Israel Gershoni and James Jankowski, *Egypt, Islam, and the Arabs: The Search for Egyptian Nationhood, 1900–1930* (New York: Oxford University Press, 1986); Nadav Safran, *Egypt in Search for Political Community* (Cambridge, Mass.: Harvard University Press, 1961). Donald M. Reid's excellent essay "Nationalizing the Pharaonic Past: Egypt 1922–1952," in *Rethinking Nationalism in the Arab Middle East,* ed. James Jankowski and Israel Gershoni (New York: Columbia University Press, 1997), pp. 127–149 explores the relationship between Egyptian nationalism and the archaeological enterprise.

205. Reid, "Nationalizing the Pharaonic Past," p. 134.

206. As Reid points out, one should not view this episode as strictly Egypt versus Britain, but also consider the Anglo-French rivalry, because Lacau seemed more than willing to curtail the success of Carter's mission. Ibid.

207. Ibid., p. 135.
208. Ibid.
209. NA, 890g.927/110, Letter from Breasted to Murray, March 8, 1935.
210. Gershoni and Jankowski, *Egypt, Islam, and the Arabs*, pp. 98–104.

CONCLUSION

1. See Seton Lloyd and Fuad Safar, "Tell 'Uqair: Excavations by the Iraq Government Directorate of Antiquities in 1940–1941," *Journal of Near Eastern Studies* 2 (1943): 131–158.
2. *Guide to the 'Iraq Museum Collections* (Baghdad, 1942), Preface.
3. Ibid.
4. See also 'Abd Allah al-Juburi, *Al-Majma' al-'ilmi al-'iraqi, nasha'tuhu, a'dawuhu wa a'maluhu* (Baghdad: Matba'at al-Ani, 1965).
5. Lamia al-Gailani Werr, "Safar, Fuad" in *Oxford Encyclopedia of Archaeology in the Near East,* ed. Eric M. Meyers (New York: Oxford University Press, 1998), p. 448.
6. Taha Baqir, "Iraq Government Excavations at 'Aqar Quf. First Interim Report, 1942–1943," in *Iraq,* supplement (London, 1944), p. 3.
7. Ibid.
8. Baqir published a total of three interim reports in *Iraq* in 1944, 1945, and 1946.
9. Samuel Noah Kramer, *The Sumerians: Their History, Culture and Character* (Chicago: University of Chicago Press, 1963), p. 30.
10. Seton Lloyd, *Foundations in the Dust* (London: Oxford University Press, 1947), p. 222.
11. See Mina Marefat's excellent article "Wright's Baghdad," in *Frank Lloyd Wright: Europe and Beyond,* ed. Anthony Alofsin (Berkeley: University of California Press, 1999).
12. On the 1958 revolution see Hanna Batatu, *The Old Social Classes and the Revolutionary Movements of Iraq* (Princeton, N.J.: Princeton University Press, 1978); and Robert Fernea and Wm. Roger Louis, eds., *The Iraqi Revolution of 1958: The Old Social Classes Revisited* (London: I. B. Tauris, 1991).
13. *Sumer,* vol. 15 (Baghdad, 1959), pp. 59ff. See also Amatzia Baram, *Culture, History and Ideology in the Formation of Ba'thist Iraq, 1968–1989* (New York: St. Martin's Press, 1991), pp. 28–29.
14. I thank Professor Benjamin R. Foster for bringing this point to my attention.
15. *Sumer,* vol. 25 (Baghdad, 1969), p. 12.
16. *Sumer,* vol. 30 (Baghdad, 1974), p. 354.
17. For the doctrines of the Ba'th party see John F. Devlin, *The Ba'th Party: A History from Its Origins to 1966* (Stanford, Calif.: Stanford University Press, 1976).

18. Cited in *Sumer*, an annual publication of the Iraqi Department of Antiquities (Baghdad, 1979), p. 9.

19. Baram, *Culture, History*, Chapters 2–4.

20. This plunder has been documented in several editions of *Lost Heritage: Antiquities Stolen from Iraq's Regional Museums* (Chicago: American Association of Research in Baghdad, 1992; London: American Association of Research in Baghdad, 1993; Tokyo: American Association of Research in Baghdad, 1996).

21. MacGuire Gibson, "Ancient Mesopotamia, World Heritage under Threat," paper delivered at Iraq: A Symposium on the History, People and Politics, Villanova University, April 9, 1999.

22. Yale Babylonian Collection (YBC), Letter from Albert T. Clay to Clyde Garbett, December 16, 1921.

23. Unpublished poem from personal correspondence between Fadel Jabr and author.

WORKS CONSULTED

ARCHIVAL MATERIAL

Great Britain

British Library, India Office
    Letters, Political and Secret: L/P&S/10/689 (1917–1921);
    L/P&S/10/742 (1917–1921); L/P&S/10/751 (1917–1918);
    L/P&S/10/756 (1920); L/P&S/10/845 (1920–1921);
    L/P&S/10/866 (1920)
British Library, London
    The Papers of Austen Henry Layard (AHL)
    The Papers of Arnold T. Wilson
British Museum, Central Archives, London
    CE 32 Excavations Papers
    Minutes of the Committee of the Board of Trustees, 1898–1935
    Misc. Correspondence 1914–1941
    The Papers of Max Mallowan
British Museum, Department of Oriental Arts, London
    Samarra Collection Folder
British Museum, Department of Western Asiatics, London
    The Papers of Reginald Campbell Thompson
Brynmor Jones Library, The University, Kingston-upon-Hull
    The Papers of Mark Sykes
Robinson Library, University of Newcastle-upon-Tyne
    The Gertrude Bell Collection
Oxford University, Bodleian Library & St. Anthony's College, Oxford
    The Papers of David Hogarth
    The Papers of T. E. Lawrence
    The Papers of Lionel Smith

Public Records Office (PRO), Kew
  CO 730 series, vols. 21 (1922), 25 (1923), 58 (1924), 59 (1924)
  FO 371 series, vols. 4148 (1918), 4183 (1919), 113 (1920), 5040
      (1920), 5230 (1920), 384 (1921), 497 (1922), 2883 (1922),
      10095 (1923), 7429 (1924), 9004 (1924), 2337 (1926), 4200
      (1926), 3744 (1933), 3755 (1933), 1831 (1934), 2204 (1934),
      337 (1935), 940 (1935), 1030 (1936), 654 (1937)
  FO 406 series, vol. 70 (1930)
  FO 624 series, vol. 14 (1939)
  WO 33 (1920)
Royal Geographic Society, London
  The Papers of Henry Creswicke Rawlinson
Warburg Institute, London
  The Papers of Henri Frankfort

United States

The Semitic Museum, Harvard University, Cambridge, Massachusetts
  Nuzi Excavation Papers
National Archives, Washington, D.C.
  Records of the Department of State Relating to Internal Affairs of
      Iraq, 1930–1944. Decimal File. 890g.927
University Museum, University of Pennsylvania, Philadelphia
  Ur Expedition Archives
Rockefeller Center Archives, Tarrytown, New York
  The Papers of John D. Rockefeller, Jr., Educational Interests. Boxes
      111, 117
Babylonian Collection, Yale University, New Haven, Connecticut
  Misc. Correspondence 1921–1931

PRIMARY SOURCES—PUBLISHED

Newspapers, Journals, and Museum Guides

Al-Ahali (Baghdad, 1933)
Al-Akhbar (Baghdad, 1939)
Al-Alam al-'arabi (Baghdad, 1934)
Al-Bilad (Baghdad, 1934)
The Antiquarian (London, 1871)
Baghdad Times (Baghdad, 1930)
Dalil al-mathaf al-'iraqi (Baghdad, 1937)
Dalil mathaf al-athar al-'arabiyyah fi khan marjan bi baghdad (Baghdad, 1938)

The Guardian
A Guide to the 'Iraq Museum Collections (Baghdad, 1942)
Hartford Courant
The Independent online
Iraq (London, 1934–1946)
London Illustrated News (London, 1848–1852)
Majallah al-tarbiyyah wa al-ta'lim (Baghdad, 1928–1932)
Al-Murshid ila mawatin al-athar wa al-hadarah (Baghdad, 1962–1966)
New York Times
Sawt al-'iraq (Baghdad, 1933)
Sumer (Baghdad, 1945; 1951; 1959; 1969; 1974; 1979)
Al-Thawra (Baghdad, 1980)
The Times (London, 1934)
Washington Post

Government Reports and Publications

Antiquities Law (Baghdad, 1924)
Antiquities Law no. 59 of 1936 (Baghdad, 1936)
Colonial Office: Correspondence Regarding the Future of Mesopotamia (London, 1920)
Cyprus Gazette Supplement (London, 1905)
Excavations at Samarra, 1936–1939 (Baghdad: Department of Antiquities, 1940)
Iraq Government, Ministry of Education, Department of Antiquities, *Report on Excavations in Iraq during the Season 1928–9* (Baghdad, 1929)
Iraq Government, Ministry of Education, Department of Antiquities, *Report on the Excavations in Iraq during the Seasons 1929–30, 1930–1, and 1931–32. Report on the Activity of the Department of Antiquities from 1st October, 1931 until 30th September, 1932* (Baghdad, 1933)
Iraqi Government Gazette (Baghdad, 1937)
Minhaj al-dirasa al-ibtida'iyya li sanat 1936 (Baghdad, 1936)
Minhaj al-dirasa al-mutawassita (Baghdad, 1931)
Report by His Britannic Majesty's Government to the Council of the League of Nations on the Administration of Iraq (London, 1925–1931)
Takrir'in al-hafariyat fi al-'iraq mu'sim 1928–9 (Baghdad: Department of Antiquities, 1929)
Takrir'in al-hafariyat fi al-'iraq mu'sim 1929–30; 1930–31; 1931–32 (Baghdad: Department of Antiquities, 1933)
Review of the Civil Administration of Mesopotamia, 1914–1920. Compiled by Gertrude Bell (London, 1920)
Al-Waqa'i al-'iraqiyya (Baghdad, 1924; 1927; 1934; 1936)

Monographs (Arabic)

Al-Ayyubi, Ali Jawdat. *Dhikrayat.* Beirut: Matba'at al-Wafa, 1967.
Al-Basir, Muhammad Mahdi. *Ta'rikh al-qadhiya al-'iraqiyya.* 2 vols. Baghdad: Matba'at al-Fallah, 1924.
Al-Haidari, Ibrahim Fasih ibn Sabghattullah. *Kitab unwan al-majd fi bayan ahwal baghdad wa al-basra wa al-najd.* Basra: Manshurat al-Basri, n.d.
Al-Hashimi, Taha. *Mudhakkirat Taha al-Hashimi 1919–1943.* Beirut: Dar al-Taliah, 1967.
Al-Husri, Sati'. *Abhath mukhtarah fi al-qawmiyyah al-'arabiyyah.* Beirut: Markaz Dirasat al-Wahdah al-Arabiya, 1959.
———. *Ara' wa ahadith fi al-qawmiyya al-'arabiyya,* 4th ed. Beirut: Dar al-Ilm lil Malayin, 1964.
———. *Ara' wa ahadith fi al-tarbiyyah wa al-ta'lim.* Cairo: Matba'at al-Risalah, 1944.
———. *Ara' wa ahadith fi al-wataniyya wa al-qawmiyya,* 4th ed. Beirut: Dar al-Ilm lil Malayin, 1961.
———. *Ma hiya al-qawmiyyah?* Beirut: Dar al-Ilm lil Malayin, 1959.
———. *Majallah al-tarbiyah wa al-ta'lim.* 5 vols. Baghdad, 1928–1932.
———. *Mudhakkirati fi al-'iraq, 1921–1941.* 2 vols. Beirut: Dar al-Taliah, 1967–1968.
———. *Yawm maysalun: safhah min ta'rikh al-'arab al-hadith.* Beirut: Maktabat al-Kashshaf, n.d.
Ibn al-Husayn, Faysal. *Faysal Ibn al-Husayn fi kutabihi wa aqwalahi.* Baghdad: Matba'at Hukumah, 1945.
Al-Jamali, Fadil Muhammad. *Al-'Iraq bayna ams wal-yawm.* Baghdad: Dar al-Kashshaf, 1954.
al-Juburi, 'Abd Allah. *Al-Majma' al-'ilmi al-'iraqi, nasha'tuhu, a'dawuhu wa a'maluhu.* Baghdad: Matba'at al-Ani, 1965.
Shawkat, Sami. *Hadhahi ahdafuna.* Baghdad: n.p., 1939.
Al-Suwaydi, Tawfiq. *Mudhakkirati.* Beirut: Dar al-Katib al-Arabi, 1969.
Al-Uzri, 'Abd al-Karim. *Ta'rikh fi dhikrayat al-'iraq, 1930–1958.* Beirut: Markaz al-Abjadiyah lil-Saffa al-Taswriri, 1982.

Monographs and Articles (European Languages)

Beauchamp, Maurice de. "An Account of Some of the Antiquities of Babylon Found in the Neighbourhood of Baghdad: Also of What Is to Have Been the Tower of Babel, and of the Yezidis." *European Magazine* 5 (1792): 4–18.
Bell, Gertrude. *Amurath to Amurath.* London: W. Heinemann, 1911.
———. *The Desert and the Sown.* London: W. Heinemann, 1907.

———. *Letters of Gertrude Bell.* 2 vols. Edited by Florence Bell. London: E. Benn, 1927.

———. *Palace and Mosque at Ukhaidar.* Oxford: Clarendon Press, 1914.

———. *Poems from the Divan of Hafiz.* London: W. Heinemann, 1897.

———. *Safar Nameh, Persian Pictures.* London: Bentley, 1894.

Botta, Paul-Emile. *M. Botta's Letters on the Discoveries at Nineveh.* London: Longman, Brown, Green, 1850.

———. *Monument de Ninive découvert et décrit par M. P. E. Botta, mesuré et dessiné par M. E. Flandin. Ouvrage publié par ordre du gouvernement sous les auspices de M. le Ministre de l'Intérieur et sous la direction d'une commission de l'Institut.* Paris: Imprimerie Nationale, 1849.

Braddon, Russell. *The Siege.* London: Cape, 1969.

Curzon, Lord. *Persia and the Persian Question.* London: Longman's Green, 1892.

———. *Russia in Central Asia.* London: Longman's Green, 1899.

Della Valle, Pietro. *The Pilgrim: The Travels of Pietro Della Valle.* Translated, abridged, and introduced by George Bull. London: Hutchinson, 1989.

Hogarth, David. *Accidents of an Antiquary's Life.* London: Macmillan, 1911.

———. *The Ancient East.* New York: H. Holt & Company, 1914.

———. *A History of Arabia.* Oxford: Clarendon Press, 1922.

Ibn Battuta. *Travels in Asia and Africa 1325–1354.* Translated by H. A. R. Gibb. London: Routledge, 1929.

Kitchener, Horatio H. *Book of Photographs of Biblical Sites.* London: The Society's Office, 1876.

Koldewey, Robert. *Das wiedererstehende Babylon.* Leipzig, Germany: J. C. Hinrichs, 1913.

———. *The Excavations at Babylon.* London: MacMillan & Co., 1914.

Langdon, Stephen. *Excavations at Kish I, 1923–4.* Paris: P. Guenther, 1924.

Lawrence, T. E. *The Letters of T. E. Lawrence.* Edited by David Garnett. London: Reprint Society, 1941.

———. *Seven Pillars of Wisdom.* London: Reprint Society, 1939.

Lawrence, T. E., and Leonard Woolley. *The Wilderness of Zin.* London: J. Cape, 1915.

Layard, Austen Henry. *Autobiography and Letters.* London: John Murray, 1903.

———. *Discoveries in the Ruins of Nineveh and Babylon.* London: John Murray, 1853.

———. *The Monuments of Nineveh.* London: John Murray, 1849.

———. *Nineveh and Its Remains.* London: John Murray, 1849.

———. *Nineveh and Its Remains.* Reprint, New York: Praeger, 1970.

Mackay, Ernst. *A Sumerian Palace and the "A" Cemetery at Kish, Mesopotamia.* Chicago: Field Museum, 1929.

Mallowan, M. E. L., and J. Cruikshank Rose. "Excavations at Tall Arpachiyah, 1933." *Iraq* 2 (1935): 1–178.

Mallowan, Max. *Mallowan's Memoirs: The Autobiography of Max Mallowan.* London: Collins, 1977.

Maurice, Thomas. *Observations Connected with Astronomy and Ancient History, Sacred and Profane on the Ruins of Babylon, as Recently Visited and Described by Claudius James Rich.* London: J. Murray, 1816.

———. *Observations on the Remains of Ancient Egyptian Grandeur and Superstition as Connected with Those of Assyria: Forming the Appendix to the Observations on the Ruins of Babylon.* London: J. Murray, 1818.

Mohl, Julius. *Lettres de M. Botta sur ses découvertes a Khorsabad, prés de Ninive.* Paris: Imprimerie Nationale, 1845.

Niebuhr, Carsten. *Reisebeschreibung nach Arabien und andern umliegenden Ländern.* 2 vols. Copenhagen: N. Möller, 1778.

Peters, John Punnett. *Nippur, or Explorations and Adventures on the Euphrates.* 2 vols. New York: Putnam, 1897–1898.

Preusser, Conrad. *Nordmesopotamische Baudenkmaler Altchristlischer und Islamischer Zeit.* Leipzig, Germany: Druck von A. Pries, 1911.

Rassam, Hormuzd. *Asshur and the Land of Nimrod . . .* New York: Eaton & Mains, 1897.

Rauwolf, Leonhard. *Aigentliche Beschreibung der Raisz so er vor dieser zeit gegen Auffgang inn die Morgenländer . . . selbs volbract.* Laugingen, Germany: Verlag G. Willers, 1583.

Ray, John, ed. *A Collection of Curious Travels and Voyages in Two Tomes: The First Containing Dr. Leonhart Rauwolff's Itinerary into the Eastern Countries . . .* London: Royal Society at the Princes Arms, 1693.

Rich, Claudius J. *Memoir on the Ruins of Babylon.* London: Longman, Hurst, Reese, Orme & Brown, 1815.

———. *Narrative of a Residence in Kooridstan, and on the Site of Ancient Nineveh, with a Journal of a Voyage down the Tigris to Baghdad etc.* London: Duncan and Malcolm, 1836.

Robinson, Edward. *Biblical Researches in Palestine, Mount Sinai and Arabia Petraea in 1838.* New York: Crocker & Brewster, 1841.

Sarre, Friedrich, and Ernst Herzfeld. *Archaeologische Reise im Euphrat- und Tigris-Gebeit.* 4 vols. Berlin: D. Reimer, 1911–1920.

Sarzec, Ernest de. *Découvertes en Chaldée.* 2 vols. Paris: E. Leroux, 1884–1912.

Smith, Eli, and H. G. O. Dwight. *Researches of the Rev. E. Smith and the Rev. H. G. O. Dwight in Armenia; Including a Journey through Asia Minor and into Georgia and Persia, with a Visit to the Nestorian and Chaldean Christians of Oormiah and Salmas.* Boston: Crocker & Brewster, 1833.

al-Tabari. *The History of al-Tabari.* Vol. 1. Translated by Franz Rosenthal. Albany: State University of New York Press, 1989.

———. *The History of al-Tabari.* Vol. 4. Translated by Moshe Perlman. Albany: State University of New York Press, 1989.

Thompson, William. *The Land and the Book; or Biblical Illustrations Drawn from the Manners and Customs, the Scenes and Scenery, of the Holy Land.* New York: Harper & Brothers, 1859.

Ward, William H. "Report on the Wolfe Expedition to Babylonia." In *Papers of the Archaeological Institute of America*, pp. 3–12. Boston: Archaeological Institute of America, 1886.

Watelin, Louis, and Stephen Langdon. *Excavations at Kish III, 1925–27.* Paris: P. Guenther, 1930.

———. *Excavations at Kish IV, 1925–30.* Paris: P. Guenther, 1934.

Wilson, Arnold T. *Mesopotamia: A Clash of Loyalties.* 2 vols. London: Oxford University Press, 1931.

Woolley, C. Leonard, T. E. Lawrence, and P. L. O. Guy. *Carcemish: Report on the Excavations at Djerabis on Behalf of the British Museum.* 3 vols. London: British Museum, 1914, 1921, 1952.

Woolley, Leonard. *As I Seem to Remember.* London: Allen & Unwin, 1962.

———. *Spadework: Adventures in Archaeology.* London: Lutterworth Press, 1953.

Secondary Accounts—Unpublished

Amin, Mudhaffar. "Jama'at al-Ahali: Its Origin, Ideology and Role in Iraqi Politics, 1932–46." Ph.D. diss., Durham University, 1980.

Bendiner, Kenneth Paul. "The Portrayal of the Middle East in British Painting." Ph.D. diss., Columbia University, 1979.

Bohrer, Frederick. "A New Antiquity: The English Reception of Assyria." Ph.D. diss., University of Chicago, 1989.

Gibson, MacGuire. "Ancient Mesopotamia, World Heritage under Threat." Paper delivered at Iraq: A Symposium on the History, People and Politics, Villanova University, April 9, 1999.

Matteson, Lynn Robert. "Apocalyptic Themes in British Romantic Landscape Painting." Ph.D. diss., University of California, Berkeley, 1975.

Secondary Accounts—Published (Arabic)

Abu al-Suf, Bahnam. "Dawr al-tanqibat al-athariyaa fi al-kashf 'an hadarat al-'iraq al-qadim." In *Hadarat al-'Iraq*, pp. 46–71. Baghdad: Dar al-Hurriyah lil-Tiba'ah, 1985.

'Attiyyah, Naim. "Ma'alim al-fikr al-tarbawi fi al-bilad al-'arabiyyah fi al-mi'at al-sanah al-akhirah." In *al-Fikr al-'arabi fi mi'at sanah*, ed. Fu'ad Sarruf and Nabih Amin Faris, pp. 515–532. Beirut: American University of Beirut, 1967.

al-'Azzawi, 'Abbas. *Asha'ir al-'iraq.* 4 vols. Baghdad: al-Tijarah wal-tiba'ah, 1956.

———. *Ta'rikh al-'iraq bayna al-ihtilalayn.* 8 vols. Baghdad: Matba'at Baghdad, 1935–1956.

Al-Barudi, Fakhri, ed. *Al-Anashid al-wataniyya.* Beirut, 1937.

Al-Bazirkan, Ali. *Al-Waqa'i al-haqiqiyya fil-thawra al-'iraqiyya.* Baghdad: n.p., 1954.

Burj, Muhammad 'Abd al-Rahman. *Sati' al-Husri.* Cairo: Dar al-Katib al-Arabi, 1969.

Al-Fayyad, 'Abdallah. *Al-Thawra al-'iraqiyya al-kubra sanat 1920.* Baghdad: Matba'at al-Irshad, 1963.

Al-Fir'awn, Fariq al-Muzhir. *Al-Haqaiq al-nasi'a fil-thawra al-'iraqiyya sanat 1920 wa-nata'ijiha.* Baghdad: al-Najah, 1954.

Al-Haraka al-islamiyya fi al-'iraq. Beirut: Muassasat al-Jihad, 1985.

al-Hasani, 'Abd al-Razzaq. *Ta'rikh al-'iraq al-siyasi al-hadith.* Sidon, Lebanon: Matba'at al-Irfan, 1948.

———. *Ta'rikh al-sihafa al-'iraqiyyah.* Sidon, Lebanon: Matba'at al-Irfan, 1971.

———. *Ta'rikh al-wizarat al-'iraqiyyah.* 10 vols. Sidon, Lebanon: Dar al-Kutub, 1933–1967.

———. *Al-Thawra al-'iraqiyyah al-kubra.* Sidon, Lebanon: 'Abd al-Razzaq al-Hasani, 1965.

Ibn Mansur, Muhammad ibn Mukarram. *Lisan al-'arab.* 6 vols. Cairo: Dar al-Marif, 1981.

Al-Jamil, Husayn. *Hayat al-siyasiyya fi al-'iraq, 1925–1946.* Baghdad: Maktabat al-Muthanna, 1983.

Al-Karkuli, Rasul. *Dawhat al-wuzara fi ta'rikh waqa'i baghdad al-zawra.* Beirut: Maktabat al-Nahda, 1963.

Ma'ruf, Naji. *Al-Madkhal fi ta'rikh al-hadara al-'arabiyya.* Baghdad: Matba'at al-Ani, 1960.

Mousa, Sulayman. *Al-Haraka al-'arabiyya: sirat al-marhala al-ula lil-nahda al-'arabiyya al-haditha 1908–1924.* Beirut: Dar al-Nahur, 1970.

Murqus, Elias. *Naqd al-fikr al-qawmi: Sati' al-Husri.* Beirut: Dar al-Taliah, 1966.

Al-Nafisi, 'Abdallah. *Dawr al-shi'a fi tatawwur al-'iraq al-siyasi al-hadith.* Beirut: Dar al-Nahar, 1973.

Rashid, Fawzi. *Taha Baqir: Hayatuhu wa-atharu.* Baghdad: Wizarat al-Thaqafah, 1987.

'Ukashah, Thawrat. *Al-fann al-'iraqi: sumar wa-babil wa-ashur.* Beirut: Al-Mu'assasah al-Arabiyah, 1970.

Al-'Umari, Muhammad Tahir. *Ta'rikh uqadarat al-'iraq al-siyasiyya.* 3 vols. Baghdad: Matba'at al-Fallah, 1925.

Al-Wardi, Ali. *Lamahat 'ijtima'iyya min ta'rikh al-'iraq al-hadith.* 6 vols. Baghdad: Matba'at al-Irshad, 1969–1978.

Secondary Accounts—Published (European Languages)

Adelson, Roger. *Mark Sykes: Portrait of an Amateur.* London: Cape, 1975.

Ahmed, Feroz. *The Young Turks: The Committee of Union and Progress in Turkish Politics, 1908–1914.* Oxford: Oxford University Press, 1969.

Akrawi, Matta. *Curriculum Construction in the Public Primary Schools of Iraq.* New York: Columbia University, 1943.

Alexander, Victoria D. *Museums and Money: The Impact of Funding on Exhibitions, Scholarship, and Management.* Bloomington: Indiana University Press, 1996.

Alsop, Joseph. *The Rare Art Traditions: The History of Art Collecting and Its Linked Phenomena Wherever These Have Appeared.* New York: Harper & Row, 1982.

Altick, Richard D. *The Shows of London.* Cambridge, Mass.: Harvard University Press, 1978.

Amanat, Abbas. *Pivot of the Universe: Nasir al-din Shah and the Iranian Monarchy.* Berkeley: University of California Press, 1996.

Andersen, Benedict. *Imagined Communities.* London: Verso Press, 1983.

Anderson, M. S. *The Eastern Question, 1774–1923.* London: Macmillan, 1966.

Andrae, Walter. *Babylon: Die versunkene Welstadt und ihr Ausgräber, Robert Koldewey.* Berlin: W. de Gruyter, 1952.

———. *Lebenserinnerungen eines Ausgräbers.* Berlin: Walter de Gruyter, 1961.

Antonious, George. *The Arab Awakening.* Beirut: Khayat's, 1938.

Arnove, Robert. *Philanthropy and Cultural Imperialism.* Boston: G. K. Hall, 1980.

Attiyeh, Ghassan. *Iraq, 1908–1921: A Socio-Political Study.* Beirut: Arab Institute for Research & Publications, 1973.

Awad, Georges. "Babil" in *Encyclopedia of Islam.* Leiden, the Netherlands: Brill, 1974.

Baikie, J. *The Glamour of Near East Excavations.* Philadelphia: Lippincott, 1927.

Balston, Thomas. *John Martin: His Life and Works.* London: G. Duckworth, 1947.

———. "John Martin and Metropolitical Improvements." *Architectural Review* 102 (1947): 2–7.

Baqir, Taha. "Iraq Government Excavations at 'Aqar Quf. First Interim Report, 1942–1943." In *Iraq,* supplement. London, 1944.

Baram, Amatzia. "A Case of Imported Identity: The Modernizing Secular Ruling Elites of Iraq and the Concept of Mesopotamian-Inspired

Territorial Nationalism, 1922–1992." *Poetics Today* 15 (2): 279–319.
———. *Culture, History and Ideology in the Formation of Ba'thist Iraq, 1968–1989.* (New York: St. Martin's Press, 1991.
Barnett, Correlli. *The Collapse of British Power.* Gloucester, UK: Eyre Methuen, 1984.
Barnett, Richard. "Layard's Influence on British Orientalism in the Nineteenth Century." In *Austen Henry Layard Tra L'Oriente e Venezia,* ed. Frederick Fales and B. J. Hickey, pp. 177–181. Rome: L'Erma di Bretschneider, 1987.
Batatu, Hanna. *The Old Social Classes and the Revolutionary Movements of Iraq.* Princeton, N.J.: Princeton University Press, 1978.
Bator, Paul. *The International Trade in Art.* Chicago: University of Chicago Press, 1982.
Baudet, Henri. *Paradise on Earth: Some Thoughts on European Images of Non-European Man.* New Haven, Conn.: Yale University Press, 1965.
Bennett, Tony. *The Birth of the Museum.* New York: Routledge, 1995.
Berkes, Niyazi. *The Development of Secularism in Turkey.* Montreal: McGill University Press, 1964.
Bjelajac, David. *Millennial Desire and the Apocalyptic Vision of Washington Allston.* Washington, D.C.: Smithsonian Institution Press, 1988.
Bohrer, Frederick. "Assyria as Art: A Perspective on the Early Reception of Ancient Near Eastern Artifacts." In *Culture and History,* 4 (1989): 7–29.
Bosshard, Walter. *Winckelmann: Aesthetik der Mitte.* Zurich: Artemis-Verlag, 1960.
Boulton, W. H. *The Romance of Archaeology.* London: S. Low Marston, 1936.
Bowler, Peter J. *The Invention of Progress: The Victorians and the Past.* Oxford: B. Blackwell, 1989.
Boyer, Paul. *When Time Shall Be No More: Prophecy Belief in Modern American Culture.* Cambridge, Mass.: Harvard University Press, 1992.
Brackman, Arnold. *The Luck of Nineveh.* New York: McGraw-Hill, 1978.
Brown, L. Carl. *International Politics and the Middle East.* Princeton, N.J.: Princeton University Press, 1984.
Burgoyne, Elizabeth. *Gertrude Bell.* London: E. Benn, 1961.
Bury, J. B. *The Idea of Progress: An Inquiry into Its Growth and Origins.* New York: Dover, 1955.
Busch, Briton C. *Britain, India and the Arabs.* Berkeley: University of California Press, 1971.
Butler, Marilyn. "John Bull's Other Kingdom: Byron's Intellectual Comedy." *Studies in Romanticism* 31 (3): 26–43.
Butterfield, Herbert. *The Origins of History.* New York: Basic Books, 1981.
Campbell Thompson, Reginald, and R. W. Hutchinson. *A Century of Exploration at Nineveh.* London: Luzac & Co., 1929.

Carena, Omar. *Historiography of Ancient Near Eastern Studies.* Darmstadt, Germany: Button & Bercker, 1989.

Caygill, Marjorie. *The Story of the British Museum.* 2nd ed. London: British Museum Press, 1992.

Carrott, Richard. *The Egyptian Revival: Its Sources, Monuments, and Meaning, 1808–1858.* Berkeley: University of California Press, 1978.

Ceram, C. W. *God, Graves, and Scholars.* New York: A. A. Knopf, 1967.

———, ed. *Hands on the Past.* New York: A. A. Knopf, 1966.

Chamberlain, Russell. *Loot! The Heritage of Plunder.* New York: Facts on File, 1983.

Chew, Samuel. *The Crescent and the Rose.* New York: Oxford University Press, 1937.

Christianson, Paul. *Reformers and Babylon: English Apocalyptic Visions from the Reformation to the Eve of the Civil War.* Toronto: University of Toronto Press, 1978.

Cig, Muazzez. "Ataturk and the Beginnings of Cuneiform Studies in Turkey." *Journal of Cuneiform Studies* 40 (1988): 211–216.

Clarke, D. L. "Models and Paradigms in Contemporary Archaeology." In *Models in Archaeology,* ed. D. L. Clarke, pp. 1–12. London: Metheun, 1972.

Clay, Albert. *Amurru, the Home of the Northern Semites: A Study Showing that the Religion and Culture of Israel Were Not of Babylonian Origin.* Philadelphia: Sunday School Times, 1909.

Cleveland, William. *Islam against the West: Shakib Arslan and the Campaign for Islamic Nationalism.* Austin: University of Texas Press, 1985.

———. *The Making of an Arab Nationalist: Ottomanism and Arabism in the Life and Thought of Sati' al-Husri.* Princeton, N.J.: Princeton University Press, 1971.

Colley, Linda. *The Britons: Forging the Nation, 1707–1838.* New Haven, Conn.: Yale University Press, 1992.

Collins, Basil Anthony. *Al-Muqaddasi: The Man and His Work.* Ann Arbor: University of Michigan, 1974.

Connor, Peter. "Cast-collecting in the Nineteenth Century: Scholarship, Aesthetics, Connoisseurship." In *Rediscovering Hellenism: The Hellenic Inheritance and the English Imagination,* ed. G. W. Clarke. Cambridge: Cambridge University Press, 1989.

Coombes, Annie. *Reinventing Africa: Museums, Material Culture, and Popular Imagination in Late Victorian and Edwardian England.* New Haven, Conn.: Yale University Press, 1994.

Cooper, Jerrold. "From Mosul to Manila: Early Approaches to Funding Ancient Near Eastern Studies Research in the United States." In *Culture and History* 7 (1992): 126–134.

Culler, Dwight A. *The Victorian Mirror of History.* New Haven, Conn.: Yale University Press, 1985.

Curl, James Stevens. *A Celebration of Death: An Introduction to Some of the Buildings, Monuments and Settings of Funerary Architecture in the Western European Tradition.* London: Constable, 1993.

———. *Egyptomania: The Egyptian Revival; A Recurring Theme in the History of Taste.* New York: St. Martin's Press, 1994.

Curtis, John, ed. *Fifty Years of Mesopotamian Discovery: The Work of the British School of Archaeology in Iraq, 1932–1982.* London: British School of Archaeology in Iraq, 1982.

Daiches, Samuel. *Lord Kitchener and His Work in Palestine.* London: Luzac & Co., 1915.

Dalley, Stephanie. *Myths from Mesopotamia: Creation, the Flood, Gilgamesh and Others.* Oxford: Oxford University Press, 1989.

Daniel, Glyn. *A Hundred and Fifty Years of Archaeology.* Cambridge, Mass.: Harvard University Press, 1976.

———. *A Hundred Years of Archaeology.* London: Duckworth, 1950.

———. *Short History of Archaeology.* London: Thames & Hudson, 1981.

———, ed. *Towards a History of Archaeology.* London: Thames & Hudson, 1981.

Daniel, Norman. *Islam and the West: The Making of an Image.* Edinburgh: Edinburgh University Press, 1960.

Dann, Uriel. *Iraq under Qassem: A Political History 1958–63.* New York: Oxford University Press, 1969.

Dannenfeldt, Karl H. *Leonhard Rauwolf: Sixteenth-Century Physician, Botanist, and Traveller.* Cambridge, Mass.: Harvard University Press, 1968.

Darwin, John. *Britain, Egypt and the Middle East.* New York: Macmillan, 1981.

David, Rosalie. *Discovering Ancient Egypt.* New York: Facts on File, 1994.

Davis, Eric. *Memories of State: Politics, History and Collective Identity in Modern Iraq.* Berkeley: University of California Press, 2003.

———. "The Museum and the Politics of Social Control in Modern Iraq." In *Commemorations: The Politics of National Identity,* ed. John R. Gillis, pp. 90–104. Princeton, N.J.: Princeton University Press, 1994.

Davis, John. *The Landscape of Belief: Encountering the Holy Land in Nineteenth-Century American Art and Culture.* Princeton, N.J.: Princeton University Press, 1996.

Dawn, Ernest C. *From Ottomanism to Arabism: Essays on the Origins of Arab Nationalism.* Urbana: University of Illinois Press, 1973.

Delitzsch, Friedrich. *Babel and Bible: Three Lectures on the Significance of Assyrological Research for Religion.* Chicago: Open Court Publishing, 1906.

Delumeau, Jean. *History of Paradise: The Garden of Eden in Myth and Tradition.* New York: Continuum, 1995.

Devlin, John F. *The Ba'th Party: A History from Its Origins to 1966.* Stanford, Calif.: Stanford University Press, 1976.

Diaz-Andreu, Margarita, and Timothy Champion, eds. *Nationalism and Archaeology in Europe*. London: University College of London Press, 1996.

Drews, Robert. *The Greek Accounts of Eastern History*. Cambridge, Mass.: Harvard University Press, 1973.

Duncan, J. E. *Milton's Earthly Paradise: A Historical Study of Eden*. Minneapolis: University of Minnesota Press, 1972.

Earle, E. M. *Turkey, the Great Powers and the Baghdad Railway: A Study in Imperialism*. New York: Macmillan, 1923.

Ehrich, Robert, ed. *Chronologies in Old World Archaeology*. Chicago: University of Chicago Press, 1993.

Einreinhofer, Nancy. *The American Art Museum: Elitism and Democracy*. London: Leicester University Press, 1997.

El-Haj, Nadia Abu. *Facts on the Ground: Archaeological Practice and Territorial Self-Fashioning in Israeli Society*. Chicago: University of Chicago Press, 2001.

Elliot, Matthew. *"Independent Iraq": The Monarchy and British Influence, 1941–58*. London: I. B. Tauris, 1996.

Erskine, (Mrs.) Steuart. *King Faysal of Iraq*. London: Hutchinson, 1933.

Fagan, Brian. *Archaeology*. Boston: Little, Brown, 1978.

———. *In the Beginning: An Introduction to Archaeology*. New York: HarperCollins, 1994.

———. *The Rape of the Nile: Tomb Robbers, Tourists and Archaeologists in Egypt*. New York: Scribner, 1975.

———. *Return to Babylon: Travelers, Archaeologists and Monuments in Mesopotamia*. Boston: Little, Brown, 1979.

Fahnestock, Polly J. "History and Theoretical Development: The Importance of a Critical Historiography in Archaeology." *Archaeological Reviews from Cambridge* 3 (1): 13–34.

Fales, Frederick Mario. "Layard's Observation of Iraq." In *Austen Henry Layard Tra L'Oriente e Venezia*, ed. Frederick Fales and B. J. Hickey, pp. 55–77. Rome: L'Erma di Bretschneider, 1987.

Falkenstein, Adam. *Archaische Texte aus Uruk*. Leipzig, Germany: O. Harrassowitz, 1936.

———. *Die neusumerische Gerichtsurkunden*. 3 vols. Munich: Verlag der Bayerischen Akademie der Wissenschaften, 1956–1957.

Farouk-Sluglett, Marion, and Peter Sluglett. *Iraq since 1958: From Revolution to Dictatorship*. London: I. B. Tauris, 1990.

———. "Labor and National Liberation: The Trade Union Movement in Iraq, 1920–1958." *Arab Studies Quarterly* 5 (2): 139–154.

Fattah, Hala. *The Politics of Regional Trade in Iraq, Arabia and the Gulf, 1745–1900*. Albany: State University of New York Press, 1997.

Feaver, William. *The Art of John Martin*. Oxford: Clarendon Press, 1975.

Fernea, Robert. *Shaykh and Effendi: Changing Patterns among the El Shabana of Southern Iraq*. Cambridge, Mass.: Harvard University Press, 1970.

Fernea, Robert, and Wm. Roger Louis, eds. *The Iraqi Revolution of 1958: The Old Social Classes Revisited.* London: I. B. Tauris, 1991.

Field, James. *America and the Mediterranean World 1776–1882.* Princeton, N.J.: Princeton University Press, 1969.

Finkelstein, Jacob. "Bible and Babel: A Comparative Study of the Hebrew and Babylonian Religious Spirit." *Commentary* 26 (5): 431–444.

Foster, Benjamin R. "Clay, Albert Tobias," in *American National Biography.* New York: Oxford University Press, 1999.

Foster, Henry A. *The Making of Modern Iraq: A Product of World Forces.* Norman: University of Oklahoma Press, 1936.

Fowler, Don D. "Uses of the Past: Archaeology in the Service of the State." *American Antiquity* 52 (2): 229–248.

Frankfort, Henri. *Art and Architecture in the Ancient Orient.* Orig. 1954; New Haven, Conn.: Yale University Press, 1996.

Fraser, J. T. *Of Time, Passion and Knowledge: Reflections on the Strategy of Existence.* New York: G. Braziller, 1975.

Fromkin, David. *A Peace to End All Peace: The Fall of the Ottoman Empire and the Creation of the Modern Middle East.* New York: H. Holt, 1989.

Al-Gailani Werr, Lamia. "Safar, Fuad" in *Oxford Encyclopedia of Archaeology in the Near East,* ed. Eric M. Meyers, p. 448. New York: Oxford University Press, 1998.

Gellner, Ernst. *Nations and Nationalism.* Ithaca, N.Y.: Cornell University Press, 1983.

———. *Thought and Change.* London: Weidenfeld and Nicolson, 1964.

Gero, Joan, David Lacy, and Michael Blakey, eds. *The Socio-Politics of Archaeology.* Amherst: University of Massachusetts, 1983.

Gershoni, Israel, and James Jankowski. *Egypt, Islam, and the Arabs: The Search for Egyptian Nationhood, 1900–1930.* New York: Oxford University Press, 1986.

———, eds. *Rethinking Nationalism in the Arab Middle East.* New York: Columbia University Press, 1997.

Ghareeb, Edmund. *The Kurdish Question in Iraq.* Syracuse, N.Y.: Syracuse University Press, 1981.

Giamatti, A. B. *The Earthly Paradise and the Renaissance Epic.* Princeton, N.J.: Princeton University Press, 1966.

Gibson, McGuire. *The City and the Area of Kish.* Miami: Field Research Projects, 1972.

Gilbert, Martin. *Winston S. Churchill, 1916–1922.* Vol. 4, *The Stricken World.* Boston: Houghton Mifflin, 1975.

Gillard, David. *The Struggle for Asia: A Study in British and Russian Imperialism.* London: Methuen, 1977.

Goldsmith, Steven. *Unbuilding Jerusalem: Apocalypse and Romantic Representation.* Ithaca, N.Y.: Cornell University Press, 1993.

Goold, Douglas. "Lord Hardinge and the Mesopotamian Expedition and Inquiry." *Historical Journal* 19 (4): 919–945.

Gould, Cecil. *Trophy of Conquest: The Musée Napoleon and the Creation of the Louvre*. London: Faber & Faber, 1965.

Grabill, Joseph. *Protestant Diplomacy and the Near East: Missionary Influence on American Policy 1810–1927*. Minneapolis: University of Minnesota Press, 1971.

Grayson, D. K. *The Establishment of Human Antiquity*. New York: Academic Press, 1983.

Gregory, Jeremy. "Anglicanism and the Arts: Religion, Culture and Politics in the Eighteenth Century." In *Culture, Politics and Society in Britain, 1660–1800,* ed. Jeremy Black and Jeremy Gregory. Manchester, UK: Manchester University Press, 1991.

Greenfield, Jeanette. *The Return of Cultural Treasures*. New York: Cambridge University Press, 1989.

Gunter, Anne. "Introduction." In *Culture and History* 7 (1992): 2–12.

Gunter, Michael M. *The Kurds of Iraq: Tragedy and Hope*. New York: St. Martin's Press, 1992.

Haj, Samira. *The Making of Iraq 1900–1963: Capital, Power and Ideology*. Albany: State University of New York Press, 1997.

Haklyut, Richard. *The Principal Navigations, Voyages, Traffiques and Discoveries of the English Nation*. 10 vols. London: J. M. Dent & Sons Ltd., 1927–1928.

Halbwachs, Maurice. *The Collective Memory*. New York: Harper & Row, 1980.

Haldane, Aylmer L. *The Insurrection in Mesopotamia, 1920*. Edinburgh: Allborough Publishers, 1922.

Hanioglu, Sukru. *The Young Turks in Opposition*. New York: Oxford University Press, 1995.

Hansot, Elisabeth. *Perfection and Progress: Two Modes of Utopian Thought*. Cambridge, Mass.: MIT Press, 1974.

Harrison, J. F. C. *The Second Coming: Popular Millenarianism, 1780–1850*. New Brunswick, N.J.: Rutgers University Press, 1979.

Hartman, Michelle, and Alessandro Olsaretti. "'The First Boat and the First Oar': Inventions of Lebanon in the Writings of Michel Chiha." *Radical History Review* 86 (2003): 37–65.

Hasan, M. S. "Growth and Structure of Iraq's Population, 1867–1947." *Bulletin of Oxford University. Institute of Economics and Statistics* 20 (1958): 339–352.

Haskell, Francis. *Rediscoveries in Art: Some Aspects of Taste, Fashion and Collecting in England and France*. Ithaca, N.Y.: Cornell University Press, 1976.

Haven, S. F. *Archaeology of the United States*. Washington, D.C.: n.p., 1856.

Hawkes, Jaquetta. *The World of the Past.* New York: Knopf, 1963.

Heizer, Robert. *Archaeology; A Bibliographical Guide to the Basic Literature.* New York: Garland Publishers, 1980.

Hill, Christopher. *Antichrist in Seventeenth-Century England.* London: Oxford University Press, 1971.

———. *Puritanism and Revolution.* London: Mercury Books, 1958.

Hilprecht, H. V. *Explorations in Bible Lands during the Nineteenth Century.* Philadelphia: A. J. Holman, 1903.

Hinsley, C. M. "Revising and Revisioning the History of Archaeology: Reflections on Region and Context." In *Tracing Archaeology's Past: The Historiography of Archaeology,* ed. Andrew L. Christianson, pp. 79–96. Carbondale: Southern Illinois University Press, 1989.

Hobsbawm, E. J. *The Age of Empire.* New York: Vintage 1987.

Hoffman, Barbara. "The Spoils of War." *Archaeology* 46 (3): 37–40.

Hole, Frank, and Robert Heizer. *Introduction to Prehistoric Archaeology.* New York: Holt, Rinehart and Winston, 1973.

Honour, Hugh. *Romanticism.* New York: Harper & Row, 1979.

Hopwood, Derek. *Tales of Empire: The British and the Middle East, 1880–1952.* London: I. B. Tauris, 1989.

Horowitz, Sylvia. *The Find of a Lifetime: Sir Arthur Evans and the Discovery of Knossos.* New York: Viking Press, 1981.

Hourani, Albert. *Arabic Thought in the Liberal Age.* Cambridge: Cambridge University Press, 1983.

———. *Europe and the Middle East.* Berkeley: University of California Press, 1980.

Hoving, Thomas. *Tutankhamun: The Untold Story.* New York: Simon & Schuster, 1978.

Hudson, Kenneth. *Museums of Influence.* Cambridge: Cambridge University Press, 1987.

———. *A Social History of Archaeology.* London: Macmillan, 1981.

Huffman, Herbert B. "Babel und Bible: The Encounter between Babylon and the Bible." *Michigan Quarterly Review* 22 (3): 309–320.

Hume, Ivor Noel. *Archaeology.* London: John Gifford, 1971.

———. *Historical Archaeology.* New York: Knopf, 1969.

Husry, Khaldun. "The Assyrian Affair of 1933 (I)." *International Journal of Middle East Studies* 5 (2): 161–176.

———. "The Assyrian Affair of 1933 (II)." *International Journal of Middle East Studies* 5 (3): 344-360.

Hutchinson, William. *Errand to the World: American Protestant Thought and Foreign Missions.* Chicago: University of Chicago Press, 1987.

Ibn Haykal. *The Oriental Geography of Ebn Haukal.* Translated by William Ouseley. Reprint of London 1800 edition. Frankfurt: Institute for the History of Arabic-Islamic Science, 1992.

Ibn Khaldun. *The Muqaddimah.* Translated by Franz Rosenthal. New York: Pantheon Books, 1958.

Impey, Oliver, and MacGregor Arthur, eds. *The Origins of Museums.* Oxford: Clarendon Press, 1985.

Ireland, Philip. *Iraq: A Study in Political Development.* London: J. Cape, 1937.

Ismael, Tariq. *Iraq and Iran: Roots of Conflict.* Syracuse, N.Y.: Syracuse University Press, 1982.

Istakhri, Ibrahim ibn Muhammad. *Kitab masalik al-mamalik.* Frankfurt: Institute for the History of Arabic-Islamic Science, 1992.

James, Lawrence. *Golden Warrior: The Life and Legend of Lawrence of Arabia.* London: Weidenfeld & Nicolson, 1990.

———. *The Rise and Fall of the British Empire.* New York: Little, Brown, 1994.

Jenkins, Ian. *Archaeologists and Aesthetes in the Sculpture Galleries of the British Museum 1800–1939.* London: British Museum Press, 1992.

Kabbani, Rana. *Europe's Myths of Orient.* Bloomington: Indiana University Press, 1986.

Kaiser, Werner. *75 Jahre Deutsches Archäologisches Institut Kairo, 1907–1982.* Mainz, Germany: D. von Zabern, 1982.

Kaminsky, Arnold P. *The India Office, 1880–1910.* New York: Greenwood Press, 1986.

Kaufmann, Milo. *Paradise in the Age of Milton.* Victoria, B.C.: University of Victoria, 1978.

Kayali, Hasan. *Arabs and Young Turks: Ottomanism, Arabism and Islamism in the Ottoman Empire, 1908–1918.* Berkeley: University of California Press, 1997.

Kaye, Lawrence M. "Laws in Force at the Dawn of World War II: International Conventions and National Laws." In *The Spoils of War: World War II and Its Aftermath: The Loss, Reappearance, and Recovery of Cultural Property,* ed. Elisabeth Simpson, pp. 100–105. New York: H. N. Abrams, 1997.

Kedar, Benjamin. *Crusade and Mission: European Approaches to the Muslims.* Princeton, N.J.: Princeton University Press, 1984.

Kedourie, Elie. *England and the Middle East: The Destruction of the Ottoman Empire, 1914–1921.* London: Mansell Publishers, 1987.

———. *In the Anglo-Arab Labyrinth.* Cambridge: Cambridge University Press, 1976.

Kennedy, Paul. *The Rise and Fall of British Naval Mastery.* London: Ashfield Press, 1976.

———. *The Rise of the Anglo-German Antagonism, 1860–1914.* London: G. Allen & Unwin, 1980.

Kent, Marian, ed. *The Great Powers and the End of the Ottoman Empire.* London: G. Allen & Unwin, 1984.

Kermode, Frank. *The Sense of an Ending: Studies in the Theory of Fiction*. New York: Oxford University Press, 1967.

Khadduri, Majid. *Independent Iraq, 1932–1958*. London: Oxford University Press, 1960.

———. *Political Trends in the Arab World: The Role of Ideas and Ideals in Politics*. Baltimore: Johns Hopkins Press, 1970.

Khalidi, Tarif. *Islamic Historiography: The Histories of Mas'udi*. Albany: State University of New York Press, 1975.

al-Khalil, Samir (pseud.). *Republic of Fear: The Inside Story of Saddam's Iraq*. New York: Pantheon, 1990.

Khoury, Philip S. *Urban Notables and Arab Nationalism: The Politics of Damascus 1880–1920*. Cambridge: Cambridge University Press, 1983.

Kimble, G. H. T. *Geography in the Middle Ages*. London: Methuen & Co., Ltd., 1938.

King, Philip. *American Archaeology in the Mideast*. Philadelphia: American School of Oriental Research, 1983.

Klieman, Aaron S. "Britain's War Aims in the Middle East in 1915." *Journal of Contemporary History* 3 (3): 237–253.

———. *Foundations of British Policy in the Arab World: The Cairo Conference of 1921*. Baltimore: Johns Hopkins Press, 1970.

Kohl, Philip L., and Clare Fawcett, eds. *Nationalism, Politics, and the Practice of Archaeology*. Cambridge: Cambridge University Press, 1995.

Kramer, Samuel Noah. *History Begins at Sumer*. Garden City, N.Y.: Doubleday, 1959.

———. "Sumerian Literature: A General Survey." In *The Bible and the Ancient Near East: Essays in Honor of William Foxwell Albright*, ed. G. Ernest Wright, pp. 12–30. Garden City, N.Y.: Doubleday, 1961.

———. *The Sumerians: Their History, Culture and Character*. Chicago: University of Chicago Press, 1963.

Kubie, Nora. *The Road to Nineveh: The Adventures and Excavations of Sir Austen Henry Layard*. New York: Cassell, 1964.

Kuklick, Bruce. *Puritans in Babylon: The Ancient Near East and American Intellectual Life, 1880–1930*. Princeton, N.J.: Princeton University Press, 1996.

Lane, E. W. *An Arabic-English Lexicon*. London: Williams and Norgale, 1863.

Lane-Poole, Stanley. *The Life of the Right Honourable Stratford Canning . . . .* London: Longman, Green, 1888.

Langdon, Stephen. *Sumerian Epic of Paradise, the Flood, and the Fall of Man*. Philadelphia: University Museum, 1915.

Larsen, Mogens Trolle. *The Conquest of Assyria*. London: Routledge, 1996.

———. "Orientalism and Near Eastern Archaeology." In *Domination and Resistance*, ed. Daniel Miller et al., pp. 97–115. London: Unwin Hyman, 1989.

————. "Orientalism and the Ancient Near East." In *Culture and History* 2 (1987): 92–115.

Larue, John. *Babylon and the Bible*. Grand Rapids, Mich.: Baker Book House, 1969.

Lawless, R. I. "Iraq: Changing Population Patterns." In *Populations of the Middle East and North Africa*, ed. J. I. Clarke and W. F. Fisher, pp. 97–127. London: London University Press, 1972.

Layton, Robert, ed. *Who Needs the Past? Indigenous Values and Archaeology*. Winchester, Mass.: Unwin Hyman, 1989.

Lenczowski, George. *The Middle East in World Affairs*. Ithaca, N.Y.: Cornell University Press, 1980.

Lewis, Bernard. *The Emergence of Modern Turkey*. Oxford: Oxford University Press, 1968.

————. *History Remembered, Recovered, Invented*. Princeton, N.J.: Princeton University Press, 1975.

Link, Arthur, ed. *Papers of Woodrow Wilson*. Vol. 65. Princeton, N.J.: Princeton University Press, 1991.

Lloyd, Seton. *Foundations in the Dust*. London: Oxford University Press, 1947.

————. *Mesopotamia: Excavations on Sumerian Sites*. London: L. Dickson, 1936.

Lloyd, Seton, and Fuad Safar. "Tell 'Uqair: Excavations by the Iraq Government Directorate of Antiquities in 1940–1941." *Journal of Near Eastern Studies* 2 (2): 131–158.

Longrigg, Stephen. *Iraq 1900–1950*. Oxford: Oxford University Press, 1953.

Lost Heritage: Antiquities Stolen from Iraq's Regional Museums. Chicago: American Association of Research in Baghdad, 1992. London: American Association of Research in Baghdad, 1993. Tokyo: American Association of Research in Baghdad, 1996.

Loud, Gordon. *Khorsabad: Excavation in the Palace and at a City Gate*. Chicago: University of Chicago Press, 1936.

Loud, Gordon, and Charles Altman. *Khorsabad: The Citadel and the Town*. Chicago: University of Chicago Press, 1938.

Lukitz, Liora. *Iraq: The Search for National Unity*. London: F. Cass, 1995.

Lundquist, John M. "Babylon in European Thought." In *Civilizations of the Ancient Near East*, vol. 1, ed. Jack Sasson, pp. 60–72. New York: Scribner, 1996.

McBryde, Isabel, ed. *Who Owns the Past?* London: Oxford University Press, 1985.

McGinn, Bernard. *Visions of the End: Apocalyptic Tradition in the Middle Ages*. New York: Columbia University Press, 1979.

Mackenzie, John M. *Propaganda and Empire: The Manipulation of British Public Opinion, 1880–1960*. Manchester: Manchester University Press, 1964.

Magnus, Philip. *Kitchener: Portrait of an Imperialist.* New York: E. P. Dutton, 1959.

Magoffin, R. V. D. *Magic Spades.* New York: H. Holt & Company, 1928.

Maisels, Charles Keith. *The Near East: Archaeology in the "Cradle of Civilizations."* London: Routledge, 1993.

Makdisi, Ussama. "Reclaiming the Land of the Bible: Missionaries, Secularism, and Evangelical Modernity." *American Historical Review* 102 (3): 680–713.

Mallowan, Max. *Twenty-Five Years of Mesopotamian Discovery, 1932–1956.* London: British School of Archaeology in Iraq, 1956.

Marchand, Suzanne L. *Down from Olympus: Archaeology and Philhellenism in Germany, 1750–1970.* Princeton, N.J.: Princeton University Press, 1996.

Marchisotto, Alan. "The Protection of Art in International Law." *Vanderbilt Journal of Transnational Law* 7 (1974): 689–724.

Marefat, Mina. "Wright's Baghdad." In *Frank Lloyd Wright: Europe and Beyond,* ed. Anthony Alofsin, pp. 184–214. Berkeley: University of California Press, 1999.

Markus, R. A. *Saeculum: History and Society in the Theology of St. Augustine.* Cambridge: Cambridge University Press, 1970.

Marlowe, John. *Late Victorian.* London: Cresset P., 1967.

Marr, Phebe. "The Development of a Nationalist Ideology in Iraq, 1920–1941." *Muslim World* 75 (2): 85–101.

———. *The History of Modern Iraq.* Boulder, Colo.: Westview, 1985.

Masters, D. *The Romance of Excavation.* London: J. Lane, 1923.

Meade, C. W. *Road to Babylon: The Development of U.S. Assyriology.* Leiden, the Netherlands: Brill, 1974.

Melman, Billie. *Women's Orients: English Women and the Middle East, 1718–1918.* London: Macmillan, 1992.

Messenger, Phyllis, ed. *The Ethics of Collecting Cultural Property: Whose Culture? Whose Property?* Albuquerque: University of New Mexico Press, 1989.

Mertz, Barbara. *Temples, Tombs and Hieroglyphs.* New York: Coward-McCann, 1964.

Metlitzki, Dorothee. *The Matter of Araby in Medieval England.* New Haven, Conn.: Yale University Press, 1977.

Meyer, Edward. "25 Jahre Deutsche Orient-Gesellschaft." In *Mitteilungen der Deutchen Orient-Gesellschaft,* no. 62, pp. 1–25. Berlin: Deutsche Orient-Gesellschaft, 1923.

Meyer, Karl E. *The Plundered Past.* New York: Atheneum, 1973.

Miller, Edward. *That Noble Cabinet: A History of the British Museum.* London: Andre Deutsch, 1973.

Mitchell, Timothy. *Colonising Egypt.* Berkeley: University of California Press, 1991.

Momigliano, Arnaldo. *The Classical Foundations of Modern Historiography.* Berkeley: University of California Press, 1990.

———. *Studies in Historiography.* London: Harper & Row, 1966.

Monkton, Norah. "Architectural Backgrounds in John Martin." *Architectural Review* 104 (2): 46–61.

Monroe, Elisabeth. *Britain's Moment in the Middle East.* Baltimore: Johns Hopkins Press, 1956.

Moorey, P. R. S. *Cemeteries of the First Millennium B.C. at Deve Huyuk, near Carchemish, Salvaged by T. E. Lawrence and C. L. Woolley in 1913.* British Archaeological Reports series # 82. Oxford: Archaeopress, 1980.

———. *Kish Excavations 1923–1933.* Oxford: Clarendon Press, 1978.

———. *Ur "of the Chaldees": A Revised and Updated Edition of Sir Leonard Woolley's Excavations at Ur.* Ithaca, N.Y.: Cornell University Press, 1982.

Mordechai, Omar. *Turner: die Landschaften der Bibel.* Bayreuth, Germany: Gondrum Verlag, 1985.

Morsey, Klaus. *T. E. Lawrence und der arabische Aufstand 1916–18.* Osnabruck, Germany: Biblio-Verlag, 1976.

Al-Muqaddasi, Muhammad ibn Ahmad. *Ahsan al-taqasim fi ma'rifat al-aqalim.* Translated by G. S. A. Ranking and R. F. Azoo. Orig. 1897; Frankfurt: Institut für Geschichte der Arabisch-Islamischen Wissenschaften, 1989.

Murray, Margaret Alice. *The Splendour That Was Egypt.* New York: Philosophical Library, 1989.

Nakash, Yitzhak. *The Shi'is of Iraq.* Princeton, N.J.: Princeton University Press, 1994.

Neillands, Robin. *The Dervish Wars: Gordon and Kitchener in the Sudan, 1880–1898.* London: J. Murray, 1996.

Newton, Douglas. "Old Wine in New Bottles, and the Reverse." In *Museums and the Making of "Ourselves": The Role of Objects in National Identity,* ed. Flora Kaplan, pp. 269–290. Leicester, UK: Leicester University Press, 1994.

Nicholas, Lynn H. *The Rape of Europa: The Fate of Europe's Treasures in the Third Reich and the Second World War.* New York: Knopf, 1994.

Nieuwenhuis, Tom. *Politics and Society in Early Modern Iraq: Mamluk Pashas, Tribal Shayks and Local Rule between 1802 and 1931.* The Hague: M. Nijhoff, 1982.

Nisbet, Robert A. *History of the Idea of Progress.* New York: Basic Books, 1980.

Nissen, Hans, Robert Englund, and Peter Damerow. *Archaic Bookkeeping: Early Writing and Techniques of the Economic Administration in the Ancient Near East.* Chicago: University of Chicago Press, 1993.

Nuseibeh, Hazem Zaki. *The Ideas of Arab Nationalism.* Ithaca, N.Y.: Cornell University Press, 1956.

Oates, David. *Studies in the Ancient History of Northern Iraq.* London: Oxford University Press, 1968.

Oates, Joan. *The Rise of Civilization*. London: Elsevier-Phaidon, 1976.

O'Leary, Stephen D. *Arguing the Apocalypse: A Theory of Millennial Rhetoric*. New York: Oxford University Press, 1994.

Olender, Maurice. *The Languages of Paradise: Race, Religion and Philology in the Nineteenth Century*. Cambridge, Mass.: Harvard University Press, 1992.

Owen, Roger. *The Middle East in the World Economy 1800–1914*. London: Methuen, 1981.

Paley, Morton D. *The Apocalyptic Sublime*. New Haven, Conn.: Yale University Press, 1986.

Pallis, Svend. *The Antiquity of Iraq: A Handbook of Assyriology*. Copenhagen: E. Munksgaard, 1956.

Patrides, C. A., and Joseph Wittreich. *The Apocalypse in English Renaissance Thought and Literature*. Ithaca, N.Y.: Cornell University Press, 1984.

Patterson, Thomas C. *Toward a Social History of Archaeology in the United States*. Fort Worth, Tex.: Harcourt Brace, 1995.

Petersen, Holger. *The Discovery of Language: Linguistic Science in the Nineteenth Century*. Bloomington: Indiana University Press, 1931.

Petrie, Flinders. *Seventy Years of Archaeology*. London: H. Holt & Company, 1931.

Phillips, Clifton Jackson. *Protestant America and the Pagan World*. Cambridge, Mass.: Harvard University Press, 1969.

Pinsky, Valerie, and Alison Wylie, eds. *Critical Traditions in Contemporary Archaeology*. Cambridge: Cambridge University Press, 1989.

Pitcher, Donald Edgar. *An Historical Geography of the Ottoman Empire*. Leiden, the Netherlands: Brill, 1972.

Plaut, F. "Where Is Paradise? The Mapping of a Myth." *Map Collector* 29 (2): 2–7.

Pollard, Sidney. *The Idea of Progress: History and Society*. Harmondsworth, UK: Watts, 1971.

Posner, Ernst. "Public Records under Military Occupation." *American Historical Review* 49 (2): 213–227.

Postgate, Nicholas. *The First Empires*. London: Elsevier-Phaidon, 1977.

Potts, Alex. *Flesh and the Ideal: Winckelmann and the Origins of Art History*. New Haven, Conn.: Yale University Press, 1996.

Prott, Lyndel, and P. J. O'Keefe. *Law and the Cultural Heritage*. Abingdon, Oxon: Professional Books, 1984.

Quynn, D. M. "The Art Confiscations of the Napoleonic Wars." *American Historical Review* 50 (3): 437–439.

Rathmann, Lothar. *Berlin-Baghdad: Die imperialistische Nahostpolitik der kaiserlichen Deutschlands*. Berlin: Dietz, 1962.

Rawlinson, George. *Memoir of Major-General Sir Henry Creswicke Rawlinson*. London: Longmans, Green & Co., 1898.

Reade, Julian. "Hormuzd Rassam and His Discoveries." *Iraq* 54–55 (1993): 39–60.

———. "Reflections on Layard's Archaeological Career." In *Austen Henry Layard Tra L'Oriente e Venezia*, ed. Frederick Fales and B. J. Hickey, pp. 47–53. Rome: L'Erma di Bretschneider, 1987.

Reeves, Nicholas. *The Complete Tutankhamun: The King, the Tomb, the Royal Treasure*. London: Thames & Hudson, 1990.

Reid, Donald M. "Nationalizing the Pharaonic Past: Egypt 1922–1952." In *Rethinking Nationalism in the Arab Middle East*, ed. Israel Gershoni and James Jankowski, pp. 122–144. New York: Columbia University Press, 1997.

———. *Whose Pharaohs? Archaeology, Museums, and Egyptian National Identity from Napoleon to World War I*. Berkeley: University of California Press, 2002.

Renger, Johannes. "Die Geschichte der Altorientalistik und der voderasi-atischen Archaologie in Berlin von 1875 bis 1945." In *Berlin und die Antike*, ed. Willmuth Arenhövel and Christa Schreiber, pp. 151–192. Berlin: Deutsches Archäologisches Institut, 1979.

Reyman, Jonathan. "The History of Archaeology and the Archaeological History of Chaco Canyon, New Mexico." In *Tracing Archaeology's Past. The Historiography of Archaeology*, ed. Andrew Christenson, pp. 41–54. Carbondale: Southern Illinois University Press, 1989.

———, ed. *Rediscovering Our Past*. Aldershot, UK: Brookfield, 1992.

Ronaldshay, Earl of. *The Life of Lord Curzon*. 3 vols. London: E. Benn, 1928.

Rose, Kenneth. *Superior Person: A Portrait of Curzon and His Circle in Late Victorian England*. London: Weidenfeld & Nicolson, 1969.

Rosenblum, Robert. *Modern Painting and the Northern Romantic Tradition*. New York: Harper & Row, 1975.

Ruskin, John. *The Works of John Ruskin*. Edited by E. T. Cook and Alexander Wedderburn. 39 vols. London: George Allen, 1903–1912.

Russell, John Malcolm. *From Nineveh to New York: The Strange Story of the Assyrian Reliefs in the Metropolitan Museum and the Hidden Masterpiece at Canford School*. New Haven, Conn.: Yale University Press, 1997.

Safran, Nadav. *Egypt in Search for Political Community*. Cambridge, Mass.: Harvard University Press, 1961.

Sahlins, Peter. *Boundaries: The Making of France and Spain in the Pyrenees*. Berkeley and Los Angeles: University of California Press, 1989.

Said, Edward. *Orientalism*. New York: Vintage Books, 1978.

Salem, Paul. *Bitter Legacy: Ideology and Politics in the Arab World*. Syracuse, N.Y.: Syracuse University Press, 1994.

Saunders, Ernest. *Searching the Scriptures: A History of the Society of Biblical Literature, 1880–1980*. Chicago: Scholars Press, 1982.

Schneider, William. *An Empire for the Masses: The French Popular Image of Africa, 1870–1900*. Westport, Conn.: Greenwood, 1982.
Schofield, Richard, ed. *The Iraq-Iran Border, 1840–1958*. Farnam, England: Archive Editions, 1979.
Schöllgen, Gregor. *Imperialismus und Gleichgewicht: Deutschland, England und die orientalishe Frage, 1871–1914*. Munich: R. Oldenburg, 1984.
Schulz, Max F. *Paradise Preserved: Recreations of Eden in Eighteenth- and Nineteenth-Century England*. Cambridge: Cambridge University Press, 1985.
Schwab, Raymond. *La Renaissance Orientale*. Paris: Payot, 1950.
Shaw, Stanford, and E. K. Shaw. *History of the Ottoman Empire and Modern Turkey*. 2 vols. Cambridge: Cambridge University Press, 1976–1977.
Shaw, Wendy M. K. *Possessors and Possessed: Museums, Archaeology, and the Visualization of History in the Late Ottoman Empire*. Berkeley: University of California Press, 2003.
Sherman, Daniel. "The Bourgeoisie, Cultural Appropriation and the Art Museum in Nineteenth-Century France." *Radical History Review* 38 (1987): 38–58.
Shorrock, William. *French Imperialism in the Middle East: The Failure of Policy in Syria and Lebanon, 1900–1914*. Madison: University of Wisconsin Press, 1976.
Silberman, Neil Asher. *Between Past and Present: Archaeology, Ideology, and Nationalism in the Modern Middle East*. New York: Henry Holt, 1989.
———. *Digging for God and Country: Exploration, Archaeology, and the Secret Struggles for the Holy Land, 1799–1917*. New York: Knopf, 1982.
Simon, Reeva. *Iraq between the Two World Wars: The Creation and Implementation of a Nationalist Ideology*. New York: Columbia University Press, 1986.
———. "The Imposition of Nationalism on a Non-Nation State: The Case of Iraq during the Interwar Period, 1921–41." In *Rethinking Arab Nationalism*, ed. James Jankowski and Israel Gershoni. New York: Columbia University Press, 1997.
———. "The Teaching of History in Iraq before the Rashid Ali Coup of 1941." *Middle Eastern Studies* 22 (1986): 37–51.
Simpson, Elisabeth, ed. *The Spoils of War: World War II and Its Aftermath: The Loss, Reappearance, and Recovery of Cultural Property*. New York: H. N. Abrams, 1997.
Sluglett, Peter. *Britain in Iraq 1914–1932*. London: Ithaca Press, 1976.
Smith, Anthony D. *National Identity*. Reno: University of Nevada Press, 1991.
Southern, R. W. *Western Views of Islam in the Middle Ages*. Cambridge, Mass.: Harvard University Press, 1962.
Spadafora, David. *The Idea of Progress in Eighteenth-Century Britain*. New Haven, Conn.: Yale University Press, 1990.

Speiser, Ephraim. *At the Dawn of Civilization: A Background of Biblical History.* New Brunswick, N.J.: Rutgers University Press, 1964.

———. *Introduction to Hurrian.* New Haven, Conn.: American Schools of Oriental Research, 1941.

———. *The United States and the Near East.* Cambridge, Mass.: Harvard University Press, 1950.

Stark, Freya. *Baghdad Sketches.* London: J. Murray, 1938.

———. *Baghdad Sketches.* Evanston, Ill.: Northwestern, 1992.

Stiebing, William. *Uncovering the Past.* Buffalo, N.Y.: Prometheus Books, 1993.

Stocking, George W. *Victorian Anthropology.* New York: Free Press, 1987.

Stoneman, Richard. *Land of Lost Gods: The Search for Classical Greece.* Norman: University of Oklahoma Press, 1987.

Streck, Maximilian. *Die Alte Landschaft Babylonien nach den Arabischen Geographen.* Orig. 1900–1901; Frankfurt: Institut für Geschichte der Arabisch-Islamischen Wissenschaften, 1986.

Sweetman, John. *The Oriental Obsession: Islamic Inspiration in British and American Art and Architecture, 1500–1920.* Cambridge: Cambridge University Press, 1988.

Tabachnick, Stephen E. "Lawrence of Arabia as Archaeologist." *Biblical Archaeology Review* 23 (5): 40–47, 70–71.

Tarbush, Mohammad. *The Role of the Military in Politics: A Case Study of Iraq to 1941.* London: KPI, 1982.

Tauber, Eliezer. *The Formation of Modern Syria and Iraq.* London: Frank Cass, 1995.

Thomas, Nancy, ed. *The American Discovery of Ancient Egypt.* Los Angeles: Los Angeles County Museum of Art, 1996.

Thompson, Michael. *General Pitt Rivers: Evolution and Archaeology in the Nineteenth Century.* Bradford, UK: Moonraker Press, 1977.

Tibi, Bassam. *Arab Nationalism: A Critical Enquiry.* London: Macmillan Press, 1981.

———. *Arab Nationalism: Between Islam and Nation-State.* New York: St. Martin's Press, 1997.

Tomkins, Calvin. *Merchants and Masterpieces: The Story of the Metropolitan Museum of Art.* London: E. P. Tomkins, 1970.

Traill, David A. *Schliemann of Troy: Treasure and Deceit.* New York: John Murray, 1996.

Trigger, Bruce. "Alternative Archaeologies: Nationalist, Colonialist, Imperialist." *Man* 19 (1984): 355–370.

———. *A History of Archaeological Thought.* Cambridge: Cambridge University Press, 1990.

———. "Writing the History of Archaeology: A Survey of Trends." In *Objects and Others: Essays on Museums and Material Culture,* ed. George Stocking, pp. 218–235. Madison: University of Wisconsin, 1985.

Tripp, Charles. *The History of Iraq.* Cambridge: Cambridge University Press, 2002.

Trumpener, Ulrich. "Germany and the End of the Ottoman Empire." In *The Great Powers and the End of the Ottoman Empire,* ed. Marian Kent, pp. 111–140. London: G. Allen & Unwin, 1984.

———. *Germany and the Ottoman Empire, 1914–1918.* Princeton, N.J.: Princeton University Press, 1968.

Tuchman, Barbara. *Bible and Sword: England and Palestine from the Bronze Age to Balfour.* New York: New York University Press, 1956.

Turner, Frank M. *Contesting Cultural Authority.* Cambridge: Cambridge University Press, 1993.

———. *The Greek Heritage in Victorian Britain.* New Haven, Conn.: Yale University Press, 1981.

Tylor, Edward. *Anthropology: An Introduction to the Study of Man and Civilization.* New York: D. Appleton and Co., 1881.

Viongradov, Amal. "The 1920 Revolt in Iraq Reconsidered: The Role of Tribes in National Politics." *International Journal of Middle East Studies* 3 (2): 123–139.

Waley, S. D. *Edwin Montagu: A Memoir.* New York: Asia Publishing House, 1964.

Wallach, Janet. *Desert Queen. The Extraordinary Life of Gertrude Bell: Adventurer, Adviser to Kings, Ally of Lawrence of Arabia.* New York: Anchor Books, 1996.

Warner, Philip. *Kitchener: The Man behind the Legend.* New York: Atheneum, 1986.

Waterfield, Gordon. *Layard of Nineveh.* London: J. Murray, 1963.

Wauchope, R. *They Found Buried Cities.* Chicago: University of Chicago Press, 1965.

Wehr, Hans. *A Dictionary of Modern Written Arabic.* Ithaca, N.Y.: Cornell University Press, 1976.

Wensinck, A. J. "Harut and Marut" in *Shorter Encyclopedia of Islam.* Leiden, the Netherlands: Brill, 1995.

Wensinck, A. J., and G. Vadja. "Fir'awn" in *Encyclopedia of Islam,* vol. 2. Leiden, the Netherlands: Brill, 1965.

Westrate, Bruce. *The Arab Bureau: British Policy in the Middle East, 1916–1920.* University Park: Pennsylvania State University Press, 1992.

Willey, Gordon, and Jeremy Sabloff. *A History of American Archaeology.* San Francisco: W. H. Freeman, 1980.

Williams, Sharon A. *The International and National Protection of Movable Cultural Property: A Comparative Study.* New York: Dobbs Ferry, 1978.

Wills, Garry. "Athens of Fifth Avenue." *New York Review of Books,* June 10, 1999, pp. 38–40.

Wilson, Jeremy. *Lawrence of Arabia: The Authorized Biography of T. E. Lawrence.* New York: Atheneum, 1990.

Wilson, Mary C. *King Abdullah, Britain and the Making of Jordan.* Cambridge: Cambridge University Press, 1987.

Winks, Robin. *Cloak and Gown: Scholars in the Secret War, 1939–1961.* New York: Morrow, 1987.

Winstone, H. V. F. *Gertrude Bell.* London: J. Cape, 1978.

———. *The Illicit Adventure: The Story of Political and Military Intelligence in the Middle East from 1898 to 1926.* London: J. Cape, 1982.

———. *Uncovering the Ancient World.* London: Constable, 1983.

———. *Woolley of Ur: The Life of Sir Leonard Woolley.* London: Secker & Warburg, 1990.

Wolf, John. *The Diplomatic History of the Bagdad Railroad.* Columbia: University of Missouri Press, 1936.

Wood, Christopher. *Olympian Dreamers: Victorian Classical Painters, 1860–1914.* London: Constable, 1983.

Woodbury, R. B. *Alfred V. Kidder.* New York: Columbia University Press, 1973.

Woolley, C. L. *Ur of the Chaldees.* London: E. Benn Limited, 1929.

Wortham, J. D. *British Egyptology, 1549–1906.* Norman: University of Oklahoma Press, 1971.

Wright, G. Ernest. "The Phenomenon of American Archaeology in the Near East." In *Near Eastern Archaeology in the Twentieth Century: Essays in Honor of Nelson Glueck,* ed. James A. Sanders, pp. 3–40. Garden City, N.Y.: Doubleday, 1970.

Yapp, M. E. *The Near East Since the First World War.* London: Longman, 1991.

Zeine, Zeine N. *The Emergence of Arab Nationalism, with a Background of Arab-Turkish Relations in the Near East.* New York: Caravan Books, 1973.

———. *The Struggle for Arab Independence: Western Diplomacy and the Rise and Fall of Faysal's Kingdom in Syria.* Beirut: Khayat's, 1960.

Zerubavel, Yael. *Recovered Roots: Collective Memory and the Making of Israeli National Tradition.* Chicago: University of Chicago Press, 1995.

Zola, Emile. *L'Assommoir.* Translated into English by A. Symons. New York: Knopf, 1924.

INDEX

Endowments and Religious
Affairs), 2, 158
Ministry of Education (Iraq), 109,
111, 126–127, 151, 172–175,
182, 186, 197–202
Ministry of Education (Ottoman),
39
Ministry of Foreign Affairs, 185,
192, 205
Ministry of Public Works, 118,
126, 153
Missionary Herald, The, 50
Mohl, Julius, 40–41
Momigliano, Arnaldo, 21, 225n10
Montagu, Edwin, 76–77, 92,
247n89
Montague House. *See* British
Museum
Monument de Ninive, 41
Moorey, P. R. S., 132
Morgan, J. P., 50
Mosul, 36, 42, 45, 47, 57, 68, 98,
114, 151
Muhammad, Prophet, 5, 107, 154
Mulkiye Mektebi, 119
Münter, Frederick, 46
al-Muqaddasi, 97–98,
253–254n11, 254n14
Muqaddimah, 32
al-Muqtataf, 59
Museum of Arab Antiquities, 202
Museum of Fine Arts (Baghdad), 3
Museum of Modern Art (Iraq),
212
Muslim Brotherhood, 210
Mustafa, Muhammad Ali, 212
Mustansirriya College, **PS**
al-Mutakwakkil, Great Mosque of,
PS
al-Mutasim Caliph, 75

Nadir Shah, 99
Nahrwan, 157
Napoleon, 55, 73–74, 102,

246n79
al-Naqib, 'Abd al-Rahman, 105,
256n38
Naram-Sin, 2
Nasir, Gamal Abd-al, 209–210, 214
Nationalism. *See* Iraq: and nationalism
National Library and Archives
(Dar al-Katub wa al-Watha'iq),
2–3
National Museum (Iraq Museum),
2–3, 76–80, 82, 92, 123, 126,
128, 187, 137–138, 143,
147–156, 159, 171–172, 176,
178, 183, 189, 191–192, 195,
202–206, 211, 222n2,
269n111, **PS**. *See also* Bell,
Gertrude: and establishment
of Iraq Museum
National museums, establishment
of in the West, 23, 149–150
Nebbi Yenus, 40
Nebuchadnezzar, 32, 36, 67, 73,
133, 216
Negev Desert, 70
Nestorian Christian Church, 167
Niebuhr, Carsten, 35–37, 46
Nilsson, Sven, 22–23
Nimrud site, 41–42, 45, 63, 149,
215
Nineveh, 2, 25–26, 28, 31, 35–36,
40–41, 45, 114, 149,
235n116, 241n16; marbles,
44
Nineveh and Its Remains, 44–45
Nineveh Gallery (British
Museum), 44
Nippur site, 11, 51–52, 57, 131,
133–134, 215, 238n147,
262n4
Nöldecke, Theodor, 169
Norton, Charles Eliot, 51
Notgemeinschaft der Deutschen
Wissenschaft, 169

Lightning Source UK Ltd.
Milton Keynes UK
UKOW04f2147110118
315929UK00001B/143/P